OBJECTS OF CONCERN

Jonathan F. Vance

Objects of Concern

Canadian Prisoners of War Through the Twentieth Century

UBC PRESS / VANCOUVER

Printed in Canada on acid-free paper ∞

ISBN 0-7748-0504-8

Canadian Cataloguing in Publication Data

Vance, Jonathan Franklin William, 1963-
   Objects of concern

   Includes bibliographical references and index.
   ISBN 0-7748-0504-8

   1. Prisoners of war – Canada – History – 20th century. 2. War (International law) – History – 20th century. 3. Concentration camps – History – 20th century. I. Title.

JX5141.V36 1994   341.6'5'0971   C94-910711-5

This book has been published with the help of a grant from the Social Science Federation of Canada, using funds provided by the Social Sciences and Humanities Research Council of Canada. UBC Press also gratefully acknowledges the ongoing support to its publishing program from the Canada Council, the Province of British Columbia Cultural Services Branch, and the Department of Communications of the Government of Canada.

Set in Scala and Scala Sans
Printed and bound in Canada by D.W. Friesen & Sons Ltd.
Copy-editor: Francis J. Chow
Proofreader: Carolyn Bateman
Designer: George Vaitkunas

UBC Press
University of British Columbia
6344 Memorial Road
Vancouver, BC v6T 1z2
(604) 822-3259
Fax: (604) 822-6083

CONTENTS

ACKNOWLEDGMENTS

WHEN I WAS STILL A TEENAGER, I developed a peculiar interest in the experiences of prisoners of war and, much to the amusement of my friends, turned the collection of POW lore into something of a hobby. Since then, hundreds of ex-prisoners have been generous with their time and assistance, and have graciously accepted my invitations to jot down their recollections on various subjects. For fostering a boyhood interest that eventually turned into serious research, my first debt must go to those old soldiers, many of whom were quite happy to help me again as this book took shape. They have been unstinting in their assistance, and have shown great understanding in allowing me to shuffle through their scrapbooks and pester them with seemingly endless questions; sadly some of them, including Percy Hampton, Gus Gruggen, and Dick McLaren, did not live to see the publication of this book. At the same time, I must thank various veterans' organizations that have provided assistance, both in locating personal papers and in tracking down ex-prisoners. Particularly helpful have been Cliff Chadderton (War Amputations of Canada), Lionel Hurd (Hong Kong Veterans' Association), Fred LeReverend and Bert Konig (National POW Association), and Bud Ward (RCAF Ex-POW Association).

When this book was a doctoral dissertation at York University, it benefited greatly from the guidance and advice of my supervisor, Jack Granatstein, whose knowledge of the archival material allowed me to utilize many sources that I would otherwise have missed, and whose always cogent criticism prevented me from straying into the realm of

POW trivia. Michael H. Kater and Albert Tucker have also been instrumental in helping me improve my historical method, and I am grateful to Chuck Roland of McMaster University for guiding me through his incomparable POW archives and helping me to work through some of the difficult problems in analyzing the features of captivity.

I would also like to express my gratitude to the Social Sciences and Humanities Research Council of Canada, whose financial support made this project possible, and to York University, for providing assistance with travel expenses.

Every historian owes a debt to the archivists who act as guides through the vagaries of finding aids and conversion lists. Many individuals have been generous with their help but I am especially grateful to Rod McFall (National Archives of Canada), Bob Fraser (Argyll and Sutherland Highlanders of Canada Archives), Ted Kelly (Department of External Affairs), Chris Petter (University of Victoria Archives), Glenn Wright (Director General History), Johanne Neville (Commonwealth War Graves Commission), and Janice Summerby (Veterans Affairs Canada).

I am also indebted to a number of my colleagues, especially Bill Wiley, who, in the course of many fruitful discussions on POWs, did not hesitate to shoot holes in some of my more fanciful theories. Penny Bryden, Andy Holman, Norman Knowles, and Dean Oliver have also been kind enough to keep their eyes open for prisoner of war material. The technical assistance of Caroline Brodie was much appreciated, and I must also extend sincere thanks to UBC Press, especially Jean Wilson for showing an interest in this project in the first place, and Laura Macleod, whose expertise and good humour made the publication process a pleasure from start to finish.

The biggest debt, though, must go to my family, who have had to do many things without me over the past few years so that this book might see the light before all of Canada's ex-POWs passed away. This project owes as much to my wife, Cheryl, and my son, Gordon, as anyone else, for giving me support, encouragement, and time to work.

BAAG	British Army Aid Group
BCFK	British Commonwealth Forces in Korea
CID	Committee of Imperial Defence
CMHQ	Canadian Military Headquarters
COPC	Canadian Overseas Prisoners of War Committee
CPOWRA	Canadian Prisoners of War Relatives Association
CPW	Committee for the Protection and Welfare of Canadian Prisoners of War in Enemy Hands
CRCS	Canadian Red Cross Society
DPOW	Directorate of Prisoners of War
DVPA	Dieppe Veterans and POWs Association
EALEX	Eclipse Air Lift Executive
GWVA	Great War Veterans' Association
HKVA	Hong Kong Veterans' Association
ICAN	Inter-Governmental Committee on Allied Nationals in Japanese Hands
ICRC	International Committee of the Red Cross
IPOWC	Imperial Prisoners of War Committee
ISCP	Inter-Service Committee on Prisoners of War
MPOWA	Maltreated Prisoners of War Association
NDHQ	National Defence Headquarters
NPOWA	National POW Association
OMFC	Overseas Military Forces of Canada
PWX	Prisoner of War Executive

RAMP	Recovered Allied Military Personnel
RAPWI	Recovered Allied Prisoners of War and Internees
RCAF	Royal Canadian Air Force
RCEB	Red Cross Enquiry Bureau
RCN	Royal Canadian Navy
SAAG	Special Assistant to the Adjutant-General
SACSEA	Supreme Allied Command, South-East Asia
SHAEF	Supreme Headquarters, Allied Expeditionary Force
UNC	United Nations Command
UNHRC	United Nations Human Rights Commission
WPA	War Prisoners' Aid of the World's Committee of YMCA's

OBJECTS OF CONCERN

HOCKEY MAGNATE CONN SMYTHE, Trudeau Cabinet minister Gilles Lamontagne, and the composer and former conductor of the Toronto Symphony Orchestra, Sir Ernest MacMillan, share something other than their public notoriety: they can all claim the dubious distinction of having been captured by the enemy during Canada's wars of the twentieth century. Like some 15,000 other Canadians, Smythe, Lamontagne, and MacMillan experienced the bewilderment that accompanied the moment of capture, the humiliation of being completely in the power of the captor, and the sense of stagnating in a backwater while the rest of the world moved forward.

Their captivity was spent in small worlds bounded by barbed wire, from which they were only infrequently allowed to emerge. Communication with the outside world was strictly controlled, as was their diet, clothing, recreational activities, and everything else that they had always taken for granted. In this unnatural habitat they spent months or years, often in the prime of life, with no way of knowing how long their captivity would last. If they were fortunate, they might make the most of a bad situation and throw themselves into study, prison camp theatricals, or sports, but when these amenities were unavailable, their existence could be almost unbearably boring. It was also immensely dangerous, and prisoners often existed in the full knowledge that their lives were of little consequence to their captors and could be ended at any time. And when it was all over, most people expected ex-prisoners to return home and drift back into civilian life as though nothing had happened.

Conn Smythe (right) relaxes in his room in prison camp in 1918.

Despite their physical isolation from friends and family, however, prisoners did not fight their battles alone. While they were carrying on their war in captivity, another struggle was under way on their behalf as an army of politicians, civil servants, and private citizens mobilized to make Canadians in enemy hands as comfortable as circumstances would allow. This task was made more difficult by a number of factors. First of all, captives were divided into various categories, each of which presented unique problems for Canadian officials. The most numerous were prisoners of war, members of the armed forces who were captured by the enemy during or after battle and who, in theory, enjoyed some degree of protection under international law. In this group can be included Canadians imprisoned by regimes sympathetic to Canada's enemies, such as Vichy France. Far less numerous than prisoners of war were civilian internees, either residents of or visitors to other countries who found themselves arrested and imprisoned for no other reason than their citizenship. Missionaries in China, clerical students in France, and businessmen in Germany were all liable to arrest and internment once war began and their places of residence were occupied.

Two smaller groups of prisoners also deserve mention. A number of Canadians were interned in neutral states, in Holland and Switzerland during the Great War and in Sweden, Switzerland, Spain, Portugal, Afghanistan, the Vatican, and Eire during the Second World War. Exchanged POWs and airmen who force-landed in neutral territory made up the bulk of this group. Finally, hundreds of Canadian merchant seamen fell into enemy hands during the world wars, and they occupied a position somewhere between civilian internees and POWs. During the First World War, merchant mariners were usually treated as civilian internees, but during the Second all sides regarded them as POWs, despite the fact that international law did not recognize them as such. This anomalous position would create problems for merchant seamen both in captivity and after the war.

Efforts to provide for these prisoners were further complicated by the fact that the conditions of their captivity varied tremendously. At the top of the scale were Canadian airmen interned in Sweden and Eire during the Second World War. In Sweden, Canadians enjoyed liberal privileges on parole, to the point of choosing their own accommodation outside the prison camp at the Swedish government's expense. Even while in the camp (which scarcely deserved the name since the main gate was rusted off its hinges and the guards' rifles had brass caps welded over the muzzles to keep the rain out) the conditions were hardly taxing.[1] The situation in Eire was no more arduous. Most internees had their own bicycles and made weekly trips into Dublin; they kept pets, became engaged to local girls, and held memberships at nearby tennis clubs. It was hardly the sort of captivity that would move the government to do much on their behalf.[2]

At the opposite end of the scale were those Canadian servicemen who had the misfortune to be captured by the Japanese in the Second World War. Their captivity was marked not by cycling trips and tennis matches but by savage beatings, systematic starvation, overwork, rampant disease, and, in some cases, summary execution. Theirs was a horrific existence and often all that sustained them was the will to live or, to borrow a phrase from the Canadian poet Alden Nowlan, the 'stubborn disinclination' to die.[3] For those who clung to life through the years of captivity in Hong Kong and Japan, V-J Day would bring only a temporary respite from their suffering. Of all the Canadians imprisoned in the wars of this century, the Far East POWs bear the deepest and most afflicting physical and emotional scars and still live

Haggard and emaciated, many of these POWs would never fully recover from the effects of nearly four years in Japanese captivity.

with the legacy of their maltreatment fifty years later.

Despite the existence of such a variety of prisoners living under conditions that could be poles apart, two basic themes ran through the Canadian government's efforts to provide for its citizens in enemy hands. For the sake of convenience, these can be termed relief and release. When a friend or relative was captured, the natural impulse was to make captivity more bearable by dispatching as many different forms of relief supplies as possible to the camp. In a sense, the relief campaigns attempted to bring all the comforts of home, within reason, to the prison camp. Some campaigns were more successful than others. During the First World War, officer POWs frequently enjoyed food hampers from the finest London shops, while POWs captured in the Pacific during the Second World War often got no more than a single food parcel in any given year. Regardless of the outcome of the campaigns, government departments, humanitarian agencies, and private citizens never stopped searching for ways to ensure the delivery of relief shipments.

Of course, it would have been preferable to obtain the release of all prisoners, and much effort went into negotiating exchanges that would return POWs and civilian internees to their homes. The First World War saw marked success in this area, not only in securing the release of sick and wounded POWs (usually known as *grands blessés*) but also in arranging for the internment of long-term prisoners of war in the more hospitable conditions of neutral Holland and Switzerland. The release campaigns of the Second World War had less happy results. In Europe, only a tiny minority of sick and wounded Canadian POWs and a few civilian internees gained their freedom through repatriation, while in the Far East only civilian internees benefited from exchanges. The Korean War represents the other end of the scale, for the United Nations Command successfully negotiated the exchange of all (or at least all that North Korea and the People's Republic of China admitted detaining) prisoners captured by Communist forces, including thirty-three Canadians. The other significant aspect of the release campaigns was the return of liberated prisoners safely and quickly to their homes after the conclusion of hostilities, a task that proved to have difficulties far greater than Canadian planners imagined.

A number of other related themes enter into any discussion of captivity. The government had an obligation to prepare Canadian servicemen for what they might encounter if captured, and to advise them of the measures that would be taken to safeguard their interests while imprisoned. Whether the private who went to Korea with the Princess Patricia's Canadian Light Infantry in 1950 was any better prepared for captivity than his predecessor who accompanied the regiment to France in 1914 is worth considering. An extension of this theme is the reintegration of ex-POWs into society after the wars, and the subsequent battles for reparations or pension benefits. To ex-POWs who reflected upon the government's success or failure in caring for them, the outcome of these battles was just as important as their experiences in captivity.

The development of international law also runs through the story, both in Canadian attempts to monitor its observance during wartime and in the government's participation in its revision during peacetime. The concept of reciprocity of treatment, always uppermost in the minds of Canadian officials seeking to ensure that the enemy observed international law in the treatment of prisoners, is a related theme. As one study has stressed, Canadians in enemy hands and enemy aliens and POWs in Canada were in a very real sense mutual hostages, something that officials in both world wars and the Korean conflict never forgot.[4]

According to the story of one Canadian airman captured in Italy, 'many of the folks back home had no real conception of what a war, or being a POW, was like.'[5] The comment is a typical one and has been applied by ex-prisoners to the postwar years as much as to the war years. Indeed, some ex-POWs consider themselves to be forgotten casualties, whose privations were misunderstood during the war and whose needs were neglected afterwards. This is a serious charge, since it suggests that the Canadian government failed to discharge its responsibilities to its citizens who were unlucky enough to be captured by the enemy in war. It also implies that the government learned nothing from the experience of war, but repeated the same mistakes over the course of the century.

The charge is, however, not entirely justified. Canadian administrators often failed to learn from past practices, but enough important lessons were heeded over the course of the century that by the time of the Korean conflict many of the mistakes from the First and Second World Wars had been identified and corrected. Furthermore, it is unfair to assert that the government was insensitive to the needs of its citizens in captivity. Certainly a marked lack of appreciation for the difficulties facing POWs and civilian internees was evident at times, but one cannot doubt the sincerity of those individuals involved in providing for Canadians in enemy hands. In most cases they did everything possible to ameliorate the conditions of captivity for the thousands of Canadian prisoners, and obstacles were more often created by an over-abundance of enthusiasm than by a lack of interest. Caring for the thousands of Canadians in enemy hands was a massive undertaking that could have been less arduous had officials not faced a host of problems largely of their own making.

However, these difficulties had little impact on the objects of all the effort, the prisoners themselves. They did not know of the many problems plaguing the campaigns for relief and release, nor did they know how much time and effort was wasted in duplication of tasks, jurisdictional confusion, and petty wrangling. Most prisoners knew only that, all things considered, they were well looked after by the people at home, and for this they were often the envy of their campmates.

ONE

Nineteenth-Century Precursors

THE NINETEENTH CENTURY provided Canada with numerous examples of the problems involved in looking after the interests of Canadians in enemy hands, although the examples were of limited utility in this century, given the drastically different characteristics of warfare. Even so, the nineteenth century did demonstrate the enduring nature of a number of themes related to captivity, themes that would increase in importance as the scale of war grew. Furthermore, experiences with captivity from the War of 1812 to the Boer War gave Canadians mistaken impressions of the developing trends in the nature of captivity and bred in them a false sense of security that would be quickly shattered in the twentieth century.

DURING THE WAR OF 1812, the government's responsibility to care for servicemen in captivity was limited by the prevalence of parole and exchange, which meant that only a small proportion of prisoners captured were actually incarcerated by the enemy. The time-honoured institution of parole was based on the assumption that an officer's honour was sufficient to guarantee his word. In some cases, an officer could return home upon giving a pledge not to participate in the hostilities until officially exchanged; alternatively, he might be given complete freedom within a certain area in the enemy state provided he swore not to escape or take part in hostilities. When an entire unit was paroled, the commander's pledge was assumed to be binding on his men. At times, the strain on resources was such that armies were granted parole under the articles of capitulation, although it was more common to take POWs into temporary captivity while the Detaining Power decided which captives were worth retaining for exchange purposes.

The concomitant to parole was exchange, which allowed paroled troops to return to active service. Whenever the British and American governments reached an agreement on the exchange of prisoners, either locally or in general, a fixed number of paroles were cancelled as part of the accord. For example, the British government might agree to release a thousand American militiamen and their officers; in return, 500 British POWs would be freed and the military authorities could also reactivate 500 ex-prisoners who were already back in Upper or Lower Canada but who had been sitting idle as a condition of their parole.

Even when soldiers were taken into captivity, the government's involvement in monitoring and ameliorating their living conditions rarely extended beyond appointing an agent to deal with any difficulties that arose over their care or exchange. Most of the time, POWs were left to their own devices by their government. Officers usually had the choice of either accepting billets in private homes or inns, provided for them at the expense of the Detaining Power, or arranging for accommodation at their own expense. Under normal circumstances, neither option was particularly unpleasant. The soldier and novelist John Richardson, captured by the Americans at Moraviantown in present-day southwestern Ontario in October 1813, lodged with a very hospitable gentleman in Chillicothe, Ohio, and later wrote that 'no individual in the character of a prisoner of war ever had less reason to inveigh against his destiny.' The officers captured at Lundy's Lane in the Niagara Peninsula in July 1814, including a young William Hamilton Merritt, future promoter of the Welland Canal, also experienced a very agreeable captivity and had almost complete freedom after pledging not to escape.[1]

However, a prisoner's lot was not entirely happy, and the isolated problems that cropped up gave hints of future difficulties. Richardson recorded a misunderstanding that forced a group of released POWs to spend a month on a marshy and fever-ridden plain near Sandusky, Ohio; many men fell gravely ill, all because no one in Upper Canada had thought to procure vessels to transport them to Long Point. Returned prisoners sometimes found that their troubles continued after they reached home. One group of soldiers who escaped to Quebec in the spring of 1814 arrived penniless and in rags, and remained nearly destitute while their regimental paymaster looked for authorization to credit their pay for the period they were in captivity.[2]

The most notable lapse in the otherwise humane treatment of POWs during the war was one that would have direct echoes over a century later. In November 1812, when Colonel Winfield Scott and nearly a thousand Americans captured at Queenston were sent to Boston on parole, British commander-in-chief in Canada Sir George Prevost gave orders to retain any prisoners who appeared to have been British-born. Accordingly, 23 American soldiers of Irish birth were detained and shipped to England to be tried for treason. The sequence of reprisals that followed is, in hindsight, almost comical. In May 1813, upon Scott's recommendation, Congress approved the close confinement of 23 British soldiers as hostages, and in October Prevost ordered the detention of 46 American soldiers in retaliation; he went on to decree that, if any of the 23 Britons were executed, twice as many Americans would be put to death. A month later, American President James Madison responded by jailing a further 46 British officers as 'a pledge for the safety of those on whom the British Government seems disposed to wreak its vengeance.' Not to be outdone, Prevost announced that 46 more Americans would be confined, bringing the number of hostages on both sides to well over 200.[3]

Although the exchange of indignant letters makes entertaining reading, the consequences for individual prisoners were dire. Richardson was crowded into a single cell with nine others in Chillicothe, and eventually suffered the indignity of being handcuffed as part of the retaliation. On the other side, American James van Horne, captured just before the surrender of Detroit, was found to be almost naked and suffering badly from lack of food and water when visited by his government's agent in Quebec.[4] The entire episode appeared even more futile when the British government revealed that it had never tried the original twenty-three Irish Americans at all, but had merely imprisoned them with the rest of its POWs. Not for the last time, Canadian soldiers suffered privations for the simple reason that Britain decided to participate in a contest of reprisals.

In the wake of the War of 1812 and the Napoleonic Wars in Europe, attention began to turn towards improving the conditions of captivity, although it was not until the 1860s that a milestone was reached. In 1863, Dr. Francis Lieber, a Prussian jurist at Columbia University, formulated a document now known as the Lieber Code, whose fifty-seven separate articles dealing with POWs made it broader in scope than any subsequent convention until 1929. Although they were innovative at the time, Lieber's provisions merely guaranteed basic rights that today are taken for granted: protection of private property; adequate medical treatment; 'plain and wholesome' food; and humane treatment without being forced to endure 'intentional suffering or indignity.' Following the Franco-Prussian War, the Brussels Declarations of 1874 reiterated the provisions of the Lieber Code, even to the point of echoing some of the language, but they were far more limited in scope. Although they were widely sanctioned by armies around the world, neither the Lieber Code nor the Brussels Declarations had any force of law through ratification.[5]

However, these developments passed largely unnoticed in Canada and reprisal continued to be an important characteristic of captivity through the rest of the century. During the 1837 rebellion in Lower Canada, a rebel mob beat to death a prisoner, Lieutenant George Weir, only to see the act come back to haunt the insurgents in December 1837, when *patriotes* trying to escape from the burning church at St. Eustace were given no mercy by troops shouting, 'Remember Jock Weir.' During the Fenian Raids, the otherwise humane treatment of the Canadians captured at Ridgeway in May 1866 was marred by Fenian General O'Neil's threat that ten prisoners would be put to death for every Fenian executed by Canadian authorities.[6]

Retaliation against captives was also a significant theme in the Riel rebellions. The most obvious manifestation of this was the storm of outraged calls for vengeance that swept English Canada after Louis Riel's execution of the prisoner Thomas Scott, but it also figured prominently in the North-West Rebellion of 1885. The second Riel uprising was also characterized by the other significant facet of captivity in the nineteenth century, the preoccupation with atrocity stories.

First reactions to the Métis seizure of prisoners were mixed, the Montreal *Gazette* calling it 'of no more consequence than a petty riot in any well settled part of old Canada,' but the fate of the hostages held in the cellar at Batoche soon captured the imagination of the public.[7] The soldiers who took part in the attack on Batoche felt that freeing the prisoners was an important part of their mission, and concern for the captives found an outlet in the excessive descriptions of their pitiable plight.[8] Writers described the cellar as a wretched dungeon where the prisoners had lived hourly expecting death, only to emerge weak, ghastly, and white as ghosts to the ringing cheers of their liberators. Charles Mulvaney, who served at Batoche with the Queen's Own Rifles, has left a typical account of the liberated captives: 'The prisoners released from Batoche's house all bear the deep imprint of the hardships they have undergone during their long imprisonment, their pale, pinched faces and emaciated forms furnishing indisputable proof of sufferings, both bodily and mental.' There were also calls for Riel to pay with his life for the suffering of both the prisoners and the soldiers who had fought to free them.[9]

The seizure of hostages by the Métis was serious enough, but news that prisoners had been taken by native bands created an outrage, and speculation immediately began to circulate about the horrors the bands might inflict upon their captives, especially the women.[10] The consequences of these rumours were well described by Dr. John Pennefather, a surgeon with the Winnipeg Light Infantry: 'While lying in Calgary the most sensational stories were circulated as to the atrocities perpetrated by the Indians on prisoners they had captured, especially on several females ... it inflamed the feelings of the men, and there was a general desire to get after Big Bear and his band and take vengeance upon them.'[11] Most soldiers realized that the fate of the captives was the major reason for the expensive and complicated campaign against Big Bear. One officer noted that plans for the expedition began as soon as Minister of Militia Adolphe Caron learned of the seizure of prisoners at Fort Pitt, while another wrote that 'if this old Chief [Big Bear] had not some white prisoners with him the troops would not be asked to follow up the wiley ruffian.'[12]

However, the tales of mistreatment that so inspired the troops were greatly exaggerated. Despite the desire of Mrs. McLean, one of the women taken prisoner at Fort Pitt, to shoot some of her captors, there is no indication that the prisoners were mishandled.[13] Major-General Frederick Middleton, commander of the force that captured Batoche, assured Caron that no indignities had been offered to the women, while Pennefather reported that the freed prisoners arrived at Fort Pitt

'bearing little trace of hardship or suffering.'[14] Inspector Francis
Dickens of the North-West Mounted Police, who escaped with the garrison of Fort Pitt after the civilians there had surrendered to the
natives, wrote that Big Bear had treated his captives well, and wondered
how the government could 'hang a man whose respect for the rules of
war would startle instructors at the Royal Military College.' Salamon
Pritchard, a Métis captured at Frog Lake, stated that his native captors
paid little attention to their prisoners, and one of the teamsters captured by Poundmaker in May 1885 recalled many years later that he too
had been treated decently enough.[15]

Once the captives had been freed and the reports of ill-treatment
had been proven false, interest in the campaign waned, although the
public did not tire of stories from the Rebellion, which almost invariably contained the requisite description of the agonies endured in the
cellar at Batoche or the murder of prisoners at Frog Lake. The apparent
popularity of such accounts, however, never progressed beyond a
somewhat prurient fascination with descriptions of violence and muti-
lation. Indeed, it failed to translate into any sustained interest in the
continuing attempts, which had been under way since earlier in the
century and had produced the Lieber Code and the Brussels
Declarations, to prevent such outrages by codifying the laws of war.

The next important step in the development of international law as
it related to prisoners of war was the Hague Convention of 1899, which
resulted from the Hague Peace Conference of that year. Initiated by the
Czar of Russia out of a desire to limit spending on armaments, the
conference also tackled the thorny problems of arbitration to solve
international disputes and the revision of the still unratified Brussels
Declarations. Though this last goal was not the most important in the
minds of the conference's planners, it provoked a certain amount of
debate. Military theorists were opposed to any such code, though not
for philosophical reasons. Their aversion stemmed from a more pragmatic desire to preserve the commander's freedom of action, as
German staff officer Lieutenant-Colonel A. von Boguslawski pointed
out in 1881 in an influential book on small wars:

> International efforts [to codify the laws of war] ... will remain powerless in
> practice in view of the obligation a commanding officer must have to pro-

tect the safety and honour of the detachments under him ... To draw up an international code would only put the screw on the individual soldier's resolve; it would not influence the conduct of a military leader beyond what he himself perceives as his duty and obligation according to the law.[16]

For these reasons, the British War Office and the Admiralty were reluctant to assent to an international code relating to the conduct of war; Prime Minister Lord Salisbury supported this position and advised against conveying any definite opinion on a code of conduct.[17] Other diplomats raised similar concerns. In 1898, the German and Italian ambassadors in Vienna opined that the Hague Conference should consist of a simple and non-binding exchange of ideas, while a Belgian jurist thought that the amelioration of suffering in war should be left to the general development of international law.[18]

Nor did this scepticism fade when the twenty-six participating nations began their deliberations on 18 May 1899. Andrew White, the head of the American delegation, characterized the mood of the conference as hopeless scepticism while Charles à Court Repington, a member of the British delegation, wrote of the 'vanity of human wishes' and the naïveté of diplomats who believed that the evils of war could be removed with the stroke of a pen.[19] The chief naysayer of the British contingent, though, was naval adviser Admiral Sir John Fisher, who was convinced that warfare would only become more barbaric and took it upon himself to lead an attack on the idea that it could be civilized. According to his biographer, Sir John wrote in journalist W.T. Stead's autograph book that the best way to avoid conflict in the international arena was to make it perfectly clear that you intended to fight with all possible viciousness, including 'boil[ing] your prisoners in oil (if you take any!).'[20]

The scepticism among the delegates at The Hague was matched by a marked lack of interest in Canada. Despite the fact that journalists enjoyed wide access to the proceedings, most Canadian newspapers devoted little space to the conference with only a few providing reasonably full coverage, usually through Associated Press reports. Some papers were moved to editorialize on the subject. In general, editors shared in the climate of scepticism surrounding the conference, the London *Free Press* doubting 'if any nation will consider itself as absolutely bound by its resolutions.' The *Canadian Magazine* found 'food for thought' in the efforts to make warfare more humane, but noted that 'where any such proposal threatens to cripple a particular service or a particular nation we find that it meets with little favour.' The Brantford *Expositor* and *Saturday Night* were equally gloomy.[21] Only the Toronto *Mail and Empire* and the *Vancouver World* tried to put a positive face on the conference, finding solace in the fact that delegates were meeting at all.[22] Furthermore, few editors mentioned the revision of the Brussels Declarations, most of them confining their remarks to disarmament or the arbitration process. Where the laws of war were considered, the use of dum-dum bullets excited more comment than protection for prisoners.

Even military observers had little interest in the proceedings at The Hague. 'Military News and Comment,' a service column that appeared in a number of newspapers, never mentioned the conference, nor does it figure in the papers of the Governor General's military secretary. After the first small wave of interest that accompanied its opening, the Hague Conference of 1899 faded from the pages of Canada's newspapers, to be replaced by the Dreyfus case or Queen Victoria's birthday celebration. Except for a few short press reports on its conclusion, the conference might never have happened, for all that Canadians cared.

Nevertheless, the Hague Convention with Respect to the Laws and Customs of War on Land, which was unveiled at the final session on 29 July 1899, was a considerable achievement.[23] Seventeen articles covered various aspects of captivity, beginning with the assumption that POWs were the responsibility of the hostile government and not of the individual units that captured them. Prisoners could be put to work, except on military projects, according to their rank and abilities; they were to be paid at the standard rate for the task, less the costs of their maintenance. The Detaining Power was bound to provide for prisoners' upkeep and, in terms of food, clothing, and accommodation, prisoners were to be considered on the same footing as the depot troops of the Detaining Power. Article 14 mandated the establishment of an information bureau by each belligerent to answer inquiries regarding POWs and maintain current information about captures, transfers, hospitalizations, and deaths. Relief societies were to be given every facility to perform their humane tasks, and could dispatch delegates to the camps to distribute relief supplies. Finally, repatriation of POWs after the close of hostilities was to take place as quickly as possible. To the delegates, the convention appeared to cover all eventualities, although Britain remained sceptical, signing largely because the other powers were so enthusiastic about it.[24] With Britain's signature, Canada was also bound by the provisions of the convention.

HARD ON THE HEELS of the Hague Peace Conference came an opportunity to test the efficacy of the new convention in South Africa. Although the applicability of the convention to the Boer War was debated vigorously, many observers were keen to see how the convention would operate in the field. Furthermore, by moving the plight of prisoners out of the sterility of the diplomatic salons and onto the field of battle, the war offered considerably more scope for public interest in POW matters, a fact recognized by publishers anxious to capitalize on this fascination by releasing gripping tales of captivity in South Africa. The most well known of these accounts is certainly Winston Churchill's tale of his capture by and eventual escape from the Boer forces.[25]

The future prime minister's reflections on the nature of captivity are deservedly famous, yet his experiences were far from typical for soldiers captured during the war. It is very difficult to determine the number of Canadians taken prisoner in South Africa, largely because service records rarely note that a soldier fell into enemy hands. The British official history lists one Canadian officer and twenty other ranks captured by the Boers, but a casualty table compiled by the Department of Militia and Defence contains no separate listing for POWs.[26] By considering the casualty reports and other accounts, it is possible to identify thirty-nine Canadians who were captured (four officers and thirty-five other ranks), although the actual figure is probably slightly higher.

There are a number of reasons for the inadequacy of POW statistics from the Boer War. In the first place, there was a real stigma attached to becoming a prisoner of war, and most soldiers regarded it as a fate to be avoided at all costs. A member of the Royal Canadian Regiment who transferred to Brabant's Horse, an irregular colonial unit, recounted an incident that must have been typical: 'Colonials know what Boers are and would rather die than be taken prisoners. They sent in word advising us to lay down our arms and if not they would "blow us to hell."

Our Commanding Officer politely replied "We prefer hell!"[27]

Furthermore, there was a tacit assumption in the contemporary military mind that a soldier was at least partly at fault for his own capture, and British military law stipulated that returned POWs should be brought before an examining board to determine whether they had fallen into enemy hands because of carelessness or neglect of duty. Captain D.M. Howard and Private Jonathan Hobson of Lord Strathcona's Horse, captured at Waterval on Dominion Day 1900, appeared at such an inquiry before being absolved of blame, and four members of the 1st Canadian Mounted Rifles captured at Nooitgedacht on 5 September 1900 underwent a similar process to determine whether the capture of their outpost had occurred because they had fallen asleep. An affidavit from the Boer commander who had led the operation (fortunately for the four, he was passing through British lines on a safe-conduct pass at the time) was required before the four were cleared of negligence.[28] Given that soldiers could expect to undergo cross-examination once they returned from captivity, some likely decided to simplify matters by not reporting their capture. Because of the operational characteristics of the Boer War, it was easy for a soldier who had been briefly held prisoner to claim that he had merely become detached from his unit and spent a day or two wandering around the veld.

Other soldiers probably did not bother to report themselves as having been captured because they were often able to return to their unit the same day. During the guerilla stage of the war, Boer commandos faced extreme shortages of supplies and often did not detain POWs at all. In most cases, prisoners were stripped of weapons, valuables, and sometimes clothes and were left to make their own way back to friendly lines.[29] Private A.E. Hilder and other members of his unit, captured at Leliefontein on 7 November 1900, were released as soon as the Boers had confiscated their arms and ammunition. Four members of the 2nd Canadian Mounted Rifles who fell into Boer hands after a hard fight at Boschbult on 31 March 1902 were divested of their arms, equipment, and clothing, congratulated on their stiff resistance, and released with safe-conduct passes. Even officers could often avoid detention. Major D.C.F. Bliss of the Royal Canadian Dragoons was taken prisoner at Witkloof on 6 November 1900, but his captors were content to remove his belt and spurs and send him on his way. Captain Dr. Eugène Fiset, the future Deputy Minister of Militia and Defence, was captured with his batman while recovering from enteric fever in a hospital at Heilbron; both were released as soon as they had regained their health.[30]

For those prisoners who were not immediately released, it was often ridiculously easy to escape. F.J. Livingston, a Canadian doctor serving as a medical officer in Zululand, was taken prisoner by the Boers on 29 October 1899. Fearing that he might be sent to jail in Pretoria, Livingston had no difficulty slipping away from his captors on the first day and making good his escape to friendly territory. A trooper of the Royal Canadian Dragoons who was wounded and captured near Belfast on 5 November 1900 was placed in an unguarded sheep *kraal*, his captors believing him to be too seriously hurt to require supervision. As soon as he was left alone, the trooper stole a horse and rode back to his unit. A private of the Lord Strathcona's Horse had a similar experience; captured at Buffelsdoorn Pass in November 1900, he feigned sleep until his single guard dozed off, then slipped out of the encampment and back to his unit.[31]

The Boers also behaved very correctly to the few prisoners they decided to detain. Despite the occasional negative account of permanent prison camps in South Africa and the horror stories that emanated from the concentration camps established to hold displaced Boer civilians, a British jurist wrote in the 1920s that 'no prisoners of war have ever been better treated than the British soldiers who were captured by the Boers in the South African War.'[32] This statement also holds true for Canadians. The Department of Militia and Defence reported that the Boers 'behaved splendidly' towards the Canadians captured at Leliefontein, and Captain A.H. Macdonell, who was detained by Boer general Christian De Wet for some seven weeks before being released, wrote that 'they [the Boers] could not have treated us as prisoners of war in a better way.'[33] Incidents of ill-treatment of prisoners on the battlefield, which occur with relative frequency in British accounts, are conspicuous by their absence in descriptions of Canadian actions.

So, all in all the Boer War was a non-event in terms of the Canadian government's need to provide for her soldiers in captivity. In most cases, there was little that the government or any other agency could do, or in fact needed to do, to ameliorate the lot of captive Canadians. Time spent as a POW was usually so short that it was counted as little more than an aberration, often scarcely worthy of mention, in a soldier's career. Nevertheless, the Boer War did mark two important developments that would influence the treatment of prisoners in the coming century.

In a transformation that had been under way in Europe since the Revolutionary era, the soldier was ceasing to be perceived as a nameless, faceless individual who generated little interest or sympathy.[34] Instead, the Canadians who went to fight in South Africa were citizen-soldiers, men who had temporarily given up their civilian lives to serve their country in war. They were students, labourers, apprentices, and salesmen; sons, husbands, fathers, and brothers; and they left at home families who passionately cared about their well-being and who were capable, in some cases, of exerting no small amount of influence to ensure that they were well taken care of. One has only to look at contemporary news accounts or unit histories from the Boer War period, with their brief biographical sketches, portrait photographs, and lengthy nominal rolls, to see that the individual soldier had become an object of considerable public concern.

The Boer War also saw the first overseas work of the Canadian Red Cross Society, which would play such an important role in the lives of POWs in the twentieth century. The Red Cross movement was the brainchild of Swiss humanitarian Henri Dunant, whose experiences organizing emergency aid for French and Austrian casualties at the Battle of Solferino in 1859 moved him to consider the welfare of wounded soldiers. In his book *Un souvenir de Solferino*, published in 1862, Dunant proposed the establishment of voluntary relief societies in all nations, and in 1864 the first such organizations were formed. The same year, Dunant was the prime instigator behind the international negotiations that led to the 1864 Geneva Convention for the Amelioration of the Wounded in Time of War. From that date, the creation of national Red Cross societies around the world continued apace.

A Canadian branch of the British Red Cross Society was established in October 1896 in Toronto on the initiative of Lieutenant-Colonel G. Sterling Ryerson, who had served as a surgeon with the North-West Field Force. The branch received the official sanction of the British Red

Cross in December, a requirement that stemmed from the fact that the terms of the 1864 convention prevented a colony or dominion from having a completely autonomous society. The Canadian Red Cross performed extensive work in South Africa, but confined its activities exclusively to the sick and wounded; the published report of Red Cross efforts in South Africa stated explicitly that the Red Cross had always positively refused to assist any men, including POWs, who were in good health.[35] Even when the Canadian Red Cross Society was incorporated as an autonomous body in 1909, the statute mentioned only the provision of aid to the sick and wounded.[36]

Fortunately for future prisoners, the policy against assisting unwounded POWs was changed at the Ninth International Red Cross Conference in Washington in 1912. After a number of attempts to convince national Red Cross societies to accept an obligation to aid POWs, the French Red Cross proposed in Washington that the national societies organize special commissions to maintain contact with and forward POW relief supplies to the International Committee of the Red Cross, headquartered in Geneva, which would arrange for their distribution in the camps. The French proposal passed unanimously and, with minor changes, the mechanism conceived in Washington remained in use through both world wars.[37]

In the years following the war in South Africa, there were also diplomatic initiatives to convene another international conference, to improve the arbitration process, amend further the laws of war, and draw up a convention governing maritime warfare. U.S. President Theodore Roosevelt had raised the possibility of such a conference in 1904, but the Russo-Japanese War intervened and, ironically, further convinced statesmen that the trend was towards greater liberality in the treatment of POWs. In stark contrast to their later conduct, the Japanese evidently took pride in the extent to which they observed the Hague Convention, a fact borne out by contemporary Japanese literature on the conflict.

Western observers were also very favourably impressed. According to one American doctor, 'Probably no prisoners of war ever enjoyed such comfort and such liberty as the Russian prisoners now sojourning at Matsuyama ... many prisoners declare frankly that they had never fared better in their lives.'[38] President Roosevelt too reacted positively, and praised the Japanese Army for showing that 'the most reckless indifference to death and the most formidable fighting capacity can be combined with a scrupulous compliance with all the modern ideas as regards the proper treatment of prisoners.'[39] A few decades later, another Roosevelt would have a rather different assessment of Japanese conduct towards POWs.

The conclusion of the peace treaty that ended the Russo-Japanese War in 1905 provided an admirable opportunity to resurrect the plan for further international deliberations. In the course of negotiations for the conference, Roosevelt agreed to transfer the initiative for issuing invitations to the Czar, who had been responsible for the 1899 gathering. Forty-four nations accepted the invitation to the Second Hague Peace Conference, which ran from 15 June to 18 October 1907.

Despite some commentators' insistence as to the extensive public input into the 1907 conference, it elicited even less interest in Canada than its predecessor had. Editorial comment was sparse, and again reports often failed to mention an improvement in the laws of war as an objective.[40] Where the conference was reported, it was greeted with scepticism. The *Halifax Herald* admitted to being unable to decide whether the gathering was a comedy or a farce, and jibed that war might even break out at the conference itself. The *Busy Man's Magazine* (later *Maclean's*) reprinted an article from the American periodical *Collier's* that called the gathering a 'clearing-house for small differences' and stated that the Boer and Russo-Japanese wars had proven there was little need for further regulation of the treatment of prisoners.[41] Just as in 1899, even informed Canadians had little to say about the laws of war. In March 1907 Ontario Premier James Pliny Whitney introduced a motion in the provincial legislature commending the work at The Hague. The resolution noted that this was the first occasion that nations had gathered during peacetime to discuss mutual relations (like many Canadians, Whitney had evidently missed the 1899 conference altogether), but failed to mention the revision of the laws of war in its declaration of support for the conference.[42] Similarly, Loring Christie, the Department of External Affairs' first legal adviser, in a chronology of events leading up to the Great War made note of the two conferences, but only with respect to attempts to control the arms race.[43]

In some ways the lack of interest was justified, since the 1907 convention that resulted differed from the 1899 version in only minor respects. The article relating to labour was amended to exclude officers from being put to work, while the duties of the information bureaus were expanded to provide for the maintenance of more detailed records on each POW and the return of those records to the prisoner's own government after the conclusion of hostilities. There were also a few minor changes in wording, but nothing that altered greatly the overall thrust of the convention.[44] Interested observers may well have drawn the conclusion that the 1907 conference confirmed what the two most recent wars had suggested: little else needed to be done to protect POWs. Indeed, the Boer War, the Russo-Japanese War, and the two Hague conferences had created a false sense of security regarding prisoners of war that is perfectly summed up in J.M. Spaight's oft-quoted comments on the subject:

> To-day the prisoner of war is a spoilt darling; he is treated with a solicitude for his wants and feelings which borders on sentimentalism. He is better treated than the modern criminal, who is infinitely better off, under the modern prison system, than a soldier on campaign. Under present-day conditions, captivity ... is no sad sojourn by the waters of Babylon; it is usually a halcyon time, a pleasant experience to be nursed fondly in the memory, a kind of inexpensive rest-cure after the wearisome turmoil of fighting. The wonder is that any soldiers fight at all.[45]

This mood of complacency evidently infected the Canadian government as well, which apparently did not consider the impact of the Hague Conventions in the prewar years. The only mention of POWs in government files before 1914 is a brief correspondence regarding the maintenance of discipline among prisoners to ensure their 'safe custody and good treatment' according to the 1907 convention. After two requests for comments, the Canadian government finally informed Britain that it had no thoughts to offer on the matter.[46] Canada's military establishment had rather more to say about POWs, but only just. British military regulations, to which Canadian soldiers were subject, continued to stipulate an inquiry whenever soldiers were captured to determine whether any wrongdoing was involved, but most other provisions in service manuals were purely administrative in nature.[47] The

Field Service Pocket Book issued to officers did include the full text of the 1907 Hague Convention as it pertained to POWs, but the text was so closely printed that one wonders whether it was ever intended to be read.

THE NINETEENTH CENTURY, THEN, provided Canadians with limited experience in the problems of captivity but, as in most other aspects of warfare, that experience would prove to be hardly applicable to the challenges of the twentieth century. The past had taught that captivity was generally a harmless episode, during which a prisoner could expect little in the way of privation. For the few Canadians who bothered to follow the two conferences convened at The Hague, the conventions produced there gave them no reason to change their minds. For its part, the army still operated under the assumption that captivity was the result of a personal failing, and only when this was discounted was it allowed that circumstances might have been beyond the individual's control. And the Canadian public was largely uninterested in the entire subject, save when tales of atrocities perpetrated against prisoners caught their imagination and drove them to demand retribution. Canada was surely not alone in possessing this combination of thought patterns in the years before 1914, but this fact did not make its government and people any more prepared for the First World War.

TWO

'EVERYBODY'S BUSINESS'

IF THE CANADIANS who flocked to answer Britain's call in August 1914 had any ideas at all about captivity, they were most likely unrealistic. They little knew that imprisonment would be counted not in days or weeks as in South Africa, but in years, or that the enemy would not always be as chivalrous towards POWs as recent experience had suggested. Nor was their government any better prepared for the four years of war that lay ahead. In coping with the problems of captivity, the government would be forced, both by the position of Canadian troops in the British Army and by its own failure to take the initiative, to rely on administrative structures that were either beyond its immediate control or hastily cobbled together. The First World War, however, would not find the Canadian people uninterested in the fate of prisoners, and, once primed by the events of 1914 and 1915, they would rush to join the relief campaign in aid of Canadians behind barbed wire. This combination of administrative unpreparedness and a widespread public desire to assist POWs, complicated by unrealistic notions of the nature of captivity,[1] would prove a troublesome mix.

I

A Canadian officer taken prisoner in 1915 likened being captured to a bastard mule, 'born of misadventure, reared in reluctance and its only virtue is its inability to beget its kind,'[2] and this unhappy fate befell thousands of Canadian soldiers and civilians during the Great War (see Table 1 in the Appendix for details). There is some variance in the statistics for the number of Canadian servicemen taken prisoner during the First World War, but the most reliable figures state that over 3800 soldiers were captured, roughly 300 of whom died in captivity.[3] In addition, an indeterminate number of Canadian civilians, primarily merchant seamen, businessmen, and students, were interned by the Central Powers for varying periods of time.

None of these individuals can be said to have been prepared in any way for the rigours of captivity. This is hardly surprising in the case of civilian internees, but soldiers were little better off because the army either consciously ignored or forgot the possibility that they might be taken prisoner, because of the persistence of the nineteenth-century military ethos, which held that to be captured could have resulted only from some personal failing on the part of the soldier. In a letter to the family of a subordinate, the commanding officer of the 100th Battalion revealed the military's attitude: 'It may be possible that he is a prisoner, but the general belief of both officers and men who knew him is that he would not be taken prisoner, he was too good a soldier for that.'[4] It is difficult to say whether this letter was meant to be comforting or invigorating. Such views were just as prevalent outside the military. In 1920, a history of Brant County stated that the local unit 'made the proud boast that of the Battalion members, but six were taken prisoner, and each and all of these were wounded first, not one unwounded man falling into German hands.' Even the British Red Cross noted (albeit erroneously) that it was to Canada's 'eternal honour' that every single Canadian soldier captured at Ypres in April 1915 was either wounded or gassed.[5]

The stigma was reinforced by army regulations and the provisions of military law. The stipulation that a board of inquiry should be held to examine every case of capture essentially assumed guilt until innocence was proved, and even in the confusion of war, the army found time to convene boards to examine POWs who had escaped and returned to England. These boards listened to evidence, often only from the ex-prisoner himself, of the events surrounding his capture, and declared their findings gravely: 'It is the opinion of the Court that No. 77930, Pte. H. Batchelor, was taken prisoner by reason of the chances of War, and through no neglect or misconduct on his part.'[6] Fortunately for ex-

POWs, the flood of returning prisoners in 1918 prevented such proceedings from being convened for every captured serviceman.

Partly because of the stigma attached to becoming a prisoner and partly out of simple neglect, soldiers received virtually no preparation for captivity. The subject was covered in various training manuals but it was apparently not stressed, so most soldiers contemplated only that they might be killed or receive a blighty wound that would earn them a stay in England for recuperation.[7] The comment of Private Bertram Ashbourne, captured at Ypres in April 1915, was typical of Canadian soldiers: 'Not knowing anything about being taken a prisoner of war, I did not know just exactly what was going to happen.'[8] Nor was much mention made of POWs' rights under international law; the Hague Convention was printed in various soldier's handbooks, but one wonders how many men were advised or bothered to read the closely printed text. Even after the first Canadians returned home through exchange, little effort was made to instruct soldiers on the reception they could expect if captured. Any advice given was confined to exhortations against revealing military secrets to the enemy.[9]

Because of the combination of these facts, the emotions experienced by soldiers upon capture ran from shame to bewilderment to depression. Private Mervyn Simmons, captured at Ypres, remembered a comrade constantly repeating to himself, 'This is the thing my father told me never to let happen,' while British Columbia native Private Don Corker, also taken prisoner at Ypres, recalled that it took some weeks to get over the disgrace he felt at becoming a POW. Captain T.V. Scudamore, captured in the same action, received a letter from his father, a veteran of the Afghan Wars, which assumed that Scudamore had been captured unconscious, the implication being that if he had been conscious, he would have fought to the death.[10] Lieutenant E.W. Mingo, taken prisoner at Regina Trench in October 1916, felt an intense depression and mental numbness that he could only liken to that felt by a tuberculosis patient being sent home to die.[11]

To add to the mental strain of capture, Canadian soldiers often faced a rough reception from their new captors, who considered them to be little better than mercenaries. Sergeant Arthur Gibbons, taken prisoner at Ypres, was accused by his captors of fighting for British gold, not for his country; the German soldiers became even more irate when they discovered that Gibbons and his fellow Canadians earned $1.10 a day to fight. One German demanded of Scudamore why Canadians had come to Europe to fight, since Germany had never declared war on Canada.[12]

Even without such ticklish questions, the first few hours of captivity were uncertain at best. Soldiers fighting savagely one hour sometimes found it difficult to become compassionate captors the next, as some Canadians learned to their discomfort. Mingo, despite the fact that he had been badly wounded in an explosion, was clubbed over the head by a German soldier brandishing a grenade, while Corporal Edward Edwards, a Princess Pat captured at Polygon Wood in May 1915, narrowly escaped injury by a huge German swinging an axe.[13] Nor could enemy medical personnel be relied upon to deal gently with wounded prisoners. A.F. Field was threatened with hanging by a German hospital orderly, who was keen to retaliate for the alleged hanging of three Germans by Canadian troops. When Private Fred Gies of the 13th Battalion was taken prisoner at Sanctuary Wood in June 1916, he received no medical attention at all for a piece of shrapnel lodged in his shoulder; when he finally reached hospital four days later, maggots had taken up residence in the wound.[14]

Other POWs were surprised by the enemy's solicitude. H.W. Macdonnell recalled that he was treated with consideration by the troops who captured him at Mount Sorrel in June 1916; they were more curious about Canadians than anything. Jack Evans of the 4th Canadian Mounted Rifles, another Mount Sorrel prisoner, expected to be butchered by his captors but got no more than a few kicks as he and his comrades were being marched to the rear.[15] University of Toronto graduate Captain J. Harvey Douglas was taken prisoner by a German soldier who had once been a waiter in an English hotel; his wounds were expertly dressed by a German doctor, he was given a hot cup of coffee, and two German Red Cross workers carefully located stretchers so that Douglas and his wounded comrades did not have to sit or stand on the train to Germany.[16]

Not all prisoners were so lucky on the journey into captivity. That trip often began with a march to the nearest major railhead, where the new captives were packed into empty buildings until transport was available. For officers, the train journey was as comfortable as could be expected under the circumstances; they usually travelled in fourth-class carriages and received meagre rations whenever the train stopped. For private soldiers, conditions were more primitive. Packed into filthy and unventilated boxcars, as many as forty or fifty men in each, they were given little in the way of food or drink, even if the trip lasted a number of days. Mounted rifleman Harry Stone got no more than three issues of water during a three-day trip to Germany. Corporal Edwards was a little luckier; along with one drink of water, he received one ration of bread and practically inedible bacon between his capture and his arrival at Giessen days later.[17]

The new prisoners were doubtless grateful to reach a more permanent home, though their relief usually faded as soon as they got a closer look at their camps. Jack O'Brien of the 28th Battalion thought that the camp at Dülmen looked like a chicken ranch, while Lieutenant J.R. Martin of Hamilton called his camp at Schwarmstadt the Swampy Camp because the three large pumps that ran constantly were incapable of keeping the compound drained. Captain Scudamore's temporary home at Halle was a condemned iron foundry with no proper sanitation and a dirt floor in the mess hall.[18] Nor was John Thorn of the 7th Battalion impressed by his first view of Bischofswerda camp, an old cavalry school that had been ringed with barbed wire; his opinion was not enhanced when he discovered that the wooden beds in the long brick barrack huts broke if one sat too heavily upon them.[19] Lieutenant N.L. Wells, a Regina bank employee taken prisoner in June 1916, was a little luckier with the camp at Friedberg. A former training school for Germans NCOs, the camp had shower baths, a gymnasium, and enough open space for the prisoners to build a football field and two tennis courts.[20]

Even prisoners living in such comparatively congenial conditions, however, faced the psychological problems of captivity. The Ottawa poet Arthur S. Bourinot, shot down and captured in June 1917, summed up the monotony of captivity in verse:

> Silently, surely, weary,
> > The sentries pace their beat,
> Silently, surely, weary,
> > The lagging hours we meet.
>
> Imprisoned, lonely, hoping,
> > The future is our goal,
> Imprisoned, lonely, hoping,
> > Time takes of us her toll.[21]

Many First World War camps had been converted from other uses.
This one at Blankenburg had been a school.

In the unnatural prison camp atmosphere, where normal human relations, privacy, and even silence were all but unobtainable, Harvey Douglas
could easily understand how long-term prisoners 'become despondent,
nervous wrecks and often go stark staring mad, or commit suicide.'
Donald Laird of the 4th Canadian Mounted Rifles suffered very badly
in this regard. Troubled by hallucinations and fits of mania, he shunned
the company of other prisoners and spent most days in his bunk; not
even Red Cross food could tempt him at times.[22] Trooper Charles
Harrison of the Royal Canadian Dragoons spent two weeks in solitary
confinement after being captured in March 1918; fearing that his reason would desert him, Harrison talked incessantly to himself, repeating every quotation he could recall learning in church and school.[23]

While all prisoners faced a struggle to keep their wits about them,
private soldiers often fought a battle for survival as well. According to
the Hague Convention, POWs could be put to work by their captors,
and the German government took full advantage of this provision,
despite the efforts of Canadians to avoid work. Private Bilson Merry of
the 7th Battalion recalled that when German labour coordinators canvassed his camp to determine the talents of the prisoners, a considerable number of them disavowed any skills at all and claimed to have

Every Day in the Week, 6 AM, Giessen Camp, by Arthur Nantel, who was captured at
Ypres in April 1915. The work illustrates the cramped conditions prevailing in many camps,
a feature of captivity which took a toll on the minds of some POWs.

been bartenders or salesmen; one enterprising fellow even claimed to
be a draught clerk, a specialist in the opening and closing of windows.[24]

In reality, prisoners had little choice but to accept the work assigned
to them. Some Canadians were lucky enough to be sent to farms or
other agricultural labour camps, where the conditions might be reasonably pleasant, but very many more were forced to work in dangerous
occupations under the control of often vicious overseers. Some, like
Sam Watson of the 102nd Battalion, were kept immediately behind
German lines to rebuild roads and railway lines. Exposed to all the dangers of the front, they lived in whatever shelter happened to be available and were given no blankets, soap, or clean clothes, and little in the
way of food; by the fall of 1917, Watson's weight had dropped to eighty-
five pounds.[25]

Of course, labour away from the front could be just as dangerous.
Jack Evans was sent to a coal mine, where he and his fellow prisoners
worked ten-and-a-half-hour days in appalling conditions, while Fred
Gies laboured for twelve hours a day in an East Prussian lumber camp

31

for the princely wage of a cent an hour. Privates Harry Drope and Bidwell Stone of the Princess Pats got into trouble with their guards at Dülmen and were sent to a work party at Goldap in East Prussia. There they lived in barracks with sand floors that had been built half underground in a sandpit, and were roused at 4:00 AM to march to work demolishing houses that had been damaged earlier in the war.[26]

With appalling working conditions and often brutal overseers, the prospects of serious injury or even death were very real. Private Arthur Wyllie of the 7th Battalion tried to keep up with the work at a salt mine at Olden, but got such bad sores on his legs that he was eventually posted to less arduous work; decades later, he still carried the scars from his labours. William Langford broke his leg when a ditch he was digging caved in on him, while prewar machinist and 3rd Battalion Lance-Corporal Thomas Bromley contracted blood poisoning when he injured his hand at a chemical factory.[27] Billy Flanagan of the 4th Canadian Mounted Rifles was not so fortunate; put to work in the notorious Auguste Victoria mine, he was killed by a fall of coal.[28]

Faster, You Schweinhund, by Arthur Nantel. The artist's subtitle noted that the sketch illustrates 'the delights of life in a straffe commando [punishment camp].'

Those who escaped accidental death or injury had to evade the ire of guards and civilian overseers, who were determined to use any means to extract as much labour as possible out of their charges. Private Thomas Noon of the 48th Highlanders lost his voice for six months when a guard struck him across the throat with a pick handle at the Beienrode salt mine. Melville Trueman of the same unit, only seventeen when he enlisted in September 1914, was beaten about the head and face and forced to sit at attention all day when he refused to work in a munitions factory.[29] Prisoners who attempted organized resistance were treated even more harshly. In 1916, eight Canadian POWs at Bokelah refused to obey the orders of the German sergeant-major and demanded to see the commandant. A brief skirmish ensued and the eight were charged with mutiny; after a trial witnessed by the American ambassador, they received prison terms of twelve to thirteen years.[30] For some, it was as good as a death sentence. Private William Brooke was sent to a prison in Cologne to serve the sentence; his cell was dank and airless, and Brooke eventually contracted pneumonia and died in March 1917. Private Francis Armstrong lasted a little longer. Picked as the ringleader of the Bokelah mutiny by the German court, he faced a death sentence but got away with thirteen years. Enduring the same conditions as Brooke, Armstrong at least made it back to England after the war before dying of the experience.[31]

The prisoners, however, were quick to learn that resistance was possible without risking one's life. Don Corker, sent to labour at a stone quarry at Rittmannshausen, found that, with the aid of a German phrase book, he could waste considerable time talking to his guards and overseers. Later, while working at a lock at Dieteheim, Corker and his comrades took every opportunity to dispose of their tools by burying them or dropping them in the river; their guards never seemed to connect such acts with the prisoners, and constantly blamed the disappearance of tools on the civilian workers.[32] Frank MacDonald of the 1st Canadian Mounted Rifles found himself on a German farm, where he and his comrades were instructed to plant cabbage seedlings. It did not take them long to learn that a deep nick made in each root would leave the farmer with a field of dead plants within a few days. Jack O'Brien discovered many abandoned tunnels in the mine in which he worked, and he and a few pals took to slipping away from their group on the way to work; they whiled away the day chatting and napping and, at the end of the shift, blackened their faces with coal dust and tagged on to the end of the line of prisoners as it passed them.[33] Acts of resistance such as these were small victories, but they were victories nonetheless.

II

While prisoners struggled with the trials and tribulations of captivity, individuals back in Canada were coming to grips with the problems associated with superintending POW affairs. The starting point of that superintendence was an accurate accounting of the number of prisoners in enemy hands and a detailed picture of conditions inside the camps; only with such information could informed decisions be made about the shape of the relief effort, based on the number of prisoners involved, their living conditions, the supplies provided by their captors, and the amenities required most urgently.

To provide accurate lists of the individuals who had fallen into enemy hands, the Hague Convention called for the establishment of information bureaus to receive and transmit personal details of all prisoners. Lists of soldiers captured by the Germans were forwarded by the German POW information bureau to the British Foreign Office through neutral governments. For Canada, the task of collating these lists fell to the Information Department, Casualties and Prisoners, established by the Canadian Red Cross Society (CRCS) at 14 Cockspur Street, London, on 11 February 1915.

Two very capable women controlled most of the department's operations. The directorship was held by Lady Julia Drummond, a prominent figure in Canadian philanthropic organizations such as the Victorian Order of Nurses and the National Council of Women. In 1908, as president of the Women's Canadian Club of Montreal, she had been the first woman to speak at a public banquet in the city. When her son, the much-eulogized Captain Guy Drummond, was killed in action in 1915, she commissioned the Canadian sculptor Robert Tait McKenzie to sculpt his figure, which was later presented to the National Archives. Lady Julia's devotion to Red Cross work was an equally tangible and considerably more valuable memorial to her son.

Evelyn Rivers Bulkeley, with son Robert

Assisting the director as head of the Prisoner of War Branch was
Evelyn Rivers Bulkeley, who had come to Canada in 1911 as a lady-in-
waiting to the Duchess of Connaught. Two years later she married
another member of the Governor General's household, but in October
1914 her husband, an officer of the Scots Guards, was killed in action at
Ypres. Like Lady Drummond, Evelyn Rivers Bulkeley consoled herself
by throwing all her energies into Red Cross work.

The methods used by the POW Branch were primitive but effective.
Because the German lists did not distinguish between soldiers from
different parts of the Empire, the nominal rolls had to be examined

carefully to sort out members of Canadian units, as well as members of British units who listed their next of kin as residing in Canada. Gradually, a card index of Canadians in captivity was compiled, and similar lists were maintained by the Department of Militia and Defence in Ottawa and CRCS headquarters in Toronto.[34] Conspicuous by its absence was any central office to which inquiries from next of kin or friends were directed. The POW Branch in London should have filled this role, but government officials were reluctant to forward inquiries to a non-governmental office. This state of affairs persisted for most of the war, and proved to be a nagging flaw.

Once the identities of Canadians in captivity were known, conditions inside the camps had to be analyzed to determine the supplies required. The vehicle for obtaining this information was the camp inspection.[35] The first such inspection occurred on 20 August 1914, when the American ambassador to Germany, James W. Gerard, visited a camp at Döbberitz and was permitted to converse freely with the British civilians interned there. Embassy staff continued similar inspections through the fall, but there was no agreed program of inspections and each visit had to be arranged on an individual basis with the camp commandant and the commander of the military district. The United States was very keen to arrange visits according to a definite schedule, pointing out that the 'most terrible accounts of the barbarous treatment' of British prisoners stood in marked contrast to the treatment of Germans in Britain. His Majesty's Government agreed to a program of visits on 27 January 1915, and on 17 March 1915 Germany granted the American request and the inspections could proceed according to a mutually acceptable schedule.[36]

The inspection reports compiled by neutral delegates discussed the living conditions, diet, clothing, and recreational and spiritual activities of the prisoners, but there was some question as to whether the inspectors' assessments gave a true picture of conditions in the camps. Many prisoners reported after the war that camp officials routinely spruced up the barracks before a neutral visit, and removed the few amenities used to brighten the huts once the visit had concluded. John Thorn, incarcerated in the damp and dismal Fort Zorndorf as punishment for trying to escape, noticed one day 'that the whole place was being cleaned up, and even curtains were being placed on the windows.' The mystery was solved when Ambassador Gerard arrived at the camp the next morning.[37] Other POWs doubted that the inspections brought any improvement in their living conditions. Ottawa pilot Russell Smith wrote in his diary of the visit of Dutch inspectors: 'Our SBO [Senior British Officer] went over all our complaints and grievances, it might do some good but I doubt it.'[38] Despite such scepticism, one must give the inspectors a certain amount of credit for possessing enough acumen to see through temporary alterations. Furthermore, there are sufficient accounts of improvements following camp visits to suggest that the inspectors did secure substantive changes for the better in the prisoners' lot.[39]

When official inspection reports were unavailable, other sources of information had to suffice. Interviews with POWs who had escaped or been repatriated from Germany on medical grounds were particularly useful in this regard, for they could provide details on the relief that was getting through and suggest ways to improve the shipments.[40] Unfortunately, when neither inspection reports nor first-hand accounts were available, officials were obliged to rely on newspaper stories (many of which were third- or fourth-hand accounts passed on by the relatives of prisoners), rumour, and hearsay.[41]

As soon as information on camp conditions was available, the relief effort could get under way. Most supplies reached the camps through the channels outlined at the Washington Red Cross Conference in 1912. Parcels destined for POWs, whether they originated with the Red Cross or with relatives who mailed them at the local post office, were forwarded by the General Post Office in Britain to one of the neutral countries, usually Switzerland. Swiss haulage companies then delivered the parcels to the camps via a number of central depots. The entire process, from the packing of a parcel to its receipt by a prisoner, took two to three months. The only exception to this pattern was bread, provided by various agencies and shipped through a Red Cross depot at Frankfurt. Despite tests of the bread's shelf life, it often reached the camps in an unappetizing condition. George Mercer, shot down and captured in the spring of 1918, reported that his bread arrived consumed by mould, while former Bank of Commerce employee Percy Hampton, another young pilot downed in 1918, recalled that bread from Berne was so hard that the prisoners had to punch holes in the loaves, fill them with water, and bake them until they were soft enough to eat.[42]

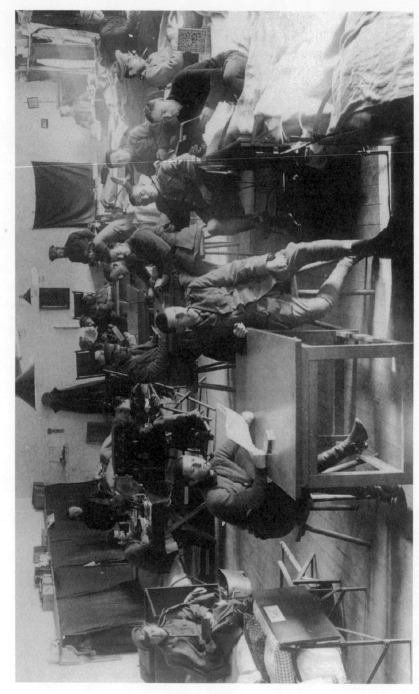

Cramped living quarters, like this officers' dormitory in the prison camp at Halle in 1918, often drew criticism from neutral inspectors.

Because of the position of the Canadian contingent within the British Army, the relief effort for Canadian POWs was circumscribed by that which developed in Britain. For the first few months of the war, no central direction of relief existed and the shipment of supplies to POWs was carried on by two types of organizations: groups associated with regimental depots, known as Regimental Care Committees, and independent local associations supplying comforts to prisoners from their area. This disparate campaign was adequate while the number of prisoners remained small, but by the end of 1914 the need for a central committee was evident. In March 1915, newspaper owner and benefactor of the blind Sir Arthur Pearson and Sir Charles Lucas, a civil servant and historian, established the POW Help Committee to coordinate the relief effort by encouraging cooperation between local groups and the Regimental Care Committees.

When the Help Committee began operations, the POW Branch of the Canadian Red Cross in London affiliated itself with the new umbrella group and began playing a dual role as an official information bureau and a relief agency. The card index used to respond to inquiries from relatives began to function as a record of relief shipments, and the volunteer workers could easily determine the date and contents of the most recent parcel sent to any prisoner. The London bureau also worked closely with CRCS headquarters in Toronto, which coordinated the relief effort in Canada.

At the time of its inception, the POW Branch had little to do because so few Canadians had been captured. Nevertheless, Canadians were far from uninterested in POW matters and quickly developed a fascination with the plight of their citizen-soldiers in captivity. Not surprisingly, the traditional preoccupation with atrocity stories soon came to the fore. As an American prison camp inspector noted, an effective way to encourage patriotism was to portray the enemy as barely human, and in this regard stories of the ill-treatment of prisoners were particularly effective.[43] A typical propaganda tactic was the publication of documents such as *The Usages of War on Land*, a manual issued by the German General Staff. In hindsight, the manual seems quite reasonable, and in fact differed little in substance from the British *Manual of Military Law*; both were essentially military codifications of the 1907 Hague Convention. However, every effort was made to portray the book in the worst possible light, and the introduction pointed out that Germany treated the Hague Conventions as scraps of paper. Lest any uncertainties remain in the mind of the reader, the excerpt chosen for the title page stated that 'certain severities are indispensible in war, nay, more, the only true humanity very often lies in a ruthless application of them.'[44]

With the groundwork laid by such publications, there developed in the Allied world a preoccupation with German atrocities, which came to be known collectively as *Kultur* or *Schrecklichkeit* (frightfulness).[45] In 1915, Britain's Committee on Alleged German Outrages submitted a report that included numerous accounts of the murder of prisoners. Like *The Usages of War on Land*, the report circulated widely in the Dominions.[46] Later that year, the execution of Edith Cavell stoked the flames of indignation. Cavell, a British nurse in Brussels, had been arrested for helping Allied soldiers escape from Belgium and was tried by a German military court. Although the case against her was clear-cut, the execution of a woman who had dedicated her life to humanitarian work horrified the Allied world. Ire was raised further by the publication of accounts of misdeeds against Canadians. Reporting on the murder of Private David Moncur of Toronto, captured in October 1914 while serving with the Gordon Highlanders, a Canadian newspaper queried, 'Was Murder of Miss Cavell any worse than brutal shooting of Toronto boy?'[47]

Occasionally, such accounts drew calls for reprisals, or at the very least a closer adherence to the concept of reciprocity of treatment. When reports surfaced that Canadian prisoners were being treated especially harshly, the government pointed out that conditions in camps in Canada provided no grounds for such treatment.[48] As the war dragged on, relatives too began to notice this contradiction and, in a few isolated cases, openly demand reprisals. One individual suggested warning Germany that, for every day prisoners were maltreated, a postwar boycott would be extended for one week.[49] Late in the war, the British government itself suggested reprisals and wrote to the Governor General accordingly: 'In connection with treatment of our prisoners in Germany I should be glad to learn whether your Ministers would if necessary arrange for reprisal treatment of selected prisoners of war, and to receive names of important German civilians or exceedingly wealthy ones.' Canada's response was cool, stating that once further details were received, the government would cooperate 'in any reasonable way.'[50]

Accounts of atrocities certainly raised emotions against the enemy, but they also bred within the Canadian public feelings of concern that were to find an outlet after two battles in 1915 and 1916. In late April 1915, Canadian troops bore the brunt of a German offensive in the Ypres Salient, and numerous battalions suffered heavy losses: the 3rd (Toronto), 7th (British Columbia), and 15th (Toronto) Battalions each lost over 200 men as POWs, while the 2nd (Eastern Ontario) and 13th (Montreal) Battalions each lost over a hundred men as POWs.[51] By August 1915, roughly 1300 Canadian soldiers were reported to be prisoners of war in Germany. The following year, on 2 June 1916, both the Princess Patricia's Canadian Light Infantry and the 4th Canadian Mounted Rifles sustained heavy casualties at Mount Sorrel, and by July another 730 names had been added to the rolls of Canadian POWs.[52]

The lengthening POW lists focused attention on the needs of prisoners, and concerned Canadians began to look for ways to assist in the provision of relief. The simplest method was through donations to any of the funds that had been established, such as the Duchess of Connaught's POW Fund or the Red Cross national appeals. These appeals always specifically mentioned CRCS work for POWs, the January 1917 campaign pointing out that it cost 35 cents for the Red Cross to feed a Canadian POW. 'In what way,' asked an advertisement, 'can a Canadian spend 35 cents better than in providing necessary, nourishing food for our Canadian brothers daily suffering for us?'[53] Furthermore, any group of concerned citizens could assemble to raise money for charitable purposes, either by securing registration under the War Charities Act or by obtaining authorization from a registered charity.[54] A wide variety of organizations solicited contributions, with most of the money eventually going to the Red Cross POW Branch in London. Donations in the form of aid also reached prisoners through the YMCA, which shipped books, clothing, food, and religious material to the camps.[55]

Another vehicle for involvement in the relief effort was the regimental committee, administered either by the regiment itself or by the ladies' auxiliary. Typical was the Relief and Casualty Committee of the 5th Royal Highlanders of Canada, which raised money to benefit men of the Montreal battalions who had been captured. In the fall of 1915, Lieutenant G.L. Ogilvie, chairman of the committee, sent a circular letter to influential Montrealers requesting cash contributions; the committee would also accept donations of clothing or non-perishable food to be shipped to camps in Germany. The first appeal raised over $400, which was remitted to the Canadian Red Cross in London with instructions that each prisoner from the 13th and 42nd Battalions receive a parcel for Christmas; the packages were to be marked as originating from 'their friends in the Home Regiment.'[56]

Perhaps the most popular method of assisting POWs was through adoption, an idea that was apparently pioneered in Canada by the Ottawa Women's Canadian Club. In July 1915, the club began encouraging individuals to adopt POWs by pledging $2 per month for their upkeep, and pointed out that the scheme had appeal for all ages: 'in order that all may have a personal share in this great effort of mercy, even the penny savings or voluntary offerings of the children will be accepted and devoted to the cause.'[57] Eventually, the scheme was picked up by many other groups, such as the Canadian Prisoners' Aid of Fort William, Ontario, the War Aid Department of the St. John Ambulance of Manitoba, and the Beaches Branch of the Toronto Women's Patriotic League. The Nova Scotia Red Cross was particularly active, arranging for the adoption of 270 prisoners in forty-eight camps. It accepted responsibility for two-thirds of the monthly cost of maintaining a POW (with the national Red Cross covering the balance), and encouraged individuals or organizations to make a monthly pledge towards that sum. The adopter kept in touch with the adoptee, with contact coordinated by an executive committee of the provincial society.[58]

Individuals could also adopt POWs without the aid of an intermediary organization, and the Department of Militia and Defence was deluged with requests from kind-hearted souls who wanted to send parcels to prisoners from their area, from the local regiment, or who had listed no next of kin. Adopting men with a local connection had particular appeal, for as one correspondent wrote when requesting a list of POWs from the 29th and 47th Battalions, 'while we are interested in *all* prisoners still our *own* come first.'[59] The volume of requests received at Militia and Defence suggested that there was no shortage of adopters; more than one organization requested further names from the department when the first list they had received was exhausted by local philanthropists.[60]

Regrettably, the government had no mechanism to handle this volume of requests. Without a central office to deal with POW matters and because few officials seemed to know that the Red Cross POW Branch in London was able to assume this role, Members of Parliament and non-military departments forwarded inquiries to various offices in the Department of Militia and Defence, each of which attempted to answer queries on its own. These offices rarely gave consistent advice. A relative who inquired about sending relief supplies might be told to approach the Women's Canadian Club, the Dominion Express Company of Canada, or Cook's Travel Agency; only a few correspondents received the correct advice, that they should contact the Canadian Red Cross.[61] In response to one query about Christmas parcels for prisoners, the Assistant Director of Supplies and Transport first replied that they were allowed, and then wrote back some weeks later saying that they were not.[62] Having received a request for supplies from three Canadian POWs, Colonel Victor Williams (himself to become a prisoner in 1916) at the Canadian Training Division, Shorncliffe, inquired of Colonel J.W. Carson, the Minister of Militia and Defence's special representative in England, whether anything could be done for them. Carson was unsure what provisions could be made, but suggested that the American Express Company be approached. The advice was given despite the fact that, less than a week before, a branch of the Overseas Military Forces of Canada (OMFC) had been instructed to forward all requests for aid to Evelyn Rivers Bulkeley.[63]

The waste and duplication to which these misunderstandings could lead became obvious in August 1915, when Lady Julia Drummond drew the attention of Militia Minister Sir Sam Hughes to a routine order advising Canadian POWs that their requirements could be supplied by the Canadian Field Comforts Commission, an organization that had gone to England with the First Contingent to distribute gifts to Canadian soldiers. Drummond was rightly indignant about this order, which flew in the face of the arrangements previously made for the dispatch of comforts by the Canadian Red Cross.[64] Hughes ordered Carson to look into the affair, and it transpired that the misunderstanding had originated in Giessen camp and had merely become compounded over time. As Carson put it, the 'matter started with somebody's blunder in Germany, and this blunder seems to have wandered through every

Government Department here and on to Canada and Back again.'[65] Once the mistake was identified, Rivers Bulkeley pressed Prime Minister Robert Borden for a public statement of the government's position that 'all Funds and matters connected with the Prisoners of War [should] be centralized as much as possible in the Red Cross.' In November, a Militia Order formalized the arrangements by stressing that all comforts were to be supplied through the CRCS.[66]

III

If the attempts to provide comforts to POWs hinted at the potential for problems inherent in the Canadian relief effort, the food parcel campaign revealed those problems in full bloom. The image of the starving prisoner of war has long been a particularly potent one, so it is hardly surprising that Canadians interested in the plight of prisoners expressed the greatest concern over their diet. Under the Hague Convention, the Detaining Power was bound to feed prisoners the same rations as its own garrison troops, but this proved to be a vain hope in many cases. The German government took full advantage of the Allied blockade to renounce its responsibility to provide adequate food for prisoners, and once parcels began arriving in the camps, some commandants reduced rations even further, believing that they no longer had the same obligation to feed POWs.[67]

Certainly in many instances, the rations were barely sufficient. The German authorities reported issuing bread, potatoes, vegetables, meat, fish, cheese, milk, and smaller quantities of other foods to prisoners each week, but in fact the rations were often less satisfactory. Don Corker recalls that a typical day's ration consisted of coffee made from scorched acorns for breakfast, a thick soup for lunch, the same soup in a much watered-down form for dinner, and a piece of rye bread (each prisoner received a small loaf, ten inches in diameter, every five days). One analysis of the bread found it to be nearly fifty per cent water, wood fibre, and ashes.[68] Prisoners at Parchim camp breakfasted on acorn coffee and bread garnished with a jam made of crushed beets that had been chemically sweetened; the bread was made of sifted sawdust, and the jam itself would remove the tin plating from a spoon in a matter of hours. For every other meal, they received pea soup, so called not because it contained any peas but because it was the colour of pea soup.[69] At Dülmen, Jack Evans lived on black bread, turnip soup, and a gritty and nearly inedible porridge known by the prisoners as 'sand storm.' Bilson Merry and his fellow inmates were issued turnips, weeds, and a mystery stew, the meat for which was reputed to have originated in the local zoo. Frank MacDonald went to the trouble of collecting the bones from one ration of stew; he later claimed that he had been able to reconstruct the skeleton of a small dachshund.[70]

POWs promptly informed relatives of the inadequacy of prison camp rations, and the provision of food parcels eventually became the single most important aspect of the relief effort. Soon after the first large groups of Canadians were reported captured, Militia and Defence forwarded a questionnaire to the camps in Germany to determine whether Canadian prisoners wished to assign a portion of their pay to cover weekly food parcels to be sent by the Red Cross. The majority agreed, and this regulation was eventually incorporated into the army paybook.[71] By early 1916, most Canadian POWs were assigning enough pay to cover two parcels per month, with adopters paying for two further parcels, so that each prisoner received at least one package a week. When the CRCS began receiving sufficient donations to enable it to supply the parcels at no cost to POWs, prisoners were given the opportunity to reconsider their pay assignments. Most prisoners, however, elected to continue their assignments; Rivers Bulkeley later pointed out that it helped a prisoner's morale to contribute to his own upkeep and not be entirely reliant on charity.[72]

The Red Cross was not the sole supplier of food parcels, though; regimental associations, local groups, relatives or friends of POWs, and anyone else, for that matter, could send packages to prison camps through licensed suppliers or through the CRCS in London. This unregulated shipment of relief resulted in a steady increase in the number of parcels moving through the Red Cross office, to the point where the volunteer workers could no longer cope with the flow. Furthermore, the private dispatch of parcels meant that relief was very unevenly distributed. A British inquiry in 1917 discovered that some prisoners had few parcels while others received up to sixteen each fortnight, besides the regular bread parcels; consequently, some POWs received considerably more food than they could eat.[73] Numerous other problems plagued the shipment of parcels: many were incorrectly or incompletely addressed, and hence were undeliverable; parcels often included perishables or foodstuffs packed in jars, which almost invariably broke in transit and ruined the rest of the contents; and other packages were so badly packed that they fell apart in transit.[74]

The relief operation to aid civilian internees was equally unsatisfactory, but for quite different reasons. At first, the Canadian High Commission in London maintained contact with civilians through government information bureaus in Denmark and Norway and the Canadian Trade Commission in Rotterdam, but such channels were clearly not suitable for shipping relief supplies. In 1915, High Commissioner Sir George Perley pointed out that, because the Red Cross served only combatants, civilians were in danger of slipping through the cracks in the relief effort and, consequently, the government should assume responsibility for their maintenance. Prime Minister Borden agreed and a number of London firms were contracted to pack supplies for the Canadians in Ruhleben, an internment camp that had been established at a race course in Berlin; eventually, twenty-seven cases of supplies were shipped via the American Express Company.[75] When more supplies were requested the following year, officials again had to scramble to find a means of shipping them. The High Commission approached the Canadian Trade Representative in Rotterdam, but he had no useful suggestions; subsequent inquiry determined that the POW Help Committee had also not been sending parcels to civilian internees on a regular basis and had no plans to do so.[76] Such confusion did nothing to soothe the worries of internees' next of kin, who began to approach government officials with concerns that their relatives were being overlooked. Their worries were not allayed by Under-Secretary of State for External Affairs Sir Joseph Pope's claim that no civilian internees were in need of aid.[77] Nor would they have been comforted by the confusion over which agency was responsible for the upkeep of civilian internees. The Canadian Red Cross at one point claimed responsibility for assisting civilians but the High Commission in London disagreed, maintaining that they were under the care of the POW Committee.[78] There is no indication that this controversy was ever resolved, and internees continued to be overlooked in the workings of the relief campaign.

With the relief program for POWs in danger of collapsing under the demands placed upon it and the effort for civilians clearly stagnating, government action was imperative. The War Office, believing that the supervision of voluntary organizations in Britain was a Home Office matter, had already once declined to assume responsibility for the POW Help Committee, and the government had also ignored the calls of one Member of Parliament to establish a 'Ministry of Prisoners.'[79] In September 1916, however, the War Office was induced to act and ordered the establishment of the Central POW Committee as a branch of the War Organization of the British Red Cross Society and the Order of St. John. The committee, which included among its members General Sir Charles Mansfield Clarke, the British Quartermaster-General during the Boer War, and former imperial adventurer Sir Leander Starr Jameson (who had been made a prisoner himself after his abortive raid on the South African republic of the Transvaal in 1895), was intended to coordinate all aspects of the relief effort. It was empowered by the British government to assume complete control of the shipment of relief supplies, and it alone could authorize other groups to work as its agents. As part of the reorganization, all Dominion aid agencies were transformed as well. The Canadian Red Cross POW Branch became the Care Committee for Canadian POWs and was authorized to act as the official agent for Canadian prisoners. As such, it was bound by all regulations emanating from the Central POW Committee.

The committee quickly made sweeping changes to the relief effort. In October 1916, it announced that on 1 December a scheme for the coordination of relief would come into force. All parcels going to POWs had to be packed by the Central POW Committee or an authorized agent; all other organizations had to discontinue shipments and confine themselves to collecting money to be turned over to the committee or one of its agents. Each prisoner could receive parcels from only one source, and the total weight of food reaching a prisoner was not to exceed thirty pounds (including bread) per week. The most controversial aspects of the new plan, though, were the stipulations that relatives and adopters could no longer send individual food parcels to POWs, and that the scheme would not apply to officers, who could still receive unlimited parcels from any source.[80] The official reason for this last exemption was that, because there were fewer officer prisoners, it was no great problem to examine and censor all parcels sent to them. Implicit, though, was the class-based assumption that the families and friends of officers could be trusted not to contravene parcel regulations; the next of kin of enlisted men, on the other hand, were not necessarily so reliable and had to be monitored more carefully.

Not surprisingly, reaction to the scheme in Canada was quick and largely negative, especially when Canadian Red Cross Commissioner Charles Hodgetts stated (incorrectly, as it later proved) that Canadian parcels reaching England after 1 December would not be sent on.[81] One correspondent expressed disbelief that other ranks would be discriminated against and stated that, if it was true, 'it is an outrage, and will not be tolerated by the fathers and mothers of the unfortunate prisoners.' The sister of a Canadian POW wondered whether the sons of those officials who issued the orders were all officers, while another concerned individual pointed out that 'this is not a time to raise obstacles in the path of relief for our unfortunate soldiers.'[82]

The greatest flaw in the new scheme was that its impact on Canadian POWs was unclear. Militia and Defence replied to inquiries that it did not apply to Canada, a view that was confirmed by the Central POW Committee, but much uncertainty characterized government correspondence on the subject. In fact, it seems that only Evelyn Rivers Bulkeley fully understood the scheme and its impact on Canadians.[83] She realized that, according to the new rules, parcels destined for Canadian POWs had to pass through the Care Committee, acting as the Central Committee's agent. However, since the other half of the scheme, the prohibition of private parcels, did not apply to Canada, all the parcels that had previously reached Germany through various other channels would now be funnelled to the Red Cross volunteer workers at Cockspur Street.

By mid-January 1917, precisely as Rivers Bulkeley had predicted, the Care Committee for Canadian POWs in London was beginning to feel the strain of being half in and half out of the new regulations. The congestion at Cockspur Street was so bad that Rivers Bulkeley advised that parcels from Canada be stopped entirely and that next of kin be instructed to send remittances instead. Sir George Perley, the War Office, and the Director of the Central POW Committee agreed, Perley pointing out that the Australian Red Cross had already taken this step. The High Commissioner admitted that the measure would cause much dissatisfaction, but agreed that the exigencies of wartime often demanded unpopular measures.[84]

In fact, when the contemplated changes were reported in the Canadian press, they elicited little editorial comment and very few letters to the editor, perhaps because the report successfully conveyed the fact that the changes were necessary and reasonable. It stated that the Red Cross in London was overwhelmed with parcels and pointed out what had apparently never been reported to the Canadian public, that all parcels, even those that were individually addressed, had to pass through the CRCS office. Furthermore, the new regulations prevented the office from forwarding more than thirty pounds of parcels to each prisoner per fortnight, so that a great many packages accumulated at the depot. The best and most likely solution, read the report, was a prohibition of the 'indiscriminate despatch of parcels.'[85]

The opinions of Rivers Bulkeley and Perley, combined with the support of various Red Cross branches in Canada, were sufficient to convince the government, and on 29 January 1917 the Post Office Department dispatched a circular to all postmasters detailing a new Canadian parcel scheme that would go into effect on 1 February. In its major provisions, it was identical to the British plan. All foodstuffs were prohibited in private parcels, and individuals could send only money to the Canadian Red Cross. Requested articles would be purchased, packed, and dispatched by the Red Cross, along with a note identifying the sender. Since all prisoners were to receive the same number of parcels (three per fortnight), pay assignments that had previously been made by POWs were cancelled. The Canadian regulations also duplicated the British position that the scheme would apply to other ranks only; officers could still receive parcels from any source and in any quantity.[86]

The reaction of prisoners to the changes was mixed. Some men praised the new rules for avoiding waste, or expressed concern only because they had received no official word of the changes. Others were glad that well-meaning friends would no longer be able to send parcels full of items that were completely unnecessary in a prison camp.[87] However, other prisoners were less enthusiastic. Five officers who had been repatriated to Switzerland wrote to complain about the new procedure and insisted that it be re-examined for the benefit of their men still in Germany. Another POW lamented that the men of his battalion felt overlooked under the new scheme.[88] Relatives and interested groups were quick to join the chorus of complaints. The Nova Scotia branch of the CRCS cited a letter from a prisoner who claimed that people in Canada did not understand the conditions of captivity. 'The implication,' lamented the Red Cross, 'is so horrible that we who are living in comfort dare not even attempt to put it into words.'[89]

These complaints eventually reached Evelyn Rivers Bulkeley, who, upon investigation, found many of them to be groundless. Two prisoners who had lodged complaints were found to have acknowledged a considerable number of parcels, although Rivers Bulkeley appreciated why they would oppose the reduction in numbers: 'It cannot be nearly as nice to get only three parcels a fortnight instead of seven or eight a week which many of them were getting.' The prisoners, she insisted, were receiving quite enough food to keep them from starvation, and she also had harsh words for some relatives: 'It is, to me, very strange how little some people appear to realise the war conditions existing on the continent. They seem to think that it is only sufficient for a parcel to be sent, to be certain that it will arrive, and if the parcel does not arrive, it merely means that it has not been sent.'[90]

Despite the efforts of Rivers Bulkeley to calm the waters, opposition to the parcel scheme refused to fade. At the end of July, the relief question was raised in the House of Commons. J.G. Turriff, the member for Assiniboia, spoke out against the 'most unfair and discriminatory' parcel regulations and criticized in no uncertain terms the efforts of the Red Cross, whose 'work in this respect has been anything but satisfactory.' Volunteer workers in London, he claimed, 'come and go just as they please,' with no one on hand to see that the work was done properly; the result was that for months Canadian POWs received no parcels or else parcels of an inferior quality.[91] Minister of Militia Sir Edward Kemp responded angrily to these largely unfounded criticisms, and praised the magnificent work of the Red Cross. He also pointed out, as gently as possible, that there could be no absolute guarantee that all parcels dispatched would be delivered; according to all accounts, however, most parcels were getting through.[92]

By this time, British authorities were also becoming concerned, not by the inequalities of the parcel regulations but by the logistics of allowing unrestricted parcels to officers. At a May 1917 meeting of the Imperial War Cabinet, the Secretary of State for War, the Earl of Derby, cited the extreme example of one officer who received over 170 pounds of food every fortnight. Based on such cases, the Secretary and the Army Council in Britain agreed that officers' parcels should be limited both in number and in weight, a decision that the Department of Militia and Defence and the Post Office in Canada applauded.[93] On 1 October 1917 the Central POW Committee released the new scheme's particulars, which were repeated almost verbatim in a CRCS memorandum the following month. Officers would receive six parcels every month, up to a maximum of 100 pounds, sent by the Canadian Red Cross. Significantly, these parcels should be packed with particular consideration for the needs of officers, a courtesy that was not extended to other ranks; in order to avoid an outcry, Red Cross Commissioner Noel Marshall advised giving as little publicity as possible to this provision. Next of kin could send a further four parcels monthly, for which they would be issued official labels. The plan was to go into effect on 1 December 1917, after which no parcels would be accepted without such labels.[94]

At the same time as the officers' parcel scheme was being publicized, another plan was revealed. In response to continued complaints that next of kin of other ranks resented the lack of personal involvement in the relief effort, the Central POW Committee decided that relatives could send an eleven-pound personal parcel each quarter; it could contain no foodstuffs, but must be confined to games, toiletries, and other personal necessities. According to the notice, the scheme was to take effect on 1 December 1917.[95] Unfortunately, to the dismay of Deputy Postmaster-General R.M. Coulter, it was not specified whether this plan would affect the parcel schemes already in place, or whether it would apply equally to officers and other ranks.[96]

In a situation that would be repeated all too often, a local Red Cross branch took it upon itself to preempt the government and place notices in the press giving details of the scheme. This action understandably sent the Post Office into an uproar. Coulter fired off letters to anyone he could think of who might have been involved, stressing that the publication of postal regulations without the approval of the Post Office

Department could only cause confusion and dissatisfaction within the public.[97] Eventually, it was revealed that the War Office had intended the next-of-kin parcel scheme to apply only to Britain, but that Rivers Bulkeley had taken up the case and secured its extension to the Dominions. She had assumed that this arrangement would be communicated to the High Commission by the War Office, and felt justified in informing Red Cross branches in Canada of the impending change. Nevertheless, the High Commission deemed it advisable to remind the Red Cross that, before any future announcements were made about postal regulations, the Post Office Department must be consulted.[98]

Despite the confusion that characterized all of the parcel schemes, only late in the war was an attempt made to bring some sort of coordination to the adminstration of the relief effort. In September 1917, in response to a request for a delegate to represent Canadian interests at the monthly conferences convened by the Central POW Committee, Perley recommended Evelyn Rivers Bulkeley for the position. It was a wise decision, but, as a British parliamentary committee pointed out, consultation with members of the various relief organizations should have been sought at the beginning of the Central POW Committee's mandate, not towards the end of it.[99]

Another year passed before anyone suggested the appointment of an officer at OMFC headquarters in London to deal solely with POW affairs. The suggestion emanated from a former prisoner, who stressed that the average POW needed to know the name of an individual to whom he could write with his problems. Despite the suggestion having been passed to the Minister of Militia and Defence, there is no indication that it was acted upon.[100] At the same time, Rivers Bulkeley began to press for Dominion representation (as opposed to representation of Dominion relief societies) on the Central POW Committee. Not until well after the Armistice did the Colonial Office reply that Dominion delegates would be welcome.[101] By this time, the Central POW Committee in London had merged with the British government's Inter-Departmental Committee on POWs, and Canadian military authorities took another three weeks to decide on the appointment of Major E.H.W. Blake to the position.[102]

IN ADMINISTRATIVE TERMS, THEN, the relief effort was characterized by poor communication between governments and departments, over-lapping jurisdictions, and a tendency to work at cross purposes instead of in unison. However, it must be said that this state of affairs had little impact on the prisoners themselves. In the first place, it was often pos-sible to get supplies to the camps surprisingly quickly. For example, in March 1916 Andrew Wolfe of Dartmouth, Nova Scotia, informed Prime Minister Borden that his prisoner son Howard of the 8th Battalion required a new uniform. The request was passed on to Perley and Rivers Bulkeley, and soon came the reply that the Canadian Red Cross had shipped the necessary uniform to Germany. The entire transaction took less than a month.[103] In 1918 a Canadian merchant sea captain informed the High Commission that he had been denied his pay for want of documents confirming his status, and had to borrow money from his fellow internees for his upkeep. The matter was investigated, and in just over a month the necessary proof was on its way to Germany.[104]

Information could sometimes be procured just as quickly. In 1917 Sir Frederick Williams Taylor of the Bank of Montreal asked Sir Joseph Pope for information on his son, who had been reported missing while serving with the 13th Hussars in the Middle East. Before Lieutenant Williams Taylor was officially reported a prisoner some seven weeks later, the inquiry had been pressed in a number of quarters, including 13th Division commander General F.N. Maude; Sir George Perley; the British ambassador to Washington, Sir Cecil Spring-Rice; Canada's Chief of the General Staff, Major-General W.G. Gwatkin; the British minister responsible for POW matters, Lord Newton; the Swiss Legation in Washington; the Dutch Legation in Constantinople; and the governments of Turkey and the Netherlands.[105] However, one did not require influence to secure prompt attention. An inquiry as to the whereabouts of three escaped POWs was answered in less than a week, something that would be inconceivable in the Second World War.[106]

Furthermore, the objects of this concern, the prisoners themselves, were largely untouched by the administrative problems. The Canadian Red Cross in London dispatched over 472,000 food and 57,000 clothing parcels throughout the war, besides handling an unknown number of miscellaneous packages sent by relatives.[107] Obviously not all of these parcels reached their destinations; estimates vary widely, from ten to ninety per cent, but probably more than half of the parcels dispatched reached the prisoners for whom they were intended.[108] Regardless of the exact figures, POWs were delighted with the relief supplies that reached them, and many took time to visit the Cockspur Street office in London after the war to extend personal thanks.[109] Probably to a man, ex-prisoners felt nothing but gratitude towards the Red Cross. John Thorn, for example, had only 'the highest praise for the splendid work of the Canadian Red Cross. If it had not been for them hundreds of prisoners in Germany would have died from starvation. Their parcels contained the necessities of life, and their work will never be forgotten by the prisoners of war in Germany.'[110] Many other ex-POWs agreed that without the Red Cross food parcels, they would surely have starved.[111]

Just as important as the sustenance provided by parcels from home was their effect on morale. Prisoners took every opportunity to display their goods from home to the German populace, to counter enemy propaganda that the Allies were slowly dying of starvation. Harry Stone recalled that POWs would invariably wear their best woollen clothes from home whenever they left the camp, and Don Corker made a point of carrying Red Cross food on train journeys and eating it in front of civilians, who always appeared hungrier than the prisoners.[112] In addition to these minor psychological victories, it was vital to the POWs' mental health to believe that they had not been forgotten by friends and relatives at home, and relief parcels proved this admirably. Canadians in enemy camps found immense comfort in the knowledge that fellow Canadians, in Britain and at home, took an interest in their well-being and attempted to improve their lot. As one prisoner put it, 'outside of the material gift, there is the grateful knowledge that the people back home remember us and that they appreciate the fact that we cannot help our predicament.'[113]

As far as the POWs themselves were concerned, then, the relief effort must be considered a success. Aid agencies, especially the Canadian Red Cross Society, and private philanthropists should receive much credit for this state of affairs. People like Evelyn Rivers Bulkeley gave unstintingly of their abilities and energies, and did everything possible to ameliorate the lot of Canadian POWs. That the government never developed a workable mechanism for utilizing their talents adequately was certainly not their fault. For this reason, the government

Parcels for the Boys, by Arthur Nantel. For prisoners, food parcels offered not only badly needed nourishment, but also a welcome reminder of home.

had less cause to be pleased with its work, and the problems it encountered were almost entirely of its own making. The capture of hundreds of Canadians in April 1915 would have been the perfect opportunity for Militia and Defence to appoint an officer to deal exclusively with POW matters, but nothing of the sort was done. Without such an officer, there was no one to coordinate the activities of various departments and to ensure that the voluntary aid societies worked in concert with, not in opposition to, government offices.

The consequences of this lack of coordination were significant. The public often received conflicting information regarding relief. Regulations emanating from the British government were misunderstood or incorrectly applied, something that was as much Canada's fault as Britain's.[114] The tendency of the Red Cross to go over the government's head and act on its own initiative was matched by a marked reluctance in some government departments to admit the Red Cross as a valuable partner in the relief effort; this mutual suspicion, for want of a better phrase, meant that the workload for bureaucrats was multiplied as everyone tried to do the same job, and no one did it particularly well. In the final consideration, John Carson's assessment of the controversy over prisoners' promotions can apply equally well to government attempts to manage the relief effort: 'What is everybody's business is nobody's business.'[115]

THREE

REPATRIATION AND LIBERATION

AN APOCRYPHAL REMARK often attributed to prisoners of war held that after six months in captivity the only appetites left were for food and freedom. The relief effort had certainly done all it could to keep prisoners supplied with food, but freedom was a far more desirable commodity to prisoners and to people interested in their welfare. Adventurous POWs could follow the lead of the great escapers of history by attempting to break out of their prison camps and make their way out of Germany by stealth and cunning, but relatively few prisoners chose this option. For the vast majority, the only real prospect of early freedom was through repatriation on medical grounds or exchange to a neutral country. Attempts to secure release in this manner began almost as early as the relief campaign, and were also dogged by a combination of public overenthusiasm and administrative confusion. Furthermore, a preoccupation with various exchange schemes diverted planners from making arrangements for the postwar evacuation of prisoners, whose liberation was consequently far from the triumphant return that some of them might have envisioned.

I

Compared with the experience of the Second World War, escaping from captivity in the Great War was a relatively easy proposition. Camp security was not as well developed as it would be in the next war, police forces were fewer and less vigilant, and Holland provided a relatively near haven for escapers. In all, a hundred Canadians broke out of camps in Germany and reached neutral territory during the First World War, and many more were continually frustrated in their attempts. Not everyone was physically or mentally suited to attempt escape; it required considerable planning, no small amount of self-confidence, the physical strength to travel overland with a minimum of supplies, and the fortitude to endure the punishment meted out to unsuccessful escapers. Nevertheless, some Canadians were willing to put their stamina and strength to the test, preferring it to an often scarcely less dangerous existence in a work camp.

The battle began in the camp, with the collection of material needed to travel across wartime Germany. At the very least, a prospective escaper would require food to see him through his journey, a rough map of his intended route, a compass if possible, and clothes to allow him to blend in with the general population. Food was often the first consideration: a prisoner had to husband his resources carefully for weeks to accumulate enough supplies. Most of the foodstuffs sent in parcels were too heavy to carry, and tinned food was traded for more portable commodities, such as hard biscuits, chocolate, and bouillon cubes. Once these ran out, the escaper had to rely on whatever he could scavenge from fields and orchards.

Maps too were relatively easy to procure in the camps, and were often duplicated on gelatine printing machines. Compasses were more difficult to obtain. Don Corker received one in the mail from a relative, but prisoners often had to do without. For clothing, many escapers used the black suits issued in camps. They were supposed to have wide coloured stripes sewn into the sleeve and leg seams, but the French tailors assigned to the job usually just sewed the stripes on top of the seams so they could be easily removed. Since most of the travelling would be done by night, such makeshift clothing was usually sufficient.

Once all of the escape equipment had been secured, the breakout itself had to be planned. Officers faced a difficult task in this regard, for permanent camps had more sophisticated security arrangements and were well guarded by vigilant sentries. Consequently, officers often had to resort to carefully constructed tunnels or complicated ruses to get out of the camp. Norman Wells worked on a tunnel at Clausthal camp that reached seventy-one feet in length and took six months of hard work to complete; the day before the tunnel was due to break, it was given away by an Irish orderly.[1] Tom Scudamore attempted to escape from Bischofswerda in a packing crate, but was discovered when the guards decided to search all of the crates and, in the process, unceremoniously dumped Scudamore and his escape gear into the middle of the compound. John Thorn was trundled out of his camp in a wheelbarrow full of manure; once free, he dressed himself in the black garb of a widow and, accompanied by a French officer dressed as her hunchbacked son, attempted to buy tickets to Berlin at the local railway station. The pair deserved to succeed, but were arrested soon after entering the station.[2]

For private soldiers attached to work details, the task of escaping was much simpler. Work detachments were often only makeshift prison camps, with a minimum of security devices, few guards, and civilian overseers who were easily duped. On his first escape, Don Corker merely had to wait until a passing truck diverted the sentry's attention, and then climb the fence to temporary freedom; on subsequent escapes, it was as easy as wandering away from his work party. Mounted riflemen Jack Evans and William Raesides had no difficulty escaping from the mine to which they had been posted; in the wash building at the mine head, they simply took the exit for civilian workers instead of the one for prisoners and walked straight out into the street.[3] Ted Edwards of the Princess Pats wandered off into the woods beside the railway embankment that he and other prisoners were grading, while Harry Drope of the same unit pretended to be walking up a lane to relieve himself but instead hid in a bake oven, with the aid of an obliging Russian prisoner.[4]

Once the escaper was away from the camp, the real battle began. Even for the fittest of prisoners, the cross-country travelling was arduous and tiring. Because few of them spoke German or possessed correct travel documents, escapers had to avoid contact with the natives as much as possible. This meant walking only at night; spending the daylight hours hidden in a deserted building, a clump of trees, or even a hole in the ground; and carefully avoiding towns or villages, even if it meant a detour of some miles.

As though these trials were not enough, escapers could face any number of other disconcerting incidents. After escaping from their camp in the fall of 1917, Jack Evans and W.L. Masters blundered into a

Don Corker (left) and two fellow prisoners, 1916

swamp early in their trek and spent hours knee-deep in mud trying to find their way to firmer ground. Despite having only ten hard biscuits each, they overcame this bad start and trudged for four days and nights before crossing the border into Switzerland.[5] Frank MacDonald and his partner crossed the frontier into Holland on their first attempt, but became disoriented in the darkness and walked back into Germany and into the clutches of border guards. Ted Edwards and Mervyn Simmons scavenged oats, milk, and raw vegetables from farms they passed and made it all the way to the Dutch frontier. The worst encounter awaited them there. They found themselves face to face with a shotgun-toting farmer and his dog, and realized that their escape would be over if the farmer raised the alarm. The stakes were too high, and in the struggle that ensued, Edwards and Simmons killed the farmer and his dog, then slipped quickly into neutral territory.[6]

Not all escapes had such tragic incidents. Don Corker finally succeeded on his seventh escape attempt. On three of those attempts, he
crossed the Rhine River at the same place and stole the same boat each
time. On the first occasion, it was sitting on the riverbank but the second time, the boat was moored in the river with the oars in it. This did
not stop the intrepid Canadian, who swam out, clambered into the
boat, and rowed himself the rest of the way across, only to be recaptured on the other side. Realizing that sterner measures were called
for, the owner then moored the boat in the river without its oars. Not to
be outdone, Corker again swam out to the boat, pulled up one of the seats
to use as a paddle, and rowed himself across. Grateful to the owner for
not moving the boat, Corker left a small amount of German money to
cover the damages and made his way across the border into Holland.[7]

Persistence also paid off for another Canadian. After leaving his
bake oven on 13 June 1918, Harry Drope headed eastward in the company of two Russians. One of them, a Muscovite, was recaptured, but
Drope and his companion pressed on, sleeping by day and walking by
night. For five weeks they walked, until after a number of close calls they
crossed the Dnieper river to freedom. Reaching Moscow, Drope was
taken under the wing of the British consul, who arranged for his transport to Archangel and Murmansk. On 13 August, a British ship carrying Drope docked at Newcastle-upon-Tyne, giving him the distinction of
travelling farther than any other successful Canadian escaper of the war.[8]

II

Of course, not all POWs were as plucky as Don Corker and Harry
Drope. Some lacked the physical or mental strength to escape, while
others thought that the odds against success were too great to warrant
an attempt. Still others probably believed that they had done their bit
and were justified in waiting out the war in captivity. These men saw a
safer way to obtain freedom, through repatriation and exchange,
despite the fact that it was not well regarded by some prisoners. As one
POW wrote, 'Escaping was a thing of nerve and adventure; passing for
repatriation was a squalid business of medical boards and, at times,
crying "pain, pain, when there was no pain."'[9]

John Thorn, a typical fire-eater, disliked exchanges because they meant that the prisoners could not return to active service; he much preferred escaping, which allowed soldiers to get back into the front lines and exact a measure of revenge for the maltreatment they had suffered in captivity.[10] However, for prisoners with less intestinal fortitude than Thorn, repatriation and exchange offered the only real opportunity to get out of a German prison camp before the war's end.

For such men, repatriation was something of a talisman, clung to as much out of desperation as anything. As Donald Laird recalled, 'such was their need of comfort that they clung to a hopeless belief, knowing it hopeless, yet not daring to admit its hopelessness.'[11] Unfortunately for those captives who pinned all their hopes on repatriation, the specifics of exchange proved to be tiresomely difficult to iron out. In late August 1914, Britain refused a German offer for a reciprocal exchange of all interned civilians because there were only 5000 British subjects in Germany, compared with 50,000 Germans in Britain.[12] Furthermore, His Majesty's Government insisted upon treating the Empire as a single unit in exchange negotiations, even if it seemed possible to arrange an exchange involving only one Dominion's citizens. High Commissioner Sir George Perley questioned the validity of the British position, noting that 'it would seem to be our duty and to our benefit to get as many British subjects out of the enemy country as possible,'[13] but British officials refused to be moved from a viewpoint that would become increasingly troublesome to Canadian officials. Even when there was a real possibility of substantive achievement, Britain refused to allow any step that compromised the principle of united action by the members of the Empire.[14]

Shortly after Britain rejected the civilian exchange proposal, the Swiss government raised the possibility of a mutual release of seriously wounded POWs between Germany and France.[15] There was no immediate agreement, but in February 1915, after the papacy had lent its support to the plan, France and Germany reached an accord. The first exchange occurred on 2 March 1915; by November 1916, over 10,000 German and French prisoners had been exchanged. The success of this scheme convinced International Committee of the Red Cross (ICRC) president Gustave Ador to suggest the exchange of less seriously wounded prisoners; France rejected the plan but agreed to the internment of such prisoners in Switzerland. In August 1915, again after the Pope's intervention, the Kaiser personally acceded to the plan, and in January 1916 the first group of prisoners, 200 French and German tubercular cases, reached Switzerland. By the middle of February, over a thousand such prisoners had arrived.

The Foreign Office began to take an interest in these exchanges in December 1915, and in the spring of 1916 the British government elected to enter into negotiations with Germany. At the end of May 1916 the first group of British soldiers, including a number of Canadians, reached Switzerland.[16] For the rest of the war, small parties of British and Empire prisoners would leave Germany, either to be repatriated directly to England (for the most serious medical cases) or to be interned in neutral countries (for other classes of repatriables). The earliest prisoner exchanges were arranged according to a schedule of ailments that justified repatriation, including tuberculosis, diabetes, pernicious anemia, malaria; poisoning by chlorine, carbon monoxide, or mercury; emphysema, bronchitis, asthma; digestive, vision, or circulatory disorders; gout, rheumatism, epilepsy, paralysis, sciatica, loss of a limb, diphtheria, and neurasthenia. As the war progressed the criteria became wider, and for many POWs the hope of repatriation became a vital source of sustenance.

It also gave sustenance to the families of prisoners. Despite the fact that the Canadian government had little input into the process, the publicity given to the exchanges created a ray of hope for many families, who began to press their cases with Canadian authorities. Many of these pleas came from individuals who believed that, for one reason or another, they had a particular claim on special treatment. Letters frequently began by pointing out that Private Johnny Canuck's father was a loyal Conservative, an old friend of the Prime Minister, or the chairman of the local recruiting association; the soldier's mother was invariably in poor health and much distracted by her son's condition.

Some correspondents went considerably further than this. In September 1916, Prime Minister Robert Borden received a letter from Clarence J. McCuaig of Montreal that deserves to be quoted at some length, if only for its bare-faced gall. McCuaig was bent upon obtaining the release of his son, Major D.R. McCuaig, who had been captured at Ypres in April 1915, and explained that he had almost arranged two deals for his son's exchange. The first had been frustrated when the War Office refused to consider the exchange of individual prisoners, while the second had come to nothing because Major McCuaig (who would surely have been mortified had he known of his father's efforts on his behalf) was not allowed to give his parole. Now McCuaig senior was proposing that the Canadian government release an interned German nobleman, Baron von Polenz, for his son, but there was a complication: the government hoped to exchange von Polenz for Dr. Henri Béland, a former Laurier Cabinet minister who had been detained in Germany since the spring of 1915. 'Hitherto I have only urged the services of my son as a reason why I am entitled to every consideration,' wrote McCuaig defiantly, 'but apparently that argument seems to have fallen on as deaf ears as those which originally listened to my warnings to the Government regarding the Ross Rifle.' Here was the rub. McCuaig went on to state that the people of Canada might one day hold Borden responsible for the doings of the Purchasing Committee, and that his correspondence with Robert Rogers might make 'very interesting reading someday for the Canadian public.' McCuaig concluded by saying that he had always attempted to be loyal to the Conservative party but that his patience was wearing thin and he required a decision in the matter of von Polenz.

Borden's reply was a study in carefully considered language. He noted that the letter had been 'couched in exceedingly peculiar terms' and rightfully accused McCuaig of blackmail, though he refrained from using the word. The Prime Minister concluded by saying that the request, put in such terms, could not possibly be considered and that McCuaig should feel free to take any steps that he felt were his duty. McCuaig's parting shot was a more detailed account of how he had tried to stop the Ross Rifle from being put into service, and he questioned whether Borden believed his intention to act upon his threat. There the matter ended, although it would have echoes later in the war.[17]

Even had McCuaig stated his case more intelligently, it would have availed him nothing, for various reasons. In the first place, raising an individual case with the Detaining Power often redounded to the detriment of that person, for it merely convinced the Germans that the individual was of some value and therefore should not be released.[18] Furthermore, as McCuaig seemed reluctant to recognize, British authorities would not consider individual cases, even if they promised success. As Lord Newton, the chairman of Britain's Inter-Departmental Committee on POWs, wrote, such cases involved 'very protracted and difficult negotiations with disproportionately small results ... it would be constantly alleged that individual exchanges were obtained by favouritism or political influence.'[19]

Nor would British officials consider cases put forward by individual Dominions. For example, in 1917 Major R.R. McKessock wrote from Bischofswerda that there were roughly fifty Canadian officers in the camp who had been captive for more than twenty months; there were also about fifty German reserve officers held in Canada. It occurred to him, quite naturally, that the two groups could be exchanged to a neutral country, given the fact that such exchanges seemed to be in vogue at the moment. The proposal seemed reasonable enough, but British authorities quickly threw cold water on it. McKessock was 'entirely misinformed,' replied the War Office, 'that any arrangement concluded between this country and Germany differentiates in the slightest degree between British forces from any part of the Empire.' Consequently, 'the [Army] Council would deprecate any departure from the policy of precisely similar consideration being accorded to all British prisoners-of-war.'[20] Again and again, the Canadian government would hear this refrain. In this case, while Britain's position had merit, it is also hard to argue with Perley's earlier statement that as many captives as possible should be freed, regardless of their circumstances or nationality.[21]

If prisoners of war were often thwarted in their efforts to secure release, civilian internees were no more fortunate. Joseph Gelin, arrested in August 1914 on his way back to Canada from Russia and detained in Ruhleben camp, wrote that he had been approved for exchange on medical grounds but had been denied a passport, a situation that had put him through considerable anxiety. He concluded his plea by stating that 'I certainly am sure that the Canadian Government will not leave a subject in distress and refuse me to come back home in my present conditions, as I always had fair treatment from my government.'[22] Gelin was to be disappointed, for he was not released until October 1917. In fact, civilian internees were generally disappointed in their efforts to regain freedom. In November 1916, when British and German diplomats began to discuss a proposal to release civilians forty-five years of age or older, the High Commission produced the names of seven eligible Canadians for transmission to the Protecting Power; however, the proposal was eventually reduced to cover only invalid civilians. Nevertheless, the fact that a civilian exchange had even been considered gave hope to relatives, who continued to press their inquiries with various government offices.[23]

Even when civilians did come up for exchange, the outcome often did not satisfy some people. Evelyn Rivers Bulkeley of the Red Cross POW Branch in London wondered whether complaints should be lodged about the identities of Canadian civilians being released, specifically the fact that various 'true Canadians' had been passed over. According to Rivers Bulkeley, 'the only two civilians who have been repatriated are A.E. Schippel, who I understand, can scarcely speak English at all, and Hyman Fischmann, who from his name would certainly also appear to be German.' Perley was quick to soothe the injured feelings of Rivers Bulkeley. He admitted that the choice of exchanged civilians was remarkable, but pointed out that Schippel at least should be regarded as a true Canadian, having lived in the country for forty years and having had eight children with a Canadian woman.[24]

Civilians, then, continued to be marginalized in the efforts to secure release, but the prospects for soldiers were fast improving. May 1917 brought new hope for POWs when France and Germany concluded an agreement for the reciprocal release of prisoners who had been captive for more than eighteen months and who were over fifty-five years of age (for officers) or forty-eight years of age (for other ranks). The publicity surrounding the plan eventually convinced the British government to seek a similar arrangement. Accordingly, in June 1917 British and German representatives met at The Hague to discuss the specifics. The eventual agreement established new criteria for repatriation, which included the release to a neutral country of all officers and NCOs, regardless of age, who had been prisoners for more than eighteen months; the priority list would be drawn up according to date of capture, regardless of nationality. Prisoners of less than eighteen months' standing who were diagnosed as having a captivity neurosis known as barbed-wire disease could also be lodged in a neutral country and would be eligible for repatriation if their condition did not improve within three months.[25] To accommodate these prisoners, the Swiss agreed to repatriate to their homelands all tubercular prisoners and any other men whose recovery was expected to be prolonged, while the Dutch government offered to intern up to 16,000 combatants in Holland, as long as Britain and Germany refunded all the costs.[26]

The agreement was a considerable breakthrough for the POWs concerned. Granted, they would still technically remain captives, held prisoner by neutral governments on behalf of Germany. Nevertheless, although Switzerland was officially neutral, the crowds who welcomed incoming trains of Allied POWs left little doubt where their sympathies lay, and the Swiss government too tried to be as helpful as possible to Empire prisoners without being blatantly one-sided. Finally, neutral internees would be allowed comparative freedom of movement within Switzerland or Holland, and would also benefit from inspections made by their own governments to ensure that they were being well looked after.

With the schedule of disabilities agreed upon, the War Office requested from the Dominions nominal rolls of all prisoners believed to be eligible for exchange; these lists would be transmitted to Germany for consideration. To draw up the lists, Canadian authorities resorted to a very primitive tactic: they sent a circular letter to the next of kin of POWs who were known to be wounded requesting detailed descriptions of wounds and physical condition, as the prisoners themselves had described them in recent letters. The pitfalls of this approach were obvious. Certainly many sincere replies were received, but the method encouraged exaggeration as relatives attempted to make the best possible case. Furthermore, other individuals who had heard of the circular letter wrote to describe why their relatives deserved consideration as well, even if they were uninjured. Then, after all the administrative work of sending out the circulars and collating the replies, Canadian authorities learned that the entire procedure of drawing up lists was 'eye-wash,' because all repatriates were subject to a medical examination in any case.[27]

Considerably more disturbing than this minor waste of time and effort was the levelling of accusations that influence was being exercised to bend the regulations and obtain the release of certain POWs. In December 1917, G. Napier Gordon, who had left the Stratford, Ontario, branch of the Bank of Commerce in the first week of the war to enlist, wrote from Heidelberg prison camp that, despite the expected medical examination, the last two parties of prisoners sent to Switzerland included officers who had been captured less than a year before and were only slightly wounded. He observed that the Canadian government must have left the matter entirely in the hands of British authorities, and wondered: 'Why does our Government neglect us? have they ceased to consider our services? Someone should ask the question in the House – Why Canadian unwounded prisoners taken in 1916 should be exchanged to Switzerland prior to wounded prisoners taken in 1915?'[28] A group of Canadians who arrived in Switzerland in November 1917 raised similar questions; they told a Red Cross representative that many POWs remained in Germany whose repatriation seemed more urgent than their own.[29]

Shortly afterwards, Clarence McCuaig re-entered the fray, claiming that his son had been disadvantaged in this manner. Obviously unchastened by his correspondence with Borden in 1915, McCuaig noted sanctimoniously that he did 'not wish to use any influence on his [Major McCuaig's] behalf except to see that he is not held back by influence used in favor of others.' In a subsequent letter, he was back to his old tricks, observing that 'I can hardly believe that this [the use of influence to secure a prisoner's release] is true, for if it is, the truth is certain to come out, and both you [Perley] and Sir Robert Borden ... will be placed in a very embarrassing position.' By this time, though, the matter had been clarified by the War Office, which pointed out that decisions regarding the repatriation of sick and wounded prisoners rested entirely with the German and Swiss medical commission, which was beyond the reach of influence from Canada; furthermore, 'any deviation from the correct order of transfer as based on official records' would be reported to the German authorities at once. McCuaig pronounced himself satisfied with this explanation, and did not trouble the High Commissioner again.[30]

The stipulation that only NCOs and officers of eighteen months' imprisonment would be repatriated also caused concern, although it had a logical explanation: the Germans refused to exchange any POW who could be used for manual labour and, because they could not be put to work under the provisions of international law, all prisoners over the rank of lance-corporal were essentially useless mouths to feed.[31]

Nevertheless, many individuals questioned the fairness of this provision. One imprisoned private wrote to a relative that 'it's a damned shame that the N.C.O.'s [sic] are all being exchanged and we're still here. It nearly break's [sic] one's heart to see them gradually going, especially those who have only been captured about 22 months. I've been here more than three years now and really think it is time that a few of the old ones were exchanged, as the French and Germans have agreed to do.' The plea was forwarded to Frank Keefer, MP, with the notation that the individual concerned had indeed been an NCO but had reverted to the ranks to join a machine gun company.[32]

Nor was the discontent felt only by those who had been left behind in Germany. Lieutenant W.G. Colquhoun, exchanged to Holland in February 1918, 'felt like a deserter, nothing more or less, and can't get over the thought that the officers are deserting their men when they leave them over there and come to Holland themselves ... if by going back it would help them in any way I, personally, and, I am sure, the majority of the rest when they arrive, would go back like a shot.' Colquhoun stressed that other ranks were treated much worse than officers, and called it a crying shame that the Canadian government did not act on their behalf. He found it particularly galling because most of the Canadian prisoners were 'sacrifice troops,' or 'men left in an impossible position and officially wiped out, and if they had been cowards and not stayed where they were put they would not have been caught.' The lieutenant concluded by writing that he was tired of polite sympathy for POWs and urged his family to 'kick up a row' to address the situation. Members of Colquhoun's old regiment forwarded his concerns to Major-General S.C. Mewburn, Kemp's successor as Minister of Militia and Defence, but there is no indication that they went any further than that.[33]

Munro and Colquhoun were certainly correct in claiming that the repatriation process was flawed, in large part because it was so exasperatingly inconsistent. Candidates for repatriation had to be recommended by a German doctor, after which they were examined by a commission of Swiss and German doctors. The commissions, particularly those with a majority of German doctors, were notoriously capricious, so much so that even the most seriously wounded prisoner could not be sure of a favourable judgment. One POW was advised by a sympathetic German to play the role of the idiot if he wished to secure repatriation; another had very little wrong with him but was fluent enough in German to win favour with the board and ensure his passage.[34] Prisoners resorted to every possible ruse to make their cases appear more worthy, even to the point of securing samples of sputum from tubercular Russian POWs to pass off as their own. As one POW wrote, horse races and elections were nothing compared to the uncertainty of the repatriation board.[35]

Because the process was so uncertain, prisoners who were lucky enough to pass for repatriation found the experience every bit as emotional as slipping across the frontier in the dead of night. When Captain Harvey Douglas and his fellow repatriates learned that they would soon be crossing into Switzerland, they 'were all running around in our pajamas, shaking hands and hugging each other.' After he passed for repatriation, Donald Laird felt completely incapable of taking care of himself; his memory deteriorated so much that he was terrified he would forget to present himself when the repatriates paraded to leave the camp in the morning.[36] Colonel H.A. Picot, the commander of the British repatriate colony in Switzerland, also observed the effect that repatriation had upon the prisoners: 'I could see that this outburst of emotion after the suppression and antagonism of the years of captivity was having a very trying effect, for all ranks looked dazed, and appeared only half conscious of what was taking place around them.' Captain Scudamore, who crossed into Switzerland in December 1916, found the attention given to the repatriates overwhelming and was overtaken by his emotions.[37] Alfred Cleeton and his comrades, leaving Germany in August 1918, expressed their gratitude by singing a doxology as they crossed the frontier, while John Thorn performed a rather different ritual. Before the repatriation train passed into neutral territory, he paid his respects to his former captors by urinating on German soil.[38]

Once repatriates entered Switzerland, they found that conditions were relatively decent, at least compared to those they had just left.[39] Canadian prisoners lived in locations throughout Switzerland, but primarily at Mürren and Château d'Oex; each camp was administered by a Swiss military officer, who was in effective control of the camp, and a Senior British Officer, whose authority was largely nominal. The

British officer in charge of the entire Empire repatriate colony was Colonel Picot, assisted by Captain W.H. Hooper of the 2nd Battalion as chief paymaster and Captain Scudamore as stores officer. The prisoners lodged in various hotels and *pensions*, paid for by the British government, and the food was sufficient in both quantity and quality. Courses of instruction were available to prisoners who wished to learn a trade, and recreational funds were established in most camps. Canadian internees even enjoyed a Dominion Day excursion in 1917, with a trip to Interlaken and Gunten and a cruise on Lake Thun.[40]

Always mindful of the possibility of improvement and the accompanying political benefits, the government decided in August 1917 to send a Canadian delegation to Switzerland to inspect conditions there and prepare a report that could be made public. Brigadier-General Lord Brooke, head of the Canadian Military Mission to France, and Major G.R. Geary of the 58th Battalion, a former mayor of Toronto, were accordingly dispatched, and their report was publicized on 9 November 1917.[41] Brooke and Geary made every effort to speak with as many Canadians as possible, and the internees were delighted to know that 'although far from home, they had not been forgotten.' After touring most of the internee enclaves, the visitors concluded that the Canadians were making the best of things and deserved the fullest recognition for what they had endured.[42] In November 1917, Lieutenant-Colonel Claude E. Bryan, assistant commissioner of the Canadian Red Cross, also visited the facilities in Switzerland and reported favourably on the lot of Canadians interned there.

Both reports stated that the only serious problem facing the administration of Canadian prisoners in Switzerland involved their pay. Although prisoners' food and lodging were paid for by the British government, there were obviously more places to spend money in Switzerland than there had been in Germany. Recently exchanged POWs were keen to take advantage of the shops, restaurants, theatres, and excursions that were available in Switzerland. Up to October 1916, POWs could secure remittances as long as their pay accounts stood in credit. However, after a number of ex-prisoners exhausted their accounts in a matter of days, Picot notified the Red Cross that in future all pay requests would have to be countersigned by the Senior British Officer.[43]

Not surprisingly, the change brought protests from Canadian prisoners. Corporal H.S. McKay of the 8th Battalion wrote that, 'as a born Canadian and ratepayer,' he should be entitled to his pay. Another repatriate was evidently more disturbed; Private F.R. McKelvey described himself as a full-blooded Canadian of good character and good credit rating who had left a $10-a-day job to join the first batch of volunteers. He complained that

> I must obtain written permission from the Commandant of this place, before you will send me the above mentioned sum £3.2.6. Did Canada or England issue this order? Is Canada looking after her own? If as I hope she is, then there is a gross mistake, and if she is not then it is time she did, or I am very much afraid many of her sons of whom she is justly proud may become army criminals.[44]

In spite of McKelvey's protests, so many internees were squandering their accumulated pay in Switzerland that the Canadian Red Cross suggested placing further restrictions on the amount that could be drawn at any one time. Eventually, the government decided that prisoners should be permitted to draw only £3 per month; requests for more required the approval of the Paymaster-General in England.[45]

After the July 1917 exchange agreement reached at The Hague, prisoners also began moving to Holland, with the first group of repatriates crossing the border in December 1917. The Canadians lived primarily at The Hague and Scheveningen, in several large sea-front hotels, and some apparently had a very pleasant internment punctuated by sightseeing, cycling trips, and dinner parties. They established a Canadian officers' club at Scheveningen, and recreational facilities were also available; an immensely successful Dominion Day sports meet drew over 6000 spectators. One nagging problem was the volume of complaints that female relatives of POWs were prohibited from visiting them in Holland, unlike in Switzerland, except in the case of dangerous illness or other unusual circumstances. Eventually, Evelyn Rivers Bulkeley took up the case, suggesting that Canadians were at risk because Holland was teeming with German women dressed as Belgian refugees, who were 'rapidly getting hold of our people,' presumably to encourage them to change their loyalties.[46]

A greater problem for internees in Holland, though, was food. Provisions were supposed to be supplied by a Dutch firm contracted by the British government, but the contract was not observed and it took some time to arrange the shipment of supplementary rations. Also, commodity prices were extremely high. In any case, it would have been difficult to buy extra food because until mid-1918 Canadians in Holland could not receive pay allowances; Canadian officers had to arrange loans with a Dutch bank to secure funds for their men. Furthermore, food parcels could not be sent to Holland because the Dutch government resented the fact that prisoners might have better rations than the populace. All things considered, Militia and Defence believed that prisoners in Holland were worse off for food than they had been in Germany.[47]

July 1918 brought the hope of imminent improvement when Britain and Germany reached an agreement that provided for the release of all prisoners interned in neutral countries; according to a preliminary schedule, all British prisoners would be repatriated from the Netherlands within roughly three months of the ratification of the agreement. Though the ratification was not a certainty by any means, a decision one way or the other was expected soon and Canadian authorities therefore decided against large undertakings on behalf of POWs in Holland until the status of the agreement was resolved. In the interim, the Canadian Red Cross would endeavour to ship supplies to internees via the British YMCA, the only means by which food was permitted to enter Holland.[48] However, growing cries that Canadian repatriates were being ignored forced the government to consider more active intervention in Holland, and Canadian officials decided to arrange an exploratory visit to investigate the possibility of a permanent Canadian presence in the Netherlands.[49] Since a British inspection party had already made arrangements to travel to Holland, the Overseas Military Forces of Canada (OMFC) opted to attach a Canadian mission consisting of Major E.H.W. Blake, his secretary, and Mrs. Cory, the wife of one of the interned officers.[50]

Blake encountered an obstacle as soon as the plan came to the attention of British authorities: the embassy in The Hague advised the Foreign Office that the British inspectors could take care of all the Dominions' requirements, so a Canadian delegation was unnecessary. Learning of the situation, Borden reacted strongly and drafted a firm letter to British Prime Minister David Lloyd George, which stated unequivocally that the Canadian delegates were going to Holland and requested that instructions be issued to all necessary officials. On the argument that Canadian representation was unnecessary, Borden admitted that he was 'utterly unable to conceive on what principle the [British] Embassy [in Holland] should undertake to pass such a judgement upon a decision of the Canadian Government.' Before the letter could be sent, British officials had changed their argument, claiming that the objection to Canadian representation originated with the Dutch.[51]

The difficulties were eventually solved, and on 20 September 1918, Blake and his delegation, accompanied by Colonel Gerald W. Birks, the Canadian YMCA's Chief Supervisor for Overseas, crossed the English Channel to the Netherlands. They spent two weeks touring the facilities and visiting with some of the nearly 400 Canadian internees there, and found conditions to be generally better than they had expected.[52] However, the delegates did have a number of recommendations. Despite the July 1918 agreement to release all POWs interned in neutral countries, the Canadian government should assume that the prisoners would be in Holland for some time and, consequently, should expand as much as possible the provision of supplies. To this end, both the Canadian Red Cross and the YMCA should be encouraged to extend their facilities in the Netherlands, staffing them with Canadians wherever possible. (This recommendation was put into effect immediately, and by war's end the Canadian YMCA had established a comforts hut that sold goods at a fraction of the Dutch prices.) Blake also recommended that a subsistence allowance payable in kind from the YMCA huts be made to all other ranks, who should be issued with full uniforms and unit badges as well, to preserve their identity as Canadians. Finally, and most significantly, Blake's report advised that a separate department at OMFC be established to deal solely with POW matters. Unfortunately this most important recommendation was never carried out.

While the discussions over conditions in Holland progressed, another reciprocal release operation was being proposed.[53] As usual, Canada was kept informed but took no part in the negotiations, so that when an agreement seemed imminent, Borden urged Mewburn and Kemp to consider what points affecting Canadians should be raised with Britain. Not until November was word received that the German government had decided to extend the agreement for the exchange of prisoners.[54] By then, events had overtaken the new accord and created a whole host of different problems.

III

In the camps in Germany, prisoners began to notice subtle changes in the atmosphere through the fall of 1918. Private Eric Seaman of the 3rd Battalion, a POW since the Second Battle of Ypres, started hearing rumours of mass desertions among troops in the North Sea ports; he also noticed that the guards were becoming rather friendlier to the prisoners.[55] When confirmation of the Armistice came, it was rarely communicated by the camp staff. On his regular escorted trip into town to collect the camp mail, W.J. Chambers met a party of soldiers hoisting a red flag who informed him that the Kaiser had departed and a revolution was under way. Fred Gies learned of the Armistice at noon on 11 November, but the prisoners were back at work the next morning and continued working for another three weeks as though nothing had happened.[56] Percy Hampton learned of the ceasefire only by reading it in a German newspaper. Eric Seaman happened to see a poster giving the terms of the Armistice affixed to the window of a butcher shop.[57]

Partly because of the continued interest in the progress of exchange negotiations and partly because of the rapidity with which the end of the war came, plans for the return of prisoners after the conclusion of hostilities were incomplete at best. In October 1917, the War Office informed the Canadian Pay and Record Office that, in preparation for demobilization, it was compiling a nominal roll of all POWs and would require a list of Canadian prisoners at some point in the future, likely on short notice.[58] By the following spring, British military officials had drawn up a preliminary plan for the handling of liberated prisoners once they reached Britain.[59] Other ranks would be housed in special reception centres at Dover and Clipstone (Ripon was later selected as a better site), where they would receive medical assessments and new uniforms and kit, and undergo a short debriefing. To process the Canadians, the OMFC provided an officer (Captain H.H. Gardner for

Dover and Major A.G. Woolley Dod for Ripon) and a staff of six for each camp. Soldiers would be granted leave directly from the reception centre if they requested it, and could apply to the Paymaster-General for pay advances; if they did not request leave, they would be dispatched to their battalion depots to await transport back to Canada. Officers avoided all of this bureaucracy; they were to report on their own to OMFC headquarters, which would make arrangements for their return home.[60]

Humanitarian agencies also made provisions for returning prisoners by establishing welcome centres along the way. The YMCA opened a centre at the Hotel d'Iléna in Paris to serve prisoners travelling through Mons and Valenciennes, while the staff of the comforts hut in Holland travelled to the Dutch border to assist Canadian POWs coming out of Germany. YMCA officials also accompanied parties of ex-prisoners from Rotterdam to England whenever possible. In London, the Red Cross converted into a hostel the building that had been used to pack parcels, and hundreds of returned prisoners passed through it in the weeks after the Armistice.[61]

The arrangements for the return of civilian internees differed slightly. They would be brought back to England by British authorities and were instructed to present themselves at the High Commission upon arrival. There they would be advanced £10 for pocket money and £13 for passage home, which would be given against a promise to repay. They were to be reminded that communication with Canada House did not imply an obligation of any sort on behalf of the Canadian government towards ex-internees, but was 'solely for the purpose of recording the whereabouts and intentions of the persons concerned.'[62]

The provisions for ex-prisoners once they reached England, then, were reasonably complete. Missing from the plan, however, was any clear notion of how to get them from the prison camps to the reception centres.[63] The immediate repatriation of all Allied POWs was stipulated in the Armistice agreement, but the conditions of that repatriation were left to be determined at some time in the future. That prisoners might try to make their own way out of Germany apparently did not occur to anyone until after the Armistice was signed, when British Quartermaster-General Sir Travers Clarke issued instructions that prisoners returning through the front lines should be provided with clothing and blankets if necessary and forwarded to a camp at Calais.[64] However, since no further arrangements had been made, least of all for the reception of large numbers of ex-prisoners at Calais, it was impossible to act on these orders and they were soon amended so that all returning prisoners would be moved to a number of forward collecting centres in France and Belgium to await onward transfer. They would then be taken by truck or train to camps at Calais, Boulogne, or Dunkirk, and from there to England, to be processed through the Dover reception centre.

These arrangements, however, applied only to the roughly 32,000 POWs who had been held immediately behind the front lines. The 120,000 British and Empire POWs scattered throughout the rest of Germany proved a bigger problem. To address the issue, a subcommission of the Permanent International Armistice Commission was established under Major-General Sir John Adye and began work on 20 November 1918. The commission agreed that prisoners in Germany should be collected at points on the Oder, Elbe, Weser, and Rhine rivers, to be moved by water to embarkation ports such as Rotterdam. At those ports, they would be met by reception parties, provided with new kit, and escorted to the docks to embark for England.

However, the agreement proved more difficult to put into force, for a number of reasons. Certainly German intransigence was a factor, but a genuine lack of resources, especially railway cars to transfer POWs to collection points, was also a problem. Furthermore, there was no organization left in Germany to hand over liberated prisoners, so most of the work had to be done by the Armistice Commission itself. This task was made more difficult by the reluctance of prisoners to remain in their camps until advised otherwise, as they had been instructed to do by way of notices in German newspapers.[65]

In fact, the delays encountered in the return of prisoners became a considerable bone of contention in the post-Armistice discussions, with the Allies threatening more exacting terms if the POW question was not solved satisfactorily. These threats seemed to have some effect, although Lieutenant-General Sir Richard Haking, who headed the British section of the Armistice Commission, and Major-General Sir Richard Ewart, the Red Cross Commissioner for the Repatriation of British POWs, both believed that German officials were doing all they could to rectify the situation and that Allied officers should be sent to each camp to handle the repatriation operation in person.[66] This apparently was never done, and it was late January 1919 before Ewart could report that virtually all British ex-prisoners had been repatriated and that any remaining cases could be handled by the British Military Mission in Berlin.[67]

For the prisoners themselves, the failure of governments to make adequate provisions for their liberation created a variety of problems. In some camps, POWs were ordered to continue working after the Armistice, and when such orders were disobeyed, the Germans responded by withholding food, electricity, or fuel to force the prisoners to cooperate. At Langensalza on 27 November, edgy guards fired on a group of prisoners. The camp staff later maintained that the POWs were fomenting revolution; prisoners reported that as many as sixteen of their comrades were killed and twenty-four wounded.[68] In other camps, guards simply deserted their prisoners, and for these POWs the situation was almost as bad. Canadians at Bohmte camp, north of Osnabrück, were abandoned by their guards and had to walk the eighty-odd kilometres to the Dutch border, while prisoners at camps deeper in Germany found the problems of evacuation even more difficult. POWs at Vehnemoor were shuttled to an assembly camp at Soltau that was packed with 20,000 other captives; disease was rampant, and many men succumbed to influenza at this late stage of the war. At least one officer died of neglect at Bad Colberg in the weeks after the Armistice, hardly surprising since the only medical man on hand was rumoured to be a veterinary surgeon.[69] In Salzerbad, McGill University graduate and captured pilot George McLeod waited patiently for transportation to friendly territory but eventually gave up and stowed away on a freight train bound for Trieste. POWs at Stralsund were caught in a dispute between the area corps commander and the head of the local revolutionary council, and got out by chartering their own train to take them to Denmark. Percy Hampton, imprisoned at Pilau on the Baltic coast, waited over a month before a Swedish passenger liner arrived to ferry the inmates of the camp to Scotland.[70] Even prisoners who had been exchanged to Holland had a long wait. Shortly after the Armistice was announced, they learned that, instead of proceeding directly to England, they were to remain in Holland to oversee the repatriation of all ex-POWs passing through the country. The task was eventually accomplished, though not without some grumbling from the neutral internees.[71]

Once these men reached England, arrangements were in some cases little better. Brass bands and cheering crowds welcomed prisoners at the debarkation ports, but the situation deteriorated after that. Occasionally no advance notice was provided for the arrival of sick or wounded POWs, who reached British ports to find no one to direct them to their next destination. There were further logistical problems at the reception centres. Despite an understanding that all necessary facilities would be provided by British authorities, the camp at Dover was sadly ill-equipped and a representative of the Canadian Red Cross had to be summoned to provide emergency furnishings for the reception rooms and barracks.[72] For the ex-prisoners, the apparent lack of organization was irritating. Russell Smith reported waiting in line for six hours for his medical exam, while Harry Howland, one of the Bokelah 'mutineers,' recalled that the 'hurry up and wait' atmosphere quickly took its toll on the discipline of the men.[73] In such circumstances, ex-prisoners can be forgiven for wondering what had become of the goodwill they had benefited from while in the camps.

FORTUNATELY, SUCH A SITUATION was not representative of Canadian efforts over the previous four years. During the war, the government dealt with relatives fairly and honestly, careful not to raise hopes unduly but always willing to pass on to British authorities the concerns of a relative. The methods used to monitor the release of prisoners from Canada's end were sometimes primitive, but there is no indication that anything more could have been done, given that Germany held most of the cards in the release game.

There were, however, some areas of concern. Civilian internees received short shrift in exchange negotiations, just as they had in the relief effort, not out of malice but simply because it was unclear where they fell in terms of administrative responsibility. Too often they fell between departments, and found that their concerns were neglected. More serious was Britain's unwillingness to compromise imperial unity by considering exchange schemes particular to any given Dominion, a fact that boded ill for the future. Canadian administrators could do little about this at the time, although the disagreement over the Canadian delegation to Holland in 1918 showed that Borden was quite willing to take a firm stand with Britain.

In terms of the postwar liberation, the picture is less satisfying. Canadian officials cannot be held responsible for the failure of Allied commanders to devise a means of evacuating POWs from Germany quickly and safely, nor were they primarily at fault for the shortcomings at the British-run liberation camps. Grumbling ex-prisoners, however, can scarcely have been expected to be familiar enough with the administrative hierarchy to apportion blame fairly, and much of their discontent was inevitably focused upon the Canadian officers staffing the camps. Unfortunately, POWs' experiences in the reception camps formed their last impressions of the government's work on their behalf, and the mishandling of the liberation process may well have erased many ex-prisoners' positive memories of the efforts made for them, at least in the short term. It was supremely unlucky for the government that some ex-POWs would enter the interwar period believing, based on their liberation experiences alone, that they had been neglected.

FOUR

THE INTERWAR YEARS

AFTER PERIODS OF INTERNMENT that ranged from weeks to years, Canadian ex-prisoners came home in 1919 to a vastly different Canada. New political parties were gaining prominence in some provinces, partial nationalization of Canada's railways was under way, women had the franchise in every province but Quebec – some returning prisoners must have found home all but unrecognizable. After the outpouring of concern lavished on them while in the camps, ex-prisoners might reasonably have assumed that their needs would receive special attention after the war. However, it soon became clear that the ex-POW would be treated no differently from any other veteran. Aside from bursts of interest in sensational stories and atrocity tales, ex-prisoners would be generally neglected in the 1920s and 1930s and would come to feel increasingly marginalized. Though in different ways, some ex-POWs would find the struggle to readjust to a normal life just as difficult as the struggle for survival had been in the camps.

THAT NEW STRUGGLE began almost as soon as ex-POWs set foot in Canada. There were enthusiastic welcomes, many returning prisoners receiving cards and sweets from local patriotic or aid societies, but little more.[1] Ex-prisoners who had refused leave in Britain, where many of them had no family or friends to spend it with, found that they could not get the same benefits in Canada, although they had never been advised that this was the case. Some liberated POWs even found it difficult to obtain an accurate account of the pay that was owed to them.[2]

Doubtless all returning soldiers experienced such administrative problems, but ex-prisoners were particularly ill-equipped to cope with them. Few people realized that ex-POWs required special handling and that to treat them as any other returned soldier could have dire consequences; one ex-prisoner even claimed that 'if you take a prisoner of war and scratch him just the least bit you have a man who is pretty close to being a mental case.'[3] Certainly many liberated prisoners had difficulty readjusting to civilian life. Private Bertram Ashbourne found himself constantly looking over his shoulder to make sure that no one was following him, while Private Stephen O'Brien had a rather different reaction to freedom: 'I walked into butcher shops and bought meat of all kinds just to realize I had meat in my possession, then I would give it to some boy or poor-looking person.' For soldiers unused to any kind of freedom, it was particularly unfortunate that Canadian authorities decided on a full payout of all back pay. O'Brien, for example, received $800 in back pay when he arrived in England; when he sailed for Canada five weeks later, he had nothing left.[4]

Nor were the provisions for the physical well-being of ex-POWs any more developed. One commentator described the total lack of consideration for the postwar welfare of ex-prisoners in Britain, despite the promises given them in the camps, and there is little reason to suppose that the situation was any different in Canada.[5] No effort was made to address the medical problems that might plague prisoners who had lived on short rations for years, and a POW organization later pointed out that few doctors understood the long-term physical effects of imprisonment. This organization estimated that the mortality rate for ex-prisoners was five times higher than that for other returned soldiers. Percy Hampton recalls that the only medical advice given was a sign on the repatriation ship that read, 'Eat Sparingly, Eat Often.'[6]

Returned prisoners might have drawn some little comfort from the attempts that had been made in the camps to give POWs a head start on the postwar job hunt by utilizing the years of captivity to train them to 'get on with the battle of life.'[7] Most of the energy in this sphere was directed at POWs who had been transferred to neutral countries. In Switzerland various schools were established for the internees, including a carpet factory at Gunten, a leather works and tailoring shop at Meiringen, and clerical schools at Montreux and Lausanne.[8] Instruction in motor mechanics had been instituted at Vevey, where the school was superintended by Lieutenant A.C. McLurg of Sault Ste. Marie; a number of Canadian graduates of the school found work in Switzerland, including one man who was employed as a driver by the American Legation in Berne. The British Red Cross in Holland organized many courses, most of which were led by internees such as Major F. Palmer of the 1st Canadian Mounted Rifles, who taught poultry and general farming to his fellow repatriates. Of the nearly 400 Canadians in the Netherlands, only sixty-seven were not occupied in either educational courses or relief work with the Red Cross or YMCA.[9] The only hindrances to these training schemes were shortages of supplies, especially in Switzerland, obstacles created by neutral authorities, and the feeling among some internees that they would be able to live on government pensions after the war.

Despite the good intentions, these courses can have benefited only a small fraction of Canadian POWs; the rest were left to fend for themselves in the difficult postwar employment situation. Private Don Corker, after over three years of captivity, found that he lacked the self-confidence to reapply for the clerk's job he had held before the war, while Private Alfred Cleeton was unable to hold a job at all for four years.[10] Walter Haight, a prisoner for nearly two years, attempted to establish a medical practice but soon discovered that the physical and psychological after-effects of his ordeal had turned him into a physical and emotional wreck.[11] Again, such problems were not particular to returned prisoners, but ex-POWs were especially ill-equipped to deal with them, and the problems became part of the burden of grievances that former prisoners would carry through the interwar years.

Returned prisoners must have found it especially galling that the public was generally less interested in their problems of readjustment than in the possibility that POWs were still being held in Germany. Just as the United States has spent decades agonizing over the possibility that Americans might still be held captive in Southeast Asia, so Canada was plagued by stories of prisoners remaining in captivity after the Armistice. Such accounts began to circulate even before the treaty was two months old, when repatriates reported that forty-five Canadians were being worked at a mine near Hameln camp as of late December.[12] More fantastic stories were yet to appear, for in January

1919 Canadian newspapers reported the release from Germany of 15,000 British prisoners who had been officially listed as dead. In short order, the story underwent a metamorphosis and eventually reappeared as an article in the *Ottawa Journal* claiming that a secret prison camp had been found in Germany with 1500 Canadian soldiers who had previously been posted as missing in action.[13]

Certainly there were problems in locating all prisoners of war after the Armistice. As the British chargé d'affaires at The Hague reported, the number of small work detachments made it difficult to be certain of reaching all camps. As examples, he reported that the parent camp at Schneidemühl had 447 work detachments with fewer than five prisoners, the camp at Bayreuth had 680 labour details with fewer than five prisoners, and the camp at Soltau had 972 work detachments with five or fewer prisoners employed.[14] Nevertheless, the account of 1500 unreported POWs was too far-fetched to be believed, and was soon revealed to the public as a hoax that did nothing but falsely raise the hopes of relatives. It transpired that the story originated with a woman who claimed to have heard it somewhere, and the rumour was then turned into an article by an overzealous reporter at the *Journal*. When the Department of Militia and Defence confirmed that there was not a single case of a Canadian being liberated from a prison camp after having been posted as missing and presumed dead, the *Journal* printed a number of corrective articles and discharged the reporter concerned.[15]

To avoid a resurfacing of such hurtful stories, the government offered a public statement on the repatriation operation, reporting to the House of Commons the findings of a POW Repatriation Commission that had been established in January 1919 to travel to Europe in search of lost prisoners. As of 31 March 1919, according to figures given by Sir Edward Kemp, the Minister of the Overseas Military Forces of Canada, only twenty-two prisoners (four officers and eighteen other ranks) were unaccounted for. By May, all but ten of these cases were resolved: the officers had been located and repatriated; seven other ranks had been confirmed dead; and one other rank was in a French hospital.[16] As a further safeguard against hoaxes, any repatriated prisoners who did not wish to return home were ordered to sign statements to that effect, so that they did not become the subject of rumours.[17]

Despite these precautions, the issue refused to die. Concerned citizens continued to approach Militia and Defence with their fears that soldiers who had been reported captured had apparently vanished, and in 1921 the controversy emerged again. The Calgary branch of the Great War Veterans' Association (GWVA) expressed its belief that many prisoners were still incarcerated in remote areas of Germany; this contention was based on statements made by a Belgian named Georges Debels, who had recently returned home from captivity and reported that prisoners of many nationalities had been held with him in Friesland until 1921. The GWVA urged the Militia Council to press Prime Minister Arthur Meighen for 'undeniable assurance' that all Canadian prisoners had been freed, because 'any proof that we had neglected an imprisoned comrade could only be regarded with dishonour.'[18] The assertion caused some concern in Militia and Defence, which admitted the remote possibility that some of the soldiers listed as missing and presumed dead might still be detained in Germany. Deputy Minister (and ex-Boer War POW) Sir Eugène Fiset could only recommend that an assurance be given to the GWVA and to the relatives of missing men that every effort had been and would be made to determine whether any Canadians remained in formerly enemy territory.[19]

In October 1921, this latest controversy was resolved. The War Office reported that rumours of missing prisoners turned up occasionally but were always found to be groundless, and expressed its satisfaction that no Allied POWs remained in Germany. Furthermore, Debels was held to be a man of notoriously bad character who had never been a prisoner in Germany but had worked there voluntarily during and after the war. The War Office also pointed out that in Germany, similar rumours of prisoners held in camps in Britain and Canada often cropped up.[20] Even this, however, did not put an end to the rumours. Over a year later, Militia and Defence continued to receive queries about reports that Germany was still holding British POWs and working them to death.[21]

If the public was preoccupied with the possibility of Canadian prisoners languishing in Germany, they were just as interested in reading about the indignities to which POWs had been exposed. A spate of captivity accounts appeared in the years immediately following the Armistice, with such gripping titles as *Into the Jaws of Death* and *Out of the Jaws of Hunland*. Opting for a relatively nondescript title, the Vancouver publishers Cowan and Brookhouse instead gave John Thorn's *Three Years a Prisoner in Germany* a lurid cover drawing showing an officer struggling to break free of a web while a huge black hand clutched menacingly at him. Publishers were quick to realize that a profit could be made. The memoirs of Henri Béland, the former Cabinet minister who had been interned in Berlin for much of the war, were the object of a bidding war between *Maclean's* magazine, the *Toronto Star* syndicate, and the Toronto publishing houses Frederick D. Goodchild and William Briggs. Nellie McClung's *Three Times and Out*, the story of Private Mervyn Simmons's escaping career, reached the top twenty of Canada's non-fiction bestseller list in 1919.[22]

The cover of John Thorn's book, *Three Years a Prisoner*

Furthermore, published accounts were rarely without grim stories of maltreatment at the hands of the dastardly Hun, and newspaper articles went even further in painting a sensational picture. The *Vancouver Daily Sun* secured a photograph of a British merchant seaman who had had a snake's head tattooed on his cheek by a U-boat commander. Another report stated that three prisoners being transferred into Germany borrowed a penknife 'to cut their throats and so end their miseries.'[23] It was bad enough when such accounts were verifiable, but some stories were completely unsubstantiated. A report that POWs were branded with tattoos of Prussian eagles on their foreheads was apparently based solely on the evidence of two visitors from England who had not actually seen the tattoos themselves but had merely heard them described.[24]

GIVEN SUCH A PREOCCUPATION with the complete repatriation of POWs and the mistreatment that they had suffered, it would seem logical that Canadians would be fascinated by the debate over the revision of the laws of war in the 1920s, directed as it was towards improving the lot of POWs. Such was not the case, however. The movement to revise international law in light of the experiences of the Great War began even before the Armistice, when in February 1918 the International Committee of the Red Cross (ICRC) suggested a diplomatic conference to 'supplement and clarify' those aspects of the Hague and Geneva Conventions relating to POWs.[25] In the early 1920s, a number of organizations prepared draft codes for the treatment of prisoners of war, but it was not until 1924 that British authorities began to consider the matter.[26] A subcommittee of the Committee of Imperial Defence (CID) dispatched its recommendations to the Dominions for their opinions, and within a month the Department of National Defence had concurred in them, suggesting only an addition to facilitate the identification of any POW who was insane or otherwise unable to identify himself.[27] In August 1925, when the Swiss proposed a diplomatic conference to revise the 1906 Geneva Convention for the Amelioration of the Wounded in Time of War and prepare a similar document for POWs, another CID subcommittee was struck, and it reported to the British cabinet in December 1925.[28] Its conclusions reached the Dominions in March 1926, and in May, Canada replied that the draft was acceptable. Only Canada and Australia had no suggestions to make; India, New Zealand, and South Africa each raised a number of issues of interest to them, many of which were acted upon by the subcommittee.[29]

The Geneva diplomatic conference to discuss the conventions had been scheduled for 1929, but the Canadian government was apparently left out of Empire discussions on the matter. When in May 1929 the CID subcommittee reconvened, representatives of Australia, New Zealand, South Africa, and Ireland, but not Canada, were invited to attend.[30] This may have been because Canada had shown little interest in the subject. In 1926, the government had had nothing to say about the proposed drafts, and when amended versions were received in Ottawa in 1928, National Defence declined to consider them because they were not printed in English.[31]

The content of the drafts apparently excited less debate than the make-up of the delegation Canada intended to send to Geneva. Specifically, the government could not decide whether to send Minister of National Defence Colonel J.L. Ralston, or whether W.A. Riddell, the permanent delegate to the League of Nations, and Lieutenant-Colonel Georges P. Vanier, Canada's representative on the Permanent Consultative Commission for Military, Naval, and Air Matters, would suffice. National Defence also considered dispatching Captain J.V. Williams, Canada's representative at the International Congress of Military Medicine, but balked when informed by External Affairs that the department would have to foot the bill for Williams. In the end the government decided that, since Riddell and Vanier were already present in Switzerland (at considerable public expense, External Affairs hastened to add), they should serve as Canada's delegates.[32]

The conference, which ran from 1 to 27 July 1929, was divided into two sections, one to consider the sick and wounded convention and the other to work on the POW convention. Canada assigned a delegate to each, with Riddell joining the deliberations on the POW code and Vanier participating in the revision of the sick and wounded convention.[33] In general, the Canadian government was pleased with the contribution of its delegates. To a large degree Canada followed the British position that the provisions should not be too specific, and that the force of the conventions should instead come from its statement of the minimum conditions achievable and the assumption that general standards of humane treatment should improve upon this wherever possible.[34] As Under-Secretary of State for External Affairs O.D. Skelton put it, 'wherever foreign proposals show an undue tendency towards rigid details and a desire to translate a matter of principle into terms of present day technique, objections should be raised.'[35] Furthermore, Deputy Minister of National Defence G.J. Desbarats crowed that in almost every case, Canadian comments or suggestions had been adopted, although he did not specify whether Canada put forward any independent suggestions or merely supported points made by other powers.[36]

Whatever Canada's input into individual clauses, the POW convention of 1929 was a marked improvement over the 1899 and 1907 Hague Conventions.[37] The Geneva version ran to ninety-seven articles and elaborated on many of the provisions that had been proven inadequate by the experience of war. Once again, the basic assumption was that POWs should be considered on par with the Detaining Power's garrison troops with respect to rations, clothing, living space, and other necessities. Reflecting those areas that had proved troublesome during the Great War, the sections dealing with work, punishment, and relief operations were all expanded, as was the section on repatriation; an annex giving a draft agreement for the repatriation of prisoners, similar to those reached by the major powers during the Great War, was also included. Finally, the article covering the speedy evacuation of POWs after the close of hostilities was made more explicit.

Once the conventions had been signed by Riddell (subject to a reservation regarding one article of the sick and wounded convention), ratification was largely a formality. One of the few dissenting voices was heard when the matter was raised in the House of Commons in February 1932. Responding to Prime Minister R.B. Bennett's comments on the steps leading to the signing of the Geneva Conventions, socialist Member of Parliament J.S. Woodsworth called the conventions anachronistic and pointed out that nearly all civilized nations had signified their abandonment of war as a means of settling international disputes. He claimed that the conventions implied that Canada did not take seriously its obligations to the Kellogg and other pacts, which denounced war as an instrument of government policy. Fortunately for future POWs, Woodsworth's remarks were ignored and the House approved Canada's signature of the conventions.[38]

During the debate on the conventions, Bennett observed that there was likely not a member in the House who, during the First World War, had not been asked to respond to a question regarding prisoners or give support to the POW relief effort. This reminder of the outpouring of concern for captives merely highlighted the fact that POWs and their problems had ceased to be of interest to the Canadian public. During the 1920s, there was virtually no comment in the Canadian press about the proposed revisions to the laws of war (the conference itself passed with scarcely a mention); where comment was made, it was sceptical. J.E. Read, later legal adviser with External Affairs, wrote in 1923 that the failure of the humanitarian lobby to reduce the suffering brought on by war was not an unmixed evil: 'War is hell, and the modern sugar-coated hell is not much better than the old fire-and-brimstone variety.'[39]

The services were not so much sceptical as uninterested. Neither the prelude to the Geneva Conference nor the conventions themselves rated a mention in the *Canadian Defence Quarterly*, and only a few postwar writers bothered to recommend any alterations to the laws of war as they related to prisoners.[40] Shortly after the conclusion of the 1929 Geneva Conference, the future official historian of the Canadian Army, C.P. Stacey, echoed Read's comments, claiming that 'the process of making war endurable by enacting rules for its waging has long since been tried and has failed miserably.'[41] Like Woodsworth, Stacey pinned his hopes on the League of Nations and the Kellogg Pact. More significantly, just a short while after the Geneva conference, Stacey was able to write an entire article on the laws of war without once mentioning the two Geneva Conventions of 1929.

FEW EX-POWS, HOWEVER, can have cared that the Canadian government and public showed little interest in the revision of the laws of war. Much more galling to former prisoners was the official attitude towards the payment of war reparations under the Armistice agreement. Four days after the Armistice came into effect, an Order-in-Council directed the Secretary of State to compile a list of people who had suffered financial losses because of the illegal warfare of the enemy.[42] In October 1921, Chief Justice of New Brunswick Sir John Hazen was appointed a Royal Commissioner to determine whether these claims were covered under the section of the Treaty of Versailles that directed the German government to make reparations payments to various categories of Allied citizens, including civilians who had been interned and prisoners of war who had suffered any form of maltreatment.[43] A fund of some $15 million was put at the disposal of the Canadian government for distribution to successful claimants.

In March 1923, Commissioner Hazen was replaced at his own request by Minister for Public Works and former New Brunswick Premier William Pugsley, who was succeeded upon his death two years later by New Brunswick lawyer James Friel. The first step in the reparations process was to reach possible claimants, and to do this Pugsley and Friel ordered the publication of newspaper advertisements advising former prisoners of the correct procedure for lodging a claim. Each claimant was sent a standard form to be completed, and medical reports were required in the case of personal injury or maltreatment. Under Pugsley, commission hearings were held in Saint John, Montreal, Ottawa, and Toronto, and in Lunenburg, Shelburne, Yarmouth, and Digby in Nova Scotia. After his death, the hearings were continued in central and western Canada by Friel, who convened sittings in Saint John, Montreal, Ottawa, Belleville, Toronto, Hamilton, St. Catharines, Galt, London, Windsor, Winnipeg, Regina, Saskatoon, Edmonton, Calgary, Kamloops, Vancouver, and Victoria.[44]

In total, seventeen former POWs and fifty-six civilian internees filed claims before the Pugsley-Friel Commission. Of the POWs, five claims were withdrawn or defaulted and three were dismissed; an average payment of $4503.56 was made to the remaining nine. Of the civilian claims, four were withdrawn or defaulted and four were dismissed, with forty-eight ex-internees receiving awards averaging $3056.20. In general, the decisions were compassionate and fair. Most of the unsuccessful claims were dismissed because they did not fall within the scope of the commission, such as claims by POWs for loss of personal effects, or because no proof of maltreatment was provided. Where maltreatment was clear, the commissioners were generous. The largest award (aside from $16,700 made to Henri Béland) was a payment of $15,000 to Arthur Boulton, who was starved and beaten for escaping and refusing to work in an armaments factory. Boulton's case was certainly tragic: 'Now a permanent cripple. No future, ill health, unable to marry, work, read, think or enjoy exercise or any other form of amusement, with probability of requiring an attendant or nurse during the remainder of his life.' Friel was evidently much moved, calling Boulton 'the most pitiful wreck of man' he had ever seen, and ordered the sizeable award 'so that during the probable limited time he has to suffer on, it may be in some degree of comfort and independence.'[45]

Friel also recognized that, despite the wide publicity given to the commission's work, some Canadians might not have heard of it; consequently, there had to be a policy to allow for claims made at a later date. At the same time, various ex-POW groups launched a challenge against the Pugsley-Friel commission, contending that the wording of the original advertisements had misled many former prisoners into believing that they were not eligible to make claims.[46] To address both concerns, a new commission was appointed under Justice Errol M. McDougall in September 1930. McDougall fixed 15 January 1931 as the closing date for claims, by which time over 700 cases had been presented, including a number of outstanding claims from the previous commission. Most civilian claims concerned shipping loss, damage to fishing fleets, or losses incurred during air raids, but the class of miscellaneous losses did include a number of former civilian internees.[47] The commission also accepted claims from 932 former POWs, of which 730 were heard.

The seeds of future discontent could be found in the preamble to one of McDougall's reports.[48] While the commissioner insisted that full legal proof would not be demanded of all claimants, he also quoted remarks from the British and American claims commissions intimating that, for an ex-POW to receive an award, he had to prove that a loss of earning capacity resulted directly from a specific incident of maltreatment; civilian internees could claim for general injuries to health but ex-prisoners could not lodge a claim based on the residual effects of captivity.

Furthermore, many factors did not constitute maltreatment in McDougall's view. Lack of food was not considered to be a form of illtreatment because food was generally scarce in Germany, nor was the use of paper bandages an acceptable basis for a claim, because German doctors often had nothing else available. 'Severe handling' or solitary confinement as punishment for an escape were not deemed to be maltreatment, for McDougall insisted that the Germans were fully entitled to take whatever disciplinary measures the situation demanded, including shooting to kill or maim a POW in the course of an escape. McDougall allowed that the Hague Conventions stipulated the proper treatment of prisoners, but expressed his doubts that any captor could live up to this 'desirable standard,' especially since Germany had millions of POWs to care for. He even dismissed the opinion of a standard legal text of the period, Oppenheim's *International Law*, which stated that the Hague Convention had been 'grievously violated by Germany in letter and in spirit.' Such an assessment, held McDougall, would involve finding maltreatment in every single case, something he considered to be 'unduly harsh and literal.'

Interestingly, McDougall's opinions were contradicted by his commission's medical adviser, Dr. J.P.S. Cathcart, Chief Neuropsychiatrist under the Director of Medical Services in the Department of National Defence. In a report that placed him ahead of contemporary medical thinking in Canada, Cathcart declared himself 'inclined to emphasize the impairment of health as [a] result of general conditions rather than the direct or indirect results of specific injuries, violence or abuses.' In examining ex-prisoners, Cathcart found a host of physical and nervous complaints, including bronchitis, pharyngitis, unusual fatigue, minor phobias, emotional instability, dizziness, and insomnia, which he originally ascribed to neurasthenia or nutritional neurosis. Eventually, though, Cathcart concluded that these disorders had a significant psychological component, based on confinement for a long period under conditions of unusual mental strain. Cathcart also flatly disagreed with McDougall's assessment of the food situation, noting that 'I am quite convinced that most of the claimants who spent long periods as employed prisoners of war in Germany, still exhibit some after effects of this service, largely attributable to prolonged deprivation of certain foods ... on which depends [sic] the preservation of good health.'[49] It would be many years before adjudicators examining the pension claims of Canadian ex-POWs accepted such opinions.

The official attitude towards conduct in captivity, an attitude that was certainly not confined to McDougall, was nowhere more evident than in the case of ex-POWs who pressed claims for ill-treatment after the Bokelah 'mutiny.' In the words of a Militia and Defence report, 'This deliberate propensity on the part of Canadian prisoners of war to be as intractable as possible does not appear to be isolated to a few solitary cases, and there appears to have been a general willingness to carry the battle right into the enemy's territory, irrespective of the punishment it entailed.'[50]

McDougall accepted this assessment entirely, pointing out that maltreatment could have been avoided by obeying camp rules and complying with the captors' wishes; provocative behaviour did not justify brutality, wrote McDougall, but it had to be taken into account when determining claims.[51] It was certainly accounted for in the claim of Harry Howland, one of the Bokelah prisoners, who was awarded the minimum payment of $500 plus interest because the brutal conditions under which he served his prison term 'can only be explained by claimant's probable attitude to his captors.'[52] Howland applied for reconsideration, calling McDougall pro-German and insisting that he had been considered a malefactor by the commission only because his name was atop the Bokelah charge list (simply because he had the lowest POW number of the group). However, since Howland could provide no further evidence, his appeal was dismissed.[53]

McDougall's decisions on POW claims were published in three separate reports, and the findings were singularly discouraging for ex-prisoners. In the first report, 208 of the 340 claims were disallowed, with an average award of just over $700. The second report included 281 claims, of which only 38 were approved, with an average award of about $580, while the third report included 213 claims, of which 31 were accepted with awards averaging under $550.[54] Furthermore, the difference between civilian and military awards was sometimes startling. Abbé Eugène Delisle, a Quebec priest studying theology in Lille when the war broke out, was awarded $5000 for impairment of health, despite the fact that the worst indignity he suffered was being struck once on the face by a German officer. In contrast, John Menear, a Boer War veteran who had suffered frequent beatings and contracted eczema, neuritis, and dermatitis while being forced to clean the latrines at Giessen camp, received only $600.[55] Countless other apparently deserving claims were dismissed, with lack of evidence being the most frequent reason cited.[56]

Faced with these apparent inequities, former prisoners and others interested in their plight began to agitate for a reconsideration of reparations cases. In an address to the Nova Scotia Military Institute, Lieutenant-Colonel E.W. Mingo drew special attention to the 'indescribable misery' suffered by other ranks; he pointed out that it was often impossible for them to prove that they had been ill in captivity, but he stressed that a man could hardly be expected to endure such conditions and not be permanently affected. W.J. Evans of Vancouver, who had been captured in March 1918 and forced to work directly behind the front lines, often under heavy shellfire, stressed his loyalty to the Con-servative party in his request for a reconsideration of his $600 award.[57]

The government was not to be moved. In a parliamentary debate on the appropriation of funds to continue the McDougall Commission's work, Secretary of State C.H. Cahan made an unfortunate comment, stating that in the years since the war, some prisoners' impressions of their suffering had become 'fantastic.' He later recanted, insisting that he had intended to say 'exaggerated,' but the damage had been done. Liberal MP and veterans' affairs critic C.G. Power, an ex-soldier whose son would become a POW in the next war, attacked Cahan for his heartless remark and criticized the government for demanding more evidence from former prisoners than from civilian claimants who had 'got their feet wet or lost a trunkful of luggage.' Power went on to point out that 'the evidence shows that the most ridiculous claims were made [by civilians] and allowed without any corroboration being necessary.'[58]

The theme introduced by Power became a central point of the ex-prisoners' case. Maintaining that McDougall had wrongly given precedence to civilian claims when such precedence was not a feature of the relevant Treaty of Versailles article, the Prisoners of War Association of Toronto contended that hundreds of claims had been improperly judged and should be reheard according to the principles of the Pugsley-Friel Commission, which they considered had been eminently fair and reasonable.[59] The head of the Maltreated Prisoners of War Association (MPOWA) in Vancouver made similar criticisms. Captain Frank Pinder, a former airman who had spent most of his captivity in German hospitals before being repatriated to Switzerland in November 1917, demanded a new commission based on the number of ex-prisoners who had not heard of the previous commissions and the contention that McDougall misled many claimants about the nature of evidence required. Former 3rd Battalion private John Kennedy, on behalf of the

Toronto branch of the MPOWA, also registered a protest, condemning the fact that corporation and civilian claims were favoured over those made by POWs.[60] Vancouver POWs Association representative D.W. Davis, another ex-pilot who claimed that lack of medical attention to his wounds had left him with permanent spinal and rib damage, criticized at greater length, citing confusion over what constituted permissible evidence and insufficient time to prepare that evidence as the most serious shortcomings of the McDougall Commission. Like Pinder, Kennedy and Davis had lodged claims with the McDougall Commission; none of the three had been successful in their first attempts.[61]

To address this mounting criticism, Cahan made a further statement on the matter in the House of Commons. He began by pointing out that the fund received from Germany out of which claims had been paid no longer existed; rather, payments for reparations awarded by the McDougall Commission came directly from the consolidated revenue fund. Furthermore, Cahan revealed that Britain did not allow any claims for injuries suffered while a prisoner but confined reparations payments to interned civilians. As to the apparent discrimination between civilian and military claims, Cahan reminded the House that POWs received their pay in captivity, were eligible for pensions if injured, and had their dependants maintained at the public expense. The civilian internee enjoyed none of these benefits, and so received generally higher reparations payments. Finally, the Secretary of State advised ex-prisoners who were dissatisfied with their awards to apply to the Pension Board.[62]

Cahan's explanation did not appease many ex-prisoners, who likely recalled his earlier comment that some claims of maltreatment were fantastic. Certainly in some cases McDougall identified a marked discrepancy between statements made during post-liberation interviews in 1918 and those made before his commission, and such discrepancies naturally led him to doubt the veracity of a number of claims.[63] However, the fact remained that McDougall demanded much less proof from civilian claimants than from POWs; furthermore, civilians had not made statements upon their return in 1918 that could be trotted out to cast doubt upon claims made in the 1930s. In this respect, the POW associations were surely correct in asserting that ex-soldiers were treated unfairly compared with civilians. POWs did enjoy a number of benefits in captivity, such as pay allowances and support for relatives, that were not available to civilians, but there was no avoiding the fact that civilians had been on the continent of their own volition and, in many cases, were amply warned that they faced internment if they remained there. Indeed, the government's policy of demanding that civilians repay their repatriation expenses implied that, in the official view, interned civilians had no one but themselves to blame for their predicament.

The Maltreated POWs Association continued to press the government for reconsideration, and in May 1936 secured permission to appear before the Special Committee on Pensions and Returned Soldiers' Problems. Harry Stone and Robert Green represented the MPOWA at the hearings. Stone, formerly a private in the 4th Canadian Mounted Rifles, had received a $500 award from McDougall for having been forced to labour in a vitriol factory when he was already in ill health; the experience had left him with pleurisy and severe bronchitis. Green, late of the 3rd Battalion, had been unable to convince McDougall that inoculations given by German doctors had permanently impaired his health.[64]

Stone and Green began by recounting the reasons why ex-prisoners were dissatisfied with the work of the McDougall Commission. They pointed out the great inequality in awards made to civilians, who received just under $8 million in payments, and POWs, who received only $160,000, despite the fact that there were roughly the same number of successful claimants in each category. Furthermore, all civilians had been granted a hearing, whereas nearly a quarter of military claimants had not been called before the commission. Stone also drew attention to McDougall's comment that a literal interpretation of the Treaty provisions would have meant that every POW could prove maltreatment, and wondered why McDougall had decided against this interpretation. He deduced that the token awards of $500 made by McDougall had been nothing but a sop to satisfy ex-prisoners for the time being. In conclusion, Stone and Green presented a brief demanding that malnutrition be considered a form of maltreatment and calling for further hearings for new claimants and claimants who wished to appeal their previous rulings or present new evidence.[65]

To keep attention focused on the fight, the MPOWA used a circular letter to exhort its members to further agitation. The letter reported that ex-prisoners who appeared before the McDougall Commission had been informed that, since the original reparations fund no longer existed, they had no legal status as claimants. Their claims were heard solely on compassionate grounds, and any payments made would be a direct charge on the Canadian taxpayer. Accordingly, McDougall's awards were not based on any notion of fairness or justice, but were 'governed by the amount of money the government was prepared to throw as a sop to P.O.W. [sic] to keep them quiet.' The MPOWA circular outlined its proposal to the Special Committee on Pensions, requesting a grant of $25 per month for life, retroactive to 1930. It advised members to place notices in local newspapers calling on other ex-prisoners to form branches of the MPOWA and write to their Members of Parliament requesting all available information on the reparations situation. The MPOWA even provided a sample circular letter to be sent to MPs, which pointed out that Armenians had received larger awards than ex-prisoners and that 'the Ex-Prisoners of War have just cause to say that the sacrifice troops in France are still being sacrificed in Canada.'[66]

Some ex-prisoners took up the MPOWA's call, and in 1938 Conservative MP Gordon Graydon asked the government for statistics on POW reparations payments awarded to date and wondered whether any provision had been made for the presentation of further claims.[67] The Liberal government considered the matter closed and informed the Ex-POW Association of Toronto that, since the portion of the Versailles reparations payment allotted to war claims had long since been exhausted, it had no intention of reopening the reparations question or of providing the machinery for further claims.[68] The election of Robert Manion, an ex-soldier, as leader of the federal Conservatives gave veterans new hope, and a number of them asked Manion to raise the matter of reparations before Parliament. An Ontario ex-POW reiterated that prisoners had been discriminated against vis-à-vis civilian and corporation reparations claims, and carefully repeated word for word the MPOWA's comment about sacrifice troops. Manion was sympathetic but admitted that he could do little beyond supporting the ex-prisoners' claims if the matter came up again in the House of Commons.[69]

Thus the efforts of Pinder, Stone, and other former POWs achieved little, in large part because they were never able to mobilize sufficient support. The MPOWA and similar organizations must have been little more than fringe groups, and former prisoners never took an active role in the more powerful veterans' organizations. For its part, the Canadian Legion had bigger fish to fry and showed little interest in the reparations issue.[70] A decade would pass before the claims of ex-prisoners would be forced upon the attention of the government by much better-organized groups.

In the years before the beginning of the Second World War, the armed forces exhibited as little interest as the government in prisoner of war matters, and apparently saw no need to amend service regulations pertaining to POWs. The British version of the *Manual of Military Law* of 1929, which was favourably reviewed in the *Canadian Defence Quarterly*, included the full text of the 1929 Geneva Convention relating to POWs, but this entire section was omitted when the manual was reproduced for use in the Canadian Army. Nor did the *King's Regulations and Orders* for Canada differ in any substantial way from the version in use before the First World War; it continued to call for a board of inquiry whenever personnel were captured.[71] Furthermore, pre-Second World War soldiers do not recall receiving instruction of any kind in the changes in international law pertaining to POWs.[72] The services had obviously learned little from the experience of the Great War and the interwar period.

THE INTERWAR YEARS must have been a great disappointment to former POWs. The objects of fairly lavish attention during the war, they found themselves quickly cast aside afterwards, by both the public and the government. For many ex-prisoners, the reparations controversy could only have been a painful insult. Future POWs would also have cause to lament the inactivity of the interwar period. Despite the claims of Desbarats, Canada played only a token role in the revision of the laws of war. Even that role elicited no interest in the general public, which remained ignorant of the Geneva proceedings, or in the military, which made no effort to incorporate the new conventions into its training. Despite the progress made at Geneva, the Canadian government and armed forces were little more prepared in 1939 than their predecessors had been in 1914 to face the rigours of captivity.

FIVE

The Organizational
Framework, 1939-45

In the maintenance of prisoners of war and internees, the Second
World War turned out to be the First World War writ large. There were
nearly three times as many Canadian prisoners to maintain, and to
achieve that end a vastly larger government organization and a much
wider range of aid groups came into existence. Furthermore, Canada
was a member of a variety of international committees more powerful
than any POW committees that existed during the Great War. In each
area, the problems that had been encountered earlier were repeated on
a correspondingly larger scale. Apart from the practical work of supplying aid to and securing the release of POWs, the purely administrative
aspects of establishing and operating a structure to monitor the interests of prisoners created problems in sufficient number to suggest that
many lessons of the First World War had been ignored.

I

During the Second World War, nearly 10,000 Canadian soldiers, sailors,
and airmen fell into enemy hands while serving with the Canadian
forces (see Table 2a to 2d in the Appendix for details); hundreds more
were captured while serving with other forces, primarily British, and
dozens of Canadians spent varying periods as internees in neutral
countries. Finally, as many as 2000 Canadian civilians, including a
large number of clerical students and missionaries, were interned by

the enemy during the war, in both Europe and the Far East.[1]

Many of the POWs still felt a real stigma at falling into enemy hands, like the captain of the Argyll and Sutherland Highlanders of Canada taken prisoner in 1944 who recalled that being captured was 'not the kind of thing that's supposed to happen' to an officer.[2] Of course, the debacles at Hong Kong and Dieppe made it difficult to argue that a prisoner should not have allowed himself to be captured alive. It is worth noting that, when the first group of wounded Dieppe POWs was repatriated in October 1943, Canadian Military Headquarters (CMHQ) in London decided that, because of the circumstances under which the men had been captured, a court of inquiry to determine whether negligence was involved was neither necessary nor desirable.[3] Nevertheless, the stigma remained, to the degree that experts considering the psychological effects of captivity agreed that ex-POWs would often feel a marked sense of guilt at having been captured.[4]

Furthermore, the armed forces still rarely considered the possibility of capture. Most servicemen never contemplated that they might fall into enemy hands, and consequently had no idea what to expect; this made the moment of capture, when new prisoners were unsure whether they would be interrogated or shot, all the more agonizing.[5] Arthur Crighton, captured in April 1942 while serving with 419 Squadron RCAF, recalled that 'it would have been comforting if I had known that I might not be shot on sight, that there were logical procedures to be followed to try to avoid capture, and that it was our right and duty to reveal only name, rank and number.'[6]

Unfortunately most lectures on captivity, when they were available, emphasized only the traditional exhortations against revealing sensitive information to the enemy; one officer recalls being given the number of the Geneva Convention article that stipulated that he was bound to provide only his name, rank, and serial number.[7] Air crews were particularly well trained in this regard, because every member of a crew could look forward to a tough interrogation at *Dulag Luft*, the German air force's transit camp through which all captured air crews passed. On the strength of information gleaned from ex-POWs who had returned to England through repatriation or escape, the Royal Canadian Air Force (RCAF) could give air crews a reasonably good idea of what to expect at *Dulag Luft*, even down to a physical description of the German officer who would try to pass himself off as a representative of the Red Cross.[8]

The RCAF also provided training in escape and evasion. The members of 1 (later 401) Squadron had at least two lectures by escapers, the first in November 1941 by an officer who had broken out of a German prison camp during the First World War.[9] The lecture obviously had the desired impact, for pilots John 'Scruffy' Weir and Wally Floody, both shot down and captured the week after, passed their time in captivity digging tunnels, most notably those used in the Great Escape of March 1944. The RCAF provided more practical instruction as well; air crews occasionally took part in an exercise consisting of being dropped off with a compass about ten miles away from the airfield with orders to make one's way back to base without using the roads.[10]

The services were clearly more interested in protecting against leaks of information or returning servicemen to action than in instructing personnel how to cope with the rigours of captivity. Some half-hearted efforts were made early in the war to rectify this shortcoming. In 1940, the High Commission in London learned that Major-General H.D.G. Crerar at CMHQ had taken steps to apprise Canadian troops overseas of their rights and obligations in war. To achieve this, Major N.E. Rodger at CMHQ arranged for a British training film to be shown to Canadian troops to illustrate what was expected of them if they were captured. The film was of poor quality, however, and was barely useful.[11] Later, in April 1942, Major John Page, Rodger's successor, asked the War Office to instruct Canadian troops in the pitfalls of captivity, and in May officers of the 2nd Division completed an eleven-day course that explained how to avoid capture, proper conduct in captivity, and equipment and techniques for escape.[12] However, based on the recollections of officers of the 2nd Division, the course apparently spent little time on conduct in captivity. Major R.E. McLaren, who commanded the Royal Hamilton Light Infantry's (RHLI) headquarters company at Dieppe, knew the generalities of the Geneva Convention but nothing more, while Captain F.J.L. Woodcock, another RHLI Dieppe prisoner, recalled that he did not learn of the convention until after reaching a prison camp.[13]

When Page left CMHQ after Dieppe, there remained no one interested in training for captivity. The course was not repeated, and two years passed before the Canadian Army took responsibility for its own POW instruction.[14] Nevertheless, knowledge of the laws of captivity did seep into the services, for certain officers appear to have had a reasonable grasp of the Geneva Convention. Captain Harry Pope, captured in Italy while serving with the Van Doos, lodged a protest under the convention based on the number of prisoners who had been packed into a railway carriage, while Allen Graham, a Canadian doctor captured at Tobruk, had a similar argument with his captors as he and other POWs were being loaded into boxcars on their way to a permanent prison camp.[15] Some soldiers found that the mere mention of the Geneva Convention was enough to calm an irate captor, at least until the moment of greatest danger had passed.[16]

The hazards inherent in that first stage of captivity eventually forced the Canadian Army to pay particular attention to preparing soldiers for the possibility of capture. Presumably Chief of the General Staff Harry Crerar's mention in 1940 of a Canadian soldier's rights and obligations in war included his right to be taken alive as a POW, and his obligation to take prisoners if they presented themselves. Nevertheless, a take-no-prisoners policy was talked of in the Canadian Army in 1940. In May, when Canadian troops were anticipating going into action in France, 1st Division General Officer Commanding (GOC) General A.G.L. McNaughton said that 'you must be absolutely ruthless ... tell the men we are not particularly interested in prisoners.'[17] Whether anyone mentioned the obverse of this, that the Germans might be just as uninterested in prisoners, is not recorded.

In 1944, these considerations suddenly became imperative. Whether or not an unofficial take-no-prisoners policy existed in the Canadian Army is a matter of some debate, but there can be no doubt that it was the practice of certain German units in Normandy.[18] On the morning of 7 June 1944, the 12th SS Panzer (Hitler Youth) Division moved into the German front line northwest of Caen, and over the next ten days was in action against units of the 3rd Canadian Infantry Division. War crimes investigators later established that during this period at least 134 Canadian soldiers had been murdered after capture by Hitler Youth troops. When these murders came to light in July, the government was forced to address the dangers surrounding the moment of capture. CMHQ had to take swift action to make soldiers aware of the new hazards facing them if captured, although Crerar, now GOC of the 1st Canadian Army, was more concerned that atrocity stories might drive Canadian soldiers to reprisals.[19] In fact, the text of a message to the troops provoked some debate. Crerar wanted to say that the prisoners had been 'murdered under circumstances of great brutality' to convince soldiers of the type of enemy they faced, but the government wanted the phrase omitted to avoid alarming relatives. In the end, Crerar compromised and said only that there must be no retaliation but that anger must be converted into a 'steel-hard determination' to defeat the enemy.[20] The impact of this incident on the training of soldiers for captivity is difficult to assess. One soldier, however, recalled that before going into action in northwest Europe, his unit was briefed on the different German troops they might face and the attitudes such troops could be expected to have.[21]

THESE THORNY ISSUES were far in the future in the early months of the war, when only a handful of Canadians were POWs in Germany. The first of these was Pilot Officer A.B. Thompson of Penetanguishene, who had joined the Royal Air Force in 1937 and was shot down on a leaflet raid over Germany on 8 September 1939, before Canada had officially entered the war. Thompson and his British navigator were regarded as curiosities by their captors and were even taken to meet *Reichsmarschall* Hermann Göring, who professed an interest in Canadian ice hockey and promised the two that captured airmen would be well treated. Some weeks later, a Red Cross inspector found the pair in Itzehoe prison camp with 2 French aviators, 600 Poles, and little to do to pass the time but play bridge. Thompson was soon joined by another Canadian, Flight Lieutenant R.M. Coste of Calgary, also a prewar RAF pilot, and by mid-1940 another two dozen Canadian airmen had been captured.[22]

The government's conduct in the first year of the war, however, revealed a distinct unpreparedness and lack of concern that a large number of Canadians might be captured. On 12 September 1939, the International Committee of the Red Cross (ICRC) placed itself at the disposal of the Canadian government, and two days later the ICRC's Central Agency established a British section to maintain records on prisoners from all parts of the Commonwealth. Casualty information

Canada's first POW of the Second World War. A.B.Thompson (foreground) enjoys a game of table tennis at *Oflag* 9A/H, Spangenberg.

emanating from Germany was directed through the British section to the POW Information Bureau at the War Office, and from there to the Dominions; after 1941, this information went from the ICRC directly to Dominion governments.[23]

In November 1939 the Canadian government established a POW Information Bureau under the Director of Internment Operations, Colonel Hubert Stethem, to collate all information pertaining to Canadian servicemen in enemy hands and enemy personnel captured by or imprisoned in Canada.[24] The same month, the Canadian Red Cross Society (CRCS) replicated the overseas organization it had used during the First World War by forming a London Advisory Committee, under the chairmanship of former Prime Minister R.B. Bennett. With the creation of these two agencies, Canada's nascent organization for safeguarding the welfare of prisoners in enemy hands was in place.

The London Advisory Committee was quick to commence operations, and within days of its creation began making plans to forward parcels to Thompson and Coste. This fast start by the Red Cross caused some concern in External Affairs, and the department's under-secretary, O.D. Skelton, promptly reminded Norman Sommerville, chairman of the CRCS Central Council, that no action regarding Canada's external relations should be taken without first obtaining the consent of the government. For this reason, Skelton asked the Red Cross to do nothing further until a meeting of the interested parties (External Affairs, Justice, the Secretary of State, National Defence, Pensions and National Health, the Post Office, and the Canadian Red Cross) could be convened.[25]

The minutes of that meeting betray a very simplistic view of the problem at hand. The participants agreed that the channel of communication for queries regarding Canadian POWs should be from External Affairs to the ICRC through the Canadian Permanent Delegate to the League of Nations in Geneva. It was also stated, quite blandly, that mail and parcels should be sent from the Canadian Post Office to the British Post Office to Germany. Despite the experience of the First World War, the minutes give no indication that the meeting's participants appreciated the problems inherent in either of these schemes.[26]

Other communications from this period demonstrate just as well how little Canadian officials grasped the extent of the problem they faced. In November 1939, Canada House political secretary Lester Pearson was searching for a copy of the 1929 Geneva Convention, despite the fact that it had been published by External Affairs and should have been in the High Commission's files. Later, Pearson had difficulty responding to an inquiry from RCAF headquarters as to what action might be required of Canada as a signatory to the Geneva Convention.[27] As late as February 1942, External Affairs and the Department of National War Services could be found comparing their map of prison camps in Germany with one published in the French illustrated magazine *Paris-Soir*, to determine which was better. After much consideration, both departments declared gravely that the Canadian government's map was superior.[28]

Of greater long-term significance were two decisions regarding Canada's POW organization, both based solely on the number of Canadians in captivity.[29] With so few prisoners, officials elected not to create a separate office in the Department of National Defence to monitor the interests of Canadians in enemy hands, preferring to leave the matter to the Director of Internment Operations. This arrangement was satisfactory with a minimum of public expense, thought Under-Secretary of State E.H. Coleman, and if the number of Canadian prisoners grew, either Colonel Stethem could be given more staff or the control of enemy POWs and Canadian POWs could be divorced from each other and a new organization established.[30]

In the absence of a separate POW office, Canadian officials decided to allow British authorities to handle the affairs of Canadians in enemy hands. In October 1940, a draft of a letter from the Dominions Office expressed the belief that 'it would be the wish of the Canadian government that the Army Council should include Canadian Prisoners of War in this responsibility [looking after British POWs], and should take all possible steps to ensure their correct treatment.' The draft reached Canada House with a covering note explaining that the letter was about to be sent, when the Dominions Office 'had second thoughts, the point being that you might very well say that you were capable of looking after your own.'[31] Two years, or perhaps even a year, later the Army Council's suggestion would have made Canadian officials bristle, but in 1940 apparently no one batted an eyelash. Coleman intimated that the Secretary of State would abide by the wishes of the service departments, but was inclined to accept the Army Council's offer. Less than a month later, Canada House also recommended accepting an offer that the British POW Information Bureau handle all inquiries regarding Commonwealth POWs, despite the existence of Stethem's bureau.[32]

In some ways it is difficult to argue with the government's decisions. By the end of 1940, perhaps only a hundred Canadians had been captured, and since almost all of these men served with British units, they were the responsibility of British authorities. Only one member of the Canadian forces was a prisoner in Germany, Private R.J. Creighton of the Hastings and Prince Edward Regiment, who had been injured in a motorcycle accident in France and captured when German forces overran the hospital where he was recuperating. Four other Canadian soldiers had been interned briefly in Vichy France but all eventually escaped.[33] Perhaps understandably, the government saw little point in creating a separate structure for Private Creighton when Britain's could be used free of charge.

Nevertheless, the decision not to establish an office in 1940 to monitor the interests of Canadians in enemy hands showed remarkable lack of foresight, especially in light of the experience of the First World War. In that war, Canadian officials had toiled away in a mass of confusion created by the absence of a single office responsible for POW affairs, and had chafed at being subject to the dictates of the British government. In 1940, the Canadian government walked into a similar situation, despite Britain's suggestion that Canada might want to look after its own POWs. In the coming years, this early reliance on British instead of Canadian structures would severely limit Canada's freedom of action, and would force the government to expend considerable effort attempting to cope with the consequences of these unfortunate decisions.

The seeds of future problems should have been apparent in the number of departments (six) represented at the November 1939 meeting to discuss POW administration.[34] This number increased a year later when Canadian officials decided to divorce the administration of Canadians in enemy hands from the control of German POWs in Canada. However, even this wise decision was flawed. In December 1940, responsibility for providing information to POWs' next of kin was transferred not to National Defence but to the Department of National War Services, which established a POW Next-of-Kin Division to maintain contact with relatives and help send relief supplies to the camps.[35] With another department now involved in POW matters, the procedure became even more complicated.

The responsibilities of various departments engaged in the administration of POW affairs were summarized in June 1941.[36] Within the Department of External Affairs' Commonwealth and European Division, a Special Section was created under Alfred Rive to administer the interests of Canadians interned abroad. Rive, a University of British Columbia graduate who left an assistant professorship at Yale to join External Affairs in 1930, had served most recently as Canada's delegate to the League of Nations in Geneva. Special Section was to act as a post box, handling all communications with the United States (and later Switzerland and Argentina) as Protecting Power, the ICRC in Geneva, and the High Commission in London. In addition, it became generally responsible for the application of the POW conventions, and also took charge of ensuring that Canadian policy was coordinated with that of the United Kingdom and the other Dominions; in both pursuits, the most important principle was reciprocity, 'to ensure that as favourable treatment is accorded Canadian prisoners of war by the enemy as Canada accords to enemy prisoners of war.'[37] Finally, Special Section was responsible for monitoring the welfare of Canadian civilians abroad.[38] In theory, the role of the Departments of National Defence and Transport was limited to providing the first notification of capture to next of kin. Further communications were to be handled by the POW Next-of-Kin Division of National War Services, which would maintain contact with relatives, transmit to them changes in postal regulations, and answer any queries they might have.

On paper, the government's organization for POW affairs appeared to be fairly straightforward, but it functioned much less smoothly in practice. Just days after Rive drew up his very tidy memorandum on departmental responsibilities, it became evident that the system for notification was not working, as members of various departments began to trade barbs over what they perceived as obstruction by other offices. Before the year was out, ICRC delegate in Montreal Ernst Maag, too, complained of problems in the Canadian system and pressed for a more efficient way of handling information.[39] However, the complaints of a few bureaucrats and a neutral diplomat were not sufficient in themselves to force improvements; the final straw was the fall of Hong Kong in December 1941, which demanded that the system be reorganized to cope with the flood of queries that Canadian officials expected to receive from anxious relatives.

The first step in that reorganization was the creation of the Red Cross Enquiry Bureau (RCEB) in Ottawa to respond to inquiries regarding POWs.[40] In an announcement of its functions, the CRCS made a special appeal to prisoners' relatives to approach the bureau with any questions about parcel regulations.[41] Perhaps because the Order-in-Council authorizing the RCEB did not stress this last role, there is no indication of concern that the new agency duplicated the functions of National War Services' POW Next-of-Kin Division.

Although government departments were directed to assist the bureau, the RCEB encountered stiff opposition from the service departments almost from its inception. Jealous of any supposed usurpation of its powers, National Defence took advantage of the Hong Kong tragedy to reclaim some of its territory by organizing its own mechanism for maintaining POWs. As a later memorandum by Minister of

National Defence J.L. Ralston stated, the department considered it an 'evasion of responsibility' to refer a relative's inquiry to either National War Services or the RCEB, something that would suggest that the department had no interest in its people once they had been captured. To discharge its obligations, National Defence deemed it essential to create an agency to monitor the welfare of Canadians in captivity, and to maintain contact both with relatives and with the rest of the world via External Affairs.[42]

Accordingly, on 12 May 1942 Colonel F.W. Clarke was appointed as Special Assistant to the Adjutant-General (SAAG) to assume responsibility for the welfare of Canadian POWs; according to the press release, his 'primary function would be to advise and assist regarding the interests of members of the Canadian Hong Kong force and their dependants, and respecting any problem relating to Canadian prisoners of war.'[43] Clarke was Honourary Colonel of the Royal Rifles of Canada (he had a son with the regiment in Hong Kong), a vice president of the Anglo-Canadian Pulp and Paper Mills, and, on paper at least, a fairly typical political choice for the position. However, he turned out to be an especially able administrator, and throughout the war demonstrated an appreciation for the problems of POWs that was shared by no one else in the Canadian government and by few others in the Allied world. Perhaps because of his ability, he was to reveal a voracious appetite for expanding the duties of his office well beyond its original mandate of safeguarding the interests of Hong Kong prisoners.

With Clarke's appointment, three agencies now performed roughly the same function: the Red Cross Enquiry Bureau, National War Services' POW Next-of-Kin Division, and the office of the SAAG.[44] A circular sent to relatives outlining the duties of the offices revealed the degree of overlap. One section instructed relatives to address all inquiries regarding mail and parcels to the Next-of-Kin Division, but the following paragraph advised next of kin to contact the Red Cross Enquiry Bureau with questions regarding parcels.[45] Relatives can surely be forgiven for not knowing which office to contact, and subsequent difficulties in this area can be ascribed to this confusing overlap of responsibility.

The appointment of Clarke as SAAG seemed to open the way for a further reorganization of the government's POW administration. Also in March 1942 came the formation of the Committee for the Protection and Welfare of Canadian Prisoners of War in Enemy Hands (CPW), consisting of representatives from the three service departments, Transport, National War Services, and External Affairs. The CPW first met on 9 April 1942, with Clarke chairing, and eventually came to be responsible for most aspects of the POW question, including the coordination of policy with other governments and the application of the Geneva Convention. Although the CPW considered itself to be simply a clearing-house for information from the departments represented on it, this was a very modest assessment, for the committee dealt with a wide range of problems. In January 1943 that range expanded further when the CPW was enlarged to take in discussion of enemy POWs and internees in Canada.[46] Unfortunately, this constructive development, which placed responsibility for all POW matters in the hands of a single committee, was only temporary; in time, the CPW would be joined by a handful of other committees intended to handle specific aspects of the POW problem.

Despite the apparent ascendency of Clarke's committee, External Affairs was still very much at the centre of things and soon found its workload increasing alarmingly. Reducing that load to make Special Section more efficient became a priority of many of the division's staffers, especially Morley Scott, a UBC classmate of Rive's who had taught history at the University of Michigan for nearly twenty years before joining External Affairs as a wartime assistant. According to one historian, Scott joined the department looking for excitement, but he cannot have found his work as a POW administrator very thrilling. He spent much of the war pushing paper, and in 1948 looked back on his tenure at Special Section with a mixture of sadness and frustration, born out of the belief that the office had achieved little of consequence during the war.[47]

One of Scott's pet projects was to improve Special Section's efficiency by clarifying the nature of its role. According to Scott, opinion on this matter was divided. Some members of External Affairs (presumably Under-Secretary of External Affairs Norman Robertson, for one) believed that Special Section should continue to shoulder most of the POW burden,[48] but the department's legal adviser, John Read, felt that National Defence and National War Services should assume most of the work; Special Section should be represented on all POW policy committees, but should act only as a post box for communication with other governments. Most of Special Section, including Rive and Scott, shared this opinion.[49]

They were clearly in the minority, though, for both National War Services and National Defence rejected Rive's proposal that External Affairs transfer more POW responsibility to them.[50] For the rest of the war, the members of Special Section grew increasingly irritated at their inability to extricate themselves from the burden of POW superintendence. On at least two occasions, Special Section had to resist being drawn into interdepartmental conflicts over POWs,[51] and in December 1944 Morley Scott blew up over the case of the wife of a Dieppe prisoner who had requested information about her husband. The woman's query had spent two months going between the Red Cross Enquiry Bureau, the Canadian Red Cross in London, the British Red Cross, the War Office, and Canada House, something that moved Scott to vent his spleen at some length:

> You will probably agree that it would be difficult to devise a method more wasteful in time and effort than has here been followed ... As I have no intention of participating in this scandalous way of doing business, ... I am not writing to the Red Cross Society but am filing these papers and passing this information to you. I presume you will telephone the S.A.A.G. to do what he can to relieve Mrs. Jessop's anxiety thus accomplishing in two minutes what Red Cross have failed to achieve in two months.[52]

Scott's point was well taken. After five years of war, the Canadian public had a right to expect that such simple inquiries would be handled with a reasonable degree of efficiency. The RCEB's decision to go 3000 miles to London for a piece of information that was located half a mile away at the SAAG's office was clearly not an acceptable way of doing business.

Government attempts to put its own house in order, then, were not entirely successful. The failure to create a single POW office in 1940 was a serious omission. Had this been done when there were few Canadians in captivity, the office could have developed experience in POW matters and would have been firmly in control of the situation by the time of the Hong Kong and Dieppe disasters. Instead, when Canadians started to fall into enemy hands in large numbers, various departments and organizations wanted to step into the void. This created an overlap of responsibility, not only between the departments themselves but between the committees that were created to handle specific problems. The result was confusion, lack of coordination, and, as the Jessop case reveals, a failure to serve the public.

II

The government's attempts to establish good working relations with the private groups involved in POW relief were little more successful than its attempts to create a functional POW bureaucracy. The problem was particularly difficult because the voluntary organizations were now much more numerous than during the First World War.[53] Most of these organizations were quite small and only needed direction, but three groups were active nationally and, more importantly, each believed it was best equipped to direct the relief effort. These organizations – the Canadian Red Cross Society, the War Prisoners' Aid of the World's Committee of YMCAs, and the Canadian POW Relatives Association – would do excellent work for POWs but would also create a host of problems for the government.

The largest of these organizations was the Canadian Red Cross Society, which had had wide experience with POW matters during the First World War. In fact, some of the key players from the Great War were still involved with the Red Cross in 1939, such as Adele Plumptre, who headed the Red Cross Enquiry Bureau. Plumptre, a Toronto municipal politician between the wars, had been the society's secretary during the Great War and had gone on to represent Canada at the League of Nations in Geneva in 1931 and the International Red Cross Conference in Tokyo in 1934. An occasional lecturer at the University of Toronto, she had a considerable reputation in Red Cross circles, not just in Canada but around the world.

The other key figure in the society was Mr. Justice P.H. Gordon of the Saskatchewan Court of Appeal. Born at Qu'Appelle, Gordon had taken a master's degree at the University of Toronto before returning

to the west, where he later served as the Chancellor of the Anglican dio-
cese of Qu'Appelle; he also represented the federal government on the
Saskatchewan Relief Commission in 1930. As chairman of the CRCS
National Executive Committee, Gordon was the de facto liaison officer
between the society and the government for much of the war.

Headquartered in Toronto, the CRCS was divided into provincial
divisions and had thousands of branches across the country staffed by
volunteer workers who were often just as experienced as the society's
executive. However, the Canadian Red Cross had more than just experience to give it a leg up on all other aid groups. On 29 April 1940
External Affairs recognized the CRCS as Canada's official voluntary aid
society under the Geneva Convention, thereby putting the Red Cross at
the top of the POW relief ladder.[54] It was a position that the society was
not keen to surrender.

In time, though, this position would be challenged by the other
major aid organizations operating in Canada. The War Prisoners' Aid
(WPA) of the World's Committee of YMCAs, although not an official
relief society under the Geneva Convention, received permission from
the Swiss government to work to improve the educational, recreational,
cultural, and spiritual life of prisoners. Over the course of the war,
WPA workers dispatched an immense variety of supplies to the camps,
from skipping ropes and golf clubs, to saxophones and harmonicas, to
wood-carving tools and modelling clay, all paid for by the various
national committees.[55] In Canada, the YMCA was recognized by
National Defence's Directorate of Auxiliary Services and originally had
full autonomy in its work. In 1942, however, the government decided
that the YMCA and a number of other volunteer groups (but not the
Red Cross) should no longer do their own fundraising.[56] This restric-
tion, combined with the fact that the YMCA had many powerful backers, would cause problems in the future.

The third organization, the Canadian POW Relatives Association
(CPOWRA), would also come to resent the most-favoured status of the
Red Cross. Also a registered war charity, the CPOWRA's aims were 'to
bring all possible comfort to our Canadian prisoners of war, and to
assist the relatives by having available for them without delay, all information regarding rules and regulations.'[57] Contact was maintained by
provincial branches, which corresponded with prisoners' next of kin

and kept a record of all POWs with relatives in that province, including non-Canadians, neutral and civilian internees, and prisoners who had been adopted by people in the province; the association's nominal rolls recorded promotions, transfers, deaths, or repatriations, and when a relative moved to another part of the country, the information was passed on to that province so that contact could be maintained.[58] The association held regular meetings to share information about news received from the prison camps, and from December 1941 published a monthly bulletin of parcel regulation updates, news items, and excerpts from prisoners' letters. It also assisted financially next of kin who could not afford to send parcels. Significantly, the association prided itself on being the only registered war charity whose sole purpose was the welfare of Canadian POWs.[59] This, combined with the fact that the CPOWRA too had a number of formidable backers (not the least of whom was its president, Beatrice Asselin, whose son had been shot down and captured while flying with the RCAF), would also bring the organization into conflict with the Canadian Red Cross.

In the early years of the war, though, the Canadian Red Cross appeared unassailable. In October 1940, the Canadian Censorship Liaison Officer recommended that the Red Cross be designated as the only agency permitted to send parcels to POWs, and the Red Cross also secured status as the sole aid organization permitted to launch independent fundraising drives.[60] This privilege was continually defended by the government. When the Navy League proposed a fund drive to send parcels to imprisoned merchant seamen, National War Services actively discouraged the plan lest it detract from the work of the Red Cross. Later, the government frowned upon similar fundraising activities proposed by the Auxiliary of Les Fusiliers de Mont-Royal and the Royal Rifles of Canada POW Association.[61] All things considered, Justice Gordon felt well able to write that 'every Department has gone out of its way to accommodate me whenever I have appealed to them.'[62]

Nevertheless, the Red Cross soon began to feel pressure from competing aid societies. The first source of conflict was the War Prisoners' Aid of the World's Committee of YMCAs, which had been sending American inspectors to prison camps in Europe since the beginning of the war. The value of having English-speaking North Americans visit

Children were encouraged to participate in fundraising drives launched by the Red Cross.

Canadian POWs was recognized, but once the United States entered the war and the American inspectors had to be withdrawn, External Affairs wondered whether the government should discontinue using the WPA as a means of reaching prisoners. The main problem was that Canada's support for WPA work in Europe gave the organization grounds to demand reciprocal rights to visit camps in Canada. This was undesirable because the YMCA had 'sent a variety of visitors into the camps, not all of whom are suitable for the work.' In the view of External Affairs, consideration should be given to forfeiting the services of the WPA for Canadian POWs in Germany in order to exert tighter control over the organization in Canada.[63]

Rive's memorandum on this subject was circulated to a number of departments and elicited a variety of responses. Under-Secretary of State Coleman, perhaps in awe of the WPA's powerful supporters, advised against restraining the organization in Canada, at least until the Protecting Power (now Switzerland) could say whether the WPA's work in Germany had been curtailed since Pearl Harbour. Naval Services agreed with Coleman's argument, although the Acting Deputy Minister admitted that his department preferred having only one organization dealing with prisoners and that the Red Cross seemed the most logical choice. The Army, on the other hand, agreed entirely with the idea of restricting the WPA's activities in Canada as a way to simplify the process of detaining POWs.[64]

External Affairs was impartial at first but soon revealed where its feelings lay. In a teletype to the Canadian Legation in Washington, External Affairs accused Dr. Jerome Davis, director of WPA operations in Canada, of 'doing everything in his power to increase the prestige and importance of his organization even, it appears, sometimes at the expense of the Canadian Red Cross.' Davis received a more restrained communication suggesting a meeting of government departments and aid groups to ensure 'that each will be doing the work for which they are most suited and all will be making a contribution without duplication or overlapping.'[65] He responded with a proposal that the WPA visit the relatives of Japanese-Canadians who had been interned at Angler Camp in northern Ontario (the WPA desired 'to do everything possible to aid the Japanese here so that we may have the best possible entré over there,' he wrote), an idea that provoked some alarm within the government. Rive claimed that Japanese families had more than enough agencies to look after them, and opined that 'the main reason for Davis' anxiety to help the Japanese is to build up the position of the PoW Aid of the World Y.M.C.A. and he is quite ready to do so at the expense of the other organizations,' especially the Red Cross.[66]

Indeed, the Canadian Red Cross soon found itself in conflict with the YMCA. When the society began a May 1942 fundraising drive, its full-page advertisements included the statement that the Red Cross was 'the only agency through which we're able to reach out to prisoners.'[67] This claim was guaranteed to anger the WPA and the organization began to mobilize its influential supporters, such as composer and Toronto Symphony Orchestra conductor Sir Ernest MacMillan (himself an internee during the First World War), former University of Toronto president Sir Robert Falconer, and former postmaster-general Sir William Mulock. Letters of complaint were sent to various Red

Cross offices, asking 'in the interests of truth and harmonious relation-ship' for a public statement that the Red Cross and the WPA comple-mented each other in POW relief work.[68] As an example of what was desired, the YMCA distributed copies of an exchange of letters between the chairman of the American Red Cross Society and his opposite number at the International Committee of the YMCA explaining how well the two organizations worked in concert.[69]

However, the Canadian Red Cross could not afford to be overly con-cerned with the complaints of the WPA, because a new contender was emerging in the battle over POW relief; for the rest of the war, the CPOWRA and not the WPA would pose the greatest threat to the ascendancy of the Red Cross. The first indication of future difficulties came over a minor National War Services press release on POW work. Adele Plumptre took exception to the statement that there were only two prisoner-next-of-kin associations, the CPOWRA and the Royal Rifles of Canada POW Association, registered under the War Charities Act, pointing out that the Red Cross had 3000 branches across Canada that had been instructed to do everything possible to assist next of kin. Plumptre went on to state that the Red Cross 'is in a position to give practical assistance in a way that neither of the other Associations are able to do.'[70]

A short time later, the Red Cross had cause to complain again, when the CPOWRA newsletter published ICRC figures on the distribution of Red Cross parcels, figures that the Canadian Red Cross had been unable to procure and that the International Committee regarded as confidential. As Red Cross Commissioner F.W. Routley wrote to Rive, 'I am sure you fully realize ... the position in which we as a Society in Canada are placed by prisoners' next-of-kin in this country when things like this happen.'[71] At the same time, the Red Cross added a POW Liaison Officers' Committee to the Ottawa Enquiry Bureau; each local branch would appoint an individual to develop personal contact with relatives and keep them abreast of changes in rules and regulations.[72] Well intentioned though it must have been, it is hard not to view this as an attempt to regain some of the territory poached by the CPOWRA.

The bad feelings between the Canadian Red Cross Society and the Relatives Association were obviously growing. In December 1942, the CPOWRA unveiled a plan to ship books to POWs, something that flew in the face of the Red Cross position that food must be the first priority. 'We do not wish to quarrel with any organization doing philanthropic work,' wrote Gordon, 'but we do feel that we know the facts and they evidently do not.'[73] The following summer, the Red Cross attempted to block the formation of a new CPOWRA branch proposed for London, Ontario. The president of the Red Cross Ontario Division assured Plumptre that the London Red Cross branch had so far successfully handled all next-of-kin matters and would oppose any 'interference or competition' from the CPOWRA. In passing these concerns on to National War Services, Plumptre was moved to write about the situation at some length:

> Difficulties ... are being occasioned in all parts of the country by the setting up of a second prisoners of war organization where the Red Cross is already active. The large majority of women whose sons become prisoners of war have previously been good members of the Canadian Red Cross Society, and there seems no reason, because their sons become prisoners, why they should be expected to join another society, especially as they still have to look to the Red Cross for the vital supplies needed by their prisoner sons.[74]

Minister of National War Services L.R. LaFlèche attempted to mollify Plumptre by pointing out that the members of the CPOWRA felt impelled to aid prisoners and explored every opportunity to do so; any attempt to restrict their work, he felt, would be misinterpreted.[75]

The Canadian Red Cross had good reason to be wary of the expanding CPOWRA, for Asselin had great plans for the association. In a letter to LaFlèche, she pressed for a new relief policy wherein POWs and men on active service would be considered as separate classes of the war effort; the CPOWRA would be given sole right in all aspects of POW relief ('other than that work which is being done by the Canadian Red Cross,' she added, almost as an afterthought). She urged that all aid organizations be called together to draw up a master plan under which they would contribute, through the CPOWRA, to the POW relief effort.[76] Asselin later attacked any attempts to restrict the welfare activities of the CPOWRA, and insisted that an excess of generosity towards prisoners would do nothing to hinder the war effort.[77]

Clearly, the poisoned state of relations between the aid groups demanded government action, and in July 1943 External Affairs suggested that Colonel Clarke use his influence to assemble representatives of the voluntary organizations into a central committee based in Ottawa. Such a move was imperative, in Rive's view, for 'it is difficult for Government Departments to avoid being drawn into these interorganization disputes, which result in hard feelings and charges of favouritism against the Departments concerned.'[78]

This assessment of the situation was pessimistic, but it took a conversation between Clarke and Rive to demonstrate to the latter that the problem was even more serious than he had imagined.[79] Clarke stated that relations between voluntary groups and some government departments were so strained that any action of the sort envisioned by Rive was hopeless. There was no possibility of any initiative coming from the Red Cross, which seemed to view itself as 'the one and only organization,' nor could the initiative come from Clarke, for National War Services might view this as an incursion into its jurisdiction; the situation was 'much too explosive' for Clarke to handle on his own. The SAAG also had harsh words for the CPOWRA, which he accused of operating a 'campaign of propaganda against the Government' and of evading export regulations and circumventing Red Cross control of parcel shipments to POWs. Clarke's insights convinced Rive that 'the whole thing is a mess and that sooner or later the stench will become too strong to bear.' Furthermore, most of the blame for future problems would inevitably fall on government departments. The only solution, as Rive and Clarke saw it, was ministerial involvement, with either Ralston or LaFlèche pressuring the Canadian Red Cross into changing its attitude and persuading other organizations to cooperate with it.[80]

It is impossible to determine what reaction Rive's memorandum provoked in government circles, but there was a realization that the organization of the Red Cross was too weak to allow it to play the role that Rive and Clarke deemed essential. The Red Cross had long been criticized (criticism that the society admitted was justified) for not moving its headquarters to Ottawa in 1939, for its Toronto office was too far away from the centre of decision-making.[81] By 1943 the internecine strife in the aid network, combined with the new problems surrounding the provision of relief to POWs in the Far East, demanded that the society's wartime organization be overhauled.

Despite pressure to reorganize themselves, however, the voluntary aid societies remained virtually unchanged, and government departments continued to struggle with them.[82] The CPOWRA remained the major offender. The most serious incident involved the shipment of capture kits, packages containing clothing and toiletries that were distributed to POWs at transit camps to supply them until they reached a permanent camp. In April 1944, Beatrice Asselin learned that the ICRC had requested additional supplies of kits, and within a week she had gathered enough material to assemble 3000 kits and was looking for ways to transport them to Geneva.[83] External Affairs was alarmed by this typically precipitate action by Asselin, but no one was willing to tackle her on the matter. While recognizing that capture kits were the sole responsibility of the Red Cross, Herbert Feaver of Special Section admitted that 'Mrs. Asselin appears to have done such a masterly job in establishing an impregnable beachhead in Red Cross territory that it seems impossible to dislodge her by any method short of total war. Be that as it may, this timid male is not so anxious to get involved in hostilities in which one army is led so ably by so redoubtable an amazon.'[84]

After due consideration, Feaver decided to leave the battlefield to Asselin and the Canadian Red Cross. National War Services, also despairing of what to do to ensure that the CPOWRA abided by government dictates, later emphasized the need to be firm with Asselin lest she exploit any sign of weakness.[85] However, none of the mandarins were willing to take a hard line with the CPOWRA president, and she continued to operate almost unencumbered by any sort of central control.

Had they been foreseen, the problems of organizing government departments and private organizations into a system of POW relief might have been daunting enough to quell the enthusiasm of even the strongest civil servant. The major aid organizations were administered by immensely capable and influential individuals, and perhaps some clash of wills was inevitable. However, the difficulties certainly could have been reduced. After the war, Rive reviewed the organizational problems of the aid network and concluded that the peacetime Red Cross structure had not been suitable to handle wartime exigencies. Rive believed that if the need were to arise again, an umbrella group should be established at the outset to bring together representatives from all interested welfare agencies. That group, and not the Canadian

Red Cross, should be at the top of the relief ladder.[86] Of course, External Affairs had advocated this in the fall of 1943; had it been implemented three years earlier, much dissension and ill will might have been avoided. Morley Scott might also have found a more rewarding outlet for his considerable talents.

III

During the First World War, the provision of aid to Canadian prisoners had been hampered by the fact that, until November 1917, there were no Canadian representatives on the British committees that administered the relief programs. This was certainly not the case during the Second World War, when Canada was a member of a number of intergovernmental POW committees, but the problems and confusion were scarcely minimized as a consequence. On the contrary, these committees merely seemed to open up a whole new range of possibilities for duplication of effort and overlap of jurisdiction.

The first of these intergovernmental bodies, the Imperial POW Committee (IPOWC), grew out of an internal British government committee which had been struck in May 1940. In 1941 the committee underwent several reorganizations that the Dominions (especially Canada) hoped would transform it into an intergovernmental body but British officials resisted such a change. To satisfy the wishes of Commonwealth governments, the Dominions Office believed that 'it is only a question of "camouflaging" a W[ar] O[ffice] Committee as "intergovernmental" and we can perhaps leave the procedure as it is.'[87] This comment explains much of Britain's future conduct regarding the organization of the IPOWC.

Dominion governments were evidently mollified by the camouflaged committee, and in November 1941 the IPOWC, chaired by the War Office's financial secretary, met for the first time to coordinate British and Commonwealth policy on POW matters.[88] The full committee convened only three times and most of the work was carried on by two subcommittees: Sub-Committee B, which handled financial matters, with Dominion representation only when necessary; and Sub-Committee A, which met 'to consider such questions affecting policy and general administration of prisoners of war as concern more than one Government within the Empire with a view to avoiding undesirable differences of treatment.'[89] Sub-Committee A, which had continuous Dominion representation, soon became the more important of the two. Canada was represented on the IPOWC and its subcommittees by the Russian-born University of Toronto graduate and Rhodes scholar George Ignatieff, who had joined the High Commission's staff in 1940.[90] Later, Morley Scott took over this task when he was posted from Ottawa to Canada House.

In Colonel Clarke's eyes, though, a committee restricted to delegates from Britain and the Dominions was not sufficient; representation from other Allied nations, especially the United States, was imperative for the future. In a long memorandum, he set out six reasons why there had to be a means of coordinating POW policy among the Allies: (1) the Axis powers were sure to try to foment discontent between the Allies by giving preferential treatment to certain prisoners; (2) the fact that there were so many Allied prisoners living in scattered locations under different conditions necessitated specialized study of the problem; (3) the immense difficulties of transportation and distribution demanded long-term planning and a centre for decision-making; (4) because so few neutral nations were available, it was important to secure unanimity respecting representations made to the Protecting Power; (5) the greater burden being shouldered by national Red Cross societies meant that governments might soon have to step in with assistance; and (6) because some of the Allies lacked the means to provide for their citizens in enemy hands, the burden of doing so fell on nations that possessed the resources.[91]

To fulfil these tasks, Clarke recommended the immediate formation of an Allied committee on POWs with a representative from each nation. The delegate would have authority to act on behalf of his government, subject to its approval, and the decisions of the committee would be final. Clarke went on to argue that the position of the United States in the war, and her probable role after the war, demanded that she be represented on the committee, perhaps as chair; for the same reasons, it was logical that the committee be permanently located in the United States. Furthermore, the SAAG recognized the importance of the principle of reciprocity, and for this reason advised that all matters concerning enemy POWs be channelled through the proposed committee as well.

Clarke had in mind for Allied governments just what he had attempted to create in Canada with the CPW: a single body responsible for all matters pertaining to POWs. However, this eminently sensible suggestion was deferred by the Cabinet War Committee pending an External Affairs review, and nearly a year of pushing for the establishment of an inter-Allied committee to serve the needs of all POWs apparently brought Clarke no closer to his goal.[92] It would take the perplexing problem of Far East relief to prove the SAAG's assertion that inter-Allied planning and coordination, in general terms rather than strictly in response to specific problems, was imperative.

External Affairs was reluctant to pursue the matter partly because of its ongoing attempts to secure a change in the organization of the IPOWC. Perhaps having realized that the November 1941 reorganization was so much window dressing, External Affairs pressed again for a truly intergovernmental committee that would emphasize external relations, perhaps under a chairman from the Dominions Office.[93] At the February 1943 meeting of the IPOWC, Ignatieff presented Canada's case. He criticized the present practice, in which the committee was responsible for both the formulation of policy and its administrative execution, and proposed the creation of a full-time secretariat to handle the latter. The new IPOWC would have a chairman of Cabinet rank, and its responsibilities would be expanded to embrace civilians in enemy territory, repatriation arrangements, the treatment of enemy aliens, and the custody of enemy property.[94] The IPOWC quickly dismissed Canada's proposal. The British government was reluctant to establish additional administrative machinery that might reduce its influence, while the other High Commissions also opposed any change in practice.[95]

Canadian officials refused to be put off by this rebuff, however, and a month later Britain agreed to recognize the IPOWC as intergovernmental in character.[96] Under this new agreement, the IPOWC would be renamed the Inter-Governmental POW Committee and would have as chairman the Secretary of State for War. Membership would consist of delegates from the War Office's Directorate of POWs, each of the British government departments concerned, and each of the

Dominions. The new committee would meet more frequently to act as the 'normal instrument for the collective consideration of policy questions,' but would also continue to be responsible for administrative execution of that policy.[97]

Although the change of name apparently never found favour and the committee continued to be referred to as the IPOWC, steps were taken to develop its intergovernmental character. In July 1943, Sub-Committee A acted upon the longstanding idea that American representatives be invited to attend committee meetings, with the request that a reciprocal invitation be extended to a British delegate in Washington. The invitation was transmitted in August; the State Department accepted and replied that a reciprocal invitation would be forthcoming.[98] The War Office Directorate of POWs used that invitation as an excuse to attach an officer to the Joint Staff Mission in Washington. This individual, Colonel R. Naesmyth, became responsible for monitoring all POW matters that came before the Combined Chiefs of Staff, and although he did not represent Canadian interests at the meetings of the Combined Chiefs, he wanted to be kept apprised of Canada's position on issues. To this end, he received copies of Canadian dispatches regarding POWs, and was also invited to attend the meetings of Colonel Clarke's CPW.[99]

IN LATE 1943, Naesmyth travelled to Ottawa to examine Canada's POW organization and attend a meeting of the CPW. He was very complimentary about what he saw, and wrote to Clarke's assistant that everything had seemed 'splendidly organized.'[100] It is difficult to say whether Naesmyth was just being polite or whether the organization actually appeared better than it was. In reality, Canada's POW structure was little better constructed than during the First World War, despite having to bear much greater burdens.

The members of Special Section did their best under difficult conditions; they certainly laboured long hours, and were thanked for their efforts by grateful Canadians.[101] The organization in which they toiled was flawed from the outset, however. The lack of a single office responsible for POW matters posed problems both for the public, which did not know where to turn for information, and for the government, which had too many departments attempting to handle POW affairs and none of them doing it very well. As Morley Scott admitted in a very candid postwar letter, Canada should have established early in the war something analogous to Britain's Directorate of POWs, under the Department of National Defence, to handle all POW matters, with other departments acting in a purely advisory capacity.[102]

Furthermore, the problems created by the enthusiasm of aid organizations had not been overcome. Doubtless they all had the best of intentions, but each major aid organization was so convinced that only it could do an effective job for Canadian POWs that each became exceedingly jealous of any incursion into its territory. Regrettably, because these organizations were voluntary and had formidable supporters, the government found it difficult to exercise the sort of control that was necessary to prevent conflict. Again, this dilemma might have been solved, or at least minimized, if all the organizations had had to answer to a single POW office.

Of course, these problems have so far been described only as they concerned the creation and operation of the bureaucracy to aid Canadians in enemy hands. When it came to utilizing the organization and doing substantive work for the benefit of POWs, there was more confusion between government departments, more committees sprang up, and more disputes with aid organizations emerged. All the basic problems were magnified, and in some ways it is a wonder that anything was achieved at all.

SIX

RELIEF AND RELEASE IN THE EUROPEAN THEATRE

ACCORDING TO A 1941 ARTICLE in a Winnipeg magazine, 'modern war, however heartbreaking it may be in some respects, pays special attention to the problems of prisoners.'[1] During the Second World War, Canadian officials took great pains to make up for having left the matter to British authorities in 1940, and over time established a structure for handling POW affairs. In purely administrative terms, however, the structure provided a recipe for chaos, as organizational problems were magnified when the network began engaging in substantive work for the benefit of POWs. As in the First World War, this work took place in three areas: monitoring of camp conditions to ensure the observance of international law; provision of various forms of relief supplies to the prison camps; and repatriation of captives, both during and after the war. In each area, the jurisdictional jungle was a constant source of frustration to Canadian administrators, who encountered the same clash of wills as when they were arranging the network in the first place.

I

An accurate picture of conditions within the prison camps was, once again, the starting point of all work for the benefit of captives. However, the bureaucrats and philanthropists who worked to provide for Canadians in enemy hands had to keep in mind an important constraint: much of what occurred in the camps came to their attention only months after the fact, while some incidents of maltreatment remained unreported until after the war. Just as the scale of the war was much larger than in 1914, so the problems of communication were more complex. No longer could Canadian officials learn of a prisoner's requirements and ship the necessary supplies within a few short weeks; no longer could information on individual POWs be secured in a matter of days. More than in the Great War, Canadian prisoners in Europe were cut off from home.

Despite much wringing of hands, Canadian officials were unable to prevent POWs from being murdered in northwest Europe, which occurred sporadically until the end of the war, and could only fall back upon vague promises of future punishment and a large measure of hope to ensure that Canadians were treated correctly by the troops who captured them. Fortunately, the soldiers murdered by their captors were exceptional cases, and most of the men taken prisoner at Dieppe, in Italy, and in northwest Europe were treated, if not generously, at least as well as could be expected under the prevailing conditions. Wounded Dieppe POW Gren Juniper recalls being lifted gingerly from the beach to the esplanade by a party of German soldiers who appeared genuinely concerned about his wounds. Herb Maxwell, badly wounded and captured in March 1945 while serving with the Argyll and Sutherland Highlanders of Canada, received exemplary medical care in a German civilian hospital. Stewart Ripley, a young officer taken prisoner in 1944, was treated quite courteously by the Hitler Youth troops who captured him; far from being beaten or starved, he was given cider and thickly buttered bread soon after his capture.[2]

The fortunes of downed airmen were more varied. As long as they were captured by military authorities, they could expect correct and even solicitous treatment. Jack Parr, a Spitfire pilot shot down and captured in June 1942, enjoyed a splendid lunch with German pilots at the airfield at Abbéville. Jim Lang, captured a few months later during a raid on Hannover, was interrogated by a First World War veteran who served him Johnny Walker and spent most of the session describing his vacations in England before the war. Bomber pilot Kingsley Brown met a number of friendly Germans in his first days in captivity; one young guard stole into his cell one day and proudly presented Brown with a huge bowl of strawberries and cream.[3]

Such niceties became less common as the war progressed and the strategic bombing campaign slowly reduced many German cities to rubble. In July 1943, the citizens of the west German town of Lingen were outraged when soldiers provided full military honours at the burial of a group of downed Allied airmen. Later that month, German guards had to clear a crowded railway carriage to prevent enraged civilians from attacking two Canadians who had been shot down during a recent raid on Münster.[4] Such protection, however, could not always be counted upon. As early as August 1943, *Reichsführer* Heinrich Himmler decreed that police officials should not prevent German civilians from dispensing *Volksjustiz* (people's justice) by lynching downed Allied airmen, an order that was reiterated periodically; the following year, security chiefs stipulated that captured aviators were liable to summary execution in certain cases.[5] Such decrees had dire consequences for Allied airmen like Vancouver native George Bolderston; downed near Nuremberg in September 1944, he and two British crewmates were beaten to death by irate civilians, who then mutilated the bodies. At least a dozen other Canadian airmen suffered similar fates at the hands of civilians or police officials. The bodies of some were discovered during war crimes investigations; others simply disappeared without a trace.[6]

Nor could Canadian officials do much to protect captives from the countless incidents of brutality that occurred almost daily. Despite the strengthened provisions of the Geneva Convention, prisoners were still forced to labour under hazardous conditions, and dozens of Canadian POWs were killed or maimed in accidents at work. Private Rufus Parent of the Essex Scottish died when he was overcome by fermentation gases in a silo at the agricultural work camp to which he had been posted. Private Paul Desautels of the same unit lost his life in a similar accident, succumbing to carbon monoxide fumes coming from the lime kiln he was tending.[7] Even away from the work camps, the threat of injury or death at the hands of the captors was ever-present. Warrant Officer H.D. Mallory of Woodstock, New Brunswick, was killed at *Stalag* 4B Mühlberg when a German aircraft swooped low over the compound and struck him and another prisoner. In March 1945, at a camp near the Czech border, Lance-Corporal E. Beaudoin of Les Fusiliers de Mont-Royal was charged with plundering; contrary to the

Canadians attached to *Stalag* 2D dig potatoes at an agricultural work detail.

Geneva Convention, he had no benefit of a trial and was apparently executed within hours after the charge was laid.[8] Another incident, known as 'The Run Up the Road,' occurred when *Stalag Luft* 6 at Bankau was being evacuated in the face of the advancing Russians. The prisoners were taken by boat to Swinemunde and were then ordered to march to their new camp four miles from the port, a comfortable walk for POWs used to longer marches. However, the sentries confiscated the prisoners' boots, manacled the men together, and forced them to run the distance while guards jabbed them with bayonets and dogs ran up and down the column snapping at the hapless prisoners.[9] Incidents of similar brutality were far from uncommon, so it was fortunate that the apparatus for dealing with breaches of the Geneva Convention was considerably more sophisticated than in the First World War.

In general, the mechanics of monitoring international law had changed little since 1918. The neutral visit was again the basic tool for securing accurate information about camp conditions to ensure the observance of the Geneva Convention. The earliest inspections of German prison camps were performed by officials from the American Embassy in Berlin, acting as the Protecting Power, and by delegates of the International Committee of the Red Cross and the YMCA, who

Many Canadians found themselves assigned to wood-cutting details since the
Germans assumed that every Canadian was a lumberjack.

attempted to visit each camp at least two or three times a year to assess
every aspect of camp life, from weekly menus to medical facilities to
reserves of blankets.

Once the inspection reports reached Ottawa, copies were distributed
to various offices, most importantly National Defence's Special Assistant to the Adjutant-General (SAAG), Colonel F.W. Clarke. One of the
SAAG's staff members collated the reports, scrutinized them to determine which features required further investigation, and maintained an
index for quick reference. He then wrote a summary of each report,
noting the number of Canadians in the camp, the unsatisfactory features, the inspector's general impressions of conditions, and the recommended action. Clarke and his assistant, Major T.P. Mackenzie,
evaluated the recommendations and initiated the protest procedure.[10]

Commonwealth policy for determining what should be protested
changed frequently, but Canada adhered to two principles throughout
the war. Officials followed a strictly functional approach, basing the
decision to protest on the number of Canadians held in the camp in
question; conditions affecting a handful of Canadians in a camp containing thousands of other Commonwealth prisoners were not
sufficient to warrant a separate protest.[11] In addition, the government

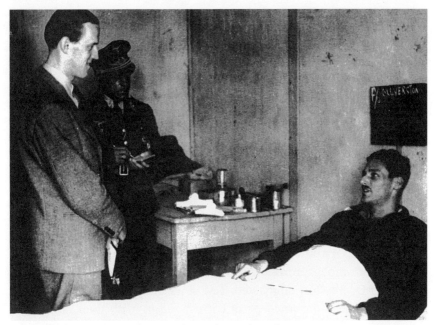

A neutral delegate inspects the camp hospital at *Stalag Luft* 3.

remained committed to the principle of reciprocity. The treatment of prisoners in Canada was seen to be inextricably linked to the treatment of Canadians in enemy hands, and the government generally lodged a protest when conditions affecting Canadians in Axis hands were markedly worse than those experienced by POWs in Canada.

Considerable public support existed for the concept of reciprocity. A 1941 magazine article called German POWs in Canada 'implied hostages to good behaviour' on Germany's part, and letters received by various government departments evinced similar sentiments.[12] In 1942, Canadian Red Cross Society (CRCS) chairman Mr. Justice P.H. Gordon wrote of stories that German prisoners in Canada received truckloads of fruit; he asked to see copies of their menus 'to be assured that they are no better than they should be.' Some Canadians obviously felt that rations for German POWs *were* better than they should be; 'we are giving our German prisoners of war better food than the average Canadian taxpayer can afford to buy,' complained a correspondent to the *Globe and Mail* in 1943.[13] A group of German prisoners arriving in Halifax were delighted to discover that their first meal consisted of white bread with butter, fried potatoes, scrambled eggs, ham, baked beans, peaches, and coffee. Such rations allowed the average POW in Lethbridge camp to gain twelve pounds during the first ten months of captivity.[14] Disgruntled Canadians could seize upon any number of other amenities, from the indoor swimming pool at Bowmanville camp to the ability of German POWs to order almost anything they could afford from the Eaton's catalogue, to highlight the disparity in treatment. The situation led the father of a POW to argue that 'in view of the generous consideration given German prisoners of war in Canada ... it seems that a persistent official effort ought to be made for reasonable reciprocity.'[15]

In fact, such an effort had been under way for much of the war. In 1940, External Affairs learned of the case of a Canadian civilian interned in Germany who had been prevented from writing to his father in Winnipeg. In response, Under-Secretary of State for External Affairs O.D. Skelton suggested that since 'Canada affords German civilian internees the privilege of corresponding with their families in Germany, and free postage, it might be thought advisable to reconsider this privilege if assurance is not forthcoming of full reciprocal action by Germany.'[16] In June 1943, a report of poor conditions in the civilian internment camp *Ilag* 8 drew a similar comment from Special Section: 'Civilian internees in Canada receive many privileges beyond those to which they are entitled under the Geneva Convention. It would not be too much to say to the Protecting Power that it would be difficult to justify the continuance of these privileges in the face of reports such as the one now before us.' Perhaps relishing the opportunity to occupy the moral high ground so soon after the shackling incident (see page 134), the Foreign Office in London threw cold water on the idea, stressing that there was little support in Britain for such reprisals and urging Canada to drop the proposed threat.[17]

To achieve reciprocity of treatment while avoiding all mention of reprisals, External Affairs' legal adviser John Read came up with a novel plan. In November 1943 he stressed to the Swiss official in charge of German interests in Canada the government's opinion that delegates who inspected camps in Canada should, as far as possible, be aware of the treatment accorded to Canadian POWs in Germany. To this end, Read proposed that the same inspectors who toured camps in

Canada should also visit camps in Germany, so that they might be acquainted with conditions in both countries before lodging protests.[18]

Sub-Committee A of the Imperial POW Committee (IPOWC) agreed to put the matter to the Protecting Power (Swiss government), the ICRC, and the US State Department; an encouraging reply came from the latter in short order, but there the proposal languished. In July, Morley Scott apologized for not having had time to bring the idea to Sub-Committee A again, and in September the Canadian Embassy in Washington wondered whether any further action had been taken. The embassy noted that the State Department was very interested in the proposal, 'but feel that where it originated with us we should lead the way and they will fall in line ... They are prepared to agree to almost any plan that we work out ... everybody concerned, including the Germans, is favourably disposed towards this plan.'[19] Despite the enthusiasm of all sides, except Canada, it appears, the proposal was never followed through.

In the effort to monitor the observance of international law, External Affairs had to remain conscious of the fact that Germany recognized the independence of the Dominions only when it could be used as a ploy to sow dissension among the Allies. Consequently, Canadians sometimes found themselves the recipients of unwanted privileges as a result of the conditions enjoyed by German POWs in Canada.[20] In the spring of 1944, German authorities announced that Canadian POWs would be moved to a new camp, *Stalag* 2D at Stargard, where they would enjoy superior facilities because of the favourable treatment of Germans in Canada. Steve Michell of the Royal Regiment of Canada, captured at Dieppe, recorded the text of the announcement made in the camps:

> Our Führer has been very impressed with the official reports of the treatment received by German prisoners in Canada. He has therefore authorized that preferential treatment be given to Canadian prisoners of war ... a new all-Canadian camp is being prepared near Stettin. There Canadians will be allowed the freedom of the town. They will be able to mix among the civilian population, and go to shows and other entertainment. Their food will be increased to double ration.[21]

Canadian prisoners at first refused to be hoodwinked by this gambit, insisting that they would accept no privileges that were not granted to all Allied POWs. However, they could not refuse the move to Stargard and were duly transferred.

The proposal also raised suspicion in Canada, where it was rightly viewed as an attempt to cause friction between the Allies by dispensing preferential treatment to selected groups. Still, it had to be taken seriously lest any of the Allies imagined that Canada had purchased this treatment by being soft on German POWs.[22] At the next meeting of Sub-Committee A, Morley Scott made it clear that 'any such action by the Germans could only be mischievously intended and would have no effect on the treatment of German prisoners of war in Canada.' The matter went no further, and it later transpired that the Germans had shifted their attention and were trying to sow discontent by telling Allied POWs that American prisoners were better treated.[23]

A more notable dispute over the concept of reciprocity of treatment was the shackling incident of 1942-3, which has often been used to demonstrate Britain's irritating tendency to take Canadian support for granted. The roots of the controversy lay in the operational orders for the Dieppe raid of August 1942, which, despite the opposition of 2nd Division GOC Major-General J.H. Roberts, recommended that prisoners be bound to prevent them from destroying their documents.[24] This provision might never have come to Germany's attention were it not for the capture of a copy of the plan after the capitulation of Canadian troops at Dieppe. The first hint of impending reprisals came in September 1942, when the German government decried the 'wild west methods' of controlling POWs and threatened to chain all Dieppe prisoners unless the binding order was rescinded.[25] A month later, the threat was revived, with renewed vigour. Citing further investigation into the Dieppe case and an instance of the binding of prisoners during a recent commando raid, the German government announced that nearly 1300 POWs would be bound the following day.[26]

At camps around Germany, the shackling began on the morning of 8 October. At *Oflag* 7B Eichstätt, Canadian officers from Dieppe were taken from the main camp to a nearby fortress, where they were handcuffed during the daylight hours. After six months, the guards tired of shackling the prisoners and merely handed them the cuffs, which were hung on hooks in the rooms until it was time to return them in the evening.[27] At Lamsdorf, prisoners were originally bound with ropes and found it very easy to sabotage the operation; some POWs removed their ropes altogether while others simply loosened the bonds and asked a guard to tighten them.[28] The handcuffs that replaced the ropes after forty-two days proved to be no more challenging; the prisoners soon learned to remove them with the key from a sardine tin, and turned the reprisal into a sort of cat-and-mouse game. It was not uncommon for a puzzled guard to find a POW standing naked in the shower, yet with his manacles firmly attached.

Though unaware of events in the camps, Britain responded swiftly to the German threat. The same day, Dominions Secretary Clement Attlee met with the Canadian High Commissioner in London, Vincent Massey, and Minister of National Defence J.L. Ralston to inform them that the British War Cabinet would begin retaliatory shackling if Germany did not back down. Massey and Ralston expressed concern at this decision. The Defence Minister thought it important to allow Germany a way out of the reprisal without losing face, whereupon the High Commissioner suggested using the Protecting Power (Switzerland) as an independent arbitrator. Ralston supported this proposal, and Attlee promised to take it up with British Prime Minister Winston Churchill.[29]

When External Affairs learned of these developments, it reacted even more negatively. The department informed Massey that the threats against Dieppe POWs had caused wide concern in Canada, and urgently requested a more detailed statement of the action intended by Britain. The department also pointed out that 'the enemy may consider this a convenient opportunity to play off one part of the Commonwealth against another.' Perhaps as an afterthought, a later cable expressed the assumption that Britain had sufficient German prisoners for the proposed reprisal and would not require POWs elsewhere to be chained.[30] The response to this last telegram was not at all what External Affairs wanted to hear. The Dominions Office stated that it would chain most of the able-bodied German POWs held in Britain, around 200, but counted on Canada to complete the reprisal by chaining up to 2000 POWs.[31]

When the matter came before the Cabinet War Committee,

Minister for Naval Services Angus L. Macdonald reviewed the circumstances leading to Britain's request and confirmed that the Dieppe operational orders had indeed stipulated the tying of prisoners.[32] He also stressed that the Canadian government had not been consulted by Britain about the reprisal, despite Canada's intimate involvement. Finally, Macdonald reported Mackenzie King's opinion that Canada would have to comply because Britain had already committed Ottawa to action. The Prime Minister did, however, emphasize the need to inform Britain that Canada was acting reluctantly, a view that the committee supported entirely.

A lengthy cable to the Dominions Office explained Canada's position. 'We feel that we have been committed without proper consultation to a course of doubtful wisdom,' read the telegram, which went on to aver that Germany was certain to win a contest based on harshness towards POWs. The missive concluded by stating that Canada had 'decided with regret' to manacle German POWs only to avoid an open difference with Britain. Ottawa later urged the British government to take every opportunity to seek a solution through the Protecting Power or the ICRC.[33]

The following day, Germany raised the stakes by announcing plans to retaliate by chaining three times the number of prisoners manacled by the Allies. Britain replied that she too would escalate the reprisal, and asked the Canadian government to approve the handcuffing of 3888 German POWs. The request was accompanied by a personal appeal from Churchill to King, hoping that 'you will stand by us in this anxious business' and expressing the belief that the retaliation would be short.[34] Despite Churchill's soothing words, the Cabinet War Committee took a hard line to the latest request and approved a draft telegram urging against further chaining until the Protecting Power had time to act. Though reluctant to involve the Protecting Power, the British War Cabinet finally agreed to lodge a protest with Switzerland over the breach of the Geneva Convention.[35]

The reluctance of Canadian officials to extend the reprisal was due in part to the difficulties experienced by internment officials trying to carry out the chaining. Problems were encountered at all four affected camps in Ontario – Gravenhurst, Espanola, Monteith, and Bowmanville, with the resistance being stiffest at Bowmanville. German POWs armed with hockey sticks and broom handles used mattresses to barricade themselves in their huts; they had to be dislodged by water cannons and guards, who were met by a hail of glass, clubs, and tableware as they rushed the barracks. In the ensuing melee, dozens of minor casualties were sustained by both sides. After the 'Battle of Bowmanville,' Internment Operations decided that it was unwise to attempt to extend the chaining.[36]

The incident at Bowmanville alarmed King and convinced him that Canada had taken the wisest course in refusing Britain's latest request, especially in view of the mounting opposition to the shackling.[37] In Canada, opinion had been mixed at first but was soon running strongly against the reprisal. Newspaper editorials were highly critical, and the government and the press began to receive a tide of letters sharing a common theme: the Allies could not win a competition of reprisals and to enter into such a contest was merely descending to the level of the Nazis. Opposition in Canada was serious enough, but criticism was also mounting elsewhere in the Commonwealth, in Britain, and in the United States.[38] King was evidently most disturbed by an article in *TIME* magazine that described in detail the battle at Bowmanville; although misleading in some minor points, the account was largely accurate.[39]

Clearly Canada had to act, and the government's hand was strengthened by the German response to the Protecting Power's protest. That reply was uncompromising, and restated the refusal to unshackle unless Britain admitted the error in ordering the tying of POWs and forbade such binding in the future.[40] This obvious stalemate moved Canadian officials to take a harder line. Massey believed that Canada should fix its own date to unshackle, but the Cabinet War Committee backed away from such a strong step, proposing instead that the Protecting Power be asked to request both sides to unshackle simultaneously on a given date.[41]

Perhaps recognizing the weakness of his position at last, Churchill accepted the Canadian suggestion. On 9 December Canadian newspapers carried a report of the Swiss request, thereby paving the way for a speedy end to the reprisal.[42] Ralston and other cabinet ministers advised that Canada unshackle immediately, to demonstrate that Ottawa could act independently of Downing Street, but King held out for simultaneous action, to show a united front to Germany and to avoid creating 'a serious feeling in Churchill's own mind.'[43] On 10 December, the Canadian and British governments announced that German POWs would be unchained without delay.

However, the situation was only half resolved; Germany maintained its refusal to end the reprisal unless the Allies gave a 'categorical and general order' forbidding the binding of prisoners of war.[44] The British government refused to promulgate such an order, and from this point the shackling incident was out of the hands of the Canadian government. Over the next few months, camp inspections revealed that some POWs had been unshackled, but there was still no end to the matter. Then in November 1943, the German Foreign Ministry accepted an ICRC suggestion that the shackles be removed discreetly, with neutral delegates on hand to witness the removal. No public statement would be issued either before or after the fact; the Allied governments would merely be informed that the shackling had ended. The Detaining Power (Germany) acted upon the suggestion almost immediately.

Although later observers were incorrect in stating that most of the affected Allied POWs were Canadian, the shackling incident was no less serious from Canada's point of view.[45] An echo of the hostage controversy of the War of 1812, the episode demonstrated starkly the tendency of Britain to act as though unified Imperial policy were still a reality. As she had done so often in the past, Britain assumed that Canada would support her unquestioningly, even in actions of dubious wisdom, an assumption that inevitably created friction in view of the need to avoid a public breach between Allies. For walking the thin line between accommodating Churchill and holding to its principles, the King government deserves credit, much of which should go to Vincent Massey. The key figure in the episode as far as Canada was concerned, his recommendations were often adopted *in toto* by the Canadian government. Ironically, it was the noted anglophile Massey, the 'imperial Canadian,' who proved to be the strongest proponent of taking a harsh line with Britain.[46] Not even Mackenzie King, Canada's lead actor of the piece in many interpretations, was willing to be as firm as his High Commissioner.

It must be said, then, that any problems encountered by Canadian officials in monitoring international law were largely due to factors beyond their control. The machinery worked very efficiently from

Canada's end, largely because it involved only a small circle of bureaucrats. Most of the initiative came from the SAAG's office, with External Affairs acting as a go-between, and matters could be dealt with quite expeditiously. The failure to pursue the proposal for camp inspections by the same delegates can perhaps be explained by the fact that such a system would have required the agreement of several government departments. By restricting discussion to the SAAG and External Affairs, officials charged with monitoring the enemy's observance of international law could accomplish their task efficiently and with a minimum of delay. When it came to the relief campaign, however, those officials were not always so lucky.

II

Propaganda photos taken in German and Italian prison camps often depicted POWs playing baseball or hockey, rehearsing the latest theatrical production, or browsing through a well-stocked library. While life behind barbed wire was considerably less idyllic than such photos suggested, prisoners in Germany and Italy did enjoy a wide variety of relief supplies from home, which helped them stave off boredom. Enterprising POWs were quick to pool their talents and plan activities to make life in captivity a little more bearable; indeed, many prisoners developed skills or interests that would stay with them for the rest of their lives.

Orchestras and bands could be found in most camps, using instruments bought from German shops or obtained through the Red Cross or the YMCA. The level of playing was exceptionally high, and groups of new POWs were invariably canvassed for willing musicians. Dieppe prisoner Steve Michell had been in a permanent camp for less than an hour before he was drafted to play trombone in the prisoners' band, the Britanniques. Calgary native Art Crighton was transferred to the North Compound of *Stalag Luft* 3 simply because the orchestra there needed a trumpet player for the march from *Aïda*, which it had scheduled for an upcoming concert; Crighton later took over the baton and conducted the orchestra until the camp was evacuated in January 1945. The camp at Belaria had regular concerts by the Belaria Dance Orchestra and the Swingtime Octet.[47]

One of the musical ensembles formed by prisoners in *Stalag* 8B, Lamsdorf

Prison camp theatrical productions were also of a particularly high standard. Gord King, young and small enough to be cast for female roles, played the daughter in *The Man Who Came to Dinner*, performed in *Stalag Luft* 3's 400-seat theatre, while Dick McLaren had a part in a production of *The Golden Boy*; the producer of the play, Michael Langham, worked at Canada's Stratford Festival after the war.[48] *Oflag* 79 at Brunswick had two theatres, the Barn and the Indian; a cinema; and a cabaret called the Rumpot. Sagan, too, had a cinema, which was equipped through the good offices of the YMCA; most of the films were German, but the POWs did see Katharine Hepburn and Cary Grant in *Bringing Up Baby* and John Wayne in *The Spoilers*.[49]

Sports provided another diversion, and teams of all sorts were assembled and named after professional clubs in North America and England. The Cardinals won *Stalag Luft* 3's softball league title in 1944, beating the Tigers, the Giants, and the Indians; at the same camp, Saskatchewan native Bev Smiley joined the Chelsea soccer squad, while Rae Guess of Westmount was drafted to play cricket for Somerset.[50] Campo 78 at Sulmona in central Italy held regular international soccer matches that drew not only thousands of POWs but also most of the camp staff, who occupied the prime viewing area at midfield and were arrayed on either side of the commandant, ensconced in a large arm-chair at the centre line. In a very successful inter-Dominion sports

The ice rink at *Stalag Luft* 3, Sagan

POWs at *Oflag* 9A/H, Spangenberg, stage a boxing tournament using equipment provided by various neutral organizations.

meet at Sagan in June 1944, the Canadian competitors finished a strong second to a much larger British team. Their reputation in camp athletics was considerable, and Canadian hockey teams (often stiffened by a few professional players who had been captured) could be counted upon to trounce all comers. Most of the equipment used in the camps came from the YMCA and the Red Cross, but some was donated by generous Canadians like Conn Smythe, who knew from personal experience the boredom of captivity and was more than happy to provide equipment for Canadians behind barbed wire. Other prisoners worked out with gymnastic or volleyball equipment, learned to box, or honed their table-tennis skills. *Stalag Luft* 3 even had a nine-hole golf course.[51]

As appealing as this sounded, it should not be imagined that captivity was anything but unpleasant, for such amenities only served to help POWs make the best of a bad situation. The prison camps themselves were usually either medievally uncomfortable or monotonously similar. The camp at Mülhausen, which held a group of Dieppe prisoners, was a dank and flea-ridden castle near Gotha, while the *oflag* at Schubin, the temporary home of a number of Canadian airmen, had been converted from a girls' school; the tree-covered grounds were quite pleasant but the barracks consisted of cavernous and drafty barns that were impossible to keep warm. Canadian officers captured at Dieppe went to *Oflag* 7B at Eichstätt, in Bavaria, where an old cavalry barracks had been converted into a prison camp. The compound was graced by well-kept gardens and two excellent tennis courts, but it also featured dingy and badly ventilated concrete barracks, overworked sanitary facilities, and an apparently inexhaustible supply of mud. In Italy, a handful of Canadians lived at Campo 35 at Padula, near Naples, a bitterly cold monastery whose eighteenth-century kitchen equipment was not up to the task of providing for the hundreds of POWs in the camp.

Other Canadian POWs spent their captivity in camps that had been specially constructed for the purpose and that shared certain common characteristics: two or more high barbed-wire fences; long, low barrack huts, built of brick, wood, or concrete; a stone punishment block, known as the cooler; primitive and barely adequate latrine facilities, known variously as the abort or the forty-holer; and a flat and dusty parade square where roll call was held. A few senior officers had private rooms, but most of the men lived in dormitories whose populations

The prisoners' domain: the temporary residence of Jim Wernham (top) in *Stalag Luft* 3. He was later murdered after the Great Escape from *Stalag Luft* 3.

increased as the war progressed. It was impossible to escape from one's fellow human beings, even on the exercise path that ran around the perimeter of the camp. Privacy, which so many men had taken for granted, was virtually impossible to obtain.

In such surroundings, it is hardly surprising that some prisoners suffered psychologically. In the winter of 1944, after rations had been reduced yet again and the prisoners lived in uncertainty about what the next week held, Ambrose Farnum suffered badly from insomnia and one night became so desperate that he thought he would have to wake a friend who would prevent him from making a suicidal dash for the wire.[52] Separation from family was just as hard to bear. A Canadian pilot confined in Colditz Castle became convinced of the need to release his wife from their marriage, and grew so despondent that he attempted suicide on at least four occasions. Another Canadian tried to help the man through his difficulties, but he too became unhinged and never fully recovered even after the war.[53]

The lavatory block at *Stalag* 8B

Guard towers were a constant presence
in prison camps.

The prisoners' compounds at *Stalag* 8B

In such circumstances, POWs became obsessed with what might seem to be trivialities. Mail from home was eagerly awaited, and some prisoners passed the time drafting complex charts or graphs to record the receipt of letters and parcels from friends and family. Some men became compulsive autograph hunters, and pursued fellow prisoners to sign their diaries or log books. Others read ceaselessly, filling their diary pages with the titles of books they had finished. But for virtually every POW, food was the paramount concern. One has only to look at the diary of a POW, with pages of ration scales, recipes, imaginary banquet menus, and exhaustive lists of foodstuffs received from home, to see where his priorities lay. As Stewart Ripley recorded in his diary, 'we lived from meal to meal, when we talked we talked of food. When we didn't talk we thought about food.'[54]

For most of the war, the staples of a prisoner's diet were potatoes and a heavy black bread whose main ingredient (according to many POWs) was sawdust; the vegetable ration included turnips, beets, carrots, cabbage, and marrows, often served in soup or stew form. Unwelcome surprises in the stews were not uncommon; Ian MacDonald of the Essex Scottish was shocked to find horse teeth in the first cabbage soup he received after being captured at Dieppe.[55] Blood sausage was doled out once or twice a week, as was a pungent and practically inedible product known as fish cheese; few POWs had strong enough stomachs to consume the latter. Small quantities of margarine and a chemically sweetened jam rendered from turnips were also issued weekly. Sugar, mint tea, and coffee made from roasted acorns or scorched grain rounded out the food provided by the captors. Rations for the hundred-odd Canadians captured by the Italians varied in content but not in quantity. Bread made up the bulk of the day's ration, with two ounces of pasta, an ounce of cheese, and smaller quantities of meat, vegetables, olive oil, tomato purée, and sugar making up the rest of each day's allotment.[56]

One of the most notorious foods issued by the Germans was known as fish cheese (sketch by R.M. Woychuk).

As the war dragged on, POWs had to live on even shorter rations. Private W.A. Sandhals of the North Nova Scotia Highlanders was captured in France in July 1944; during his journey into Germany, he lived for five days on one-seventh of a loaf of bread and a few cups of water. Fred LeReverend, taken prisoner in October 1944 while serving with the Lincoln and Welland Regiment, had to labour in a German salt mine on a daily ration of one cup of synthetic coffee, a bowl of soup, a slice of bread, and two potatoes. In an attempt to curb the hunger pangs, LeReverend and a few other prisoners tried smoking dried horse manure, but found it a singularly unsatisfying experience. Ambrose Farnum had a different way of coping with hunger; to avoid generating an appetite, he spent most of the day in bed, emerging from his bunk only for roll call and meals.[57] It is little wonder, then, that prisoners developed an almost obsessive attachment to food parcels from home.

Because of the experience of the Great War, when the shipment of foodstuffs from well-meaning relatives had overwhelmed the resources of the Red Cross in London, the Canadian government decided in 1940 that only the Red Cross could dispatch food parcels to the prison camps. Registered next of kin could send a personal parcel to POWs once every three months, but it could contain no food other than chocolate; clothing, toiletries, and recreational material made up the bulk of these packages. The prohibition of food in the quarterly parcels soon became a contentious issue, largely because no such ban existed in the United States. Consequently, an early version of cross-border shopping started in the summer of 1941, when some POWs instructed relatives to send personal parcels from the United States. By the end of the year, so many relatives and friends were shipping parcels through the United States that the Canadian Red Cross, always jealous of being bypassed in relief work, began to complain. External Affairs, however, could see no solution to the dilemma until the same provisions for individual food parcels existed in Canada, a change that Britain resisted on the grounds that allowing one member of the Commonwealth to send personal parcels when the others could not was exceedingly unfair.[58] The other option, trying to cajole the United States Postal Service (USPS) into tightening its parcel regulations, seemed just as unlikely.[59]

The capture of nearly 2000 Canadian soldiers at Dieppe in August 1942 made a quick resolution to the problem imperative, especially since many of these soldiers came from regiments based close to the American border. In October, External Affairs reported that over a third of the POWs from one regiment had asked that their first parcels be sent through an agency in New York. Even more serious, External

Affairs reported that an unnamed group (probably the Canadian POW Relatives Association [CPOWRA])

> has opened a violent attack on the Government against the prohibition of including food in next-of-kin parcels and has begun its campaign by advising all its members to send forward next-of-kin parcels containing nothing but chocolate ... Further it appears that the same organisation have written letters to the prisoners denouncing the Canadian authorities for the restrictions. These letters appear to be written with the intention that the Censors will stop them and return them to the senders. Whereupon the members of the organisation will bring pressure on members of Parliament.[60]

When the USPS announced in October that it would continue to allow foodstuffs in POW parcels mailed in the United States, External Affairs realized that action was imperative. The only solution, as far as the department could see, was to bring Canadian rules in line with American and permit the inclusion of the same food items, such as dried fruit, nuts, macaroni, and soup powders, in personal parcels. Unless Britain had any objections, Canadian officials proposed to issue new regulations as soon as possible.[61]

In fact, His Majesty's Government raised strong objections to the planned announcement. Over the next few weeks, Britain presented a number of arguments in support of its case, including the belief that inequalities of food had a negative effect on camp morale and could produce divisions along national lines, and the fact that the Germans had already reduced rations twice, claiming that too much food was being wasted on account of the number of parcels reaching POWs.[62] British officials also wondered whether relatives would be satisfied with quarterly parcels, and thought that opening the door to personal food parcels would merely bring demands that such parcels be allowed more frequently.[63]

Canada responded firmly to all of these arguments. External Affairs was sympathetic, but maintained that it was 'politically impossible' for Canadian and American parcel regulations to be at significant variance, if only for simple reasons of geography.[64] Accordingly, on 9 November 1942, the department published a list of ten food items now allowed in quarterly parcels, the press release pointing out that Canadian and American parcel regulations were now 'substantially the same.'[65]

Despite the apparent solution, the controversy did not entirely disappear, for the changes did, as Britain feared, open the door to demands for an even greater liberalization of parcel regulations. As late as November 1944, External Affairs had to fend off an attack by Beatrice Asselin of the CPOWRA, who continued to push for individual food parcels instead of the standard, unaddressed parcels that the Red Cross had been supplying so successfully since January 1941.[66]

Such disputes over major aspects of policy were not uncommon, but even more frequent were the quarrels and delays over minor administrative matters that cropped up almost weekly. In the absence of an established procedure for determining parcel contents, National War Services, External Affairs, National Defence, and the Post Office were often at odds over who should be responsible for final decisions. Consequently, even the most mundane task could take months to complete. In June 1943 Deputy Postmaster-General P.T. Coolican reported that the revision of an eight-page pamphlet outlining the rules for sending parcels to POWs in Germany had been under way for fifteen months and was still not completed. A seven-page information leaflet to be sent to prisoners took over sixteen months to complete.[67] Much of the delay was the fault of the service departments, which demanded a say in all matters concerning POWs but were unable to handle them with any degree of dispatch; the Royal Canadian Air Force, for example, once took over seven months to decide how it would deal with the replacement of damaged uniforms for POWs.[68]

HAPPILY, SUCH DIFFICULTIES did not unduly hamper Canada's greatest relief effort, the provision of standard Red Cross food parcels to Allied POWs.[69] Any conversation with a former POW invariably comes around to the Canadian food parcel, its superiority to packages provided by other national Red Cross societies, and the fact that such parcels often made the difference between life and death. Long after the war, the Canadian Red Cross continued to receive requests from former prisoners for parcel replicas as keepsakes. Indeed, the Red Cross food parcel has become the symbol of Canada's relief effort in aid of POWs.

Preparations for this massive aid campaign began in the summer of 1940, after the British Red Cross asked the Canadian society to begin packing 5000 food parcels weekly, to be shipped via New York.[70] To decide on the contents of the parcels, the CRCS turned to a research team under Dr. Frederick Tisdall, of the University of Toronto's Department of Pediatrics. The team began by examining the rations supplied by the Germans, as listed in camp inspection reports, and endeavoured to supplement these rations to provide the optimum daily allowance of essential vitamins and minerals. After much consideration, Tisdall and his staff created an eleven-pound parcel that provided 2070 calories per day for seven days, from thirteen food items: whole milk powder, butter, cheese, corned beef, pork luncheon meat, salmon, sardines, dried apples, dried prunes, sugar, jam, biscuits, and chocolate. Other items included salt, tea, and soap.[71]

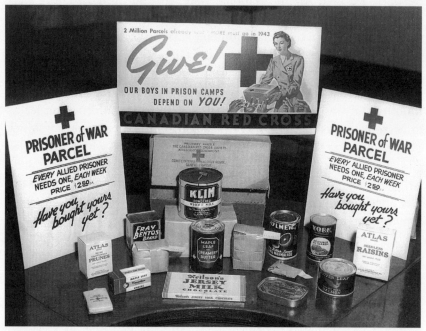

The contents of a standard Canadian Red Cross food parcel

In January 1941 the CRCS struck the Red Cross POW Parcels Committee, under Toronto businessman Norman C. Urquhart and Harold Leather, a member of the CRCS Central Council and the president of a Hamilton cartage company, and opened the first parcel-packing plant in the ballroom of the Ontario lieutenant governor's residence at Chorley Park in Toronto.[72] The parcel campaign grew by leaps and bounds. By June 1941, the Chorley Park facility was packing 10,000 parcels weekly, and the following month production increased with the opening of a new plant in Montreal; soon the two facilities were assembling 40,000 parcels each week. In 1942 and 1943 plants opened in Hamilton, Windsor, and Winnipeg, and on 5 June 1944 the Canadian Red Cross announced proudly that it had packed its 10 millionth food parcel.[73] The operation continued to expand until May 1945, when most of the plants were closed, with only the Winnipeg plant remaining ready to assemble further parcels for the Far East if necessary.[74]

Volunteers assemble Red Cross food parcels at the plant in Hamilton, Ontario, April 1943.

The packing was done entirely by volunteers. The Hamilton plant, in a building leased from an automobile dealership, used fifty volunteers daily, with the Imperial Order of Daughters of the Empire, the Catholic Women's League, the Royal Hamilton Light Infantry Women's Auxiliary, the Order of Scottish Clans, and the Jewish Charities supplying workers on different days. The operation was exceedingly efficient, one source estimating that a parcel could be packed in seventeen seconds. The pace was so quick that when a dignitary dropped her watch in a parcel during a tour of the Toronto facility, the box was sealed before she realized her loss. The watch was eventually returned by the prisoner who found it in his weekly parcel.[75]

After being assembled, the completed parcels were then packed in wooden crates for shipment overseas.

Once packed, the parcels began their long journey to the camps. At first the USPS ferried them to Lisbon, but in December 1941 the ICRC assumed responsibility for transporting relief shipments and established the Foundation for the Organization of Red Cross Transport. For the rest of the war, all relief supplies travelled in forty-three Spanish, Swiss, Portuguese, and Swedish vessels operated by the Red Cross.[76] Parcel shipments entered the continent at various ports, primarily Lisbon, Marseille, and Gothenburg, and were then transported to ICRC depots in Geneva or Lübeck in trucks or specially chartered trains. From there, they moved to a number of Red Cross-operated central facilities in Germany for distribution to local prison camps. Each camp maintained a reserve supply of parcels (some only a week or two, some as much as three months), and weekly distribution was performed by members of the camp staff under the watchful eye of a senior prisoner. At Lamsdorf, Jack Garswood of the Essex Scottish was elected to monitor the distribution; at Sagan, the task fell to Ottawa pilot Keith Ogilvie.[77] Pilferage was rare, although occasionally the camp staff withheld parcels as a form of collective punishment; on other occasions, POWs were required to open all food tins at the time of issue, so that tins could not be stockpiled in preparation for an escape attempt.[78]

Crates of Red Cross food parcels were stored in huge warehouses to await transport
to the camps. This one was in Geneva.

The standard parcel campaign proceeded with very few hitches,
although the government occasionally ran into difficulty because of the
tendency of the Canadian Red Cross to act on its own, without consulting the government. For example, in May 1941 the CRCS informed
External Affairs that it had granted a British Red Cross request to
increase Canadian parcel capacity to 45,000 per week. The fact that the
society accepted such a large commitment without prior consultation
disturbed the department, as Special Section noted in a later cable:
'The practice of the Canadian Red Cross of acting on communications
received from the British Red Cross without consulting the departments of the Canadian Government concerned ... has been a constant
source of trouble ... They have several times made large commitments
at London involving the expenditure of millions of dollars without consulting Ottawa.' Despite the efforts of the government to convince the
CRCS to act 'as a national society in accordance with their charter and
not as a branch of the British Red Cross,' similar incidents occurred
throughout the war.[79]

Every POW looked forward to the issue of Red Cross food parcels.

There was also a lengthy controversy, in which Canada played a significant and creditable role, over the extension of standard parcel delivery to other Allied POWs. Although initially concerned about expanding parcel supply beyond Commonwealth POWs, the Canadian government eventually came to support the diversion to Allied prisoners of parcels from the Geneva stockpile. Despite resistance from the British Red Cross, the Canadian society succeeded in having the quota for Allied prisoners raised from 1300 to 2000 parcels per week.[80] However, CRCS officials realized that this increase could be only the beginning. In September, Mr. Justice Gordon reported to R.B. Bennett the American belief that Britain was being selfish in its allocation of parcels to Allied POWs. American figures showed that for every 10,000 grams of food shipped to a British prisoner, a Frenchman received 850 grams, a Belgian 500, a Pole 280, and a Yugoslav a mere 175 grams. Furthermore, Gordon revealed that Allied groups were 'exerting terrific pressure' to have these figures raised.[81]

In September 1943, the subject of parcels for Allied POWs came up at a Washington meeting of national Red Cross societies, and again the CRCS took the initiative. Major-General C.B. Price, the society's overseas commissioner, pointed out that for the benefit of postwar relations between the Allies, all POWs should be accorded as equal treatment as possible. Price strongly believed that every Allied POW should receive one Red Cross parcel each month; this was far less than the weekly parcels being issued to Commonwealth prisoners as it did for other American POWs but far more than the American and British societies were willing to provide. While insisting that the British Red Cross would do what it could, that society's chairman, Sir Ernest Burdon, pointed out that Britain had already done much to support foreign Red Cross societies temporarily headquartered there, and consequently had 'a clear conscience as to past performance.' The American Red Cross was sympathetic but also declined to increase the present quota.[82]

Canadian authorities did not lose sight of Price's goal, and in 1944 the Cabinet War Committee considered his proposal. The committee saw three reasons in favour of it: to allay the bitter feelings created by the difference in treatment accorded to Commonwealth and European prisoners; to give Europeans tangible proof that Canada was assisting; and because anything that could be done for Europeans during the war would make it easier to provide for them after the liberation. Furthermore, shipments to Allied POWs could begin immediately from existing stocks.[83] The committee eventually accepted these recommendations, and in October 1944 the CRCS parcel program was reorganized so that Canada produced the same number of parcels for Commonwealth prisoners as it did for other Allied POWs in Europe.[84] In terms of Canadian input, the goal of treating all Allied prisoners equally was realized.

The Red Cross parcel campaign, then, was a resounding success. Through the course of the war, volunteer workers packed over 16 million parcels at a cost of over $47 million, and a number of doctors, including Tisdall, attributed the excellent health of returned POWs to the quality of Red Cross food parcels.[85] Prisoners insisted that Canadian parcels were the best that they received in captivity, a fact borne out by Tisdall's analysis of questionnaires completed by liberated POWs in 1945. He discovered that over 80 per cent of Canadian POWs and over 70 per cent of British Army POWs rated Canadian parcels as superior to all others, largely because of their bulk and because they contained white-flour biscuits (white flour was all but unobtainable by POWs) and butter (most other Red Cross parcels contained only margarine).[86]

Prisoners were effusive in their praise, and took every opportunity to extend heartfelt thanks to the organization. One repatriated POW called the parcels 'the gift of life itself,' and wrote that 'there are Canadians behind the German fronts who tonight, tomorrow night and every night till victory will dream of Red Cross Parcels.' Stewart Ripley carefully wrote in his diary a paean to the Red Cross that summed up the thoughts of many POWs: 'Enough can not [sic] be said in tribute to the wonderful work of the RED CROSS. Without the Red Cross we would be living on meagre German rations ... All in all life in a P.O.W. camp would be intolerable.'[87]

ALTHOUGH CANADA'S RELIEF PROGRAM as a whole had been bedevilled by a number of difficulties, such problems were confined to the minor facets of the campaign. The major part of Canada's effort, the provision of standard Red Cross food parcels, went remarkably smoothly, largely because few offices were involved in it. Dr. Tisdall and his team controlled the contents of the parcels (subject to the approval of the government's Food Requirements Committee), and Swiss authorities exercised the same degree of control over shipping arrangements. There was no question of other aid agencies intruding into the operation, because the standard food parcel was recognized as the exclusive preserve of the Red Cross. Just as important, departments that were notorious for slow decision-making, especially National Defence and National War Services, played no role in the provision of standard parcels. Unfortunately, the same could not be said of the campaign to secure the release of prisoners.

III

As in the First World War, Canadian prisoners had two options if they wanted to regain their freedom before the end of hostilities: escape or repatriation. Because of the proliferation of escape stories in the interwar period, many Canadian soldiers were familiar, even if only vaguely, with the exploits of their predecessors who had broken out of the Kaiser's prison camps. In general, the problems faced by the two generations of escapers were similar; the Third Reich, however, had a significantly greater problem with escaped prisoners and took much more severe measures to prevent breakouts and deal with them when they occurred.[88]

Those who tried to duplicate the feats of the Great War escapers were doubtless influenced by similar motives. A.B. Thompson, Canada's first POW of the Second World War, tried to escape because 'I don't feel that I've pulled my weight in this war, getting bounced in the first week,' while pilot Pat Langford, the son of an Alberta park ranger, could not abide the role of bystander and found in tunnelling the only way to get back into action. Most prospective escapers were unconcerned by the risk. Leo Heaps, a Canadian paratrooper seconded to the British Army and captured at Arnhem in September 1944, decided that his personal freedom was of more value than his life, and immediately after capture, turned his thoughts to escape.[89]

Of course, the easiest time to escape was during this first stage of captivity, before transfer to a permanent camp, and those soldiers who made their attempts at this time stood a reasonably good chance of success. Dozens of Canadian soldiers, such as Corporal A.G. Johnson of the Lake Superior Regiment, escaped soon after being taken prisoner. Johnson was reluctant to be marched away to captivity, so he turned on his captors, killed them after a brief struggle, and returned to his unit. North Nova Scotia Highlander Captain Jack Veness and a number of other Canadians captured in Normandy cut their way out of the boxcar carrying them to captivity. Veness made contact with the resistance, returned to Allied lines, and was back with his unit at the front by November. Leo Heaps joined with two sergeants and broke out of a train carrying them to Germany; he linked up with the Dutch resistance and helped other survivors of the botched Arnhem operation to escape.[90]

However, few prisoners considered escape at the time when it was easiest to achieve. Hungry, exhausted, often demoralized or disoriented, their thoughts turned instead to food and rest, and for many the relative comforts of a permanent POW camp seemed much more appealing than the uncertainty and privations of escape and flight. Once they reached a camp and regained their strength, many must have reasoned, they would think seriously about escape. Unfortunately, the battle to escape was immeasurably more difficult once a POW reached a permanent camp. In general, prospective escapers from

Hitler's Germany faced the same basic obstacles as their predecessors: maps, clothing, compasses, food, and identity papers had to be procured; the escape from the camp itself had to be planned and executed; and the ground between the camp and neutral territory had to be covered.[91] To accomplish any one of these goals was a feat; to put them all together was a considerable achievement.

In the first place, security measures within the prison camps were far more developed than they had been in the Kaiser's Germany. The camp commandants and security officers were usually specially trained for the task, and had a hierarchy of experts above them to ensure that the security provisions were as complete as possible. Many of the camp officers had been POWs themselves during the Great War and had considerable insight into the ruses that prisoners might employ.[92] Physically, the camps were much harder to get out of. Since many of them were built for the purpose, they lacked the loopholes, boarded-up rooms, and secret staircases that had been so helpful to prospective escapers in the Great War. The compounds were usually plain and barren, with few places to hide from guards posted in look-out towers. Technology, too, played a role; more than one escape tunnel was uncovered when underground microphones connected to the camp security office picked up the sounds of digging.

As determined as the Germans were to keep them in, however, the prisoners were bent on getting out. Tunnelling was a favourite means of escape, and some compounds became so riddled with tunnels that the captors were forced to evacuate them. Soft sand, well-packed earth, and even heavy clay proved little deterrent to tunnellers armed with small shovels crafted from stove parts or empty food tins. Toiling away in the dim glow of fat lamps or makeshift electric lights, breathing fetid air, and enduring the constant danger of cave-ins, Canadian prisoners assisted in the construction of hundreds of escape tunnels. Many were discovered and destroyed by the camp staff and others collapsed of their own accord, but there were some notable successes. In June 1943 nine Canadians, including Victoria Cross winner Lieutenant-Colonel Cecil Merritt of the South Saskatchewan Regiment, and fifty-six others escaped by tunnel from *Oflag* 7B Eichstätt. All nine were recaptured, albeit totally unchastened by the experience; a few weeks later, two of the Canadians escaped from their punishment cell by cutting the window bars and lowering themselves on stolen ropes to the ground below.[93] Just under a year later, in March 1944, nine Canadians joined sixty-seven other Allied airmen in the Great Escape from *Stalag Luft* 3 at Sagan, an incident that ended tragically with the execution of fifty of the recaptured escapers.

Other prisoners opted for less labour-intensive escape schemes. In August 1940 three airmen – Howard Wardle of Ottawa, Keith Milne of Qu'Appelle, and Don Middleton of Brandon – made short-lived bids for freedom from Spangenberg Castle; disguised as painters, Milne and Middleton found a ladder and walked straight through the prison gate before being recognized just outside the camp.[94] C.D. Noble, a bomber pilot who survived fifty-six operations before being shot down, attempted to escape from *Stalag Luft* 3 by hiding in a bin used to carry ashes away from the camp. Unfortunately, Noble buried himself too deeply and could not free himself from the wet ashes when the time came. He struggled as the bin was wheeled out of his compound, past his intended escape point, and into an adjoining compound. Much to his chagrin, Noble had neatly exchanged the frying pan for the fire. Don Thom, an Edmonton native who joined the RAF before the war, had little better luck. In August 1941 he and a British officer escaped from Colditz Castle dressed as members of the Hitler Youth, but were recaptured because they were unable to give a convincing Hitler salute.[95]

Once an escaper got free of his camp, the most difficult part of the task began. Besides a very vigilant population, escapers had to avoid the many different police officials, from the dangerous Gestapo and Kripo officials to the lowly town constables to the Hitler Youth, who, according to one former prisoner, 'spent their weekends looking for escaped prisoners.'[96] Even if the police were evaded, it was another matter altogether to enter neutral territory. Switzerland was relatively close to many camps, but the Swiss-German border was over 90 per cent water that was easily patrolled; the 'green' border was no less an obstacle, for it followed a very erratic course and was difficult to negotiate.[97] Sweden could be reached only by ship, from ports that were often teeming with police. Spain was many weeks of travelling from Germany and, realistically, could be reached only with the aid of the French resistance; even then, the Pyrenees mountains were a daunting barrier to an escaper who had been on the run for months.

For these reasons, very few Canadian POWs succeeded in escaping from permanent camps. Of the 2500 members of the RCAF who were captured, only three escaped successfully. Two of them, Sergeant C.E. McDonald and Warrant Officer H.L. Brooks, changed identities with army privates so that they could be posted from the camp at Lamsdorf to working parties. They had little difficulty escaping from the work detachments, McDonald in August 1942 and Brooks in May 1943, and both eventually linked up with organized resistance movements. McDonald was conveyed to Paris by the Polish underground and crossed into Spain in June 1943, after nearly a year at large in occupied Europe. Brooks too made contact with Polish resistance workers, and remained with them until the area was liberated by Russian troops in January 1945. The third Canadian, Sergeant J.L.N. Warren, escaped from the camp at Mühlberg in April 1944 and received assistance from French labourers, who helped him and his comrades cross into Holland. There they linked up with the Dutch resistance, and in September 1944 Warren was spirited through Allied lines to freedom.[98]

It is uncertain how many Canadian soldiers escaped successfully from permanent camps, but at least three broke out of Stargard in the summer of 1944. On 9 June, Nova Scotian Sergeant S.L. McMullen and Corporal Gus Nelson of the Calgary Tanks cut the wire to freedom and, assisted by French workers, stowed away on a bombed-out freighter that was being towed to Sweden; they spent sixteen days hiding in the engine room before the vessel reached neutral territory on Dominion Day. Private J.H. Kimberley of the Royal Hamilton Light Infantry made even faster progress. On 3 August, he slipped away from a work party in the city of Stargard, made his way onto a ship bound for Sweden, and, just eight days after his escape, swam ashore on neutral territory.[99]

Sadly, Nazi Germany was a very dangerous environment for the unsuccessful escaper. The military authorities usually treated recaptured escapers correctly, but those who fell into the hands of one of the police organizations often faced a different fate. Indeed, once the so-called Bullet Decree of 4 March 1944 had ordered the execution of recaptured non-British and American escapers, it was a relatively small step to extend its provisions to members of the Commonwealth.[100] The most notable such incident was the Great Escape of March 1944, which so outraged German officials that they ordered the execution of fifty of the recaptured airmen. Among the victims were six Canadians: Henry Birkland, a miner from Sheep Creek, British Columbia; Jimmy Wernham, a Scottish-born employee of John Deere in Winnipeg; George Wiley, a young Windsor fighter pilot captured in 1943; two former University of Toronto students, Gordon Kidder and George McGill; and Pat Langford, who had turned to escape to avoid the idleness of captivity.[101]

The *Stalag Luft* 3 case culminated in a well-known war crimes trial in 1948, but other crimes went unpunished. After breaking out of *Stalag* 3E Kirchhain, Sergeant Harold Calvert of Victoria and his British companion were recaptured while sleeping at a railway siding near Dresden; Calvert asked permission from the police to put on his boots, but when he pointed down at his feet, the police shot him dead. Toronto native Private G.M. Johnston, a Dieppe prisoner, was apprehended in the course of an escape in November 1944; he followed the guard's command to raise his hands but was immediately shot dead. In January 1945 three airmen tried to cut through the perimeter fence at *Stalag* 3A Luckenwalde; they were fired upon and two of the escapers were hit, including Flying Officer Percy Crosswell of Prince Albert, Saskatchewan, who was killed instantly. The fate of other Canadian escapers remains shrouded in mystery. In January 1944 Lieutenant W.A. 'Dopey' Millar, a Canadian engineer captured at Dieppe, slipped through a window and disappeared from Colditz Castle, never to be seen again. The same month, Private H.J. Boultinghouse of the Essex Scottish vanished without trace from *Stalag* 8B; he too likely escaped, but nothing was ever heard of him again. Millar and Boultinghouse probably died at the hands of the Gestapo some months after escaping.[102]

Nor was the danger only from the German authorities. Many prisoners were buried alive in collapsed escape tunnels, only to be pulled out in the nick of time by fellow workers. Wally Floody, a miner in northern Ontario before the war, was badly burned when a cave-in trapped a hot fat lamp against his leg; another digger was electrocuted by the makeshift electrical wiring that had been rigged up in a tunnel. In April 1943 Polish railway workers found the legless body of Private Robert Wignes of the Royal Regiment of Canada, a persistent escaper, lying beside the tracks. He had fallen while trying to jump from a railway car; his legs severed by the train wheels, Wignes had apparently bled to death.[103] These were not isolated incidents, and for many prisoners the hazards of escaping were too great to be risked.

IF ESCAPING WAS a very risky way to secure one's freedom, repatriation was hardly more certain. Negotiations aimed at exchanges of civilian internees were complex and protracted, with very limited results to show for the effort. By the same token, despite lengthy discussions, it proved impossible to arrange an exchange of long-term prisoners such as had occurred during the Great War. Consequently, only POWs who had been badly wounded in battle, who had fallen seriously ill in captivity, or who exhibited symptoms of psychological illness could hope to gain repatriation.

Efforts at securing release began even before the major part of the relief campaign. In that early period, Canadian officials were most interested in obtaining the freedom of interned civilians. Not only were civilian internees more numerous than POWs but their repatriation would also lighten the workload of External Affairs and reduce the financial burden upon the Canadian government, which supplied civilians with money that it had little hope of recovering. Repatriation would determine which so-called Canadians were actually interested in maintaining ties with the country; those who were not willing to return might be made ineligible for further financial assistance.[104]

As in the First World War, Canada tried to avoid charges of favouritism by resisting head-to-head exchanges in favour of exchanges by category; for example, Canada would consider the repatriation of all interned clergymen by both sides, regardless of number, but would not consider releasing a specific German cleric in return for a specific Canadian cleric.[105] The government held to this policy throughout the war, despite suggestions for individual exchanges put forward by interested groups and despite the fact that, because there were far more Germans in Canada than Canadians in Germany, any exchange by category would greatly favour Germany.[106]

In the early years of the war Canadian authorities did secure the release of Canadians in a number of categories. In 1941 a group of women who had been interned in France was released after the government gave assurances that Canada did not intern German women based on nationality alone, but only if they contravened the Defence of Canada Regulations.[107] The following year, Richard Grew and T.J. Monty, trade officials in Oslo who had been interned with their families after the German invasion of Norway in April 1940, returned to Canada as part of an exchange of diplomats.[108] Later in 1942, External Affairs secured the release of another category of civilian internees, eight women from the Egyptian ship *Zam Zam*, which had been bound for South Africa with a complement of missionaries, including twenty-three Canadians, when it was sunk in the South Atlantic and its passengers interned.[109]

In spite of the success in securing the release of specific categories of civilians, the major players could not agree on a formula for a general exchange of civilians. The United States wanted to repatriate all civilians, a policy that found favour with the German government, but Britain and the ICRC believed that exchange should include only certain categories of civilians, such as women and children, men of non-military age, doctors, and clerics.[110] This inability to agree on principles made civilian exchanges more difficult to negotiate, and consequently they became mere adjuncts to military exchanges.

As the prospects of release for interned civilians faded, the repatriation of sick and wounded POWs became the focus of Canada's release campaign. Military repatriation became possible in May 1940, when Britain and Germany agreed upon the appointment of Mixed Medical Commissions to examine prospective repatriates, but the first round of negotiations broke off in October 1941 over the question of numerical equality. Unfortunately, the talks collapsed while a group of Commonwealth prisoners was on its way out of Germany with high hopes of returning home; when they learned that the repatriation had been cancelled, the disappointment was a bitter blow.[111]

In June 1942 Ottawa learned the provisions of a new tentative agreement reached by Germany and Britain. The accord allowed the repatriation of all sick and wounded POWs (*grands blessés*), all surplus medical personnel, and all civilians who wished to leave, whether or not they were interned, except those serving penal sentences or deemed to be dangerous to the Detaining Power.[112] Canada, however, was soon throwing up obstacles to the plan, the most serious of which was an interest in future exchange schemes that the United States was likely to negotiate. As Norman Robertson wrote, 'there is a great deal to be said for our pursuing the same general policy in this field as the United States and the other American belligerents.'[113] Despite warnings from alarmed British authorities that the negotiations could be 'vitally prejudiced' if the German government learned that a member of the Commonwealth was attempting to make separate arrangements, External Affairs insisted that Britain's communications with the German Legation in Switzerland include the caveat that participation in Britain's scheme did not signify Canadian disavowal of any scheme negotiated by the United States.[114]

As it turned out, Canada's view had precisely the effect on negotiations that British authorities had feared. The German Legation reported that, in view of the number of German POWs transferred to Canada (and the belief that Britain intended to concentrate all prisoners it captured in Canada), Germany would not consider any agreement with Britain that did not have the full and unqualified support of Canada. In Germany's view, Canada's reservation 'would imply ... that Canadian Government would not be bound by the agreement under negotiation,' and the legation refused to forward Britain's telegram to Berlin while the reservation stood.[115] Of course, Germany would likely have found another reason to break off negotiations had Canada's reservation not been presented. Nevertheless, the incident betrayed a serious failure on the part of External Affairs to grasp a fundamental feature of the captivity problem. It should have been obvious that Germany treated the Commonwealth as a single political unit, and was not willing to deal with any one Dominion unless it furthered the aim of sowing dissent among the Allies. External Affairs admitted this fact in December 1941, when exchange negotiations were in their infancy, yet just six months later it was either ignored or forgotten.[116] Regardless of the domestic political imperatives stressed by Robertson, it should have been realized that Canada's stand played directly into the hands of the Germans by allowing them to blame Canada for the collapse of talks.

Repatriation negotiations remained in abeyance for much of the fall and winter of 1942-3 because of the shackling incident, but in the spring of 1943 discussions reopened. These talks continued for the rest of the war, and resulted in four separate repatriations involving

Canadians. The first took place at Gothenburg, Sweden, in October 1943 and included 66 Canadians in a group of nearly 4200 Commonwealth POWs; the second, at Barcelona in May 1944, included 48 Canadians among just over a thousand Allied prisoners; the third operation, in September 1944, again at Gothenburg, involved 2560 Allied nationals, including 42 Canadians; and the last, at Marseille in January 1945, brought home 81 Canadians in a group of 2500 Allied POWs.[117]

The repatriation process was identical to that employed during the First World War. Sick and wounded prisoners were recommended by their doctors, and were then examined by a board of German physicians. The stakes were again very high, and the POWs and their physicians made every effort to present a favourable case. Dick McLaren, badly wounded in the arm at Dieppe, was told by his doctor to run his hand under cold water on the morning of his examination; by the time he came before the commission the hand had turned blue and looked decidedly unhealthy. Two airmen, both amputees, were examined by the commission before McLaren and failed, but McLaren was passed for repatriation. Lloyd Gruggen, nursing a bad shoulder wound sustained at Dieppe, healed quite well and amused himself by playing volleyball; his doctor spotted and roundly scolded him, as he had been recommended for examination by the Mixed Medical Commission. He gave up volleyball, affected an air of general unhealthiness, and was passed for repatriation by the commission.[118]

While prisoners and their doctors were doing their best to dupe the medical commissions, Canadian officials were working assiduously to improve their administrative mechanism for monitoring exchanges. Britain and the United States had established two bodies, the Combined Repatriation Committee in London and the Washington Repatriation Committee, to assume responsibility for negotiating exchanges, but Canada had no permanent representation on either body.[119] To fill a perceived void, the Canadian government decided to create a new committee of its own, the Inter-Service Committee on POWs (ISCP). Made up of representatives of the SAAG, the three services, Transport, External Affairs, and Internment Operations, the ISCP was intended to deal with all administrative and operational matters pertaining to the repatriation of Canadian POWs. Mindful of past delays in decision-making, the chairman hoped that the three service representatives would be empowered by their departments to reply promptly to routine queries.[120] The ISCP was apparently entirely superfluous, however; its membership was similar to that of the Committee for the Protection and Welfare of Canadian Prisoners of War in Enemy Hands, which continued to discuss repatriation matters in its meetings. It is unclear why Canadian officials felt that the new committee was necessary at all.

Indeed, the ISCP played little role in the October 1943 repatriation, which brought home 66 Canadians (50 soldiers, 12 airmen, and 4 seamen). Perhaps because it was the first operation in which Canada actively participated, a number of difficulties arose. Aside from the fact that the RCAF was terribly put out when its band was denied permission to play at the welcoming ceremonies, the most serious problem involved finding and segregating the Canadian prisoners after they had embarked in Gothenburg.[121] Because they were divided among three repatriation ships and disembarked at three different English ports, a reception party had to be dispatched to each port to search out Canadians and apprise them of the arrangements made for them. Inevitably, some were overlooked and entrained with the other repatriates for various hospitals, where they were examined and given leave passes; once British authorities realized that this should have been done at a Canadian base, the leave passes were revoked. Some ex-prisoners were understandably reluctant to surrender their new freedom, and it was four or five days before all of them could be located and transferred to #7 Canadian General Hospital at Taplow, where they should have gone in the first place.

In light of these difficulties, a number of exchange post mortems called for a more efficient way of handling Canadian repatriates. The best solution was to place an official on the repatriation ship at the exchange port to sort out the Canadians and notify them of the procedure to be followed once they reached the United Kingdom. As one member of a Canadian reception party wrote, repatriates 'would then feel that they were being cared for and looked after by their own representatives and not left with the feeling that Canada takes no interest in their well being.' Not only was this important for the repatriates themselves but it was also vital to preserving the domestic peace. At one post mortem, the SAAG mentioned the CPOWRA, which he called 'an energetic and outspoken organization who could cause severe repercussions in political circles if, in their opinion, the repatriates did not receive every possible consideration.'[122]

Shortly after the first repatriation, Canadian Military Headquarters (CMHQ) forwarded a list of proposed procedural changes, including the placement of Canadian officials on the hospital ships for the entire voyage, the embarkation of all Canadians on a single ship, and the immediate removal of all Canadians to a Canadian hospital in Britain. The War Office agreed to most of the proposals, but they became academic when External Affairs suggested that Canadian repatriates on the next exchange proceed directly to North America, rather than disembark in the United Kingdom. In the department's view, 'from the political angle, ... it would be dangerous to insist that the Canadians be delayed in the United Kingdom while the US repatriates return directly to their own country.'[123]

The American and Canadian repatriates would return on the SS *Gripsholm*, and George Magann, attaché to the Canadian Embassy in Washington, and a small team were assigned to the ship to process all Commonwealth repatriates.[124] This arrangement worked admirably, and the High Commission, the War Office, and the medical officer in charge of the repatriation for Britain had nothing but praise for the work of Magann and his staff.[125] The Canadian repatriates were very complimentary as well, and appreciated the cocktail party Magann hosted for them after the *Gripsholm* left Barcelona. They also praised him for taking charge of the physical aspects of the exchange at Barcelona, where the Spanish dockworkers were clearly a little overwhelmed by the logistics of getting the Allied POWs off the German ship and onto the *Gripsholm*, and the German POWs off the *Gripsholm* and onto the German ship, both at the same time.[126]

The smoothness that characterized the second repatriation was generally repeated on the third. Magann again took charge of all Commonwealth prisoners, and again the major problem of the exchange involved the segregation of repatriates. The returning POWs reached Gothenburg on a number of trains arriving throughout the day, so Magann and his staff were forced to search every carriage for Canadian servicemen.[127] Because of the confusion, they went a little overboard in trying to apprise Canadians of what they should do when they reached the dock: 'Canadians, who drifted through on the third train, had received all kinds of instructions and some of which had frightened one soldier into the declaration that he was British.'[128] In total, 42 Canadians came out on the repatriation trains: 1 seaman, 24 soldiers, 16 airmen, and 1 civilian.[129] Fortunately, they encountered no serious difficulties once they embarked on the *Gripsholm*.

With the success of the third repatriation, Canada promptly agreed to a fourth, despite the fact that the administrative machinery was still dreadfully mixed up. Most seriously, the service headquarters were delinquent in double-checking the lists provided by the Mixed Medical Commissions to ensure that all eligible Canadians had been considered for repatriation. Canada House was unsure of the procedure used by the services to achieve this, but clearly despaired of what could be done to improve things:

> If we were in the middle of the war I should say we should have a talk at the Sub Committee [Sub-Committee A] and agree upon what sort of persons we should ask for and by what machinery. Sub Committee would recommend we should refer to our Services and within nine months they would be able to decide upon their answer. What to do at this stage I do not pretend to know.[130]

Evidently, the formation of the ISCP had done nothing to improve the handling of exchanges from Canada's end.

The fourth exchange, performed at Marseille in January 1945, experienced only minor problems. Despite some reluctance on the part of the senior British officer present (described as 'a doughty warrior of the "Eh, what what" school'[131]) to admit that arrangements had been made for Canadians to return to New York instead of Britain, the operation went smoothly on the whole. The 81 Canadian repatriates (53 soldiers, 26 airmen, and 2 merchant seamen) were most grateful that Canada had sent officials to look after them, and were also pleased that the Minister to France, General Georges P. Vanier, came on board at Marseille to speak to every Canadian.[132]

The only other hitch occurred at New York, where the ex-prisoners came under the control of National Defence Headquarters (NDHQ). To greet the repatriates, NDHQ had dispatched a huge party, which 'swarmed over the Gripsholm, did no useful work ... and were nothing but a nuisance.' As J.K. Cronyn, an External Affairs staffer assigned to the voyage, reported, 'it is reasonable to expect such personnel as a doctor, dentist, intelligence officer, publicity [officer] and chief greeter ... but it was not clear what the other fifteen were doing.'[133] External Affairs had nothing good to say about the efforts of National Defence: 'nobody from NDHQ showed any disposition to arrange for their [the repatriates'] disembarkation ... Once the ship docks, it becomes an NDHQ show, and if they insist on making fools of themselves, is there anything we can do to restrain them?' Assistant Under-Secretary of External Affairs Hume Wrong believed that there was not, and was perhaps thankful that there was little chance of another repatriation at this late stage of the war.[134]

EXTERNAL AFFAIRS might also be forgiven had it expressed gratitude that the military played no role in civilian exchanges, exchanges which created a different set of problems to be addressed. With the conclusion of the October 1943 POW exchange, the negotiation of a civilian repatriation could proceed, and in January 1944 Canada agreed to associate itself with a proposed exchange of all civilians, interned or not, except those under penal sentence or those who did not wish to leave.[135]

With this agreement in principle, it was imperative to address a number of matters, including the determination of priorities. For instance, Scott thought that Canada might suggest clerics as a high-priority group. 'Mathematically doubtless it would be very beneficial to us supposing people of that sort actually want to come back,' he mused. 'It would, however, give you a very large proportion of French speaking people.'[136] More important than this was the problem of determining who should be eligible for admission to Canada. External Affairs official Margaret Meagher proposed the exclusion of any Canadian nationals who had lost their 'moral claim' on Canada, including anyone who had taken up permanent residence outside the country, whether naturalized Canadians, alien widows of Canadian citizens, or Canadian-born citizens.[137] To facilitate such decisions, the High Commission considered it essential to secure lists of prospective repatriates as soon as possible, because 'the question of whether a self-styled Canadian is really a Canadian can normally be answered only in

Ottawa.' This matter had to be settled in advance to avoid difficulties at the exchange site in Lisbon, especially as only two Canadian officials (Oscar Cormier from Immigration and Max Wershof from Canada House) were available to meet the repatriates.[138] To Wershof and Cormier would fall the task of verifying the identity of 'self-styled Canadians' and issuing certificates to those who qualified; they were also instructed to obtain from each repatriate a signed statement promising to reimburse the Canadian government for the cost of their repatriation.[139]

When the exchange ship, the *Drottningholm*, arrived in Lisbon on 11 July 1944, Wershof and Cormier expected to find only three confirmed Canadians on board, but the registration procedure revealed eleven more individuals who claimed to be Canadians. Most of these people wanted to go to Canada only until they could return to their homes on the continent; some had no wish to go there at all. One of the few repatriates who expressed a desire to travel to Canada was later arrested in Liverpool on an old charge of embezzlement.[140] External Affairs admitted that these results were far from satisfactory:

> Disappointment over the small number of Canadians repatriated and the fact that a large proportion of these have had little claim on Canada, should be kept in mind for further discussions with London ... If very few Canadians are received in the Gothenburg exchange (especially if most of these few are doubtful Canadians or undesirables) we anticipate popular complaint and that the Government may have to make an explanation.[141]

The Gothenburg exchange of September 1944 was just as disappointing. Eighteen Canadians were repatriated. Four of them went to New York on the *Gripsholm*; the rest remained in Britain, and only one of these expressed a desire to go to Canada.[142] These figures drew another pessimistic letter from Alfred Rive, who wrote that 'It was a very disappointing haul and we had quite a lot of complaint from relatives of Canadians in German hands both direct and through members of Parliament. The estimates of External were about to come up in the House and the Under-Secretary took the situation sufficiently seriously to enquire whether we could not do better in bringing back the Canadians.'[143]

When the next civilian exchange was considered, in January 1945, External Affairs attempted to head off a repeat of the same situation. Having received a list of Canadians nominated for exchange by the Swiss, the department declared it most unsatisfactory, as it consisted largely of German-born naturalized Canadians who had returned to Europe with the intention of taking up residence there. Realizing the necessity of decisive action, External Affairs stated that such individuals would not be accepted by Canada and that if the Swiss list was not revised, those Germans who had been sent to the United Kingdom for the coming exchange would be returned to Canada and reinterned.[144] Luckily, circumstances changed before Canada was forced to act on the threat.

The attempts to secure the release of prisoners during the war, then, were considerably less successful than in the First World War. Only a tiny percentage of POWs were repatriated for medical reasons, and the picture was not much brighter for civilian internees. These disappointing results were due largely to circumstances beyond the control of Canadian officials. The Canadian government might have handled repatriation arrangements more efficiently by centring them in the CPW instead of creating the superfluous ISCP. This would have lessened the burden on civil servants, but it certainly would not have brought home any more Canadian prisoners. The German government was clearly more interested in getting the most out of its captives as pawns than in freeing them on humanitarian grounds, and the best organization in the world would not have changed that fact.

IV

Unlike during the First World War, however, negotiations for exchanges did not divert planners from considering the problems surrounding the evacuation of liberated POWs after the hostilities were over. With the lessons of 1918 firmly in their minds, Allied authorities were determined not to repeat the confusion that had stemmed from the lack of advance planning and the absence of a mechanism to move prisoners from their camps to safety.

Canadian officials began contemplating the problem as early as March 1942. By October, Britain and the Dominions had agreed on the necessity of a stay-put order instructing prisoners to remain in their camps once hostilities had ended, to avoid the problems of tracking down masses of scattered POWs that had been encountered after the Great War.[145] In December 1942, the Cabinet War Committee received from the War Office a draft plan for the postwar repatriation of POWs. The plan envisioned each member of the Commonwealth assuming responsibility for the evacuation of all Commonwealth POWs in a certain area; Britain was to be responsible for Europe, India for Singapore, Australia for the Dutch East Indies, and Canada for China. In short order, the committee approved the draft.[146] A year later Sub-Committee A circulated a revised plan for the postwar liberation that was in some ways a response to the difficulties encountered in the liberation of Italian camps, an operation in which Canada played no role. This draft dealt largely with the minutiae of the liberation operation, but it did reveal the principles that were important to British planners, including the stay-put order and the secondment of Commonwealth liaison officers to forward armies to deal with liberated POWs.[147]

Canadian officials were enthusiastic about these principles. The Army was especially pleased with the posting of Dominion delegates to the headquarters staffs, and further intimated that it would welcome a Dominion presence in the Allied planning group, whatever form it took.[148] Ironically, in light of National Defence's traditional demand to be consulted in all POW matters, the services displayed a marked reluctance to assume any more responsibility than this. That some of the burden should be transferred from Special Section to the services was admitted in September 1944, but the only result was the secondment of an officer to Canada House.[149]

Far from assuming greater responsibility, the services insisted instead upon the establishment of yet another interdepartmental committee.[150] Obviously hoping that this would be a first step in a transfer of duties, External Affairs agreed, and the Canadian Overseas POW Committee (COPC), with delegates from the three services, External Affairs, and Transport, was struck on 30 January 1945. Again, the need for this committee must be questioned. The membership was almost identical to that of the CPW and the ISCP, the only difference being that the COPC was based in London; even so, all decisions would surely have to be referred back to Ottawa for confirmation. Even if it was only intended as the first step in a transfer of duties, the COPC was a broken reed for it played no such role, largely because of inter-service jealousy.[151] Rather than be drawn into such wrangles at this late stage, External Affairs took the line of least resistance and continued to shoulder most of the burden.

Canada's difficulties in coordinating her own internal machinery for handling the liberation were matched by problems in securing an entrée into the decision-making process. By the summer of 1944, Britain had accepted an American proposal that planning for the liberation be left to the two Supreme Commanders; accordingly, responsibility for the operational details for western Europe was conferred on the POW Executive (PWX) of the Supreme Headquarters, Allied Expeditionary Force (SHAEF). Headed by a British brigadier, PWX included two Canadian representatives, Colonel B.M. Clerk (later replaced by Lieutenant-Colonel J.H. Mothersill) and Group Captain F.A. Sampson.[152] The appointment of Clerk and Sampson did not of itself bring a say in the arrangements, however. On 1 December 1944 Allied representatives met at the War Office to discuss in detail the liberation arrangements. The content of that conference was less important than the fact that Dominion representatives were not invited to take part. Colonel Mothersill, who surely should have been kept apprised of the plans, knew nothing of the meeting and received very little information about the arrangements as they progressed.[153] Despite the appointment of Dominion liaison officials to PWX, the evacuation plan was obviously being formulated without their input.

Part of 'Eclipse,' the code name given to Allied arrangements for dealing with a German surrender, the plan assumed that liberated POWs would remain in their camps after the capitulation until specially trained liaison teams arrived to control the evacuation process. There would be two types of liaison teams. Contact teams consisting of liaison officers from every Allied nation were to be attached to all Army Group headquarters to arrange the evacuation of camps liberated by forward troops before the enemy capitulated. The bulk of the work would be done by the *Wehrkreis* (military district) liaison teams, similarly organized but including only officers from those nations with POWs in that *Wehrkreis*. After hostilities had ceased, these teams would be transported to each *Wehrkreis* to make an accounting of all

Allied POWs, take any steps needed to ensure their safety and food supply, and prepare them for the evacuation.[154] To avoid having to ship large quantities of food to the camps, the evacuation would be accomplished largely by air. To this end, SHAEF created an Eclipse Air Lift Executive (EALEX) to coordinate the supply of transport aircraft to remove ex-POWs from the continent. Under this arrangement, the PWX liaison teams would request aircraft from EALEX as and when they were needed, and then lead liberated prisoners to the nearest available airfield. In the EALEX plan, all Canadian POWs were to be flown to the Fighter Command base at Odiham.[155]

The evacuation of prisoners liberated by the Soviets created a different set of problems. Diplomatic approaches to Moscow on the subject were acknowledged to be difficult, and prolonged negotiations were necessary to reach an agreement for the repatriation of ex-POWs from the eastern zone. The Soviet government's insistence that liberated prisoners be put to work until they were evacuated was the most serious obstacle to an accord, but all parties eventually came to terms and signed a treaty covering the matter at the Yalta Conference.[156]

Canada had little input into the negotiations, but on 7 March 1945, Major Nelson Darling and Squadron Leader C.G.E. Leafloor arrived in Moscow to act as Canadian observers to the evacuation of Allied POWs freed from camps in eastern Europe.[157] Leafloor travelled to Odessa, the main concentration point for POWs in the southern half of the Russian zone, while Darling was sent to Volkovysk in Poland, the northern concentration centre. The Soviet authorities in Moscow did much to hinder the work of Darling, Leafloor, and the other observers by withholding travel permits and ignoring requests for assistance, but the authorities in Volkovysk and Odessa were as helpful as they could be. They endeavoured to provide ('in their own inimitable way,' noted Leafloor) what they considered to be the best facilities, and the fact that this was considerably less than what the western contact officers desired was merely a reflection of cultural differences. Indeed, Leafloor believed that 'everything humanly and physically possible is being done ... to make the life of prisoners of war as bright, cheerful and comfortable as circumstances permit.'

Still, when the numbers were taken into account, the operation was only a mixed success from the Canadian standpoint. Darling encountered just three Canadians at Volkovysk, all of whom were serving with British units, while 122 Canadians (97 soldiers, 16 airmen, and 9 civilians) were processed through Odessa; another 20 POWs from the eastern zone were unaccounted for. Leafloor reported that the number of Canadians encountered was 'disappointingly low,' but considered that the Canadian presence was justified by the assistance rendered to other Allied POWs.

AS THE OPERATION IN THE EAST proceeded, a hitch appeared in the Allied planning for western Europe. All the arrangements had made provision for stay-put orders to be transmitted to prison camps, but there were no contingency plans for coping with the forced transfer of prisoners. In the fall of 1944, the Germans began moving columns of POWs westward, away from the advancing Russians; later, as the operational situation changed, the same POWs found themselves marching eastward, away from advancing American and British troops. One camp commandant gave his charges the option of staying in the camp to be liberated by the Russians or marching west towards American lines; the prisoners, with the exception of 200 Poles, chose the former alternative, much to the discomfort of the camp guards, who cannot have relished the prospect of falling into Russian hands. Other camp commanders dispensed with such democratic niceties and simply marched their POWs away from the Russians into the hands of British or American troops. One column of prisoners was led around in such a haphazard manner that it quickly became apparent the guards had no idea where they should be taking the POWs.[158]

From January 1945, thousands of prisoners were constantly on the move across Europe as part of a German plan to concentrate them in three pockets, in northern, central, and southern Germany.[159] Despite the confusion that reigned, it is possible to recreate roughly the routes taken by Canadian POWs. Most officers of the Canadian Army were lucky enough to remain in their camps until liberation, but the airmen and other ranks held in Lamsdorf began marching on 22 January and covered the 240 kilometres to *Stalag* 8A Görlitz in about two weeks. They rested there for ten days before beginning the second leg of the journey, a 512-kilometre trek to *Stalag* 9A Ziegenhain. From there, they moved again, north to the huge camp at Fallingbostel, and then west towards Hamburg.[160]

Prisoners in *Stalag Luft* 3 began their trek on 27 January; a five-day march brought them to the railhead at Spremberg, where they entrained for various locations around Germany. Some headed for *Stalag* 3A Luckenwalde, south of Berlin, and the remainder of the Commonwealth POWs moved to *Marlag und Milag Nord*, a naval camp near Bremen. The camp at Stargard, to which many of the Dieppe prisoners had been transferred, was evacuated on 2 February 1945, and the prisoners endured a forty-four day march across the top of Germany, which took them to a camp for political prisoners at Sandbostel. Days later they were on the move again, some to Fallingbostel and some to join the Canadian airmen at *Marlag*.[161]

Regardless of the specifics of each march, the conditions were similar. Dragging makeshift sledges stuffed with all the food they could take away from the camp, the POWs trudged up to thirty kilometres each day, frequently in blinding snowstorms. It was often so cold that all foodstuffs, including jam and margarine, froze solid, and clothes and boots soon became heavy with ice. The guards, many of them elderly *Volkssturm* men who had been assigned to prison camp duties to free up soldiers for the front, suffered just as badly as the prisoners, and some had to be helped along, with the POWs carrying their packs or rifles.[162] Shelter was difficult to find, and the prisoners spent many hours waiting in the cold while their guards searched for billets in barns or farm outbuildings. Even the strongest POWs found the treks heavy going, and countless men never made it. Some were shot by guards for contravening minor regulations, some succumbed to illness, and others simply collapsed by the roadside and went unnoticed as the rest of the column passed.[163] To compound the agony, dozens of prisoners were killed when their columns were strafed by Allied aircraft. A typical incident occurred on 19 April 1945, when a group of airmen evacuated from the camp at Gross Tychow neared the tiny village of Burnorf. Just after noon, four British fighter-bombers came upon the column and, assuming it to be hostile, strafed it with rockets and machine guns. By the time the attack ended, nineteen guards and thirty-four prisoners, including three Canadians, had been killed.[164] With the cold, hunger, lack of shelter, and ever-present danger from above, the forced marches were the worst experience of captivity for many POWs.

Officials in Ottawa, who knew little of the specifics of the marches, wondered how the POWs would fare during the Nazi collapse. Alfred Rive thought the Allies would be lucky to get any of them out alive; he would have been even more concerned had he known of an SS suggestion to turn thousands of Allied prisoners over to the chief administrator of the concentration camps.[165] On a more practical level, because of the marches and Germany's apparent determination to fight to the death, it soon became evident that much of the planning, including the effort to secure Canadian participation in the execution of the operation, had been fruitless. Most Allied POWs were liberated before Eclipse conditions prevailed, so PWX's exhaustive plan was quickly jettisoned in favour of hastily improvised arrangements.[166] PWX, originally envisioned as an operational unit, never worked as such because the speed of events prevented it from acting in anything but an advisory capacity. Instead, the bulk of the work, and most of the important decisions, fell to the trained liaison teams, which were divided among various forward units and headquarters. In Canada's case, army and RCAF liaison officers were attached to 6th, 12th, and 21st Army Group Headquarters, and also to four Recovered Allied Military Personnel (RAMP) camps at Namur, Epinal, Rheims, and Brussels, which had been established as concentration points for stragglers recovered by forward units.

The considerations of national representation, so highly prized by Canadian officials in the original plan, also fell by the wayside. The situation envisioned in the PWX plan bore no resemblance to the chaotic conditions in Europe during the spring of 1945, and the orderly dispatch of specific liaison officers to specific locales was simply not possible. Dominion or service contact officers could not confine their activities to only those POWs for whose interests they had been appointed, nor was it practical to move a contact officer to join large concentrations of POWs for whom he was theoretically responsible. Each officer had to assume responsibility for the prisoners in his area, regardless of their service or nationality.[167]

Furthermore, the situation on the continent made rapid air evacuation even more crucial than originally anticipated. Because of the forced marches, many prisoners were concentrated in huge camps, some of which, like *Stalag* 7A at Moosburg, held over 100,000 POWs.

In the original plan, PWX officers at the camps were to compile complete nominal rolls of liberated POWs for transmission back to the various governments involved, so that facilities could be prepared for the arrival of prisoners in England. However, to avoid the problems of supplying these huge camps, the prisoners had to be evacuated as quickly as possible, even if it meant that administrative details were downgraded in importance. There was certainly little point in taking time to register the prisoners, sort them into national groups, and draw up nominal rolls if an airlift could begin immediately.

Although the evacuation of a camp did not proceed exactly as PWX had intended, it was no less efficient. Once liberating troops reached the camp, the liaison officer contacted the POWs' leader to procure accurate statistics of the camp's population. The officer then took these figures to the commander of the forward unit to arrange for temporary supplies, while the airlift was arranged with EALEX. When transport aircraft had been assigned, the liberated POWs were assembled at the nearest airfield, to be flown either directly to England or to one of three staging airfields at Le Havre, Rheims, and Brussels. Flights left continually, as long as weather permitted, and once the camp had been cleared, liaison officers remained behind to collect any stragglers and direct them to RAMP camps for transport to England.

Obviously there were occasional snags, many of which were related to the excitement of the moment.[168] According to PWX official A.J. Evans, who had been a POW in the Great War, 'prisoners of war are not fit to be given uncontrolled liberty – certainly not during the intense excitement which follows the liberation of a camp ... Once outside ... liberty goes to their heads and often all sense of responsibility departs.'[169] At Fallingbostel, near Hamburg, liberated POWs swarmed the countryside and got in the way of advancing Allied armies, drawing an appeal from Field Marshal Bernard Montgomery, GOC of the 21st Army Group, that they restrain themselves and be patient.[170] More typical was the tendency of prisoners to commandeer cars and drive around using gasoline provided by well-meaning Allied troops. A member of the Scots Guards told Argyll and Sutherland Highlander Clifford Foulds that he could get out of Germany much faster if he commandeered a car, and Roy Clute of the same unit liberated an armoured vehicle to pass the time until his camp was evacuated.[171] W.A. Wilson

An American soldier opens the gates to liberate *Stalag* 7B, 26 April 1945.

Moments later, POWs stream out of the camp.

and his comrades, freed near Hamburg, appropriated the local burgermeister's Mercedes convertible and drove to the reception centre in Brussels, while Dieppe prisoner John Grogan and his party drove out of the Russian zone in two cars that they later sold to brothel-keepers in France.[172] The practice, however, was not without its hazards. HMCS *Athabaskan* crewman Roy Westaway was badly injured when the car he and a few friends had commandeered ran off the road and overturned while trying to avoid a column of British tanks.[173]

Even with these minor difficulties, the service officers were uniformly pleased with the evacuation operation. Group Captain Sampson reported that the success of the air evacuation surprised even SHAEF and the army commanders, and that the prisoners were moved from the camps to England much more quickly and efficiently than they had anticipated.[174] The liaison officers, even those who encountered no Canadians, also reported that the operation was well managed, and expediently handled, and that the recovered POWs were grateful for the way in which they were brought home.[175] The POWs could hardly have asked for a quicker return to England. Regina-born bomber pilot Keith Pettigrew reached England just seventy-six hours after being liberated at Zarrentin near Hamburg. At Brunswick, Stewart Ripley, another prisoner, and the RCAF contact officer left the camp briefly to look at the surrounding area; when they returned a short time later, they found that the entire compound had been evacuated. Some POWs got home more quickly than they wanted. Maxwell Bates, an artist from Alberta who had joined the Middlesex Regiment only to be captured at the fall of France, wished there had been a slower way to return to England, so that he would have had more time to adjust to freedom.[176]

Alfred Rive was less impressed with the process. In April he complained to Norman Robertson that PWX was not working and that Canadian POWs were being returned to Britain as soon as they were liberated; he pointed out that CMHQ sometimes did not learn the identities of liberated POWs until they reached the reception camps in England.[177] The three service headquarters and the COPC accepted readily that such administrative niceties were less important than rapid evacuation, and Rive's complaint revealed a serious misunderstanding of the prevailing conditions. Delays on the continent simply to sort prisoners into national groups, register them, and inform the relevant authorities in Britain would have created serious difficulties. Quite apart from the problems of supplying POWs while they were processed, liberated POWs would have had to be confined in their camps, most likely under guard, because of their tendency to wander off whenever they believed that events were not moving quickly enough. Furthermore, many of the liberating troops were more sympathetic to the POWs' desire to return home quickly than to the administrators' desire for correct accounting. General George S. Patton visited the *stalag* at Moosburg two hours after it had been liberated and promised the inmates that they would be evacuated from the camp in two days. Dieppe POW Howard Large was handed a sheaf of forms by a British liaison officer, who said that the prisoners would be out of the camp in about two weeks. Upon hearing this, an American army sergeant offered to drive Large directly to the nearest airfield, and he was back in England within forty-eight hours.[178] Prisoners who had evaded German regulations for years were not about to be inconvenienced by Allied administrators in their moment of triumph.

TAKEN AS A WHOLE, the efforts directed towards relief and release in the European theatre were plagued by a number of flaws. Jurisdiction was confused, largely because of the number of offices that felt they had a role to play in POW superintendence. Notable in this regard was the conduct of National Defence, which apparently could not decide whether it wanted to play a wide or a limited role; the department constantly demanded that it be consulted in all POW matters, but unfailingly balked at accepting more responsibility in practice. Colonel Clarke would probably have been happy to assume the entire burden, but the unsuccessful attempt of External Affairs to shift responsibility for postwar repatriation to National Defence proved that Clarke was a minority in the department.

A marked preoccupation with committees muddied the waters further, for the committee became something of a panacea to Canadian officials. The fact that new committees might only duplicate the functions of existing bodies was of no concern; the very creation of a new committee was apparently considered by Canadian officials to be a step in the right direction. The CPW was quite sufficient to handle all POW matters, and there was no need to establish either the Inter-Service Committee or the Overseas Committee, which only succeeded in adding more layers to an already overly complex bureaucracy.

However, two positive facts must be taken into consideration. In the first place, these problems apparently had little effect on the objects of the effort, the prisoners themselves, who were almost unanimous in the belief that everything possible was being done for them. Canadian ex-prisoners who visited the High Commission in London before returning home were lavish in their praise of the Canadian government and Red Cross Society, and expressed gratitude for the fact that they had not been forgotten. As one senior officer wrote, 'our comrades from other parts of the Empire feel that Canada has looked after us in our exile exceedingly well.'[179] It is unlikely that supplies could have reached the camps more quickly or in greater quantity if Canada's organization had been the paradigm of efficiency. The most that can be said is that the problems merely multiplied the work for government departments and private agencies.

Second, most POWs left the continent feeling that they had been evacuated as efficiently and quickly as possible. There was little unnecessary waiting, thanks to the decision to postpone the administrative aspects of the evacuation until the POWs reached England, and few prisoners had reason to complain about bureaucratic red tape at a time when they were least able to be patient with it. Unlike after the First World War, few former prisoners felt that they had been left to fend for themselves by an uncaring government, or forced to wait while the bureaucratic wheels turned slowly to get them home. Whether this goodwill would be carried over into the postwar years remained to be seen.

SEVEN

A Tougher Nut:
Prisoners of the Japanese

In August 1945, in a message relayed to liberated prisoners of war in the Far East, Prime Minister Mackenzie King said that 'you have been forced to endure untold hardships, indignities, and in some cases barbarous cruelties. We have known of your sufferings and in thought have shared them with you.'[1] Some prisoners seriously doubted the degree to which Canadians shared their sufferings even in thought; one former POW recalled receiving the Prime Minister's Christmas card one year, and noted gloomily that 'we were starving and he was sitting back here eating turkey.'[2] Regardless of its sincerity, King's statement did hint at the relative impotence of Canadian officials in ameliorating the hardships of prisoners of the Japanese. The simplest tasks, such as securing the names of POWs or obtaining accurate information on camp conditions, required months of persistent prodding, and even then only partial success was realized. More complex problems, such as shipping relief supplies and securing the release of prisoners, were all but insurmountable. For the Canadian government, the problem of POWs in the Far East would bring little more than disappointment and exasperation.

I

Roughly 2000 Canadians experienced the horrors of Japanese captivity during the Second World War (see Table 2a to 2d). Most were from the Royal Rifles of Canada and the Winnipeg Grenadiers of C Force, who were taken prisoner in Hong Kong in December 1941. Much has been written about the fall of Hong Kong and the experiences of Canadian POWs in the camps at Shamshuipo and North Point in Hong Kong, and later in camps in Japan. The story of Canadian efforts to provide for these prisoners is an interesting counterpoint to that tale of suffering.

Reflecting upon his time in Japanese captivity, one prisoner recalled that 'it was as if we had known no other life, the daily routine, the inadequate food, the shabby clothes, the daily humiliations, seemed to be the real and only life we had known. All else seemed a dream and Canada just a name on some dimly remembered map.'[3] The isolation, not just from family and friends but from all normal modes of human existence, felt by these POWs was virtually complete, yet Canadian officials devoted just as much time and effort to their problems as they did to those of POWs in Europe. Indeed, Canadian officials began to contemplate the problems of providing for captives in the Far East even before the capitulation of Hong Kong. Perhaps sensing that an unfortunate fate might befall C Force, External Affairs took steps to determine whether Japan could be relied upon to observe the Geneva Convention. Despite never having ratified the agreement, Japan had a reasonably good history of treating captives humanely. The exemplary treatment of POWs during the Russo-Japanese War has already been mentioned, and the living conditions of German prisoners in Japan in the First World War, while rather harsh, were little different from conditions in camps in Germany. There had certainly been no systematic brutality and wilful neglect.[4] However, Japan's view of captives was evidently changing, and events during the invasion of Manchuria suggested that Japan was adopting a much less liberal attitude towards prisoners. In light of this fact, the Commonwealth decided that the British government should initiate discussions through Argentina, the Protecting Power designated for Commonwealth interests in the Pacific, to determine Tokyo's position.[5] In January 1942 Japan replied that it intended to observe the Geneva Convention *mutatis mutandis*; with this false sense of security, Canada approached the problems of maintaining POWs in the Far East.[6]

This task was complicated by the existence of widespread antipathy in Canada towards Japanese-Canadians and Japanese nationals living on the West Coast. As the Canadian government admitted on a number of occasions, any outbreaks of violence against these groups could jeopardize the lives of Canadian prisoners in the Far East; conversely, favourable treatment of Japanese in Canada might conceivably be used to secure better treatment for Canadians in Japanese prison camps.[7] No less than in the European theatre, the government's dealings with the enemy over POWs and internees were governed directly by considerations of reciprocity.

Such considerations were important from the beginning of Canada's effort to provide for Canadians imprisoned in the Far East. According to the Geneva Convention, the Detaining Power had to provide complete casualty lists without delay, and in January 1942 Japan undertook to transmit this information, provided that Canada reciprocated with information on Japanese nationals who had been interned. External Affairs promised that lists would be prepared promptly, and waited patiently for further developments.[8] A month later, Japan confirmed the capture of 1689 Canadians in Hong Kong (the numbers of other Commonwealth POWs were provided as well), but no names were given and there was no indication where the POWs were detained.[9] Six months later, Ottawa was still searching for such information and reminded the Japanese, in the spirit of reciprocity, that Canada had adhered to both the spirit and the letter of the Geneva Convention in the treatment of interned Japanese and expected a similar show of good faith in the transmission of lists of Hong Kong POWs.[10]

The impasse continued until April 1943, when Japan requested from Canada information on Japanese nationals who had been moved inland from the British Columbia coast. Ottawa replied that it was willing to provide such information once Japan had discharged its obligations by forwarding accurate lists of POWs. This shrewd play of the reciprocity card was effective; less than two months later, the High Commission reported to Sub-Committee A of the Imperial POW Committee (IPOWC) that External Affairs had received the names of all Canadian POWs in the Far East.[11]

The effort to secure the names of Canadians in Japanese hands had taken eighteen months, but at least it ended in success. Attempts to obtain accurate information on camp conditions were just as frustrating and much less fruitful. Furthermore, they revealed that Canadian officials, in an attempt to balance consideration for the feelings of prisoners' relatives with the need to take a firm public stand with Japan, adopted a curiously ambivalent attitude towards reports of camp conditions.

Within a month of the collapse of Hong Kong, sketchy atrocity stories began to circulate, such as an item in the *Manchester Guardian* describing the torture of POWs by the Japanese, a story that External Affairs reported 'appears to have some confirmation.' In early February, further disturbing reports reached Allied officials. The British vice consul in Macao relayed an account from an escaped Hong Kong Police official that conditions in the camps were bad, that POWs were 'dying like flies' from dysentery, and that the Japanese had refused to allow Red Cross workers access to the prisoners.[12] Days later, the British military attaché in Chungking transmitted a report by Colonel L.T. Ride, an Australian doctor who had escaped from Hong Kong shortly after the capitulation. Ride stated that doctors had been whipped and nurses raped after the collapse, and that dozens of POWs had been bayoneted to death. Camp conditions were described as deplorable, the huts lacking doors, windows, light, or sanitation, and dysentery was rampant, with no medical supplies to check it. Rations were restricted to two bowls of rice and a few vegetables each day. The report concluded that the Japanese were employing 'studied barbarism undoubtedly ... with [the] object of breaking morale.'[13] Ride's account was immediately followed by an almost identical report from a representative of the International Friends Mission, which Allied officials also judged to be reliable.[14]

In March 1942, once these stories had been confirmed as much as possible, Britain and the Dominions issued public statements about Japan's treatment of prisoners. In Ottawa, Mackenzie King read to the House of Commons a statement made by Foreign Secretary Anthony Eden in the British Parliament describing the wave of murder and rape that had followed the capitulation of Hong Kong. The Prime Minister went on to say that Canadians had not been specifically mentioned in the atrocity reports, but that there was no reason to assume they had been treated differently from other prisoners. King added that vengeance must not be taken against Japanese in Canada lest it rebound against Canadian POWs in Hong Kong.[15]

The Canadian press, however, was less moderate in its comments. Ironically, western Canadian editors reacted relatively calmly to the announcement, urging that the treatment of Japanese in Canada 'should be exemplary of the rights and principles of a Christian country.'[16] The response of central Canadian newspapers was quite different, as editors racked their brains for every imaginable term of opprobrium. The Hamilton *Spectator* managed to come up only with 'soulless pagans who have made a culture of barbarism' to describe the Japanese, an epithet that paled in comparison to remarks by the editor of the *Globe*:

> The inherent corruption has oozed to the surface. They have outdone the bestiality, the barbarism, the shocking cruelty of the Nazi Huns. In the light of their terrible deeds, ignorant and unbridled cannibals beyond the fringe of civilization are revealed ... Can there be a red-blooded human that would not give all he has, his wealth, his life if need be, to wipe this scum out, to cleanse God's green earth of its foul presence?[17]

The government's statement on atrocities certainly provided a catharsis for newspaper editors, but it evidently had some substantive impact as well; intercepted Japanese diplomatic communications suggested that the publicity had encouraged the Foreign Office in Tokyo to press the Army to allow camp inspections.[18]

This in itself did not improve the treatment of prisoners, and horror stories continued to reach Canadian officials from sources such as the British Army Aid Group (BAAG), which had been formed by Colonel Ride in China. The BAAG employed Chinese agents who travelled to Hong Kong, made contact with prisoners, and returned to Chungking with details on camp conditions.[19] Other reports came from the few escapers who got out of Hong Kong, and they confirmed the stories brought back by BAAG agents. One escaper stated in late 1942 that three-quarters of the prisoners in Shamshuipo were suffering the effects of long-term malnutrition, including wet and dry beriberi, pellagra, skin diseases of all sorts, failing eyesight, dysentery, and weight loss; diphtheria alone was reported to have killed over a hundred prisoners. A month later a report from a similar source claimed that an average of four to five prisoners died each day, and that beriberi, a disease of the heart and peripheral nerves caused by nutritional deficiency, had stricken most of the POWs.[20] These reports were at least partially confirmed by the International Committee of the Red

Cross (ICRC), which in July 1943 transmitted a list of dozens of POWs who had died, most of them from diphtheria or deficiency diseases.[21]

However, reports from the ICRC and the Protecting Power were few and far between because the Japanese were extremely reluctant to allow delegates to inspect the camps. Even after the Japanese Army consented to camp visits, the inspectors' freedom of action was severely restricted. Only two hours could be spent in any camp, and the delegate was prevented from talking with any prisoner except the appointed camp leader; that interview was monitored by Japanese officers. Many commandants refused even a supervised interview, and frequently declined to answer any questions put by the inspector.[22] Furthermore, camps were often dramatically altered before inspectors arrived. As a Winnipeg Grenadier recalled,

> Truckloads of shiny new sports equipment came zooming into camp one morning. Baseball bats, gloves, balls, boxing gloves, sports togs. Ration trucks arrived with meat and other exotic food supplies. Crews set up a baseball diamond on the parade square. We were ordered to clean up, shave, organize teams, sports squads ... The mystery was soon solved. That afternoon a party of Red Cross officials arrived to inspect the camp.

Captain Norris of the Grenadiers took the risky step of informing the inspectors that it was all a sham, and the delegates promised to lodge a protest. Once the party left, the camp staff took everything away, and guards beat Norris severely for speaking to the neutral visitors.[23]

Incidents like this explain why camp inspection reports often painted a rosy picture, but Canadian officials had some inkling that such reports were misleading. In July 1942 ICRC delegate Edouard Egle visited camps in Hong Kong, and in a newspaper account of his inspection gave 'a most cheerful picture of conditions in camps.' This assessment sounded warning bells for Canadian officials, and the High Commission in London pointed out that 'it is a strange coincidence that he [Egle] uses or is made to use precisely the same words as previous Japanese article on the subject.'[24] Six months later the incident was repeated. Red Cross delegates visited camps in Japan and reported that conditions were improving, the treatment was very good, the camps were clean and orderly, and the captors supplied drugs and recreational equipment. Reports of camps in Hong Kong were similar in tone.[25]

According to External Affairs, these accounts were too good to be true: 'It is noted particularly that Intercross [ICRC] reports emphasize effusive benevolence of Japanese authorities in terms so nearly identical as to suggest possibility of Japanese tampering with telegrams.'[26]

Because of the dubious authenticity of these reports, Canadian officials cautioned against taking them at face value. In 1942 External Affairs warned against the unauthorized publication of camp reports describing idyllic conditions, which the department insisted were in no way typical.[27] A year later, when a public statement on conditions was contemplated, both the Minister of National Defence and the Special Assistant to the Adjutant-General (SAAG), Colonel F.W. Clarke, advised that reports received from official sources in the Far East were likely over-optimistic.[28] At the same time, Mackenzie King presented to the Cabinet War Committee the latest cable from 'unofficial sources' in China containing new horror stories of camp conditions; the report originated with Lieutenant-Colonel J.H. Price, the commanding officer of the Royal Rifles of Canada, and the Prime Minister stressed that it should be taken seriously.[29]

In light of such stories and the doubts cast on neutral reports, Allied governments began to contemplate a more extensive publicity campaign on atrocities in the hopes of shaming the Japanese government into improving camp conditions. The matter came before the Cabinet War Committee, but King and Minister of National Defence for Air C.G. Power were dubious; both wondered whether it would lead to anything but retaliation against Allied POWs.[30] For Power, the decision must have been especially agonizing; his son had been wounded and captured in Hong Kong while serving with the Royal Rifles of Canada, so he had a special reason to be sensitive to the impact on Canadian POWs of any publicity campaign. An interdepartmental committee took a contrary position, however. Stating that conditions for some POWs could hardly be made worse, the committee agreed that Canada should join the publicity campaign; furthermore, a government statement of facts would be more comforting to next of kin than the present rumours.[31] With the British and American governments already having decided to participate in the campaign, the Canadian government too elected to take part.

The campaign in Canada began with a statement by the Prime Minister before the House of Commons.[32] 'The evidence of Japanese brutality and organized sadism,' said King, 'is so horrible and over-whelming as to be almost incredible.' As an example, he cited the case of the *Lisbon Maru*, a freighter in which hundreds of Allied POWs died when the vessel was torpedoed and the Japanese sealed the hatches, forcing the prisoners to go down with the ship. While stressing that conditions for Canadian prisoners were perhaps a little better than for British or American POWs, he insisted that Canadians were suffering terribly, in large part because of Tokyo's intransigence regarding relief shipments. King concluded with the mutual hostages theme by point-ing out that Japan's conduct stood in marked contrast to the treatment of Japanese nationals in Canada.

The conduct of the Canadian government thus far had been consis-tent with the information available to it; in official statements, the posi-tive neutral reports were downplayed in favour of the far more accurate accounts from unofficial sources. However, in the late summer of 1944 Canada's position changed. Perhaps in a misguided attempt to comfort the families of POWs in the Far East, Canadian authorities elected to reproduce the substance of the ICRC accounts for public consumption. Doubtless they believed it advisable to put at ease the minds of Canadians who had relatives in Japanese camps, but they can only have succeeded in confusing next of kin or, worse, falsely raising their hopes by suggesting that conditions in the camps were not so bad after all.

Indeed, descriptions of camp conditions printed in the Wartime Information Board's *Facts and Figures Weekly* were so glowing that they might have been written by the Japanese. A camp at Osaka was described as having new wooden barracks with electric lighting, run-ning water, bedding, and washing facilities, and rations that included meat, fish, potatoes, and sweets. Prisoners were allowed to go on hikes when they were not at work, and could also cultivate vegetable gardens and raise rabbits. A week later, a new camp at Niigata was reported to be in a healthy district; food and clothing supplies were adequate, and the conditions had brought 'considerable improvement' in the prison-ers' health.[33] Then, just a month after this report was published, the Canadian government lent its support to another publicity campaign detailing Japanese atrocities against POWs.[34]

Such contradictions characterized the government's conduct for the rest of the war. By 1945 the Allies had decided on full and immediate disclosure of all reports of the maltreatment of Allied POWs.[35] However, as late as August 1945, after receiving photographs ostensibly taken at a camp in Taiwan showing sugar-beet harvesting, cattle farming, and fowl raising by prisoners, Canadian officials showed an astonishing willingness to pass on these patent falsehoods. Alfred Rive of External Affairs even suggested making copies of the photos available to the Wartime Information Board, the Canadian Red Cross, and the Canadian POW Relatives Association.[36]

As the government must have known, the reality of life in Osaka, Niigata, and all the other camps run by the Japanese was rather different. The prisoners received no fresh beef or poultry, although occasionally a porpoise carcass or chunk of whale meat, usually well picked over and far from fresh, was doled out. POWs who wanted fresh meat had to catch their own; some trapped doves to eat, while others killed any dogs, cats, snakes, or rats they could catch. Private Bill Savage of the Winnipeg Grenadiers passed a swamp every day on his way to work at a Japanese coal mine; he took to stuffing his pockets with as many frogs as he could find, then roasted and ate them during the day. Another prisoner calculated that his meat ration averaged roughly one teaspoon a month.[37] Camps for officers often had small vegetable gardens, but other ranks had neither the time nor the energy for gardening and had to make do with what the Japanese provided. This usually consisted of a truckload of weeds, flowers, and other unidentifiable greens, which was dumped in the compound and mixed by the prisoners into a soup known as Green Horror. The other staples of the prisoners' diet were rice (which sometimes tasted strongly of gasoline because of the barrels in which it had been cooked), sorghum, and radish soup; seaweed, fish heads, and grasshoppers were rare luxuries. Despite the disgusting offerings, POWs were so desperate for food that they occasionally fainted before meals, simply because of the excitement and anticipation of eating.[38]

On these short rations the prisoners were expected to labour for the Japanese war effort. Contrary to the reports in *Facts and Figures Weekly*, the work to which Canadian prisoners were put was so arduous that few of them could have managed a hike, even had it been offered. POWs in Hong Kong were put to work levelling hills and mixing concrete to extend the runway at Kai Tak airfield, and later dug storage tunnels for gasoline and ammunition in the mountains surrounding the city; the Japanese had no compunction about forcing POWs to work on military projects, although this was strictly prohibited by the Geneva Convention.[39] In 1943, when drafts of Canadian prisoners began moving from Hong Kong to Japan, they found the labour conditions there to be just as brutal. Some men went to coal mines, others to shipyards or steel mills. At Niigata, POWs were put to work moving tons of coal each day or hauling 100-pound acetylene tanks six or seven miles to the steel mill.[40] Regardless of the tasks, the prisoners all faced the same long hours and gruelling work. They typically worked for about fourteen hours a day, fourteen days in a row, and then were granted a day of rest; getting a day off for sickness was discouraged because prisoners who did no useful work because of illness received no rations. Weakened by disease and lack of food, many prisoners were simply unable to carry on the struggle; once they lost the will to live, they died in a matter of days.[41]

Nor were the camps themselves as hospitable as the reports suggested. North Point camp in Hong Kong had been built in 1937 as a detention centre for refugees from mainland China, but had been badly damaged in the fighting in 1941. When the Canadian POWs were first transferred there, they discovered that most of the pipes and fixtures had been looted and the floors were covered with horse carcasses and manure, refuse from the veterinary hospital that the Japanese had established in the compound. Shamshuipo was little better. A military barracks that housed C Force when it reached Hong Kong, it too had been stripped bare, and even the wooden door and window frames had been taken. Conditions in Hong Kong eventually improved, but only slightly; Shamshuipo, for example, had no electricity from September 1944 until the end of the war.[42]

Many of the prisoners who went to Japan did not believe that conditions could be any worse there but they were mistaken, for living conditions in the labour camps were just as primitive. The barracks consisted of long huts, often with earthen floors, in which the POWs slept on low wooden platforms; rush mats were usually placed on the sleeping platforms, but a blanket was a rare commodity. The prisoners' lot was made more miserable by bitter Japanese winters. Bob Manchester of the Winnipeg Grenadiers recalled that prisoners froze to death at

Niigata because they were issued only grass capes to keep out the winter cold. In another camp, a number of POWs were killed when the roof of their flimsy hut collapsed under the weight of snow.[43]

That death was a constant presence in the camps is obvious from a week's entries in a diary kept by Sergeant Lance Ross of the Royal Rifles while a prisoner in Hong Kong in 1942:

Sept. 7th Another man died. 4 Japanese fighter planes here.

Sept. 8th 7 British soldiers escaped but they were caught –
5 were shot.

Sept. 9th C.R. died today. Cause of death, Dakkina Itch.
Germans haven't got Stalingrad yet.

Sept. 10th Another man died. Half have dysentery or beri-beri.
We will all die soon.

Sept. 11th 100 degrees in the shade. More men falling sick every day.

Sept. 12th Another died today; we wrapped him in a sheet,
buried him across the road.

Sept. 14th Another death in my platoon, pneumonia.[44]

Ed Horton, a Canadian pilot captured at the fall of Java, recalled seeing corpses piled up like cordwood at his camp at Moji; Japanese carpenters had been assigned to make cremation boxes for the bodies, but they quickly fell behind in their work.[45] As the months dragged on, the line between life and death became more indistinct; for many men, it was easier to die than to live. When the Japanese asked for volunteers to make radio broadcasts to North America for propaganda purposes, George Soper put his name forward, and his carefully scripted broadcast captured the anguish felt by countless prisoners of the Japanese. He said, innocently enough, how much he wanted to be with his father. His captors could not have known that Soper's father had died when he was four years old.[46]

Such grim impressions are confirmed time and time again by statistical evidence. Winnipeg Grenadier Frank Martyn recorded in his diary the deaths of members of his regiment in Hong Kong, including 17 in October and 11 in November 1942, while C Force Senior Medical Officer Dr. John Crawford's monthly returns of sick prisoners in Hong Kong note that 128 men died of disease in Shamshuipo and North Point camps.[47] Tropical illnesses were rife, and the sketchy statistics included in unofficial reports received in 1942 proved to be very accurate. In January 1945, Sub-Committee A of the Imperial POW Committee received a lengthy and sobering memorandum on the prevalence of certain tropical diseases among POWs in the Far East, a memorandum that postwar medical examinations would prove to be grossly under-stated. Of 100 Hong Kong POWs examined after their liberation, nearly three-quarters had suffered from beriberi and experienced serious sensory disorders as a consequence.[48] They were the lucky ones; 290 of the Canadians captured by the Japanese never came home.[49]

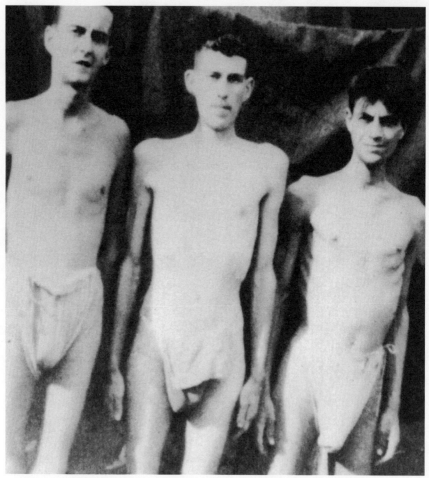

The physical effects of years of maltreatment show on three members of the Royal Rifles of Canada.

II

Fortunately, the Canadian government's ambivalent attitude towards reports of camp conditions did not prevent it from making great efforts to ship the relief supplies that POWs so desperately needed. In late 1941 Britain asked the ICRC to secure Japanese approval for the shipment of relief supplies to Commonwealth prisoners (in return for reciprocal privileges for Japanese in Canada, an External Affairs cable hastened to add), a request that started a flurry of preparations.[50] In January 1942, at a meeting of the national Red Cross societies, the Foreign Office, and the War Office, Canada was asked to help provide 50,000 Red Cross parcels weekly to feed POWs in the Far East.[51] Clarke met with representatives of the Canadian and American Red Cross societies and the State Department to discuss the details, and all agreed that the Americans should try to secure a relief ship to ferry supplies to Japan, Hong Kong, and Shanghai.[52]

Despite this decision, the relief effort was not coordinated, and Allied officials began formulating a variety of sometimes conflicting schemes, most of which came to nothing and only served to waste time and energy. Immediately upon learning of the ICRC approach to the Japanese, the American Red Cross chartered the Swedish ship *Kanangoora*, berthed at San Francisco, and loaded it with a million dollars worth of American and Canadian supplies. However, the Red Cross had neglected to ensure that Japan would provide a safe-conduct pass for the ship, and the *Kanangoora* waited in San Francisco while negotiations proceeded. Finally, in August 1942 Japan announced that a safe-conduct pass would not be granted; the American Red Cross charter was cancelled and the ship was unloaded.[53]

At the same time, British authorities directed their efforts towards using the Vatican to secure permission to ship relief supplies. Canada supported this approach, and initiated discussions with the Apostolic Delegate in Ottawa, intending to grant the delegate permission to work for Japanese internees in Canada in exchange for reciprocal privileges in the Far East. This attempt was no more successful than the *Kanangoora* debacle, however. By June 1942, with nothing to show for considerable effort, Britain concluded that the Vatican was of no use as a channel for relief supplies.[54]

The most promising of these early schemes was a plan to load supplies on the Swedish vessel *Gripsholm*, which was due to exchange Japanese and American diplomats in the summer of 1942. The Canadian and American governments decided to provide some 300 tons of food, clothing, tobacco, and medical supplies, but even this positive achievement drew criticism from Britain, for typical reasons: the Foreign Office considered that it involved preferential treatment for one group of Commonwealth POWs.[55] Canada declined to reconsider her decision, as Britain requested, and the *Gripsholm* left New York in June 1942, arriving in Japan via Lourenço Marques (now Maputo, in Mozambique) in August. The supplies reached only the Philippines and Shanghai, because Japan refused to allow the *Gripsholm* into Hong Kong or Singapore.[56] In 1943 a second small load of relief supplies was transported when the *Gripsholm* made another voyage to exchange Japanese and Allied civilians.

One of the few letters received by Captain Lionel Hurd while a prisoner in Hong Kong. Part of a shipment carried on the *Gripsholm*, the letter reached him nineteen months after it was mailed.

In September 1942 the Allies received their first big break, when Japan agreed in principle to accept shipments of clothing and medical supplies via the ICRC.[57] It was now imperative to establish a means of coordination of the sort that had been lacking in the spring. To this end, the Canadian government proposed to invite representatives of the American and British Red Cross to Ottawa to reach a 'general understanding of the magnitude of the problem' of Far East relief. The Foreign Office reacted positively to the idea, having no desire to repeat the disturbing lack of coordination of the previous spring.[58]

Gradually the Commonwealth's preferred scheme for Far East relief emerged. A committee, based in Washington and including representatives of the governments of the United States, Canada, Britain, Australia, India, and the Netherlands, as well as the Canadian, American, and British Red Cross societies, would arrange for the distribution of relief on a collective basis, with Canada and the United States assuming full responsibility for assembling shipments to all Allied POWs in the Pacific. In return, Britain would accept responsibility for servicing all Allied POWs in Europe. To iron out the details, the interested parties should meet in Ottawa.[59]

The American response, both to the proposed Ottawa meeting and to the Commonwealth's draft relief scheme, was unenthusiastic. Breckinridge Long of the State Department supported the principle behind the plan but was not optimistic about its chances in practice; some months earlier he had recorded in his diary that relief efforts were in vain and strictly 'for the record,' as Japan would never agree to them.[60] American officials were willing to discuss the matter only informally with Clarke, although they agreed to consider his proposal that two Allied ships be turned over to the ICRC; these ships would be loaded with relief supplies and sailed to Lourenço Marques, where they would be taken over by Japanese crews for the voyage to Japan. Long said that the first step was to secure the approval of the Admiralty and the Navy Department, and then the opinion of Japan would have to be obtained. If all were favourable, the United States might then consider the Ottawa meeting as a means to finalize these plans.[61]

Support for the plan came relatively quickly. The British Shipping Mission in Washington allowed that the difficulties inherent in the scheme were not insurmountable, while the Canadian defence departments (Air, Army, and Naval Services) endorsed it as well. Even Breckinridge Long seems to have had a slight change of heart, and now gave more active support to the plan.[62] The Admiralty and the British

Ministry of War Transport raised serious objections, however. The Admiralty was concerned over security at Lourenço Marques, while War Transport worried about setting a precedent that might eventually weaken the war effort; the ministry feared that the Axis might refuse to accept relief unless it was carried on Allied ships. British naval officials preferred locating two neutral ships for the same journey.[63]

Progress on relief shipments was so slow that Canadian officials suggested, as an interim solution, transferring money to neutral delegates in the Far East to purchase supplies for POWs locally. This option was first suggested in early 1942, but nothing was achieved until the end of the year, when Canadian POWs were given ten yen each as a Christmas gift from the government.[64] Predictably, the British government raised strident protests against the move. 'We had thought,' wrote the War Office, 'that it was agreed between various members of the British Commonwealth that we should seek to avoid discrimination in treatment between prisoners from various parts of the Commonwealth.' The POWs, in contrast, appreciated the gesture. One rifleman dissipated his Christmas gift in two hours shooting craps, but considered it money well spent because it took his mind off his physical agonies for a short period.[65]

Within a month, the controversy over money payments recurred. After complaining strongly about the failure of the ICRC to make reasonable progress for POWs in the Far East (a complaint that the War Office and the Foreign Office called 'typically over-stated' and a 'typical piece of selfishness on the part of Canada'[66]), George Ignatieff of the High Commission raised the subject of cash payments before Sub-Committee A. Ignatieff insisted that the neutral inspection reports were over-optimistic and that urgent action was required before conditions worsened. To address the situation, Canada intended to authorize payments to the Protecting Power, beginning at $5 per month for privates, to be used to purchase relief supplies locally. The chairman, the representative of the Exchequer, and the Australian delegate all deplored this action, insisting that the payments could create friction between prisoners. Under Canadian pressure, however, the committee agreed to release £10,000 from a fund for the relief of civilians to be used to aid all POWs in Hong Kong.[67]

The provision of funds was clearly a divisive issue, so it was fortunate that plans for shipping relief supplies were progressing. In January 1943 Commonwealth officials translated the current plan, to carry aid shipments on neutral ships, into a draft proposal for transmission to Japan by the Allies. That draft began by stressing the assumption that Japan had no desire to penalize interned Allied nationals, and went on to recall Japan's earlier willingness to observe the Geneva Convention. It then proposed that the two neutral ships would return to North America carrying supplies for interned Japanese nationals in Canada and the United States.[68]

At this point, the lack of coordination between Allies again created problems. On 18 February 1943, George Brandt of the State Department informed the Canadian minister in Washington, Leighton McCarthy, that the American Red Cross had concocted a plan to charter a vessel and ship relief supplies from an American port; the American society had asked the State Department to submit this offer to the ICRC. Brandt apologized for the fact that the plan had apparently come out of nowhere, but insisted that the State Department could not refuse to transmit it, in view of the number of prominent Americans behind it.[69] The many months of trying to persuade the United States that relief shipments should be coordinated had evidently been in vain.

Canada's reaction to the new development, that the Commonwealth had no alternative but to drop its own plan for now and support the American Red Cross scheme, was mild compared with Britain's.[70] Recalling the embarrassment of the failed *Kanangoora* scheme of the previous year, the British minister in Washington savaged the United States for such precipitate action, which hindered all the Allies, and insisted that 'our scheme does at least put the horse before the cart.' The Foreign Office drafted a letter of complaint to the United States government, and asked that McCarthy be authorized to lend his support to it.[71]

While the Canadian government regretted the American action, it was reluctant to back any strident British protest.[72] Ralston's assistant deputy minister opined that Canada might be able to benefit from the new development by taking a major part in both plans; Canada must obviously be a prime actor in any Commonwealth approach, but in all likelihood the Canadian Red Cross could also join the American society's plan on a fifty-fifty basis. There were two other pressing reasons for not criticizing American action too strongly: such criticism might imperil future Canadian-American relations vis-à-vis Far East relief; and Canadian POWs might actually secure a greater per capita allotment of relief under the American than under the Commonwealth plan. In the end, National Defence advised against joining Britain's protest while External Affairs informed the State Department that Canada 'expect[ed] and/or accept[ed]' equal participation in the American Red Cross plan.[73]

Despite the fact that these recommendations ran counter to the principle of distribution according to need, which the Cabinet War Committee had embraced just a week earlier, they were taken up as the government's position; the British protest went ahead without Canadian support, External Affairs informing Leighton McCarthy that 'no breath need be wasted on recriminations, expressed or implied.'[74] The government's decision was significant in many ways. In the first place, it revealed that Canada's commitment to the pooling principle was hardly firm, and that the desirability of any plan would in part be determined by the amount of relief it provided to Canadian prisoners. Sending one ship of supplies would be preferable to sending two ships if Canadians got a greater share of that one ship's load. Furthermore, the decision reflected Canada's willingness to exploit her long-cherished role as linchpin between Britain and the United States. National Defence admitted quite candidly that Canada could keep one foot in each camp, wait on events, and then support whichever plan offered the best advantages. As Ralston's deputy put it, Canada could play an 'independent, can't lose role.'

As it turned out, the American Red Cross scheme was a non-starter. By April 1943, Japan had still not replied to the proposal, and the society was beginning to see the wisdom of closer cooperation between Allies, particularly between the United States and Canada. Towards the end of the month, the American Red Cross single-ship scheme was finally declared a dead letter, and was replaced by a much more promising but in some ways more far-fetched plan.[75] The possibility of shipping supplies via the Soviet Union had been broached earlier in 1943, and in April Japan agreed to accept relief shipments either overland through Asia, or through Vladivostok. When the Soviets agreed in principle to the plan, all that remained was to secure Japanese approval.[76]

Or so it appeared. However, lack of coordination between the Allies continued to plague the relief effort. Britain made known a preference for small loads to be shipped via Russia at regular intervals, while the United States favoured occasional large shipments; External Affairs instructed Canada's minister in the Soviet Union, Dana Wilgress, to support the American position.[77] With no inter-Allied committee to settle the disagreement, Britain took the regrettable step of making a separate appeal to the Soviets for small, regular shipments of essential drugs and food concentrates. To this overture Canada reacted cautiously. External Affairs reiterated its support for the American position, and also stated that it was premature to discuss the contents of relief shipments until a quantity had been agreed upon.[78]

The disagreement over shipment size seemed only to divide efforts further. With Britain and the United States now apparently putting forward separate plans to the Soviets, Canadian officials began to express concern that the American plan might have been altered to benefit only American prisoners. These concerns surely grew out of the knowledge that the Soviets had recently approved Britain's plan to ship drugs and food concentrates, not to all Allied prisoners but to British subjects.[79] It was now more important than ever that the Allies establish a means of coordination so that their efforts did not cancel each other.

The dispute over load size forced the Foreign Office to admit that 'some confusion and misunderstanding [existed] because of a certain lack of proper coordination,' and Britain responded enthusiastically to a Canadian proposal for discussions in Washington between representatives of the American, Canadian, and British Red Cross societies, the British Embassy, the Canadian Legation, the State Department, and the Dutch government.[80] Once again, the Americans were unenthusiastic about Canada's plan. Still insisting that there was no point in conferring until Japan's reply had been received, the State Department suggested that the Washington meeting be confined to delegates of the three Red Cross societies.[81] Commonwealth officials made every effort to change the mind of the State Department, but as the British ambassador in Washington wrote, 'it would be almost impossible to displace Long by argument from his position that a permanent organization is not necessary until the means of transport for supplies to the Far East exist.'[82]

While the bickering over a central organization continued, the Allies drifted further apart in their views of the Far East relief problem. Britain and the United States now disagreed on the two most important aspects of the problem, the method of distribution and the contents of parcels. Britain believed that shipments consisting entirely of food and medicine should be off-loaded at various points for the benefit of all Allied POWs. The United States, on the other hand, wanted to send supplies only to those camps that held American prisoners, and planned to include clothes, cigarettes, books, and next-of-kin parcels in the shipments. The American position was in fact producing cracks within the Commonwealth. Faced with the prospect of American supplies for American prisoners, the Australian government decided that it too would make a separate approach to the Soviets, asking to be associated with any American plan that was worked out.[83]

In Clarke's view, the situation was becoming dire and could be addressed only by the formation of an inter-Allied committee. He believed that a meeting of Red Cross societies in Washington without government involvement might in fact delay this goal, and was therefore undesirable. Once again, however, Clarke's goal eluded him, and in September representatives of the three societies met in Washington; no government officials took part in the meetings.[84] The delegates discussed a wide range of topics, but the conference in fact achieved little of substance. The Red Cross officials shied away from coming to a general agreement on the relief operation, and reached an accord only on the supplies to be shipped via Vladivostok. For that route, the conference agreed upon a number of principles: the Canadian and American societies would pack parcels on a fifty-fifty basis; food would be the first priority, given that drugs had been shipped on recent exchange ships; and the standard European food parcel should be used, subject to minor adjustments in content.[85] No attempt was made to turn these provisions into general principles for the relief operation; the assumption was that similar conferences would be held to decide the specifics of each separate shipment as necessary. On other important matters, the conference was just as vague. The delegates agreed that distribution of relief supplies should be according to need, but watered this down with the statement that American POWs would get American parcels and Commonwealth prisoners would get Canadian parcels wherever possible. On the necessity of taking steps to pressure the

Japanese into discharging their obligations under the Geneva Convention, the delegates said only that they were not convinced such action was yet called for.

Still, the accord regarding the Vladivostok route was a small victory, especially as the Soviets had agreed to accept 1500 tons of supplies monthly, to be stockpiled at Vladivostok until the arrangements were finalized.[86] By early October, the United States had dispatched the first load of supplies from Portland, Oregon, to the Soviet Union; for subsequent shipments to Vladivostok, the Canadian and American Red Cross societies would each supply half of the parcels, which would be distributed according to need.[87] In early November, however, Soviet authorities requested that shipments be halted temporarily, pending confirmation that Japan would accept the supplies. Loads remaining at Portland, including 120,000 Canadian Red Cross parcels, would be accepted at Vladivostok, but nothing further would be transported to Oregon at present. This meant that approximately 3000 tons of supplies would be available at Vladivostok: 100 tons of medical supplies, 250 tons of clothing, and 2750 tons of food (the 120,000 Canadian parcels, in addition to 90,000 American parcels sent with the first shipment).[88]

Perhaps because of the Allies' most recent campaign detailing Japanese atrocities, the negotiations regarding the onward shipment of relief from Vladivostok progressed maddeningly slowly. At the same time, Canadian officials were having difficulty remaining apprised of the current state of negotiations, for Canada's attempts to play the 'independent, can't lose role' were beginning to create problems: in trying to keep irons in both the American and the British fires, Canada was in danger of being left out of both. It was obvious that the United States was quite willing to go ahead with its own plans without consulting anyone, least of all Canada; now Britain, perhaps growing weary of Canada's insistence on working within both the American and the Commonwealth spheres regardless of the contradictions this might entail, appeared willing to do the same. Morley Scott feared as much, and presented his concerns in a memorandum to High Commissioner Vincent Massey. Scott foresaw a situation in which Britain avoided Canada altogether in favour of direct discussions with the United States; any Commonwealth plan would be submitted to the Dominions only after American concurrence had been obtained. Furthermore,

Scott pointed out that the locus of POW activity was now firmly in Washington. Both the War Office's Directorate of POWs and the British Red Cross had permanent representatives in Washington, and all operational matters concerning POWs were referred to the Combined Chiefs of Staff there. Because of these developments, Scott feared that Canada would be left out in the cold: 'Whatever rules are laid down by Canada [regarding consultation on matters affecting Canada], I suspect that if they impede free conversation on Allied POW matters between Washington and London they will be broken, and when not broken, evaded.'[89]

Just as Scott feared, negotiations for the Vladivostok route continued with little Canadian input. By October 1944, Japan had agreed to send a ship to the port of Nakhodka to collect one load of relief supplies; future loads might be carried overland via Manchuria or from the port at Petropavlovsk. Canada's involvement in the operation, aside from the supplies already at Vladivostok, was confined to accepting forty-one tons of books and tea for distribution to Japanese internees in Canada.[90]

On 3 November 1944, a Japanese steamer docked at Nakhodka and loaded just over 2000 tons of relief supplies. Fifty tons were allotted to prisoners in Chosen and 100 tons to camps in Manchuria; the remainder was to be unloaded at Kobe for distribution to camps in Tokyo, Osaka, Hakodate, Zentsuji, and Fukuoka. With this minor success, Colonel Clarke was quick to inquire about the likelihood of future shipments, and in December 1944 a further 115,000 Canadian Red Cross parcels were readied for transport to Portland in case another opportunity presented itself.[91] In April 1945 the Soviets offered to dispatch a ship to a United States Pacific port to be loaded with 1500 tons of relief supplies, but days later this avenue too was closed off. On 1 April 1945, an American submarine torpedoed a Japanese freighter carrying a portion of the Nakhodka relief supplies for distribution in the southern Pacific. With this, Japanese authorities refused to consider the shipment of further relief supplies, despite continued efforts by the Allies to persuade them otherwise.[92]

FOR ALL OF THE ADMINISTRATIVE EFFORT and frustration, then, the relief effort had exceedingly disappointing results. The exchange voyages carried roughly 150,000 Red Cross parcels, while the Nakhodka operation brought in another 75,000, besides a limited quantity of medicine and clothing.[93] Supplies acquired locally by Red Cross representatives for distribution to POWs rounded out the results. The overall totals were small enough, but the amount of aid that actually reached the prisoners was less still. Many of the parcels found their way into Japanese hands, where they were either used or traded on the black market. Many were apparently sold quite openly in Kowloon shops. The majority, however, were likely just left to rot. A reporter who entered Hong Kong after the war reported finding stacks of Red Cross parcels, some of which had been there for up to two years.[94]

Regular issues of parcels were few and far between, and it was usually senseless for prisoners to demand that parcels be distributed. At Moji, when the prisoners demanded a share of 350 Red Cross parcels that arrived at Christmas, the Japanese responded, not by confiscating the parcels but by forcing the prisoners to eat the entire shipment within twenty-four hours and return all empty containers, under threat of dire punishment. Prisoners were heartbroken at having to destroy what they could not eat.[95] Winnipeg Grenadier Tom Forsyth recorded the receipt of six and one-seventh Red Cross parcels throughout the war; a personal parcel mailed by his parents in 1941 reached Forsyth after he had returned to Winnipeg in 1945.[96] Grenadier Red Windsor received a total of three parcels, the last of which was shared among eight prisoners; another soldier had to share the last of his four parcels with seventeen other POWs. In Fukuoka camp, two parcels were once divided among the sixty occupants of one hut.[97] Nevertheless, the parcels that arrived had a psychological impact perhaps greater than the physical. The comments of a Canadian doctor imprisoned in Hong Kong are revealing: 'God Bless the Red Cross! They helped in a small way, to nourish starving men but they represented something as important as food: hope. They came from home – we were not entirely cut off, but had friends who cared and could help us. The outlook never seemed quite as black again.'[98]

III

The campaign to supply relief was a major disappointment, if not to the prisoners then at least to officials in Canada, and the campaign to secure the release of prisoners was scarcely less so. Unlike in Europe, where escape was dangerous but promised a slim chance of success, escape was not a realistic option for most prisoners of the Japanese. Nor did repatriation on medical grounds give reason for greater hope, despite prolonged efforts by Allied administrators. For Canadian POWs in the Far East, freedom would come only with death or the end of the war.

Although it was obviously out of the question for prisoners who had been transferred to Japan, escape from the camps in Hong Kong was not impossible. A number of men (mostly British and Australian) were able to get beyond the barbed wire, onto the mainland, and into the hands of friendly Chinese natives or BAAG operatives. However, the odds against success were enormous. Unlike in Europe, the fleeing POW could not hope to blend in with the population, nor could he count on catching convenient trains towards neutral territory. An escape meant attempting to link up with sympathetic natives and then travelling hundreds of miles northward to meet friendly forces in Nationalist China.

Furthermore, the Nazi reaction to escape was tame compared with that of the Japanese. In response to a number of successful breakouts in the months following the capitulation of Hong Kong, Japanese officials forced all POWs to sign affidavits swearing that they would not attempt to escape. All the Canadian prisoners eventually signed the oaths, albeit under protest, but this did not stop four Winnipeg Grenadiers from making an attempt. On the night of 19 August 1942, Sergeant John Payne, Corporal George Brezinski, Corporal P.J. Ellis, and Private J.H. Adams purloined a ladder and climbed out of Shamshuipo camp. They planned to steal a boat, sail to the mainland, and make their way towards Chiang Kai-Shek's forces, but they got no further than the harbour. The four were recaptured and summarily executed, and Japanese authorities later divided the remaining Canadians into groups of five, letting it be known that collective punishment would be inflicted upon the entire group if one of its members tried to escape.[99] Two Canadian airmen who had been taken prisoner in Java met a similar fate. Warrant Officers Howard Low of Vancouver and Russell Smith of Kamsack, Saskatchewan, escaped from a camp in Batavia and made their way to a nearby airfield, where they hoped to steal a Japanese aircraft. They located a suitable aircraft and had managed to start one engine when they were discovered and recaptured. Both were executed the same day.[100]

Since escape was, for all intents and purposes, impossible for Canadian POWs, repatriation was their only hope of returning home before the end of hostilities, but it too was a vain one. In January 1942 rumours ran rife in the POW camps in Hong Kong that Canadian prisoners would be exchanged for Japanese nationals from the west coast of North America, or for their fishing vessels, but the rumours proved groundless.[101] Later the United States and Britain made a number of separate and unsuccessful proposals to Japan for the exchange of sick and wounded POWs. In May 1944 American, Canadian, and British officials arrived at a common repatriation plan: a series of continuing exchanges at Bikini until all military repatriables were released, after which civilians would be turned over. To make the plan more appealing, the Allies agreed to free all interned Japanese civilians who wished to return home.[102]

This common front was soon breached, however. In June 1944 the United States announced its intention to offer Japan an exchange of the isolated garrisons on Wake, Wotje, Mili, Maloelap, Jaluit, Ocean, and Nauru islands for 25,000 American POWs from Bataan, Corregidor, Guam, Wake, and Tientsin.[103] Realizing that it might be difficult to dissuade the United States from making the proposal, the British War Cabinet decided to ask the Americans to expand it to embrace all Allied POWs on a proportionate basis. If that failed, the Commonwealth would devise a similar exchange plan to present to Japan, involving Commonwealth sick and wounded prisoners for an equal number of Japanese civilians, or all Commonwealth POWs for surrounded Japanese garrisons in New Guinea and the southwestern Pacific.[104]

In September the United States announced another unilateral approach, the exchange of 25,000 Japanese civilians captured on Saipan for an equal number of American, Latin American, and Canadian POWs and civilians.[105] Canada joined Britain's protest that all exchanges should be negotiated collectively by the Allies, and the Foreign Office considered the time ripe for putting forward one of the schemes formulated in July.[106] With this prospect, Canada found itself caught in the middle. External Affairs considered requesting that Canada be dropped from the American scheme, but the government decided to try again the 'independent, can't lose role' and remain a part of both.[107]

As it happened, Canada was deprived of the opportunity to see whether the double game would work. In November the Americans rejected the Commonwealth's idea of an exchange of POWs for the New Guinea garrison, stating that such a plan would free up some of the best Japanese troops in the Pacific. To soothe Commonwealth feelings, the Americans agreed to include other Allied prisoners in its original scheme, but not on a proportionate basis. Reluctantly, the British government accepted the plan, though still lamenting the way that events had transpired.[108] In the end, all the agonizing was fruitless, as no military exchange was ever achieved. This was partly due to the fact that the Allies had so few Japanese POWs to offer in exchange, but perhaps more to the fact that Japan probably did not want them back in any case. As the government in Tokyo said, 'our Army maintains the position that Japanese prisoners of war do not exist.'[109]

There was considerably more success in the repatriation of civilians, although Canada played little role in either of the exchange operations. In May 1942 External Affairs learned from the British minister in Berne that Japan had decided to release a number of Canadians; these individuals, including Herbert Norman and the rest of the Canadian diplomatic staff in Tokyo, were freed at Lourenço Marques in July 1942.[110] In October 1943 another civilian exchange occurred, this one at Mormugao in the Portuguese Indies; included in the 1500 Allied nationals were 221 Canadians, mostly clerics and businessmen and their families. Also in this group were Kay Christie and Maye Waters, two Royal Canadian Army Medical Corps nurses who had been captured at the fall of Hong Kong.[111] A third civilian exchange, which was discussed in 1944, came to nothing.

After the collapse of these talks, Margaret Meagher of External Affairs began considering the possibility of arranging a direct exchange with Japan; mindful of the relative care with which Canada had treated Japanese evacuated from British Columbia, Meagher believed that

Tokyo would find no reason to refuse a direct exchange with Canada.[112] Alfred Rive was keen on the idea, but other members of the department were not so enthusiastic. Morley Scott expressed doubts about the scheme, and did not think that Canada would gain much from the effort: 'A lot of our folk don't want to come back, nor do we much care if we get them back; one of our chief aims is to get rid of a boatload of Japanese.' Scott also believed that the plan would cause problems with Britain and the United States, both of which had carefully included Canada in previous exchange schemes they had formulated. In view of this, Scott believed that the two countries would not take kindly to being left out of a Canadian plan.[113] Perhaps because of the points Scott raised, Under-Secretary of State for External Affairs Norman Robertson too declared against a separate Canadian proposal, and it was never carried through.[114]

WITH LITTLE HOPE of successful repatriations while hostilities were in progress, Allied officials might have devoted considerable effort to the problems of evacuating POWs after the war. However, even with the European example to work from, planning for the return of prisoners at the end of hostilities in the Pacific was incomplete at best. The general evacuation scheme presented by the War Office in the winter of 1942 (giving Canada responsibility for the repatriation of all Commonwealth personnel in China) received approval from Sub-Committee A, but all delegates admitted that operational considerations demanded that it be expanded to include other Allies, especially the United States.[115] Despite this very wise decision, evidently nothing was done. In September 1944 External Affairs inquired of Leighton McCarthy whether the Americans had addressed the evacuation question yet. McCarthy replied that the United States had appointed a committee to study the problem, but no report had been produced. All he could say was that the planning was likely to be a cooperative effort between the United States and the Commonwealth.[116]

Six months passed, and again External Affairs wondered what action was being taken. Finally in April 1945, after the American invasion of Okinawa, the last stepping-stone to Japan, Britain's War Cabinet decided that the time was ripe to make plans for the liberation of POWs in the Far East.[117] The British Chiefs of Staff advised that the protection, maintenance, and evacuation of all POWs be left to the commanders of forward units. Each Commonwealth government would assemble statistics on its prisoners in the Far East; British authorities would collate these statistics and prepare to transmit to forward commanders information on the estimated requirements of all Commonwealth POWs.[118] These arrangements drew protests from External Affairs and the Army, both of which believed that Canada would do better to make her own arrangements (presumably with the Americans), since she was closer to the affected areas than Britain.[119]

Canada's concerns were apparently ignored, for a draft plan for the handling of recovered POWs made no mention of Canadian involvement in the operation. This plan envisaged that Recovered Allied POWs and Internees (RAPWI) would be administered by the Green Service, established jointly by General Headquarters in India and the Headquarters of the Allied Land Forces in South-East Asia. All RAPWI would be moved to central collecting depots to be fed, clothed, and medically examined, and would remain at those centres until they were well enough to travel. Since their health would be worse than that of European POWs, most of them would have to remain at the depots for a fortnight.[120]

External Affairs was frustrated at the absence of Canadian input into this plan. To address the lack of inter-Allied coordination that had plagued the relief effort, the department proposed the formation of an Inter-Governmental Committee on Allied Nationals in Japanese Hands (ICAN).[121] The Canadian government's view of this body was characteristic of its attachment to the committee structure: the ICAN should not replace any of the other intergovernmental bodies, but would exist in concert with the Washington and London repatriation committees and Sub-Committees A and B of the IPOWC. More significantly, External Affairs believed that planning for liberation in the Far East could not proceed until there had been a decision on the proposed ICAN.[122]

Canada House was a little put off by this decision. The High Commission informed External Affairs that other governments would not likely defer their liberation planning pending a decision on the ICAN, and that the options facing Canada were really quite simple: either Canadian POWs would be covered by the directives of an ICAN, if it ever came into being, or they would not. In either case, Canadian planning should proceed. External Affairs was clearly not prepared for such an assessment. While mulling the matter over, the department directed Massey to inform Supreme Allied Command, South-East Asia (SACSEA) that, pending other arrangements, Canadians should be returned home by the quickest method possible.[123] The Inter-Service Committee on POWs (ISCP) stood behind External Affairs: unless an ICAN were formed, the American military commanders might make all the decisions themselves, without consulting the other Allies. As a further sign of Canada's preoccupation with the committee structure, the ISCP admitted that it had given no thought to arrangements for the evacuation of Canadians from Hong Kong.[124]

In the absence of such plans, Canadian officials drifted, apparently unable to maintain any policy decision for longer than a few days. Having informed SACSEA in late June that Canadians should be returned home by the fastest route, Scott told Sub-Committee A in early July that Canadian military authorities might not be willing to work within American plans after all.[125] A day later, External Affairs informed the Canadian Embassy in Washington that it would not agree in advance to any arrangements being made regarding Canadian POWs. Furthermore, External Affairs, having maintained in late June that an ICAN had to be established before planning could continue, stated in early July that planning should proceed, but must be referred to the ICAN when it came into existence.[126] With no repatriation plans to speak of under consideration, the Canadian government could not even say whether it approved of a stay-put agreement of the sort used in Europe or whether it could provide liaison officers to work with Commonwealth POW contact teams.[127]

Fortunately, Canadian officials soon came to their senses and admitted that the Americans were likely to move so quickly in the repatriation that consultation through the proposed ICAN would not be possible. As a result, Canada intended to deal directly with American authorities on a bilateral level. As the Inter-Service Committee said, 'Unilateral action at variance with the Commonwealth policy was undesirable, but as Canada was the only member so closely concerned with American operations, our decision should not have any particular bearing on other Dominions or on the United Kingdom.'[128] The upshot of this decision was a directive that effectively recognized the status quo by placing

Canadian POWs under the authority of American commanders.[129]

With this directive, the repatriation operation (and Canada's place in it) was finally clarified. Because it would take some time for each camp to be reached and evacuated, they were to be contacted by small recovery teams, drawn from Britain's Special Operations Executive, the American Office of Strategic Services, and the Australian forces under MacArthur's command, and supplied by air drops of food, medical supplies, and clothing. The recovery teams would organize the evacuation operation from the camps so that it could proceed swiftly once air, ground, or water transport was available to take the POWs to reception centres elsewhere. Able-bodied Commonwealth POWs were to be transported from Forward Disposition Centres near their camps to a main reception centre in Hong Kong. From there, Allied ships would ferry the ex-prisoners to the Philippines, where personnel would be processed and examined before returning to their homelands. Sick POWs were to be taken by American hospital ship directly from the Forward Disposition Centres to the Philippines or the Marianas, and from there to North America.[130] Canada's contribution to this operation was limited to personnel who would join the recovery teams and staff a Canadian reception centre for POWs returning through the Philippines; a senior officer to be attached to MacArthur's staff for liaison work; a joint party of External Affairs and the Canadian Red Cross, under Herbert Norman, to assist with repatriated civilians at the Manila reception centre; and an External Affairs official in San Francisco, to deal with any Canadians who arrived there.[131]

Not surprisingly, the evacuation from the Far East encountered significantly greater difficulties than the operation in Europe. The work of the recovery teams was made much more difficult by the lack of information about the camps. The location of only a portion of the camps was known, and others were happened upon purely by accident. William Allister of the Winnipeg Grenadiers, held in a coal yard at Sumidagawa, was told after the liberation that the Americans had known there was a camp in the vicinity but could not locate it for some days. George Soper and a few friends waited in their camp for the Americans to arrive, then finally decided to strike out on their own to locate their liberators. They travelled unmolested through Japan until they found American forces in Yokohama. Leonard Birchall, the

Canadian pilot dubbed 'The Saviour of Ceylon' for his role in warning British forces of a Japanese invasion force steaming towards the colony, had a similar experience. He and his fellow prisoners waited in their camp for two weeks to build up their strength, then set out for Tokyo, commandeering trucks or railway carriages as the occasion demanded. They too finally located Allied troops in Yokohama.[132]

The air drops were only a mixed success as well. The containers, usually fifty-gallon drums welded together at the ends, were too heavy for the parachutes and killed a number of POWs and Japanese civilians when they crashed to the ground.[133] Furthermore, the food was too great a temptation to POWs who had been living on starvation rations for years. Ignoring the advice of their doctors, they gorged themselves on chocolate bars, tinned fruit, and condensed milk. Because their stomachs were unused to the rich food, they would immediately vomit, and then repeat the cycle until they had tried everything. Angus McRitchie of the Winnipeg Grenadiers was given a large bowl of butter by his liberators, which he promptly ate in a single sitting; later, he consumed an entire carton of twenty-four marshmallow chocolate bars. Other prisoners smoked incessantly, for cigarettes were dropped along with the food; with their new-found bounty, they continued to smoke long after their mouths had gone raw.[134]

Canadian POWs in Hong Kong greet one of their liberators in August 1945.

There were also delays in moving prisoners out of their camps. Oss Luce spent nearly two weeks at a RAPWI camp after being liberated in . Singapore. Frustrated at the delays in the evacuation, the POWs started a rumour that RAPWI actually stood for 'Retain All Prisoners of War Indefinitely.' Within a few days, they were all on their way out of the camp.[135] Many ex-POWs felt that such delays were a feature of the Commonwealth evacuation process but not of the American. As one POW liberated in Hong Kong said, 'We feel that if this was a former American possession we would have been out of here days ago; probably the English have to turn back the history pages to find out what the precedent was at Crécy and Ladysmith.'[136]

The experiences of John Tayler, a Canadian in the RAF, bear this out. After a British recovery team reached Tayler's camp in Batavia in early September 1945, a USAF aircraft arrived to remove the American POWs. Tayler and two other Canadians secured permission from the British camp commander and the ranking USAF officer to be evacuated with the American POWs, who were scheduled to reach North America within a week. However, when the aircraft stopped in Calcutta to refuel, British Army intelligence officers removed the three Canadians, insisting that they had to return home through British channels. Had he been allowed to remain on the American aircraft, Tayler would likely have been home in Edmonton by the end of September; as it was, he reached Alberta on 6 December.[137]

In contrast, the Canadian reception camp in Manila was a model of efficiency. Each arriving ex-POW received a message of welcome from the camp commander directing him to inform a member of the staff of any requirements. Inside the reception camp, ex-prisoners received a duffel bag containing toiletries and clothing, and were at liberty to visit the mess halls (called Fort Garry and Frontenac) or showers whenever they wished. To make the surroundings seem more familiar, the camp roads had signposts that read Sparks Street, Portage Avenue, Yonge Street, and the like.[138] Also available were films, edited from newsreels, showing the main events of the war so that the ex-prisoners would not feel left out of conversations once they returned home.

OF COURSE, IT REMAINED TO BE SEEN whether such provisions would be sufficient to acclimatize liberated POWs from the Far East, who had endured conditions very different from those encountered by prisoners in Europe. Even so, the situations in the two theatres shared certain common features. Canadian officials showed the same preoccupation with committees, to the point of being unwilling to act without one; in the case of the ICAN at least, the concern with establishing a committee prevented planning from getting under way. Furthermore, the lack of coordination between Allies was far more serious than anything encountered in Europe. In this, Canada and the United States were at opposite ends of the spectrum. Canada was overly concerned with establishing a means of consultation between Allies on policy, while the United States saw no value at all in coordination before the fact, preferring to wait until an arrangement had been reached with Japan on relief shipments before convening an inter-Allied meeting. Britain occupied a position somewhere between the two, keen that there be some means of coordination but unwilling to postpone action until that means was arrived at.

Finally it must be said that, as in Europe, little more could have been done for POWs. It is one thing to lament the amount of effort wasted because of lack of coordination between Allies, but quite another to suggest that a more coordinated effort could have substantially improved conditions in the camps. Such was obviously not the case. The Japanese government clearly had little interest in treating its prisoners better, and allowed relief supplies in only when it suited them. Blandishments and threats had almost no impact, and even the concept of reciprocity of treatment was largely ineffective against a nation that believed that the prisoner of war did not exist. Despite the number of people of Japanese descent in Canada and frequent Canadian offers to allow aid workers to visit the internment camps, the Japanese government could not be enticed into making any more than token improvements in the living conditions of Canadian POWs.

The most disturbing aspect of Canada's campaign to care for prisoners in the Far East, however, was the oddly ambivalent attitude towards atrocity stories. On the one hand, the government was privy to reliable reports of horror stories of prison camp life, and also expressed private doubt as to the authenticity of more positive neutral reports. These facts are consistent with Canada's full participation in the various campaigns to publicize Japanese atrocities. Even while these campaigns were being planned, however, Canadian officials actively publicized glowing accounts of camp conditions, accounts that on numerous occasions the government had admitted were of dubious legitimacy. For its public statements, then, the Canadian government can be criticized on two levels. At most, it is open to censure for knowingly misleading the public about camp conditions in the Far East; at the very least, the government was guilty of failing to fully appreciate or understand the privations undergone by POWs of the Japanese. After 1918, the charge that the government did not and had never appreciated the sacrifices of prisoners became a rallying cry for ex-prisoners of war; after POWs from the Far East returned to Canada in 1945, it seemed entirely possible that the same situation would recur.

EIGHT

'THE DEBRIS OF PAST WARS'

IN 1944 AN ARTICLE ABOUT three Canadian sergeants held in a German prison camp in Silesia concluded with the comment that 'the three have the unanimous wish of all Stalag VIIIB that they will return home at last to a great future, earned through weary months by the expenditure of patience, selflessness, and courage.'[1] Certainly liberated POWs had high hopes of catching up on the time they had lost while in captivity, and looked forward to a future that had been put on hold for years. Reintegration into society would not be easy for all ex-prisoners, and a few would find reason to criticize their treatment by the government in the years after 1945. Most former POWs, however, would have little to complain about in the decades after the Second World War, and the events of the postwar period demonstrated that the Canadian government had taken to heart many of the lessons from the past.

I

In a poignant letter to a friend in 1944, one Canadian prisoner of war summed up what many of his fellow captives must have thought as the prospects of freedom brightened: 'A prisoner's life stands still while the world he knows travels on. I can't help but think of all the things we are going to have to learn before we will feel at home. Will we feel lost, frightened by the things we see?'[2]

Allied officials admitted quite freely that governments had largely ignored the problems of readjustment encountered by ex-POWs after the Great War, and all agreed that the neglect of these modern-day Rip Van Winkles (as some observers called them) could not be allowed to recur.[3] Fortunately, most officials recognized that ex-prisoners would face different readjustment hardships than other servicemen. As Morley Scott pointed out, 'the problems of rehabilitating a soldier who has been 2 or 3 years in a prison camp may be quite different from the general problem [of military rehabilitation].'[4] Significantly, Allied officials admitted from the outset what ex-POWs in the 1920s and 1930s had argued for years with little success.

As early as 1941, British administrators began to consider the problems that would face returned POWs, and in June 1943 the Committee for the Protection and Welfare of Canadian Prisoners of War in Enemy Hands (CPW) tackled the rehabilitation question.[5] The RCAF member stressed that action had to be taken immediately, while the prisoners were still in enemy hands, to maintain their morale and apprise them of the programs and opportunities available to them after the war. Without such consideration, their postwar rehabilitation would be that much more difficult. Morley Scott supported this opinion, and recommended that a panel of experts be convened to determine what should be done for imprisoned Canadians to prepare them for peace.[6]

In this endeavour, Canadian officials had access to a number of first-hand accounts by Allied medical personnel who had been repatriated and who had devoted considerable thought to the integration of ex-POWs into society. In a June 1943 article in the British periodical *The Fortnightly*, Dr. George Collie pointed out that the ex-POW would be 'to a greater or less degree unfit for immediate return to civilian life ... [he] is incapable mentally of adjusting himself to the problem of his homecoming and to the sudden and complete change in his environment.' Collie went on to propose a comprehensive scheme for dealing with the liberated POW, including a stay at a specially equipped rehabilitation centre, films and lectures for re-education, and frequent psychological and medical assessments.[7] Some months later, another repatriated doctor, Major P.H. Newman, put forward a similar scheme for the readjustment of ex-POWs. After discussing the symptoms that returned prisoners might exhibit, including restlessness, irritability, disrespect for authority, fear of crowds or enclosed spaces, a tendency to quick temper, and rebellion against restrictions, Newman recommended the establishment of an advice organization to which ex-POWs could turn in times of need. The organization would include a number of ex-prisoners' clubs, each staffed by doctors who understood the POW mentality, and a rehabilitation centre for the more difficult cases. Newman also advised that the organization be available to relatives of ex-prisoners who found the period of adjustment stressful.[8]

In June 1944 National Defence received a précis of a lengthy report on the psychological aspects of rehabilitation written by a British Army doctor recently repatriated from Germany.[9] The report began with the contention that ex-POWs would have more difficulties, primarily psychological, in readapting than any other body of servicemen, and reminded planners that 'the idea that a military authority may be benevolent has largely vanished from the minds of the prisoner of war'; as a consequence, military authorities had to tread very carefully around the '*Stalag* mentality' to avoid alienating ex-POWs.[10]

As the war moved through northwest Europe, Canadian officials kept themselves apprised of British and American rehabilitation plans. In December 1944 the Canadian Overseas Prisoners of War Committee (COPC) reviewed the British plans, and the following month, Group Captain F.A. Sampson, the RCAF member of the Supreme Headquarters, Allied Expeditionary Force (SHAEF) Prisoner of War Executive, transmitted to his headquarters a United States War Department directive on the subject. The document noted the likelihood of 'active or potential maladjustments' because of captivity, and commented at length about the proper treatment for ex-POWs:

> Routine handling should be avoided. The procedures which are applied to troops who have not been subjected to extended confinement under enemy control may not be found suitable, without appropriate adaptation, to recovered prisoners of war ... prisoners should be given to feel that their problems and future welfare are matters of interest to the military establishment and the country.

Sampson forwarded the directive so that Canadian authorities 'may know and include, if they have not already done so, such considerations in their planning.'[11]

" *I just want to be alone* "

The lack of privacy was a very serious problem for many POWs, and one that contributed to the '*Stalag* mentality.'

With this wealth of information, the government began making concrete plans, and in March 1945 the Inter-Service Committee on Prisoners of War (ISCP) convened a special meeting to discuss the resettlement of ex-prisoners of war and hear reports from various experts on the scope of the problem.[12] Squadron Leader F.H. Boulton, a recent repatriate from Germany, said that most ex-POWs would arrive home in a 'highly strung' condition, while Colonel H.N. Streight of Internment Operations cited the case of long-term German POWs to infer that a high percentage of prisoners from Hong Kong and Dieppe would experience some form of mental breakdown. The meeting decided to appoint a subcommittee to examine the matter in greater detail. Canadian rehabilitation plans eventually developed into a three-stage program: measures to be taken in the prison camps while the men were still captive; provisions to begin after liberation, at reception camps in England; and programs to be implemented in Canada.

The first stage had, in fact, been under way for much of the war. External Affairs and National Defence had sent various information brochures to the camps so that POWs would be aware of current events in Canada and of the general demobilization plans, though only so much could be sent because of censorship restrictions. Observers also recognized that one of the most important aspects of the rehabilitation process was to ensure that the ex-prisoner secured gainful employment, so that he could feel that he was doing something useful in society. As one POW wrote to his wife, 'I must have a steady job as soon as I get out of here or I think that I will go and drown myself as I have had enough hardship in the last 2½ years.'[13]

Consequently, an even greater emphasis than in the First World War was placed on using time spent in captivity for education and training. As one report said, effort had to be devoted to 'turning this incarceration to good account by improving his [the POW's] education and by preparing himself for rehabilitation on his return home.'[14] In 1941 the Canadian Legion Educational Services secured permission from the Swiss and German governments to supply educational materials to POWs, and over the next few years built a large and highly successful extension education program in conjunction with the War Prisoners' Aid of the World's Committee of YMCAs (WPA). By the end of the war, POWs in Europe could take elementary and high school courses through provincial departments of education, as well as university-level courses through a number of institutions, including Queen's, McGill, and Saskatchewan. Course materials and examinations were dispatched through a depot in Geneva, and the completed work was returned for marking to the University of London, whose grades all institutions had agreed to accept.[15]

By the time the war ended, Canadian officials could say that they had done everything possible to use the POWs' time behind barbed wire to prepare them for the rigours of peacetime. With the liberation of the camps, the second battle of the rehabilitation program could begin. In this stage it was vital to avoid the mistakes of 1918 and 1919, when the process for handling returned POWs had been hopelessly disorganized in many ways. In this endeavour, Canadian officials succeeded completely: the procedure for handling liberated prisoners in the United Kingdom was the paradigm of efficiency.

Upon arriving at airfields in England from the continent, ex-POWs received a snack (that is, after squirts of DDT powder had been liberally doled out to each man) while they were sorted into services and registered. In less than an hour, the ex-POWs had completed this initial processing and were on their way to the reception camps, #4 Canadian General Hospital at Aldershot for Canadian Army personnel, #3 Personnel Reception Centre at Bournemouth for members of the RCAF, and HMCS *Niobe* at Greenock, Scotland, for Canadian seamen. Immediately after their arrival at the camps, the ex-prisoners were informed of the arrangements made for them, including pay and leave provisions, medical procedures, mail services, and advice on eating and drinking in the weeks after liberation. They also had access to a number of welfare agencies, such as the Canadian Red Cross, the Knights of Columbus, and the Canadian Legion, all of which had huts in the reception camps.[16] To bring ex-prisoners up to date on current events, the camp staff distributed copies of *Canada in the Last Five Years*, a twenty-one-page pamphlet that provided a comprehensive but easily digested summary of Canada's war, including the growth and actions of the armed forces; industrial, agricultural, and scientific developments; wartime controls; and the new social welfare legislation.[17]

Liberated prisoners greatly appreciated these provisions, and most had nothing but praise for their experiences in England. However, the greatest desire of most ex-POWs was to return to Canada as soon as possible, and they were delighted to learn that anyone who had been in captivity for more than six months received top priority for transport to Canada by sea.[18] Most ex-prisoners hoped that there would be no fanfare for them at home and that they could get on with their lives as quietly as possible. As one wrote, 'No parties, please, and no fuss, and please don't meet us at the station. Let us find you at home among familiar things, as we remember you. Let us get home quickly with the minimum of routine so that we can be alone with the ones we love.'[19] Few Canadians would heed this advice, and the third stage of Canada's repatriation program, the one that had been identified as the most important, would be the least satisfactory.

Many ex-POWs, particularly those from the Far East, who were accustomed only to abuse, found the homeward trek a bewildering affair. William Allister recalled being put 'on the home train, stomach inflamed, fingers trembling, nerves shot ... My cousin, a wealthy mogul in Winnipeg, had prepared a lavish reception in my honour, with a slew of relatives and friends waiting to pounce. The whole prospect appalled me. My only desire was to crawl into a hole like a groundhog and close out the human race.'[20] Another returning Hong Kong prisoner had a similar reaction to the welcome home: 'I was in a very nervous condition. I was the only Hong Kong survivor on that particular train, and at every stop the Red Cross girls would come on because they heard there were Hong Kong men on the train, and they would ask, did I want to phone home, here's candy. It was just too much. Piles of attention, more than my share. It was very upsetting.'[21]

Unfortunately, the medical treatment and counselling that some ex-prisoners needed and that so many of the wartime reports had stressed was almost non-existent. Again, POWs from the Far East bore the brunt of this oversight. The medical care given to John Tayler, a prisoner in Java for over three years, consisted of a quick physical examination, a dose of the anti-malarial drug mepacrine, and the advice 'Don't overdo it'; other ex-POWs suffering from tropical maladies were told by doctors that nothing was wrong with them. Because so few physicians in Canada had any experience with tropical medicine, the health problems of Tayler and others went undiagnosed.[22] Furthermore, intended annual check-ups were rarely carried through, even for ex-POWs from the European theatre who had less exotic ailments. Port Hope, Ontario, native George Sweanor, a prisoner in Germany for two years, could not get the doctors to take seriously his pulse rate of 180; one advised him to avoid all exertion, while another told him to find the nearest tavern and tie one on. Wes Clare, a doctor captured at Dieppe, received an examination in 1946 that consisted of an X-ray and a blood pressure test; he was never called back for a follow-up exam the next year.[23] The lack of psychological care was just as serious. As William Allister recalled, 'there was no counselling, no advice, no awareness that we might act or feel differently. It was sink or swim, you're on your own boys. Like good Canadians, we expected nothing, got nothing.'[24]

Almost every ex-prisoner had some difficulty readjusting to freedom. Hong Kong POW Harold Englehart recalled that it took years before he felt at ease with other people; the first year was especially difficult 'because I didn't know what anybody was talking about.'[25] Gren Juniper, captured at Dieppe, could not abide crowds, while Dick McLaren found it difficult to cross the street. Gord King, a prisoner for nearly three years after being shot down over western Germany, was unable to settle back into his clerk's job at the Winnipeg civic offices, and eventually quit to become a salesman.[26] Other ex-prisoners admitted that, with hundreds of dollars in back pay accumulated, they drank far more than they should have. At the very least, all ex-POWs returned home with an almost obsessive appreciation for food.[27] To a large degree, they had to cope with these problems on their own, without the benefit of professional help. Dieppe prisoner Stanley Darch was troubled by nightmares and taut nerves upon arriving home, and found that driving around the countryside was the only thing that settled him down. Melvin Junck, taken prisoner with the Argyll and Sutherland Highlanders in northwest Europe, was unable to go to bed at night because he could not stand being closed up in a dark room; not knowing what else to do, he spent countless nights just walking the streets.[28]

Despite the good intentions of various committees, then, most ex-prisoners were left to fend for themselves in the difficult transition to freedom, for a number of reasons. With a scarcity of experts in the field, the government must have been a little daunted by the prospect of providing special rehabilitation assistance for about 10,000 ex-prisoners among the hundreds of thousands of other veterans; it was one thing to talk about such programs in the committee room, but quite another to put them in place once the time came. Furthermore, at least one National Defence official foresaw a public backlash if ex-POWs received special treatment compared with other soldiers.[29]

However, government inaction was only part of the reason, and perhaps not the largest part. Many ex-POWs began to manifest serious physical and psychological problems only years after their release, and may have appeared reasonably healthy in 1945. At the very least, many doubtless assumed that their minor aches and pains would subside after a few months at home. Other ex-prisoners knowingly concealed health problems during their medical exams, in the belief that requesting treatment might delay their demobilization or force them to spend months in a military hospital.[30] In sum, the failure to implement the third stage of the rehabilitation plan was due as much to ignorance and circumstance as it was to government neglect.

THE GOVERNMENT WAS CERTAINLY NOT BLIND to the abuses POWs had suffered in captivity, however, and took steps to investigate and punish crimes against prisoners. In November 1943 it established an interdepartmental committee on war crimes, and later created a war crimes section under Lieutenant-Colonel Bruce Macdonald at Canadian Military Headquarters in London. Although a member of the United Nations War Crimes Commission, Canada did not join the twenty-three other nations that signed the charter drawn up by the International Conference on Military Trials in 1945, or participate in the deliberations of the International Military Tribunal at Nuremberg.[31] As John Holmes put it, 'Canada was prepared to leave this matter to the countries that had had the Germans on their soil.'[32]

Nevertheless, the government pressed war crimes prosecutions in the most serious cases. At Aurich in northern Germany, Kurt Meyer, the commander of the 12th SS Panzer Division, was tried in a Canadian military court for the murders of Canadian soldiers in Normandy in June 1944. On 27 December 1945, after a trial that lasted just over two weeks, Meyer was acquitted on two charges but found guilty of inciting his troops to deny quarter and of responsibility for the murder of eighteen Canadian POWs at his headquarters. He was sentenced to hang, but despite an outcry in Canada, the sentence was commuted to life in prison and Meyer was released in 1954.

Canada took a greater role in war crimes trials in the Far East. With no occupation forces in Japan, the government could not convene military courts there, but made arrangements for British or American courts to try cases involving offences against Canadians. The government also nominated two Canadians to sit as members of the International Military Tribunal in Tokyo, Mr. Justice E.S. McDougall of Quebec as Canada's judge, and Brigadier H.G. Nolan, the Vice Adjutant-General at National Defence Headquarters, as an associate prosecutor. In addition, the Canadian war crimes unit in Tokyo assisted in the prosecution of twenty-three defendants accused of committing crimes against Canadian POWs, while the detachment in Hong Kong secured eleven convictions for crimes committed there.[33] The most well known of these was the prosecution of Kanao Inouye, a guard at Shamshuipo camp in Hong Kong. Known as the Kamloops Kid because he had been born and raised in British Columbia, Inouye exacted revenge for the discrimination he had suffered as a child in Canada by savagely beating Canadian POWs. Inouye was originally tried by a war crimes tribunal, but after the defence pointed out that he was a Canadian citizen, the trial moved to a civilian court in Hong Kong. The Kamloops Kid was tried for treason, convicted, and hanged in August 1947.[34]

II

Just as important as these trials, at least in the view of the Canadian government, were the attempts to revise the laws of war that culminated in the Geneva Conventions of 1949. Even before the war's end, the ICRC began making official approaches by canvassing all national Red Cross societies regarding the planned revisions. The signatories to the 1929 Geneva Conventions were then invited to participate in the process, and most governments, including Canada's, began to assemble teams of diplomats and experts to consider the matter.[35]

Two gatherings were eventually convened to lay the groundwork for the upcoming conference in Geneva: the April 1947 Conference of Experts held in Geneva; and the 17th International Red Cross Conference, held in Stockholm in August 1948. Canada sent delegations to both sets of discussions, and in each case the government's instructions were similar to its position in Geneva in 1929. Any 'idealistic and impracticable' amendments were deemed unacceptable, and should be strongly opposed; instead, 'a practical viewpoint must to some extent temper the idealism of the conventions,' which 'should set out only the *minimum* standard of treatment to be accorded to war victims and allow for any degree of improvement in the interests of humanity.'[36]

In specific terms, Canada attempted to address problems encountered during the Second World War. For example, Canada's delegate in Stockholm, Captain W.B. Armstrong, endeavoured to secure an amendment stipulating that full responsibility for transferred POWs rested with the government to which they had been transferred instead of the government that had captured them. Obviously a response to the jurisdictional wrangles that had plagued Allied internment officials during the last war, of which the shackling incident was only the most well known, the amendment was unfortunately lost. On the other hand, the conference accepted the view that merchant seamen should be treated as POWs, thereby recognizing in legal terms what had been the actual case, as far as Canada was concerned, during the war.[37]

At least one official, Major E.H. Barber of National Defence's Directorate of POWs, believed that Canada's position did not adequately account for the realities of the current situation. Instead of merely amending the conventions to protect the interests of personnel who fell into enemy hands, he advised a 'wider and more forward looking approach' based on the assumption that Canada would probably be involved in the next major war, which could conceivably be fought on Canadian soil. Barber believed that the conventions, rather than 'protecting the prisoner of war who has been regarded entirely as a person in misfortune,' should lay more emphasis on the obligations of the POW: 'He should be regarded as a person who has been granted a concession by the Detaining Power, in that his life has been spared ... It is not suggested that prisoners of war should be inhumanely treated but it is thought that a much greater responsibility for their welfare, while in captivity, might rest with themselves and the country in whose service they are.'[38] Barber's notions of the nature of captivity harkened back to the previous century, but his view would prove eminently realistic in light of later experience.

In October 1948 Canada received an invitation to the diplomatic conference to be held in Geneva, and named a delegation the following spring. It would be headed by M.E. Vaillancourt, the ambassador to Yugoslavia, and include Max Wershof of the High Commission in London; Lieutenant-Colonel J.N. Crawford, a former Hong Kong POW; Captain Armstrong; Captain J.W. Kerr of Transport; and Dr. E.A. Watkinson of National Health and Welfare.[39] It was a strong delegation, with wide experience in the matters to be discussed. Crawford and Armstrong had both spent some years working on revisions of the conventions, while Wershof and Kerr also had experience with POW matters from the last war, Wershof with Canada House and Kerr as a member of the CPW.

In preparation for the Geneva conference, the government convened an interdepartmental committee to consider the four proposed conventions, covering the sick and wounded, POWs, maritime matters, and civilians.[40] Based on these meetings, External Affairs drew up a memorandum to Cabinet outlining Canada's suggested position. To a large degree, the memorandum simply repeated earlier recommendations. The conventions should set only minimum standards, and 'account must be taken of the consequences of total war and a realistic viewpoint should temper the idealism of the revised texts.' Merchant seamen should be covered under the conventions, and, to address the problems created by competing aid agencies in the last war, External Affairs advised against preferential treatment for the Red Cross; all humanitarian agencies should be treated equally.[41]

The diplomatic conference in Geneva ran from 21 April to 12 August 1949 and brought together delegates from fifty-nine governments. The discussions on the POW convention, in which Armstrong represented Canada, were overshadowed by other, more contentious issues, and the POW code that emerged was not radically different from the 1929 version.[42] It grew to 143 articles, with the largest single section covering the definition of a prisoner of war, and generally the changes attempted to address specific anomalies (such as rates of pay for POWs) that had been the subject of prolonged debate during the war. Max Wershof signed the conventions on behalf of Canada in December 1949, and they were ratified in the House of Commons in 1965. The reason for the delay is not entirely clear, although it was apparently related to Canada's reservation regarding one article of the convention on civilians, and the need to secure certain statutory amendments to allow the conventions to be put into effect in Canada.[43]

Despite the delay in ratification, the Department of National Defence lost no time instructing its troops on the new code. In a five-part article in the *Canadian Army Journal*, Armstrong described the conventions in detail 'with a view to enabling Canadian Army personnel to become cognizant of the salient points of these Conventions.'[44] In 1950 the department printed a small guide to the conventions for distribution to the troops, to draw attention to those articles most likely to concern front-line soldiers and to summarize the rights of personnel who might be captured. With this guide, according to Mr. Justice P.H. Gordon of the Canadian Red Cross, Canadian troops were among the best trained in the world with respect to their rights and obligations under international law.[45]

III

The opportunity to test that training was not long in coming. For the United States, and to a lesser extent Britain, the experiences of servicemen captured during the Korean War led to enormous controversy. Attempts to brainwash and convert United Nations prisoners forced American authorities to take a hard look at the conduct of their men in Communist prison camps; lengthy reports bearing witness to the disappointing inability of many Americans to resist Communist propaganda were followed by studies that attempted to show how well American POWs had withstood the test under exceptionally difficult conditions. More difficult to deal with was the fact that twenty-two American and one British servicemen elected to remain in Communist China after the war ended.

Canadian officials were doubtless grateful that the problems of this nature that they encountered were on a much smaller scale, for only thirty-three Canadians (three officers and thirty other ranks, mostly from the Royal Canadian Regiment [RCR] and the Van Doos) were captured during the war (see Table 3 in the Appendix for details). Furthermore, the privations endured by these prisoners were mild compared to those experienced by other United Nations captives.[46]

They did not die in the same numbers as American POWs, largely because none were captured during the initial stages of the war, before February 1951, when POW death rates were highest.[47] Nor were they subject to the same intense political indoctrination as their British and American comrades, for the Communists had little to gain by converting Canadians and did not try very hard; in this instance, the fact that Canada was a relatively minor player paid off for her POWs.[48]

The first Canadian soldier fell into enemy hands in the autumn of 1951; the rest were captured in isolated engagements over the course of the war. The largest group of prisoners was a party of fourteen men of the Royal Canadian Regiment, captured at a position known as Little Gibraltar in October 1952; one member of this group, Cape Breton Islander Private Elmer McInnis, had just come up with a reinforcement party, only to be taken prisoner in his first day in the front lines. By most accounts, Canadians were more often ignored than mistreated. Because they were perceived as mere cannon fodder for the Americans (Manitoban Lance-Corporal Stan Badowich was told by a Chinese interrogator that he and his comrades were 'running dogs for American war mongers'), minor infractions committed by Canadians were often overlooked by guards who would have punished American POWs severely for the same deeds.[49] What abuse Canadians suffered frequently appeared to be more incidental than calculated. Lieutenant C.G. Owen, the sole RCR officer captured, spent four weeks in solitary confinement in a small hut with a mud floor and only a pile of straw and a small flat stone as furnishings; nevertheless, he began to resent his captors only when they confiscated the stone after seeing that Owen was using it as a pillow.[50]

The camps in which Canadians were confined were primitive, but again there was little evidence of a studied attempt at brutality. One camp at Chungsong consisted of a village that had been commandeered by military authorities to serve as an open prison camp. The small huts, constructed of mud and wattle with straw roofs and earthen floors, had recently been vacated by the villagers, who had apparently taken their furnishings with them. Captain Joe Liston, an artillery spotter captured when his observation aircraft was shot down, lived in a camp in a small valley ringed by hills; there was no fence when the prisoners arrived and the POWs declined an invitation to erect one themselves.[51]

Though not generous, the rations were generally adequate and often differed little from the food given to the guards. One of the soldiers captured at Little Gibraltar, Private Tom Rothwell of Dundas, Ontario, recalled that the rations in Camp 3 at Songsa-dong, a camp on the Yalu River established in August 1952, consisted of boiled potatoes, turnips, rice, and broth. Private J.A. Bellefeuille of the Van Doos noted that the prisoners could monitor the progress of armistice talks by the quality of food they received; when the food improved, they surmised that the talks had been going well.[52] Most prisoners lost weight, but none as much as their predecessors who had suffered the hospitality of Imperial Japan.

In most cases, however, few of these soldiers were ever reported as prisoners. As late as March 1953, Canadian authorities knew of only one Canadian who had been officially reported a prisoner, although they were aware that others may have been captured. Bellefeuille and his comrade, Private J.T. Allain, in the hopes that their names would be publicized and come to the attention of their families, had signed a peace petition circulated by an Australian journalist with Communist leanings. When the petition reached Canadian military authorities, they matched the signatures with those on file and accepted that the two Van Doos might indeed be alive.[53] Oddly enough, the fact that Canada had so many soldiers listed as missing and only one official POW raised no apparent concern in the government and public. The matter never came up in the House of Commons, nor did it become an issue in the press.

To prepare for the possible capture of large numbers of Canadians, however, the Canadian Red Cross Society (CRCS) was quick off the mark to set up its POW organization. In February 1951, just four months after the arrival of Canadian troops in Korea, the CRCS appointed Colonel Cuthbert Scott to act as its Ottawa Special Liaison Officer with the Canadian government.[54] With this, the society demonstrated its determination to avoid one of the most serious shortcomings of the last war, the lack of a senior executive close to the centre of decision-making in Ottawa. Although he could not have known it at the time, Colonel Scott would have little to do, for a relief effort was never undertaken. One Member of Parliament asked about provisions for sending parcels to prisoners, only to be told that no mechanism existed and no queries had been received.[55] In the absence of a relief effort, all attention focused on the possibility of securing release.

There is no need to recount the tortuous negotiations that led to the eventual exchange of prisoners in 1953, as they have been examined in some detail by others.[56] It is enough to say that the talks were long, complicated, and exasperating, and centred around whether North Korean POWs should be repatriated from United Nations Command (UNC) camps against their will. Initially, the United Nations was reluctant to adopt the policy of non-forcible repatriation, but the United States soon committed itself to giving Communist prisoners the option of returning home or staying in UNC hands. With this decision, UN prisoners were sacrificed to the larger political objective; as one historian put it, 'the fate of enemy non-repatriates was accorded a higher priority than the safety of captured UN soldiers.'[57]

This was certainly the case as far as Canada was concerned. Correspondence going to and from External Affairs during the exchange negotiations contained few mentions of UN prisoners, as did parliamentary debates, and the notes of UN General Assembly president Lester Pearson on the Korean discussions are silent on the place of United Nations POWs in the negotiations.[58] The talks were at an impasse until 30 March 1953, when Chinese Premier Chou En-Lai stated on Peking radio that the Communist governments would discuss an exchange of sick and wounded prisoners under the Geneva Convention. The statement gave great encouragement to the United Nations; the chairman of Canada's delegation to the general assembly stated that no previous proposal had raised hopes so high.[59]

Even with only one confirmed prisoner, Canadian officials began to make preparations for the return of released POWs. The Canadian Military Mission in Tokyo stated that representatives of the British Commonwealth Forces in Korea (BCFK) should meet exchanged POWs as soon as possible, and that no delay would be accepted in the evacuation of ex-POWs to Canada. However, the commander of the mission, Brigadier R.E.A. Morton, added the caveat that the overall plan and its execution were in the hands of the 8th Army, and that Canadian officials could only hope that its wishes would be accommodated.[60]

Communist and UNC officials signed the agreement for the repatriation of sick and wounded prisoners on 11 April 1953, and the exchange operation, code-named Little Switch, began on 20 April at Panmunjom. The first Canadian, and indeed the first Commonwealth POW, to return was Lance-Corporal Paul Dugal of the Van Doos; four days later Dugal was followed by another Van Doo, Private Arthur Baker of Montreal. Dugal brought out with him a list of more than a dozen members of the Royal Canadian Regiment who had been reported missing in action at Little Gibraltar but who were actually POWs in North Korea.[61] For many next of kin, this was the first indication that they had a relative in Communist captivity, and National Defence quickly wrote to the families of newly reported POWs, instructing them on how to correspond with their relatives.[62]

The hundred UNC prisoners who returned in Operation Little Switch were found to be in reasonably good physical condition; all had lost weight and some had minor maladies (Private Baker had laryngitis when he reached Panmunjom but nevertheless managed to give a radio interview upon his release), but the prisoners were healthier than the UNC had expected.[63] They also provided the first accounts of captivity in North Korea; previously, the only information about UNC prisoners had come from the British Communist organ the *Daily Worker*.[64] In his radio interview, Baker briefly recounted the steps leading up to his repatriation, and said that he had learned of his exchange only thirty minutes before leaving his hospital. Dugal described how 200 POWs in his camp had had to share a single straight razor; he was, however, grateful to Chinese doctors for tending his head wound.[65]

Eventually, more sinister stories of maltreatment, starvation, and mass deaths came from American repatriates, giving the press plenty of grist for the atrocity story mill. With the possibility that many soldiers previously listed as missing might in fact have been captured, the failure to report soldiers as prisoners of war became a minor cause célèbre: 'The Communists, who care nothing for the humane principles of the Geneva Convention, have not only refused to permit visits to the camps but have withheld the names of the prisoners.'[66] The *Hamilton Spectator* lamented that the 'upsurge of relief and hope' that had accompanied the arrival of the first repatriates at Panmunjom had been cruelly shattered by subsequent revelations.[67]

After Little Switch, the Communists insisted that they had repatriated all of the UNC sick and wounded prisoners, but the UNC cited evidence of nearly 400 eligible repatriates still in detention in North Korea and China.[68] The dispute was solved, and in June 1953 both sides reached an agreement for the repatriation of all prisoners of war. Evidently the Communists were reluctant to accede to any accord until UNC prisoners had been fattened up, and the food given to prisoners improved markedly in the period between the two exchanges; Tom Rothwell's rations now included eggs, ham, pork, beef, and powdered milk. The treatment in general improved as well. After the armistice agreement was signed in July 1953, the POWs in Corporal Ernest Taylor's camp were allowed to perform religious observances; an assembled church service was still forbidden, but the prisoners were permitted to engage in individual prayer while an American soldier read the Bible aloud from his hut. George Griffiths, a prisoner since October 1952, suddenly began receiving medical attention for a battle wound when word of his impending release reached the camp.[69]

Once again, as another exchange became imminent, Canadian military authorities prepared to receive the repatriates. Prisoners were to be met at Panmunjom by American troops and escorted to Freedom Village, where they would receive a quick medical examination and a new uniform, be documented by a Canadian records officer, and get a light snack. From Freedom Village, Commonwealth repatriates would move to Britannia Camp for a more thorough medical exam and a night's accommodation. The following day, the Canadians would be moved to #38 Canadian Field Ambulance, where debriefing would take place; intelligence officers would also monitor news interviews to ensure that overzealous journalists did not take advantage of ex-POWs. The final legs of their journey would take the men to Japan, and from there to Vancouver on Canadian Pacific Airways. Between 30 and 40 Commonwealth prisoners were expected to arrive each day of Operation Big Switch, but there were facilities for as many as 400 a day.[70]

The POWs who came out of North Korea in Big Switch provided further details about the experiences of Canadian captives, but authorities were perhaps most interested in determining whether Canadians had been subjected to the same rigorous indoctrination as other UNC prisoners, especially Britons and Americans. Subsequent investigation proved that this was not the case. They were forced to attend the occasional large propaganda meeting, and Communist officials did subject

Canadians to individual interviews in an attempt to demonstrate the error of their ways, but reports suggested that the pressure was comparatively mild and not difficult to resist. Montreal native Georges St. Germain of the Van Doos told his captors that he spoke no English, which apparently discouraged them from spending too much time on him; Bellefeuille and Allain were also able to take advantage of the language barrier to reduce the pressures of indoctrination.[71]

Canadian prisoners arrive at Freedom Village during Operation Big Switch, August 1953.

However, the BCFK had already decided that no program of counter-indoctrination would be instituted under any circumstances. As one official wrote, ex-POWs would be returned home as soon as possible 'in the belief that the influence of their families and friends will go as far as anything to restore their political balance.'[72] Still, Cold War suspicions could not be banished entirely. One newspaper questioned the 'cloak of secrecy' (as it called the restrictions on interviews with repatriates) thrown around Gunner Orval Jenkins of Hamilton, which was interpreted as political in origin for the simple reason that some members of the soldier's family had joined the 'pink-tinged Labour-Progressive Party.'[73] In fact, the extra debriefings given to Jenkins probably had no more sinister explanation than the fact that he had been a POW for two years, longer than any other Canadian soldier.

Operation Big Switch brought back the rest of the Canadian prisoners in Communist hands with the exception of Squadron Leader A.R. MacKenzie of the RCAF, who remained in captivity in China, the only Canadian POW transferred out of North Korea. MacKenzie, a Second World War veteran, had been on secondment to the US 5th Air Force when he was shot down over North Korea by an American aircraft on 5 December 1952. He spent eighteen months in solitary confinement and lost over a hundred pounds before he was forced into 'confessing' that he had been shot down over China; after that, the treatment improved somewhat. His freedom was apparently secured through the intervention of Chester Ronning, one of Canada's delegates to the Korean conference in Geneva, who made a personal request to Chou En-Lai for MacKenzie's release. The Chinese did not haggle, and MacKenzie was freed two years to the day after he had been shot down.[74]

Coming as it did so soon after the Geneva Conventions were signed, the Korean conflict demonstrated the pitfalls of legislating the conditions of captivity. Canada's official campaign historian summed up the difficulty neatly: 'None of the Articles of the Geneva Convention relating to hygiene, medical care, food, accommodation, or supervision was observed, but in the primitive circumstances under which the Chinese lived, their observance would have meant actual preferment of prisoners over their own soldiers.'[75] So, while the Canadian government had been wise in insisting that the Geneva Convention stipulate only a minimum standard of treatment, no one had apparently considered what to do if even that minimum was beyond the physical resources of the Detaining Power. Major Barber had come close to the mark by suggesting that a nation had to assume greater responsibility for the welfare of its personnel in enemy hands, but even this pragmatic comment did not address the situation in the Korean conflict, when Canada had no way of knowing that more than one of its soldiers was in captivity.

IV

While the Korean War was going on, ex-prisoners in Canada were engaged in another battle, an extension of the one that their predecessors had fought in the 1920s and 1930s. The struggle for POW pensions would be fought over the same ground as the struggle for reparations payments, and much of the same rhetoric would be used. Perhaps because of the example set by ex-POWs from the Great War, the second battle for pension rights would have a happier outcome.

By 1949, after a number of attempts to secure special gratuities for Hong Kong veterans, attention had focused on the possibility of convening a War Claims Commission of the sort established after the First World War. This raised the prospect of reopening old wounds, for an early report advised that war claims from members of the Canadian armed forces should not be entertained. As one National Defence official stated, 'the loss to the military personnel did not measure up to the loss occasioned civilian persons.'[76] However, the Canadian government was spurred into action by an announcement in February 1950 that the United States would make payments to ex-POWs of $1 for every day spent in captivity. News of this gratuity brought a storm of queries from Canadian ex-POWs. A member of the Van Doos captured in Italy maintained that conditions there had been 'below living standards,' and then made an oft-heard comment: 'I can't say the same for P.O.W. camps here in Canada, some of which I have seen at Farnham, P.Q.' The correspondent went on to request for Canadian POWs the same grants that Americans had been awarded.[77]

National Defence, however, strongly opposed payments to ex-POWs, the Adjutant-General Major-General W.H.S. Macklin maintaining that 'from a military viewpoint I view such a policy as obnoxious. Why fight if you can get paid more as a P.O.W.?' Furthermore, Macklin was clearly not interested in dealing with the matter and wanted it all shifted to the Department of Veterans Affairs: 'It is a DVA matter and if we are to take up time dealing with the debris of past wars, we are unlikely to get ready efficiently for the next.'[78]

The Canadian government took a more liberal attitude than Macklin. Article 16 of the peace treaty with Japan made available certain assets to compensate Allied POWs for maltreatment while in captivity, and the government appointed former Justice Minister and now Chief Justice of Nova Scotia J.L. Ilsley as Advisory Commissioner for War Claims to determine the best way to distribute reparations payments. Ilsley examined evidence from Canada, Britain, and the United States, and concluded that POWs in the Far East had experienced general and continuous maltreatment during their internment; for this, they should receive an automatic award of seventy-five cents for every day spent in captivity, or roughly $1000 for the average Hong Kong prisoner. He could make no similar assumption for POWs from the European theatre. If they could prove a specific instance of maltreatment, they should be awarded $1 for every day that maltreatment persisted; if they could not, they would receive nothing.[79] The government took the unusual step of improving upon the commissioner's recommendation, and on 9 October 1952 Prime Minister Louis St. Laurent announced that reparations payments of $1 for each day of captivity would be made automatically to all POWs from the Far East and to any European prisoner who had been held by an illegal organization, such as the SS or the Gestapo. Any other men who had been held in German or Italian camps could make claims as well, but those claims would be assessed on an individual basis. By mid-December 1952, more than 1200 ex-POWs had received compensation payments totalling over $1.6 million.[80]

The Hong Kong Veterans' Association (HKVA), however, maintained that it had agreed to the dollar-a-day payment on the understanding that it covered maltreatment by starvation only and that a further award would be made at a later date as compensation for forced labour.[81] Consequently, in 1958 the organization submitted a brief to Veterans Affairs requesting a payment from seized Japanese assets of $1.50 for each day of captivity.[82] In subsequent submissions the HKVA put forward a number of points echoing those made by ex-POWs after the Great War. Despite the fact that civilian internees enjoyed better living conditions than POWs and had not been used as slave labour, they received higher awards than ex-POWs. Furthermore, civilians had been in Hong Kong by choice, while the members of C Force had been 'sent to Hong Kong by the Canadian government, under conditions which the Hon. George Drew later proved (more or less) were adverse from the start.' For these reasons, the HKVA asked again for compensation for slave labour.[83] Perhaps bristling at the mention of George Drew (whose strident allegations that the dispatch of C Force to Hong Kong had been badly mismanaged had caused considerable embarrassment to the King administration), the Liberal government stood firm. The Secretary of State pointed out that Far East POWs had already received awards nearly three times larger than their European counterparts, who had also been subjected to forced labour, and noted that ex-POWs were entitled to various veterans' benefits that former civilians could not claim.[84]

In 1962 the HKVA won a small victory when the Department of Veterans Affairs agreed to establish the Prisoners of War (Far East World War II) Trust Fund to distribute the nearly $17,000 remaining from Canada's portion of the Japanese peace treaty payment. Minor grants from the fund could be made by DVA district officers, while larger awards required consultation with the HKVA. Since 1962, the grants have varied in size, with rarely more than two dozen being made in any one year. By 1990 the fund was over twice as large as when it was established.[85]

After the creation of the POW Trust Fund, Hong Kong veterans shifted their focus away from reparations payments. They began to push for amendments to the Pension Act to grant them a minimum 50 per cent pension for the residual effects of malnutrition, which had been given the term *avitaminosis* in the absence of any recognized medical nomenclature. Over the next few years, the HKVA made a number of submissions to the Standing Committee on Veterans Affairs, always presenting a forceful and well-constructed case. The association began with the presumption that the residual effects of captivity did not manifest themselves until some years after release, and cited a long list of medical studies detailing the effects of captivity on the central nervous, cardiovascular, genitourinary, and gastrointestinal systems.[86] One of the most convincing studies, a 1965 report by Dr. H.J. Richardson, examined 100 Hong Kong POWs whose brothers had served in the European theatre and found that Hong Kong veterans experienced a significantly higher rate of blindness, heart disease, hypertension, and premature death than their brothers.[87] The HKVA also based much of its claim on the circumstances of C Force's dispatch to Southeast Asia, and asked the government to consider whether C Force should have been sent to Hong Kong at all: 'If this was an error on the part of the

Government and/or the Military Authorities, it is significant that the total cost of this error was and is being borne by the survivors of the Hong Kong Force and their dependants.'[88] With this statement, the HKVA again echoed the comments of First World War POWs, who had demanded reparations payments on the grounds that they were 'sacrifice troops' put into hopeless situations by Allied governments.

The case of the HKVA was strengthened by the presentation in March 1968 of the report of the Committee to Survey the Work and Organization of the Canadian Pension Commission (the Woods Report), which had been commissioned by Minister of Veterans Affairs Roger Teillet, himself an ex-POW. The section of the Woods Report dealing with POW claims expressed complete sympathy with the case made by the HKVA; it took into account the difficulties of establishing the residual medical effects of malnutrition and the circumstances under which C Force had served, and recommended a basic minimum pension of 50 per cent for Far East POWs.[89] In the 1969 White Paper on Veterans' Pensions the government finally signalled its acceptance of the HKVA's case and announced the institution of a 50 per cent minimum pension for all Hong Kong POWs; widows and orphans would also be eligible for pension benefits in certain cases. When the necessary legislation passed in 1971, the HKVA achieved its main goal: the automatic attribution of the death of any ex-Hong Kong POW to his service, making his next of kin eligible for benefits under the Pension Act.[90]

Ex-prisoners from the European theatre watched the struggles of Far East POWs with considerable interest. They believed that they too deserved the benefit of the doubt in reparations claims, and in 1953 secured the appointment of Chief War Claims Commissioner Thane Campbell to consider their claim. His report devoted much attention to the work of the McDougall Commission in the 1930s, and implied that McDougall's awards had been, at the very least, unfair because of too rigorous an application of the criteria for determining maltreatment.[91] Instead, Campbell believed that every Canadian POW had experienced some degree of maltreatment and recommended the payment of a general basic award of twenty cents for each day of captivity, as well as additional sums for 'aggravating incidents,' such as having been shackled or transported by boxcar, or having endured one of the forced marches of 1945. Unlike the ex-POWs who went before the McDougall

Commission in the 1930s, European-theatre POWs who received payments under the provisions of Campbell's report do not recall having difficulty convincing the commission of the merit of their cases.[92]

With the success of the HKVA in obtaining relief under Canadian pension legislation, POWs from the European theatre moved in the same direction, and in 1971 established their own organization to press their case. Admitting that the plight of European POWs had been overlooked in the concentration on the problems of Far East prisoners, the National POW Association (European Theatre) (NPOWA) wanted what Hong Kong and American ex-POWs enjoyed: the presumption that their health problems were incurred or aggravated by captivity.[93] With the help of the HKVA and the Dieppe Veterans and POWs Association (DVPA), the NPOWA secured the commissioning of a study of European POWs to determine the long-term physiological and psychological disorders they experienced because of captivity. The study, completed by Dr. J. Douglas Hermann in 1973, canvassed over 2000 ex-POWs and examined their health, education, employment, and income levels. Hermann concluded that compensation should be awarded to Dieppe POWs and other former prisoners 'who, because of extraordinary stress and trauma related to capture and imprisonment, also suffer from significant physiological and psychological disadvantages.'[94]

With the Hermann Report as evidence, the ex-POWs appeared before the Standing Committee on Veterans Affairs. Like the Hong Kong veterans, ex-prisoners who had been captured at Dieppe based much of their case on the circumstances of their capture and believed that many of their problems stemmed from 'the fact that the Dieppe prisoner feels that he was abandoned on the beach at Dieppe.'[95] The DVPA rejected the government's suggestion that further study of ex-prisoners be undertaken, insisting that such a course was time-consuming and unnecessarily expensive. The delegates believed that sufficient data was available from previous Canadian, British, and American studies, and recommended an immediate pension of 50 per cent for all POWs held for more than thirty months.[96]

The government acted reasonably promptly, and on 1 April 1976 the Compensation for Former Prisoners of War Act came into effect. Under this legislation, Far East POWs would receive an additional 30 per cent pension, with their total rate not to exceed 100 per cent. Other

Second World War and Korean War POWs would be pensioned at three rates: 10 per cent for those who had been in captivity between 3 and 18 months; 15 per cent for those imprisoned between 18 and 30 months; and 20 percent for anyone detained for more than 30 months. The following year, the benefits were extended to First World War POWs and servicemen who had evaded capture.[97] In July 1980 the government extended the benefits to widows and orphans, and in 1986 removed the pension ceiling of 100 per cent and increased the basic pension rate for European POWs who spent more than 30 months in captivity. With these changes, Canada now had the most generous and extensive benefits for ex-POWs in the world.[98]

Over the next few years, two more groups were brought under the scheme's coverage. After a long campaign waged by James Templeton, a Newfoundlander in the RCAF who had spent over a year in Laghouat prison camp in Algeria, the government agreed in 1987 to extend POW benefits to prisoners of the Vichy regime.[99] This decision left merchant seamen as the only group of ex-POWs not covered by pension benefits. Despite the government's wartime policy of equating the treatment of merchant seamen to that of POWs, they were classified as civilian internees and were therefore deemed ineligible for the benefits paid to other POWs.[100] Only after extensive lobbying by veterans' groups did the government decide in 1991 to extend veterans' benefits to merchant mariners.

AT PRESENT, IT APPEARS that Canada has learned most of the lessons from the past about preparing servicemen for captivity, providing for them in enemy hands, and meeting their needs after their release. That capture remains a distinct possibility in the post-Cold War world was made clear by the detention of Canadian peacekeepers in the former Yugoslavia in the spring of 1994, but at least Canadian military personnel are now well prepared for captivity should they be unlucky enough to experience it. National Defence's post-Korean War training manual *Conduct after Capture*, which consisted of a series of six lectures on how to resist Communist propaganda and blandishments, has been replaced by manuals of more general utility.[101] Furthermore, military regulations now stipulate that a board of inquiry is not necessary in every case of capture, but only when that capture is suspected of having resulted from want of due precaution, disobedience of orders, or wilful neglect of duty.[102]

More importantly, various aspects of captivity are frequently discussed in defence circles. A 1979 *Canadian Defence Quarterly* article reviewed recent changes in international law as they pertained to captivity, and students at the Canadian Forces Staff College have regularly considered the problems of captivity in a changing world.[103] In a 1980 paper, Major Barry Read stressed that geography, race, and culture would affect the experiences of future POWs but that ideology would be the major determinant. If future POWs are to resist ideological attacks, they must be certain that the nation supports and remains loyal to them. For this reason, Read advised that a Canadian code of conduct for POWs state that members of the armed forces 'will keep faith with Canada regardless of doubters, knowing she will neither forget nor abandon them.'[104]

Fortunately, the Gulf War of 1991 did not afford the Canadian Forces the opportunity to test Major Read's assertions. It did, however, prove once again that the Canadian Red Cross Society would be quick to act in aid of POWs. When the war broke out, the society moved promptly to establish a means of communication with Canadians who might be captured by Iraqi forces. ICRC workers would distribute to Coalition POWs Red Cross Message forms. After completion, the forms would be forwarded to the Canadian society's provincial divisions. The divisions would then pass on each message to the local Red Cross branch, which would arrange for a volunteer to deliver it to the prisoner's next of kin; the process would be reversed for communications going to POWs. With this scheme, the Red Cross would duplicate the personal contact that it had deemed so valuable in the Second World War.[105]

The treatment of POWs after hostilities, what Major-General Macklin had called the 'debris of past wars,' remains an item of considerable interest. As in the 1920s, allegations continue to surface that prisoners were left in enemy hands after the Second World War and the Korean conflict. In 1989 an American study claimed that thousands of Allied POWs, including a number of Canadians, remained in the Soviet Union after the Second World War; the charges have never been satisfactorily answered, though they must be judged far-fetched, at least as far as Canadians are concerned.[106] Virtually all of the

Canadian POWs in Europe were accounted for; the few who were never traced were more likely casualties of the confusion of a disintegrating German Reich than of a massive Communist conspiracy.

More recently, the break-up of the Soviet Union has brought suggestions that Canadians posted missing in Korea might actually have been made prisoner but never reported as such by the Communist forces. In one case, Corporal Richard Toole of Hamilton was reported missing after a North Korean attack on 11 October 1951; subsequent accounts placed him in a Communist prison camp in Siberia. Despite reports to the contrary from North Korean sources and other UNC prisoners, Toole was officially listed as presumed killed. His family never gave up hope, and in 1992 secured a promise from Russian President Boris Yeltsin that the case would be investigated.[107] The theory of Toole's disappearance is considerably more plausible than the Second World War version, but it seems unlikely that it will ever be satisfactorily proved or disproved.

Nor has the war crimes controversy subsided. Canada has been reasonably active in searching out individuals suspected of crimes against civilians in Europe, but less well known is the aftermath of the Kurt Meyer case. In 1990 the television program *The Fifth Estate* broadcast an investigation into Wilhelm Möhnke, one of Meyer's subordinates who had been responsible for the murders of three Canadian POWs but who had not been tried due to lack of evidence. After some assiduous investigative journalism, the program located a member of Möhnke's unit who was willing to testify against his former commander if the case were tried. The matter was brought to the attention of a German war crimes prosecutor, but there has been no further action yet.[108]

Far East POWs continue to press their demands for reparations payments, and in May 1987 the chairman of the War Amputations of Canada, Cliff Chadderton, made a claim before the United Nations Human Rights Commission (UNHRC) on behalf of the HKVA for roughly $13 million from the Japanese government. While the claim was being considered, various Allied POW associations banded together and appointed Chadderton to represent the interests of ex-Far East POWs in the Netherlands, Britain, the United States, Australia, New Zealand, and Canada. In February 1991 he made a further submission to the UNHRC, requesting compensation for war crimes,

crimes against humanity, and gross human rights violations committed by the Japanese government during the Second World War.[109]

In May 1991, perhaps sensing that the UNHRC would decide in
favour of the ex-POWs, Japanese Prime Minister Toshiki Kaifu issued
an official apology for the sufferings inflicted on Canadian POWs by
Japan during the Second World War. While Kaifu's statement was satisfactory to Prime Minister Brian Mulroney, it was less so to Hong
Kong veterans. Lionel Speller of the HKVA called it a 'bloody insult,' a
comment that was echoed by many other Hong Kong POWs.[110] Far
from accepting the Japanese apology, Far East POWs went ahead with
their campaign; as of February 1993, they were still pursuing a claim
with the UNHRC asking Japan for billions of dollars in compensation
for former Allied POWs.

THE POST-1945 ERA has been more satisfying in terms of the treatment of POW issues than the interwar period, for the Canadian government has taken to heart most of the important lessons from the
past. Prisoners of war liberated in 1945 found the physical arrangements for their return to be efficient and complete; the failure to provide medical and psychiatric assistance when it was needed most was
unfortunate, but the government cannot be held entirely responsible
for this. Similarly, in Geneva in 1949 and Korea in the 1950s,
Canadian agencies made every effort to avoid the mistakes that had
been so troublesome during the Second World War.

The struggle for pension benefits reflects somewhat less favourably
on the government, and ex-prisoners' groups were often frustrated at
how slowly the wheels of bureaucracy turned. However, governments
rarely open the treasury without a fight, and ex-POWs were probably
treated no differently from dozens of other deserving groups who had
to wait years for satisfaction. Furthermore, it must be said that the final
settlement gave the benefit of the doubt to the former captive and, if
anything, erred on the side of generosity. Individual ex-prisoners may
have felt disadvantaged in some specific way, but they are the exceptions that prove the rule. During the Second World War, most
Canadian POWs considered themselves better looked after than their
campmates from other nations, and in the postwar years most ex-prisoners must admit that they were just as fortunate.

THE PHRASE 'FORGOTTEN MEN' has been used so often to describe prisoners of war that it has become almost a cliche.[1] Certainly the stereotype evokes a degree of pathos: the POW, thrown into the enemy's hands by chance of war (or perhaps through some fault of his own), whose link with home is tenuous, who realizes that his friends and family little understand what he is going through, and who returns home after the war to find few people interested in his problems. Compelling though this picture may be, it is not entirely accurate.

Certainly few people in Canada appreciated the realities of captivity. Virtually every POW diary and memoir contains a section of excerpts from the letters of friends and relatives that reveal the depth of misunderstanding. 'Darling I have found a fantastic new diet for losing weight, would you like me to send it to you?' inquired one well-meaning relative, while another correspondent suggested to a prisoner that 'if you are ever near Heidelberg be sure to see "The Student Prince."' Just as bad was a 1942 magazine article that stated at the outset that POWs had not suffered like civilians from rationing and cuts in food allowances.[2]

Even government officials who dealt with POW matters on a daily basis admitted an imperfect understanding of the realities of captivity. Of course, there were exceptions. Evelyn Rivers Bulkeley had the keenest grasp of the problems facing prisoners during the First World War, and Colonel Clarke was certainly head and shoulders above anyone else in the Canadian government during the Second World War, but most of the other bureaucrats and relief workers had less insight. Even Morley Scott, one of the ablest External Affairs officials engaged in the POW effort and the bureaucrat most deeply involved in the matter, admitted after nearly six years of war that he little understood the complexities of the aid program:

> I don't see why they [the International Committee of the Red Cross] can't get bandages and baking soda from Geneva to North Germany in less than four months. Hodson [of the Canadian Red Cross] went into a long song and dance about governmental red tape, clearance through half a dozen ministries and so on, all of which mystified me completely ... The longer I am at this game, the more I realize how little I know about the Red Cross set up.[3]

However, such comments suggest only that POWs were misunderstood, and in no way imply that Canadians did not care about their citizens in enemy hands. There is no gainsaying the good intentions of the government, or of any of the private agencies that turned their attention to the plight of POWs. In both world wars, private citizens, civil servants, and Members of Parliament gave unstintingly of their time and energy to reduce the hardships experienced by POWs. Beatrice Asselin, Justice Gordon, and many others may have acted rashly or irresponsibly at times, but only because they believed so strongly that they were best able to do the most for Canadians in enemy hands.

Unfortunately that enthusiasm did not have an efficient outlet, for in neither war did the Canadian government establish an effective means of administering POW affairs. During the First World War, this was hardly surprising, for no example existed to instruct bureaucrats on the pitfalls of the matter. There was no such mitigating circumstance during the Second World War. Officials knew of the problems that had hampered Canadian efforts during the last war, yet they demonstrated little willingness to address those problems. Instead of creating a single POW office within the Department of National Defence, as Morley Scott later admitted would have been the best solution, Canadian officials struck committee after committee to maintain relations between the host of government departments and semi-official agencies that felt they had a role to play in POW affairs.[4]

All departments must share in the blame for this state of affairs, but National Defence was perhaps the most culpable. Time and time again, the department insisted that it must be consulted on all matters pertaining to Canadian servicemen in enemy hands, yet just as frequently it resisted assuming the responsibility that it should have borne. Colonel Clarke would gladly have accepted the burden of safeguarding the interests of all Canadian POWs, and doubtless he would have accomplished the task exceedingly well. However, his superiors and the heads of other government departments never gave him the chance.

Centralizing POW affairs in a single office would have solved much of the problem, for matters could be dealt with quite efficiently when only a few officials were involved. The speed with which certain relief problems were solved during the First World War was due to the fact that only a handful of individuals needed to be consulted. Similarly, the Red Cross standard parcel campaign of the Second World War was so successful because only a few departments were engaged in it. Much has been made of the growth of Canada's civil service from 1939 to 1945, but the superintendence of POW affairs would have benefited from a leaner bureaucracy.

In fairness to Morley Scott and the many others who laboured with the task of caring for POWs, it must be admitted that the enemy held most of the cards in the game. One would be hard-pressed to state that, in either of the world wars or the Korean conflict, more could have been done for Canadian prisoners had the government's organization been more efficient. The German government during the First World War was positively munificent compared with later regimes, for Nazi Germany, Imperial Japan, and Communist North Korea and China clearly had little interest in treating POWs kindly in the interests of humanity. An efficient organization in Ottawa would not have changed this fact; it would merely have reduced the number of headaches experienced by bureaucrats.

In this situation, Canada had to pin its hopes on the concept of reciprocity in attempting to ameliorate the lot of Canadian prisoners; only by linking the treatment of prisoners in Canada to that of Canadians in enemy hands could the government attempt to exert some influence over the enemy. However, even this sensible position was weakened by the fact that the concept of reciprocity functioned only when the enemy valued its citizens in captivity as much as Canada did. Such was the case during the First World War, when the belligerents were able to draw on nineteenth-century military traditions of honour and chivalry to make reciprocity of treatment function. The case of POWs in the Far East reflects the other side of the coin, for the mutual hostages thesis had little impact on them. It is impossible to speculate what fate might have befallen the members of C Force had widespread violence against Japanese nationals in Canada broken out in early 1942. However, the argument of External Affairs that Canada treated Japanese nationals and Japanese-Canadians humanely, respectfully, and generously carried little weight with the Japanese government. In its eyes, POWs had dishonoured themselves by surrendering; they were beyond the pale and suitable only for forced labour.

The experience of Canada and its POWs also sheds light on Canada's evolving international position. As External Affairs grew in size and competence through the two world wars and the Korean War, the department must have found it a little galling that the enemy paid no heed to Canadian independence. Despite the best efforts of the mandarins, both Germany and Japan treated Canada as a colony of Britain, except when singling out Canadians to sow dissent among the Allies. The attitude of North Korea and Communist China, who viewed Canada as a lackey of the United States, was just as bad, but ironically had positive ramifications for Canadian POWs. In this regard, External Affairs might have made greater allowances for the enemies' view of Canada's constitutional position. There was no use insisting on Canada's independence of action when enemy governments would happily seize upon this as an excuse to create trouble.

The POW problem also showed the Canadian government adapting to changes in influence within the North Atlantic triangle. In various situations during the Second World War, Canada, rather than being pushed into the arms of the Americans by Britain's weakness, coolly and rather clinically evaluated the pros and cons of aligning with Britain or the United States in any given policy. In this, External Affairs was not entirely successful, for in making these calculations the department invariably took more time than Canada's two ranking allies were willing to wait. The American government did not worry about consulting Canada before pressing ahead with any plan, and as the war progressed, Britain showed a growing willingness to do the same. Canada's insistence on independent action created no small amount of friction within Commonwealth committees, and Britain was perhaps glad when the centre of POW affairs moved to Washington, where their staff could work unhindered by Canadian officials.

Canadians behind barbed wire in Germany, Japan, or North Korea knew little of these matters, and probably cared as much. Their interest lay not in whether the government had a single official responsible for POWs, or whether Canadian influence in London or Washington was waning. They cared only that people at home did not forget them. Despite the problems that plagued the liberation process in 1918 and the failure to provide adequate rehabilitation assistance after both world wars, Canadian prisoners were generally grateful for the efforts made on their behalf. Indeed, they frequently took pains to point out that they were better looked after by their government than many other Allied POWs. H.S. Ferns, who accompanied Canadian repatriates to Britain in May 1944, reported that Canadian ex-POWs were grateful for the work of the government and people of Canada in keeping up their spirits, and that prisoners from Britain, Australia, and New Zealand often felt forgotten by their governments. In 1945 a recent Canadian repatriate confirmed that 'we received more from our people than any other POW in Germany.'[5]

Canadian ex-prisoners still receive better treatment from their government than most other former POWs. The battle for prisoners' pensions spanned many decades, but after the Second World War, Canadian officials admitted the mistakes that had been made in the 1920s and 1930s and eventually gave ex-POWs the benefit of the doubt in pension claims. The generous veterans' benefits available now were not secured without a battle and a certain amount of political foot-dragging, but government benefits rarely are. Indeed, some ex-POWs are a little embarrassed at receiving a special pension for having been captured.

Only a handful of government officials who were involved in POW affairs are still alive, and the ranks of Canadian ex-POWs are thinning by the year. In 1993 only a dozen First World War ex-prisoners and 4200 from the Second World War drew pensions.[6] As the slogan for a 1987 reunion, the RCAF Ex-POW Association chose 'Stay out of Heaven till '87,' only half in jest. Except for former Far East POWs, the survivors generally look back on their time in captivity as a valuable experience. They may say that imprisonment robbed them of the best years of their lives, and none will go so far as to emulate the German ex-POW who titled his memoirs *Thank You, Canada* in gratitude to the country that had been his host during the war. Nevertheless, many Canadian ex-prisoners aver that captivity provided them with an education, in human nature and in themselves, that they could not have gained in any other circumstances.

To say that Canadian prisoners were forgotten, then, is misleading. They were frequently misunderstood and occasionally subordinated to larger political objectives, but they were rarely forgotten. The fact that so many government departments, aid agencies, and private individuals wanted to play a role in caring for prisoners certainly created a wide range of headaches for Canadian bureaucrats through the two world wars and the Korean conflict. However, that fact should also prove to the ex-prisoner that, in spite of the bickering and administrative confusion, Canadians regarded their soldiers and civilians in enemy hands as objects of concern.

A Note on Statistics

The statistics for Canadian POWs are very difficult to deal with, for a number of reasons. In the first place, soldiers who succumbed to battle wounds while in captivity are generally not listed as prisoners of war but as having died of wounds. By the same token, some statistics list all POWs who died in enemy hands not as prisoners of war but as battle or ordinary casualties. To take an example from Canadian Army official historian Colonel C.P. Stacey's figures on the Second World War, a soldier who was taken prisoner at Dieppe and died during an escape attempt in 1944 is not listed as having been captured in 1942, but as a 1944 battle casualty. Using unit histories and other sources, it has been possible to make allowances for this fact in Second World War statistics, but not in First World War statistics.

Second, Colonel Stacey's figures for POW casualties are low by quite a wide margin. For example, he lists 51 captured Canadian Army personnel as having been killed by the enemy in the European theatre, but war crimes investigations revealed that 134 Canadian POWs were murdered by German troops in Normandy alone. The discrepancy may lie in the fact that these soldiers may have been considered battle casualties, since they may not have been in captivity long enough to fit the military's criteria for having been a POW (usually forty-eight hours in enemy hands). Again, Colonel Stacey's figures have been adjusted to count these soldiers as prisoners.

Finally, official sources rarely agree on the figures for Canadian

POWs. This is particularly true for the First World War. The Overseas
Military Forces of Canada report gives two different sets of figures in
two different places, and the Red Cross POW Branch provides a
different figure again. Even the tables reproduced by Desmond Morton
vary widely; for example, one table lists 855 POWs captured in 1918,
while another lists only 481. Statistics for the Second World War are a
little better. Various RCAF sources agree on the number of Canadian
airmen captured during the war, but the official history of the RCN and
the Director General History give different numbers of Canadian seamen captured. Most sources agree on the number of soldiers captured
in Hong Kong, but Colonel Stacey and the Director General History
figures disagree on the number of Army personnel captured in Europe
and North Africa. Fortunately, the small number of Canadians captured in Korea allows for exact statistics for that war. The following
tables, then, can represent only the most plausible combination of a
variety of sources.

Tables

Table 1

First World War POWs: Canadian Expeditionary Force

	1914	1915	1916	1917	1918	Total
Officers		39	41	42	10	132
Other Ranks		1370	995	495	855	3715
Total		1409	1036	537	865	3847

Sources: Overseas Military Forces of Canada, *Report of the Ministry, Overseas Military Forces of Canada, 1918* (London: 1918), 58; Desmond Morton, *Silent Battle: Canadian Prisoners of War in Germany, 1914-1919* (Toronto: Lester Publishing 1992), app. A; Max Aitken, *Canada in Flanders*, vol. 1 (Toronto: Hodder & Stoughton 1916), app. 6

Table 2a

Second World War POWs: Canadian Army

	1940	1941	1942	1943	1944	1945	Total
ETO[a]	1		1948	264	2675	511	5399
PTO[b]		1689					1689
Total	1	1689	1948	264	2675	511	7088

[a] European Theatre of Operations (including Mediterranean)
[b] Pacific Theatre of Operations
Sources: Department of National Defence, Director General History (DG Hist): f. 113 3R2 009 (D21); Col. C.P. Stacey, *Official History of the Canadian Army in the Second World War*, vol. 1, *Six Years of War: The Army in Canada, Britain and the Pacific* (Ottawa: Queen's Printer 1955), 524-5; National Defence, *Canadian Prisoners of War and Missing Personnel in the Far East* (Ottawa: King's Printer 1945)

Table 2b

Second World War POWs: Royal Canadian Air Force

	3 Sept. 1940 to 2 Sept. 1941	3 Sept. 1941 to 2 Sept. 1942	3 Sept. 1942 to 2 Sept. 1943	3 Sept. 1943 to 2 Sept. 1944	3 Sept. 1944 to 8 May 1945[a] 14 Aug. 1945[b]	Total
European Theatre						
BC[c]	43	205	525	833	274	1880
Other[d]	23	121	189	130	139	602
Total	66	326	714	963	413	2482
Pacific Theatre						
Total		30	3	1	8	42
Total (both theatres)						
	66	356	717	964	421	2524

[a] European Theatre
[b] Pacific Theatre
[c] Bomber Command
[d] Other Commands, including Fighter, Coastal, Transport, etc.
Sources: Sir Charles Webster and Noble Frankland, *The Strategic Air Offensive Against Germany, 1939-1945* (London: HMSO 1961), 6:440; DG Hist: f. 113 3R2 009 (D21); T.W. Melnyk, *Canadian Flying Operations in South East Asia, 1941-1945* (Ottawa: Department of National Defence 1976), passim.

Table 2c

Second World War POWs:
Royal Canadian Navy and Royal Canadian Naval Volunteer Reserve

	1940	1941	1942	1943	1944	1945	Total
ETO[a]		3	3	2	84[b]		92
PTO[c]			2				2
Total		3	5	2	84		94

[a] European Theatre of Operations (including Mediterranean)
[b] Survivors of HMCS *Athabaskan*, which was sunk by German destroyers off Brittany on 29 April 1944.
[c] Pacific Theatre of Operations
Source: DG Hist: f. 113 3R2 009 (D21)

Table 2d

Second World War: Canadian POW Casualties

	Army	RCAF	RCNVR	Total
European Theatre				
Died of wounds	114	18	1	133
Killed by enemy	149	22		171
Killed by Allied aircraft	17	4		21
Died of disease	25	4		29
Died of injury	3			3
Other/Unknown	15	8		23
Total	323	56	1	380
Pacific Theatre				
Died of wounds	9	1		10
Killed by enemy	4	2		6
Died of disease	253	3		256
Died of injury	13			13
Other causes		5		5
Total	279	11		290
Grand Total	602	67	1	670

Sources: DG Hist: f. 113 3R2 009 (D21); Col. C.P. Stacey, *Official History of the Canadian Army in the Second World War*, vol. 1, *Six Years of War: The Army in Canada, Britain and the Pacific* (Ottawa: Queen's Printer 1955), 524-5; Les Allison and Harry Hayward, *They Shall Grow Not Old: A Book of Remembrance* (Brandon, MB: Commonwealth Air Training Plan Museum n.d.)

Table 3

Korean War POWs

	1951	1952	1953	Total
3rd PPCLI[a]			I	I
RCAF[b]		I		I
RCHA[c]	I	I		2
1st RCR[d]		14		14
3rd RCR			7	7
1st R22eR[e]		I		I
2nd R22eR	3			3
3rd R22eR			4	4
Total	4	17	12	33

[a] Princess Patricia's Canadian Light Infantry
[b] Royal Canadian Air Force
[c] Royal Canadian Horse Artillery
[d] Royal Canadian Regiment
[e] Royal 22nd Regiment
Source: DG Hist: f. 410 B25.065, 'Prisoners of War – Korea'

Introduction

1 'How Interned Allied Airmen Fare in Sweden,' *Saturday Night* 60/14 (9 December 1944):4; George Williams, interview by author, Milton, ON, 27 May 1992.
2 National Archives of Canada (NAC): Department of External Affairs Records, vol. 2866, f. 1841-40, John D. Kearney, Canadian High Commissioner in Dublin to External Affairs, 10 August 1943.
3 'Ypres: 1915,' in Alden Nowlan, *The Mysterious Naked Man* (Toronto: Clarke, Irwin 1969), 41-3.
4 Patricia Roy, J.L. Granatstein, Masako Iino, and Hiroko Takamura, *Mutual Hostages: Canadians and Japanese During the Second World War* (Toronto: University of Toronto Press 1990).
5 Gladys E. Smith, *Forty Nights to Freedom: The True Prisoner of War Escape Story of Wing Commander Stewart F. Cowan (Ret.)* (Winnipeg: Queenston House Publishing 1984), 72.

Chapter 1: Nineteenth-Century Lessons

1 A.C. Casselman, *Richardson's War of 1812* (Toronto: Historical Publishing 1902), 249; Capt. W.H. Merritt, 'Journal of Events Principally on the Detroit and Niagara Frontiers,' in *Select British Documents of the Canadian War of 1812*, vol. 3, pt. 2, ed. William Wood (Toronto: Champlain Society 1928; repr., New York: Greenwood Press 1968), 623-48.
2 Casselman, *Richardson's War of 1812*, 289; Lt. R. Matheson, Paymaster, Glengarry Light Infantry, Three Rivers, to Noah Freer, Military Secretary, Quebec, 8 March 1814, in Wood, ed., *Select British Documents of the Canadian War of 1812*, 3/2:742.
3 Prevost's General Order of 27 October 1813; Secretary of State to the Governor of Kentucky, 27 November 1813; General Order from the Adjutant-General's Office, Montreal, 12 December 1813, in Casselman, *Richardson's War of 1812*, 251-4. See Ralph Robinson, 'Retaliation for the Treatment of Prisoners in the War of 1812,' *American Historical Review* 49/1 (October 1943):65-70.
4 Casselman, *Richardson's War of 1812*, 261; James van Horne, *A Narrative of the Captivity and Sufferings of James van Horne* (Middlebury, VT: 1817; repr., New York: Garland Publishing 1977), 18.

5 The Lieber Code and the Brussels Declarations are reproduced in Howard S. Levie, ed., *Documents on Prisoners of War* (Newport, RI: Naval War College Press 1979), 37-44, 58-60.

6 Joseph Schull, *Rebellion* (Toronto: Macmillan 1971), 121; William Hodgson Ellis, 'The Adventures of a Prisoner of War,' *Canadian Magazine* 13/3 (July 1899):203.

7 *Gazette* (Montreal), 25 March 1885, in Desmond Morton and Reginald H. Roy, eds., *Telegrams of the North-West Campaign* (Toronto: Champlain Society 1972), xxvi.

8 Charles Pelham Mulvaney, *The History of the North-West Rebellion of 1885* (Toronto: A.H. Hovey 1885), 285.

9 Ibid., 277; *Saskatchewan Herald* 7/18 (18 May 1885), in William L. Clink, ed., *Battleford Beleaguered* (Willowdale, ON: W.L. Clink 1984).

10 Being captured by natives was a favourite phobia of whites in North America until well into the nineteenth century. Enough accounts were published to fill 111 volumes of the Garland Library of Narratives of North American Indian Captives.

11 John Pennefather, *Thirteen Years on the Prairies* (London: Kegan Paul, Trench, Trubner 1892), 21-2.

12 Harold Penryn Rusden, 'Notes on the Suppression of the Northwest Insurrection,' in *'Reminiscences of a Bungle by One of the Bunglers' and Two Other North-West Rebellion Diaries*, ed. R.C. Macleod (Edmonton: University of Alberta Press 1983), 245; Lt.-Col. H.J. Grasett to G.F. Hagarty, 7 June 1885, in Maj. D.J. Goodspeed, *Battle Royal* (Toronto: Royal Regiment of Canada 1962), 54. North-West Field Force commander Maj.-Gen. Frederick Middleton was less sympathetic about the fate of the captives and believed that the factor at Fort Pitt should have been hanged for choosing surrender over resistance. Middleton to Caron, 13 June 1885, in Morton and Roy, eds., *Telegrams of the North-West Campaign*, 344.

13 Diary of Robert K. Allan, 90th Battalion, 22 June 1885, in Iris Allan, 'A Riel Rebellion Diary,' *Alberta Historical Review* 12/3 (Summer 1964):23.

14 Middleton to Caron, 6 June 1885, in Morton and Roy, eds., *Telegrams of the North-West Campaign*, 334; Pennefather, *Thirteen Years on the Prairies*, 36.

15 Letter of 12 August 1885, in Eric Nicol, ed., *Dickens of the Mounted* (Toronto: Douglas Gibson 1989), 258; National Archives of Canada (NAC): Salamon Pritchard Papers, MG30 E127: interview with S. Pritchard; John W. Shera, 'Poundmaker's Capture of a Wagon Train,' *Alberta Historical Review* 1/1 (April 1953):9.

16 Quoted in Walter Laqueur, ed., *The Guerilla Reader* (Scarborough, ON: New American Library 1977), 108. Von Boguslawski apparently assumed that a commander would not hesitate to order an illegal act if he deemed it essential in a military sense. In this way, the onus of committing the crime would fall on the individual soldier, who would then have to deal with the psychological consequences of his action.

17 Admiralty to Foreign Office, 16 May 1899; War Office to Foreign Office, 17 May 1899; Salisbury to Pauncefote, 16 May 1899, in G.P. Gooch and Harold Temperley, eds., *British Documents on the Origins of the War* (London: HMSO 1927), 1:225-6.

18 Sir Horace Rumbold, British Ambassador, Vienna, to Salisbury, 14 September 1898, in ibid., 219; Andrew D. White, *Autobiography of Andrew Dickson White* (New York: Century 1905), 2:292.

19 R.B. Mowat, *The Life of Lord Pauncefote* (London: Constable 1929), 231; Charles à Court Repington, *Vestigia* (London: Constable 1919), 183-4.

20 Richard Hough, *First Sea Lord: An Authorized Biography of Admiral Lord Fisher* (London: George Allen & Unwin 1969), 115.

21 *Free Press*, 18 May 1899, 4; *Canadian Magazine* 13/3 (July 1899):283; *Expositor*, 25 May

1899, 2; *Saturday Night* 12/27 (20 May 1899):1.

22 *Mail & Empire*, 18 May 1899, 4; *Vancouver World* editorial, in *Alberta Tribune* (Calgary), 27 May 1899, 4.

23 The text of the portion of the 1899 convention pertaining to POWs is in James Brown Scott, *The Hague Peace Conferences of 1899 and 1907* (Baltimore: Johns Hopkins Press 1909; repr., New York: Garland Publishing 1972), 2:117-25.

24 Public Record Office: CAB 37/87, #42, 'Report of the Inter-Departmental Committee appointed to consider the Subjects which may arise for discussion at the Second Peace Conference,' 21 March 1907, 30.

25 Winston Churchill, *London to Ladysmith via Pretoria* (Toronto: Copp Clark 1900), 96. As a war correspondent, Churchill was technically a civilian internee, but he never used the phrase, preferring the more romantic ring of 'prisoner of war.'

26 Capt. Maurice Harold Grant, *History of the War in South Africa* (London: Hurst & Blackett 1910), 4:697; Department of Militia and Defence, *Supplementary Report: Organization, Equipment, Despatch and Service of the Canadian Contingents During the War in South Africa, 1899-1900*, Sessional Paper #35a (Ottawa 1901).

27 NAC: J. Frederick Ramsay Papers, MG30 E231, letter dated 8 May 1900.

28 NAC: Department of Veterans Affairs Records, series IA, vol. 47, service record of #456 Pte. J. Hobson; Report G by Lt.-Col. S.B. Steele, 23 March 1901, in Militia and Defence, *Supplementary Report*, 163; E.W.B. Morrison, *With the Guns in South Africa* (Hamilton: Spectator Printing 1901), 219.

29 The Boers often asked prisoners to give an oath of parole before being released, which bound them not to reveal any information to their commanders or to take up arms again against the South African republics. Needless to say, most ex-prisoners broke their parole as soon as they had the chance. A copy of an oath is in NAC: A.H. Macdonell Papers, MG30 E399.

30 NAC: A.E. Hilder Papers, MG30 E339, f. 2, 'Comrades All: A Narrative of the South African War,' 65; P.R. Marshall, 'Two Near VCs of the South African War,' *Organization of Military Museums of Canada Bulletin* 3 (1974):49; Morrison, *With the Guns in South Africa*, 263; Carman Miller, *Painting the Map Red: Canada and the South African War, 1899-1902* (Montreal: McGill-Queen's University Press 1993), 130.

31 F.J. Livingston, *My Escape from the Boers* (Toronto: William Briggs 1900), 25; Morrison, *With the Guns in South Africa*, 256; Col. S.B. Steele, *Forty Years in Canada* (New York: Dodd, Mead 1915), 353.

32 See, for example, W. Hart-McHarg, *From Quebec to Pretoria with the Royal Canadian Regiment* (Toronto: William Briggs 1902), 227; NAC: John Barton Heron Papers, MG30 E355, J.B. Heron to Maggie, 1 July 1900; J. Fitzgerald Lee, 'Prisoners of War,' *Army Quarterly* 3/2 (January 1922):356.

33 Report of 2nd Contingent, in Militia and Defence, *Supplementary Report*, 96; Macdonell Papers, 'South Africa,' 4.

34 George L. Mosse, *Fallen Soldiers: Reshaping the Memory of the World Wars* (Oxford: Oxford University Press 1990), 17-19; Geoffrey Best, *Humanity in Warfare* (New York: Columbia University Press 1980), 148. I am grateful to Professor Desmond Morton for his insights on this point.

35 [Canadian Red Cross Society], *Report by the Canadian Red Cross Society of its Operations in the South African War* (Toronto: Central Canadian Council 1902), 11. Ryerson's own account contains only a passing reference to POWs. See Lt.-Col. G. Sterling Ryerson, 'The

Red Cross,' *Canadian Magazine* 14/6 (April 1900):564.

36 An Act to Incorporate the Canadian Red Cross Society. *Statutes of Canada*, 1909, 8-9 Edward 7, vol. 2, c. 68.

37 André Durand, *From Sarajevo to Hiroshima: History of the International Committee of the Red Cross* (Geneva: Henry Dunant Institute 1978), 20-2.

38 Ilza Veith, 'Humane Warfare and Inhuman War: Japan and Its Treatment of War Prisoners,' *Bulletin of the History of Medicine* 19/4 (April 1946):359-60.

39 Roosevelt to Ian Hamilton, 24 January 1906, in Calvin DeArmond Davis, *The United States and the Second Hague Peace Conference* (Durham, NC: Duke University Press 1975), 125.

40 William I. Hull, *The Two Hague Conferences and Their Contributions to International Law* (Boston: Ginn 1908; repr., New York: Garland Publishing 1972), 26; see, for example, *Canadian Magazine* 28/5 (September 1907):471-2.

41 *Halifax Herald*, 18 June 1907, 6; Frederick Palmer, 'The Farce at the Hague,' *Busy Man's Magazine* (Toronto) 14/3 (July 1907):82-3.

42 Ontario, Journals of the Legislative Assembly, 17 March 1907, 209.

43 NAC: Loring Christie Papers, MG30 E44, vol. 2, f. 3, p. 1154.

44 The text of that portion of the 1907 convention pertaining to POWs is in Scott, *The Hague Peace Conferences*, 2:379-87.

45 J.M. Spaight, *War Rights on Land* (London: Macmillan 1911), 265.

46 NAC: Office of the Governor General Records, series G21, vol. 630, f. 34564, Colonial Secretary to Governor General, 24 September 1913 and reply, 12 March 1914.

47 War Office, *King's Regulations and Orders* (London: HMSO 1912), para. 675; War Office, *Manual of Military Law* (London: HMSO 1914), Rules of Procedure (1907), Pt. II, Sec. 124 (H).

Chapter 2: 'Everybody's Business'

1 On this aspect, see Richard B. Speed, *Prisoners, Diplomats and the Great War* (New York: Greenwood Press 1990), 9. For a typical example of what Canadians were led to expect regarding the treatment of POWs, see Thomas S. Russell, *The World's Greatest War* (Brantford: Bradley-Garretson 1914), 363-6.

2 Lt.-Col. E.W. Mingo, 'Prisoners of War 1914-18,' *Journal of the United Services Institute of Nova Scotia* 6 (1933):35.

3 National Archives of Canada (NAC): Department of National Defence (DND) Records, vol. 1845, f. GAQ 11-16c, Canadian Record Office report, 12 February 1919.

4 OC 100th Battalion to the family of Capt. J.A.B. McClure, August 1917, in William Smith Duthie, ed., *Letters from the Front* (Canadian Imperial Bank of Commerce 1920), 2:319.

5 F. Douglas Reville, *History of the County of Brant* (Brantford, ON: Hurley Printing 1920), 2:590; 'Canadian Prisoners of War,' *The British Prisoner of War* 1/5 (May 1918):57. Cf. M. Stuart Hunt, *Nova Scotia's Part in the Great War* (Halifax: Nova Scotia Veteran Publishing 1920), 81.

6 NAC: Department of Militia and Defence (DMD) Records, series III D1, vol. 4739, folder 155, f. 5.

7 Don Corker Diary, Richmond, BC, 3. Corker recalls that the subject of capture never came up at any time during training.

8 Gordon Reid, *Poor Bloody Murder* (Oakville, ON: Mosaic Press 1980), 87.

9 William Ready Division of Archives and Special Collections, McMaster University: World War I Collection, Miscellaneous Material Box 1, f. 8, General Routine Order #95 by General Sir William Robertson, 30 April 1918.

10 Nellie McClung, *Three Times and Out* (Toronto: Thomas Allen 1918), 10; Don Corker, interview by author, Campbellville, ON, 29 June 1992; T.V. Scudamore, 'Lighter Episodes in the Life of a Prisoner of War,' *Canadian Defence Quarterly* 7/3 (April 1930):398. Scudamore wrote that 'the most disappointing and unexpected ending to a military career, especially to one reared in all the traditions of the British Army, was to find oneself a wounded prisoner.' Ibid., 394. Cf. Desmond Morton, *Silent Battle: Canadian Prisoners of War in Germany, 1914-1919* (Toronto: Lester Publishing 1992), x.

11 Mingo, 'Prisoners of War,' 39.

12 Sgt. Arthur Gibbons, *A Guest of the Kaiser* (Toronto: J.M. Dent & Sons 1919), 130, 148; NAC: William Quinton Papers, MG30 E162, 'Twenty Months in Germany,' 2; H.W. Macdonnell and T.W. Morse, 'Canadian Prisoners of War in Germany,' in *Canada and the Great World War*, vol. 4, *The Turn of the Tide* (Toronto: United Publishers of Canada 1919), 334; Scudamore, 'Lighter Episodes,' 398.

13 Mingo, 'Prisoners of War,' 38; George Pearson, *The Escape of a Princess Pat* (New York: George H. Doran 1918), 48.

14 A.F. Field, 'Wounded and Captured,' *University Magazine* 18/2 (April 1919):266; Fred Gies, untitled MS, 2. I am grateful to Bert Konig for providing me with this manuscript.

15 Macdonnell and Morse, 'Canadian Prisoners of War in Germany,' 335; Jack Evans, 'Sixteen Months a War Prisoner,' in Francis J. Reynolds, ed., *World's War Events* (New York: P.F. Collier & Son 1921), 2:143.

16 Lt. J. Harvey Douglas, *Captured: Sixteen Months as a Prisoner of War* (Toronto: McClelland, Goodchild & Stewart 1918), 41, 44, 53.

17 House of Commons, Special Committee on Pensions and Returned Soldiers' Problems, Minutes of Proceedings and Evidence #14, 6 May 1936, 360; Pearson, *The Escape of a Princess Pat*, 80.

18 Jack O'Brien, *Into the Jaws of Death* (Toronto: McClelland & Stewart 1919), 124; Hamilton Public Library Special Collections: Martin Family Papers, scrapbook, unidentified newspaper clipping, 400; T.V. Scudamore, *Lighter Episodes in the Life of a Prisoner of War* (Aldershot: Gale & Polden 1933), 46.

19 John C. Thorn, *Three Years a Prisoner in Germany* (Vancouver: Cowan and Brookhouse 1919), 7-8.

20 Duthie, ed., *Letters from the Front*, 1:272.

21 From 'Christmas at Holzminden, 1917,' in Arthur S. Bourinot, *Poems* (Toronto: T.H. Best 1921), 32.

22 Douglas, *Captured*, 95; Donald Laird, *Prisoner Five-One-Eleven* (Toronto: Ontario Press n.d.), 75.

23 Oliver Hezzelwood, ed., *Trinity War Book: A Recital of Service and Sacrifice in the Great War* (Toronto: Ontario Press 1921), 116.

24 D. Bilson Merry, 'My Escape from a German Prison: A Thrilling Experience,' *The Gold Stripe* 1 (1918):85.

25 The Watson Family, '1917,' in Tony Strachan, ed., *In the Clutch of Circumstance: Experiences of Canadian Prisoners of War* (Victoria: Cappis Press 1985), 106-7.

26 Evans, 'Sixteen Months a War Prisoner,' 146; Gies, 3; Hezzelwood, ed., *Trinity War Book*, 243; Harry Drope, 'Escape through Russia,' *Legion*, June 1993, 15.

27 Royal Commission for the Investigation of Illegal Warfare Claims and for the Return of Sequestered Property in Necessitous Cases, Errol M. McDougall, Commissioner (cited as McDougall Commission), *Maltreatment of Prisoners of War* (Ottawa: King's Printer 1932),

case #1994; Morton, *Silent Battle*, 79; McDougall Commission, *Reparations, 1932: Further Report* (Ottawa: King's Printer 1933), case #2378.

28 O'Brien, *Into the Jaws of Death*, 143.

29 McDougall Commission, *Maltreatment of POWs*, cases #2083 and #2105.

30 DND Records, vol. 1205, f. HQ 240-1-40, CEF Records Office to Militia Council, 9 January 1917.

31 NAC: William Brooke Family Papers, MG24 I94, f. 14, p. 1794; Morton, *Silent Battle*, 116-17.

32 Corker diary, 8; Corker interview, 29 June 1992.

33 Frank C. MacDonald, *The Kaiser's Guest* (New York: Country Life Press 1918), 92; O'Brien, *Into the Jaws of Death*, 150.

34 Iona K. Carr, *A Story of the Canadian Red Cross Information Bureau during the Great War* (1920), 9; Mary MacLeod Moore, *The Maple Leaf's Red Cross* (London: Skeffington & Sons n.d.), 112-13; DND Records, vol. 859, f. HQ 54-21-13-5, pt. 1, Adele Plumptre, Canadian Red Cross Society to DMD, 29 August 1917.

35 On the mechanics of the inspection, see Daniel J. McCarthy, *The Prisoner of War in Germany* (New York: Moffat, Yard 1918), ch. 4.

36 Ambassador W.H. Page to British Foreign Secretary, 15 March 1915, in James Brown Scott, ed., *Diplomatic Correspondence between the United States and Germany* (New York: Oxford University Press 1918), 40; McCarthy, *The Prisoner of War in Germany*, 3; James W. Gerard, *My Four Years in Germany* (New York: George H. Doran 1917), 160.

37 Fred McMullen and Jack Evans, *Out of the Jaws of Hunland* (Toronto: William Briggs 1918), 84; Mingo, 'Prisoners of War,' 48; Thorn, *Three Years a Prisoner in Germany*, 29.

38 NAC: Russell M. Smith Papers, MG30 E409, diary for 29 June 1918.

39 Statement by Cpl. J. Finnimore, in Reid, *Poor Bloody Murder*, 86; Thorn, *Three Years a Prisoner in Germany*, 30; Douglas, *Captured*, 108; Alonzo Englebert Taylor, 'The Diet of Prisoners of War in Germany,' *Journal of the American Medical Association* 69/19 (10 November 1917):1579.

40 For a typical report by a returned prisoner, see DND Records, vol. 1845, f. GAQ 11-16, statement by L/Cpl. A.H. Jones.

41 Speed, *Prisoners, Diplomats and the Great War*, 18. For an example of the often contradictory accounts that found their way into government files, see '"English Swine" for Prisoners,' *Montreal Gazette*, 4 November 1915, 4, and 'Well and happy in his German prison,' *Toronto Daily News*, 29 July 1916, 4.

42 NAC: George Albert Mercer Papers, MG30 E323, diary for 18 June 1918; Percy Hampton, interview by author, Toronto, 25 November 1991.

43 McCarthy, *The Prisoner of War in Germany*, 1-2.

44 J.H. Morgan, ed., *The German War Book: Being 'The Usages of War on Land' Issued by the Great General Staff of the German Army* (London: John Murray 1915), xiii.

45 Robert Jackson, *The Prisoners, 1914-18* (London: Routledge 1989), 7; Morton, *Silent Battle*, 18.

46 United Kingdom, House of Commons, *Report of the Committee on Alleged German Outrages*, Chairman, Viscount Bryce (London: HMSO 1915).

47 NAC: Arthur Meighen Papers, MG26 I, reel C-3226, vol. 30, p. 17068, undated clipping.

48 DND Records, vol. 859, f. HQ 54-21-13-5, pt. 1, Foreign Office to American Ambassador, 10 September 1915; James Wilford Garner, *International Law and the World War* (London: Longmans, Green 1920), 2:51.

49 NAC: Department of External Affairs (DEA) Records, series A3, vol. 355, f. A/141, Mary S. Aston, Pocklington, Yorkshire, to Borden, 27 April 1917; DND Records, vol. 1206, f. HQ 240-1-56, A. Burnett, Yuma County, AZ, to DMD, 13 July 1918.
50 NAC: R.L. Borden Papers, MG26 H1a, reel C-4307, vol. 59, p. 29330, Colonial Office to Governor-General, 1 November 1918.
51 Max Aitken, *Canada in Flanders* (Toronto: Hodder & Stoughton 1916), app. 6.
52 DEA Records, series A2, vol. 302, f. POW 90/15 pt. 3, Accountant-General, OMFC to High Commission, 29 March 1917.
53 Ad for the Canadian Red Cross Serve by Giving Campaign. *Globe* (Toronto), 13 January 1917, 7.
54 NAC: Secretary of State Records, series H2, vol. 782, f. 294, Under-Secretary of State to Gertrude A. Smith, POW Committee, New Westminster, BC, 23 January 1916.
55 Clarence Prouty Shedd, *History of the World's Alliance of Young Men's Christian Associations* (London: SPCK 1955), 547-56.
56 NAC: G.L. Ogilvie Papers, MG30 E279, f. 1, Relief and Casualty Committee to W.R. Miller, President, Canadian Red Cross Society, Montreal Branch, 13 November 1915.
57 'Adopting a Prisoner,' *Saturday Night*, 17 July 1915, 22.
58 Hunt, *Nova Scotia's Part in the Great War*, 361.
59 DND Records, vol. 859, f. HQ 54-21-13-5, pt. 1, Mrs. Peter McDougall, New Westminster, BC, to Adjutant-General, [April 1917].
60 Ibid., Mrs. J.M. Knowlson, Lindsay, to DMD, 24 April 1916; Sally Warnock, War Aid Department, St. John Ambulance of Manitoba, to Robert Rogers, 15 July 1916.
61 Ibid., f. HQ 54-21-13-4, DMD to Mrs. H. Beckett, Montreal, 18 January 1915; DMD Records, series III B1, vol. 1121, f. P-47-4, Canadian Pay and Record Office (CPRO), London to Dominion Express Co. of Canada, London, 29 April 1915; DND Records, vol. 860, f. HQ 54-21-13-7, pt. 1, DMD to Miss M. Linghorne, New Liskeard, Ontario, 16 January 1917; f. HQ 54-21-13-7, pt. 2, Adjutant-General to Mrs. B. White, Toronto, 11 October 1917.
62 F. HQ 54-21-13-7, pt. 2, Assistant Director of Supplies and Transport to Mrs. L.P. Dayton, Niagara Falls, New York, 11 October 1917 and 26 October 1917. One hopes the Assistant Director did not give the same incorrect advice to his immediate superior, whose brother was a POW.
63 DMD Records, series III A1 serial 4, vol. 40, f. 4-2-13, Carson to Williams, 3 June 1915; series III B1, vol. 1121, f. P-47-4, Hodgetts to CPRO, 31 May 1915.
64 Ibid., series III A1 serial 8, vol. 40, f. 8-3-3, Drummond to Hughes, 12 August 1915.
65 Ibid., Carson to Hughes, 14 August 1915.
66 DEA Records, series A2, vol. 150, f. C9/49, Rivers Bulkeley to Perley, 20 September 1915; Militia Order #511, 22 November 1915.
67 Taylor, 'The Diet of Prisoners of War in Germany,' 1575.
68 Corker interview, 29 June 1992; *The Veterans Journal*, Spring 1978, 76.
69 Mingo, 'Prisoners of War,' 43.
70 Evans, 'Sixteen Months a War Prisoner,' 144; Merry, 'My Escape from a German Prison,' 85; MacDonald, *The Kaiser's Guest*, 89.
71 Carr, *A Story of the Canadian Red Cross Information Bureau*, 49; DMD Records, series III A1, vol. 3, f. 2-2-27, Chief Paymaster to Carson, 22 November 1916.
72 Ibid., vol. 69, f. 10-4-15, Rivers Bulkeley to CPRO, 26 August 1917.
73 United Kingdom, House of Commons, *Report of the Joint Committee to Enquire into the Organisation and Methods of the Central Prisoners of War Committee*, Cmd 8615 (1917), 2;

Public Record Office (PRO): CAB 23/2, minutes of War Cabinet meeting #122, 18 April 1917. A YMCA inspector estimated that in May 1916, Münster camp received 264,000 parcels for the 30,000 prisoners interned there. Conrad Hoffman, *In the Prison Camps of Germany* (New York: Association Press 1920), 69. Corker recalls writing to Canadian authorities, advising them to take steps to solve the inequities. Corker interview, 29 June 1992.

74 DND Records, vol. 860, f. HQ 54-21-13-7, memo 'Despatch of parcels from Canada to British and Allied Prisoners of War' by Major E. Bristol, 12 July 1917.

75 Correspondence regarding contact via Canadian offices in Europe is in DEA Records, series A7, vol. 556, f. 265; series A2, vol. 264, f. P4/58, Perley to Borden, 5 October 1915, and reply, 7 October 1915; Perley to T.H.W. Idris, Camden Town, 12 October 1915; Perley to W. Stanes, London, 23 October 1915.

76 Ibid., vol. 229, f. M61/23, High Commission to Canadian Trade Representative, Rotterdam, 14 July 1916; POW Help Committee to High Commission, 22 September 1916; Canadian Trade Representative, Rotterdam, to High Commission, 4 October 1916.

77 Ibid., vol. 150, f. C9/49, DMD to High Commission, 9 December 1916; series G1, vol. 1165, f. 1395, Pope to James Young, Copp Clark Co., 8 November 1915.

78 Ibid., series A2, vol. 302, f. POW 90/15, pt. 2, Coulter to Plumptre, 20 December 1917.

79 Arthur Marwick, *The Deluge* (London: Bodley Head 1965), 136; CAB 24/58, GT 5152, A. Stanley to Lloyd George, 16 July 1918.

80 DND Records, vol. 860, f. HQ 54-21-13-7, pt. 1, 'Scheme for Co-ordination of Relief for British Prisoners of War.'

81 DEA Records, series A2, vol. 302, f. POW 90/15, pt. 1, Hodgetts to Noel Marshall, Chairman, CRCS, [October 1916].

82 DND Records, vol. 860, f. HQ 54-21-13-7, pt. 1, W.J. Thompson, Sault Ste. Marie to DMD, 5 November 1916; Mrs. A.F. Miller, Hartford, CT, to DMD, 26 November 1916; Borden Papers, MG26 H1c, reel C-4400, vol. 212, p. 119423, W.E. Saunders, London, ON, to Borden, 6 November 1916.

83 Ibid., p. 119429, Marshall to Borden, 9 November 1916; Rivers Bulkeley to High Commission, 8 December 1916.

84 Ibid., 18 January 1917; series G1, vol. 1193, f. 1917-3, Perley to Borden, 18 January 1917; DEA Records, series A2, vol. 302, f. POW 90/15 pt. 1, 'Memorandum regarding the Despatch of Parcels from the Dominions to British and Allied Prisoners of War,' 22 December 1916.

85 *Globe*, 13 January 1917, 5.

86 DEA Records, series A2, vol. 302, f. POW 90/15, pt. 1, Post Office Department circular 'Communication with Prisoners of War Interned Abroad,' 29 January 1917.

87 Letter from Sergeant T.S. Ronaldson, 16 February 1917 in Duthie, ed., *Letters from the Front*, 1:217; DEA Records, series A2, vol. 302, f. POW 90/15, pt. 1, CSM W.E. Thomson to High Commission, 1 May 1917; MacDonald, *The Kaiser's Guest*, 124.

88 DEA Records, series A3, vol. 302, f. POW 90/15, pt. 1, letter to Perley, 12 April 1917; DND Records, vol. 859, f. HQ 54-21-13-5, pt. 1, CSM J.W. Bentley, Camp Rennbahn Münster II to Mrs. P. McDonald, 3 April 1917.

89 DEA Records, series A2, vol. 302, f. POW 90/15, pt. 1, Nova Scotia Branch, CRCS to Borden, 15 May 1917.

90 Ibid., Rivers Bulkeley to High Commission, 19 June 1917.

91 House of Commons, Debates, 31 July 1917, 3958.

92 Ibid., 3959, 3961.

93 CAB 23/2, minutes of War Cabinet meeting #131, 3 May 1917; CAB 24/13, GT 769, memo by Secretary of State for War, 19 May 1917; DEA Records, series A2, vol. 302, f. POW 90/15, pt. 3, Borden to Perley, 29 July 1917.

94 Borden Papers, MG26 H1c, reel C-4400, vol. 212, p. 119567, Marshall to Borden, 13 July 1917; DEA Records, series A2, vol. 302, f. POW 90/15, pt. 3, 'Memorandum on Officers' Parcel Scheme,' from CRCS, London, 1 November 1917.

95 Ibid., Central POW Committee Regulation #104, 26 October 1917.

96 Ibid., Coulter to High Commission, 27 December 1917.

97 Ibid., f. POW 90/15, pt. 2, Coulter to Marshall, 29 November 1917; series G1, vol. 1193, f. 1917-3, Coulter to Plumptre, 20 December 1917; Coulter to Perley, 21 December 1917.

98 Ibid., series A2, vol. 302, f. POW 90/15, pt. 2, Hodgetts to High Commission, 4 February 1918, and reply, 4 February 1918.

99 Ibid., f. POW 90/15, pt. 3, CRCS to High Commission, 29 September 1917; United Kingdom, House of Commons, *Report of the Joint Committee to Enquire into the Organisation and Methods of the Central Prisoners of War Committee*, 3.

100 DMD Records, series III A1, vol. 94, f. 10-12-59, Lt.-Col. D.R. McCuaig to Lt.-Gen. R.E.W. Turner, OMFC, London, 29 October 1918.

101 Ibid., Rivers Bulkeley to Blaylock, 28 October 1918; Colonial Office to High Commission, 25 November 1918.

102 DEA Records, series A2, vol. 303, f. POW 90/15, OMFC to High Commission, 16 December 1918.

103 Ibid., vol. 266, f. P5/70, Wolfe to Borden, 9 March 1916; Rivers Bulkeley to High Commission, 6 April 1916.

104 Ibid., vol. 281, f. P8/86, Capt. C.O. Allen to High Commission, 3 February 1918, and reply, 20 March 1918. Civilian internees, like POWs, were fed by the Germans but often resorted to other means to live in the style to which they were accustomed. For some internees, their regular pay was the only resource enabling them to live above the bare subsistence level provided by their captors. J.D. Ketchum, *Ruhleben: A Prison Camp Society* (Toronto: University of Toronto Press 1965), 101.

105 The correspondence is in NAC: Joseph Pope Papers, MG30 E86, vol. 27, serial 736.

106 DND Records, vol. 859, f. HQ 54-21-13-5, pt. 2, Morris Scovil, Gagetown, NB, to DMD, 3 February 1918, and reply, 9 February 1918.

107 Carr, *A Story of the Canadian Red Cross Information Bureau*, 50.

108 NAC: Stephen O'Brien Papers, MG30 E426, MS, 10; Moore, *The Maple Leaf's Red Cross*, 112.

109 Pearson, *The Escape of a Princess Pat*, 206.

110 Thorn, *Three Years a Prisoner in Germany*, 148.

111 William D. Mathieson, *My Grandfather's War* (Toronto: Macmillan 1981), 237; Evans, 'Sixteen Months a War Prisoner,' 147; Moore, *The Maple Leaf's Red Cross*, 109; O'Brien, *Into the Jaws of Death*, 130.

112 Special Committee on Pensions and Returned Soldiers' Problems, 361; Corker interview, 29 June 1992.

113 Thorn, *Three Years a Prisoner in Germany*, 150; letter from Sgt. T.S. Ronaldson, 16 February 1917, in Duthie, ed., *Letters from the Front*, 1:217.

114 In 1917 the *Canadian Annual Review* noted that 'there was not always in Canada a due regard for the many-sided nature of the problems before the War Office.' J. Castell Hop-

kins, *The Canadian Annual Review* (Toronto: Canadian Annual Review Publishing 1917), 514.

115 DMD Records, series III B1, vol. 1121, f. P-47-4, Carson to Chief Paymaster, 2 March 1916. The controversy centred around whether or not prisoners should receive promotions while in captivity. Carson criticized OMFC for avoiding the issue, but it was eventually decided that POWs should not be promoted until they returned home.

Chapter 3: Repatriation and Liberation

1 William Smith Duthie, ed., *Letters from the Front: Being a Record of the Part Played by Officers of the Bank in the Great War, 1914-1919* (Canadian Imperial Bank of Commerce 1920), 1:278-9.

2 T.V. Scudamore, *Lighter Episodes in the Life of a Prisoner of War* (Aldershot: Gale & Polden 1933), 41; John C. Thorn, *Three Years a Prisoner in Germany* (Vancouver: Cowan and Brookhouse 1919), 36-8.

3 Don Corker Diary, Richmond, BC, 14; Jack Evans, 'Sixteen Months a War Prisoner,' in Francis J. Reynolds, ed., *World's War Events* (New York: P.F. Collier & Son 1921), 2:154.

4 George Pearson, *The Escape of a Princess Pat* (New York: George H. Doran 1918), 108; Harry Drope, 'Escape through Russia,' *Legion*, June 1993, 15.

5 Evans, 'Sixteen Months a War Prisoner,' 156-7.

6 Frank C. MacDonald, *The Kaiser's Guest* (New York: Country Life Press 1918), 146; Pearson, *The Escape of a Princess Pat*, 169ff.

7 Don Corker, interview by author, Campbellville, ON, 29 June 1992.

8 Drope, 'Escape through Russia,' 15-16.

9 H.W. Macdonnell and T.W. Morse, 'Canadian Prisoners of War in Germany,' in *Canada and the Great World War*, vol. 4, *The Turn of the Tide* (Toronto: United Publishers of Canada 1920), 342.

10 Thorn, *Three Years a Prisoner in Germany*, 125.

11 Donald Laird, *Prisoner Five-One-Eleven* (Toronto: Ontario Press n.d.), 77.

12 Richard B. Speed, *Prisoners, Diplomats and the Great War* (New York: Greenwood Press 1990), 152.

13 National Archives of Canada (NAC): Department of External Affairs (DEA) Records, series A7, vol. 556, f. 265, Foreign Office to High Commission, 26 December 1914; High Commission to Borden, 31 December 1914.

14 Some Canadians supported Britain in this connection. Chief of the General Staff Maj.-Gen. W.G. Gwatkin wrote in 1916: 'I do not like the idea of distinction being made between Canadian and other British prisoners of war – all one in adversity.' NAC: Department of National Defence (DND) Records, vol. 860, f. HQ 54-21-13-7, pt. 1, memo from Gwatkin, 11 July 1916.

15 The following paragraphs rely on Speed, *Prisoners, Diplomats and the Great War*, 33-8.

16 Public Record Office (PRO): CAB 37/139 #50, note by H.J. Tennant, 23 December 1915; CAB 37/149 #20, note from Foreign Office, 9 June 1916.

17 NAC: Robert Borden Papers, MG26 H1a, reel C-4307, vol. 59, pp. 29062-5, Clarence J. McCuaig, Montreal, to Borden, 8 September 1916, and reply, 15 September 1916; McCuaig's reply, 21 September 1916.

18 House of Lords Record Office, Historical Collection: Beaverbrook Papers, BBK A/248, Perley to Beaverbrook, 24 September 1915.

19 CAB 37/147 #9, memo by Lord Newton, 3 May 1916.

20 DEA Records, series A2, vol. 273, f. P7/85, Department of Trade and Commerce to Borden, 22 February 1917; War Office to High Commission, 7 April 1917.

21 British ministries also disagreed over government policy regarding exchanges. The Foreign Office disliked shouldering the blame for failing to secure exchanges when the War Office and the Admiralty were often responsible for that failure. If those ministries accepted public responsibility for securing exchanges and got a closer view of the privations endured by POWs, thought Earl Grey, they would be more amenable to exchanges. CAB 37/155 #36, note by Grey, 23 September 1916.

22 DEA Records, series A2, vol. 305, f. S9/21, Finkelstein, Levinson & Co., Winnipeg, to Secretary of State, 26 February 1916.

23 Ibid., vol. 229, f. M61/23, High Commission to Colonial Office, 11 November 1916; NAC: Secretary of State Records, series H3, vol. 798, f. 294, Under-Secretary of State to Mrs. J.E. Roop, Bear River, NS, 16 February 1917. See also Borden Papers, MG26 H1c, reel C-4372, vol. 165, p. 90082, Alex MacMillan to Borden, 28 February 1917.

24 DEA Records, series A2, vol. 303, f. POW 90/15, Rivers Bulkeley to Perley, 16 January 1918, and reply, 18 January 1918. Fischmann was apparently released unilaterally by Germany in late 1916. Ibid., vol. 229, f. M61/23, Colonial Office to High Commission, 13 December 1916.

25 A contemporary expert described barbed-wire disease as a psychological disorder brought on by a complete lack of privacy, an ignorance of the duration of captivity, irregular communication with friends and family, and restrictions on all aspects of human activity. The disorder's symptoms included irritability, an inability to concentrate, restlessness, memory loss, violent mood swings, insomnia, nightmares, and impotence. See A.L. Vischer, *Barbed Wire Disease: A Psychological Study of the Prisoner of War* (London: John Bale, Sons & Danielsson 1919), 50-2.

26 Speed, *Prisoners, Diplomats and the Great War*, 37-8; *Times* (London), 26 May 1917, 5, and 1 August 1917, 7; United Kingdom, House of Commons, *An Agreement Between the British and German Governments Concerning Combatant and Civilian Prisoners of War*, Cmd 8590 (July 1917).

27 NAC: Department of Militia and Defence (DMD) Records, series III B1 serial 4, vol. 1124, f. P-49-4, pt. 3, War Office to Canadian Pay and Record Office (CPRO), 3 September 1917; Capt. G.R. Johnson, CPRO to DAAG, CPRO, [September 1917]; f. P-49-4, pt. 4, unsigned memo, 15 September 1917.

28 DEA Records, series A2, vol. 303, f. POW 90/15, G. Napier Gordon to his mother, 30 December 1917.

29 Ibid., report by Lt.-Col. Claude E. Bryan, December 1917.

30 Ibid., vol. 279, f. P8/31, McCuaig to Perley, 30 January 1918 and 14 March 1918; Perley to McCuaig, 25 February 1918, and reply, 18 March 1918.

31 Ibid., vol. 303, f. POW 90/15, memo 'Conditions Governing the Repatriation or Transfer to a Neutral Country of British Combatant POWs Captured by the Germans,' 16 August 1917; William Ready Division of Archives and Research Collections, McMaster University: P.T. Caiger Papers, Caiger to Mrs. Caiger, 19 July 1918.

32 DEA Records, series A2, vol. 303, f. POW 90/15, Borden to Perley, 8 March 1918; Keith Munro to Grace Munro, 16 May 1918; John Munro to Keefer, [May 1918].

33 DND Records, vol. 859, f. HQ 54-21-13-5, pt. 2, Colquhoun to Mrs. E.A. Colquhoun, Hamilton, ON, 1 March 1918 and 17 May 1918; Mess of the 91st Regiment, Canadian Highlanders, Hamilton to Mewburn, 25 June 1918.

34 Macdonnell and Morse, 'Canadian Prisoners of War in Germany,' 343; Desmond Morton, *Silent Battle: Canadian Prisoners of War in Germany, 1914-1919* (Toronto: Lester Publishing 1992), 122; T.V. Scudamore, 'Tales of an Interné,' *Canadian Defence Quarterly* 8/1 (October 1930):98.

35 Macdonnell and Morse, 'Canadian Prisoners of War in Germany,' 343.

36 J. Harvey Douglas, *Captured: Sixteen Months as a Prisoner of War* (Toronto: McClelland, Goodchild & Stewart 1918), 156; Laird, *Prisoner Five-One-Eleven*, 80.

37 Col. H.A. Picot, *The British Interned in Switzerland* (London: Edward Arnold 1919), 76; Scudamore, 'Tales of an Interné,' 99.

38 Oral History Archives, Hannah Chair for the History of Medicine, McMaster University: f. HCM-R 21-81, Alfred J. Cleeton, interview by C.G. Roland, 2 December 1981; Thorn, *Three Years a Prisoner in Germany*, 138.

39 This account relies on the following sources: DND Records, vol. 1848, f. GAQ 12-6, report by Brooke, 6 September 1917; DEA Records, series A2, vol. 303, f. POW 90/15, report by Lt.-Col. Bryan, December 1917.

40 *BIM* (British Interned Mürren) 1/2 (July 1917).

41 Borden Papers, MG26 H1c, reel C-4407, vol. 228, p. 127952, Perley to Brooke, 7 August 1917; *Globe*, 9 November 1917, 12.

42 *BIM* 1/5 (August 1917); DND Records, vol. 1848, f. GAQ 12-16, report by Brooke, 6 September 1917.

43 Ibid., vol. 860, f. HQ 54-21-13-10, Chief Paymaster to Accountant-General, OMFC, 30 March 1917.

44 Ibid., McKay to Hughes, 27 November 1916; DEA Records, series A2, vol. 302, f. POW 90/15, pt. 1, McKelvey to Central POW Committee, 3 March 1917.

45 DMD Records, series III A1, vol. 66, f. 10-2-48, Accountant-General, OMFC to Deputy Minister, OMFC, 22 October 1917; Deputy Paymaster-General, War Office to OMFC, 9 July 1918.

46 DEA Records, series A3, vol. 357, f. G/95, Sir John Gibson to Perley, 12 April 1918; NAC: Sir Edward Kemp Papers, MG27 II D9, vol. 154, f. P11, Maj. R.Y. Cory, Holland to Béland, 7 June 1918; DEA Records, series A2, vol. 303, f. POW 90/15, Colonial Office to High Commission, 14 January 1918; DMD Records, series III A1, vol. 94, f. 10-12-59, Rivers Bulkeley to Borden, 3 March 1918.

47 Kemp Papers, vol. 154, f. P11, Major Osborne to Béland, Rotterdam, 5 June 1918; DEA Records, series A2, vol. 302, f. POW 90/15, pt. 3, War Office POW Department to High Commission, 19 June 1918; Borden Papers, MG26 H1a, reel C-4307, vol. 59, p. 29289, A.R. Paton, The Hague to Borden, 14 May 1918; DMD Records, series III A1, vol. 94, f. 10-12-59, memo 'Canadian Prisoners of War in Holland,' [August 1918].

48 Ibid., memo 'Canadian POWs in Holland.'

49 Ibid., Helen McGillivray, IODE to Kemp, 7 June 1918; GWVA Resolution #33 adopted at national convention, 29 July to 3 August 1918.

50 Ibid., Private Secretary, Minister of OMFC to HQ, OMFC, 9 July 1918; Kemp Papers, vol. 154, f. P11, Adjutant-General to War Office, 11 July 1918.

51 Ibid., Kemp to Milner, Secretary of State for War, 9 August 1918; Kemp to Borden, 9 August 1918; Borden to Lloyd George (draft), 13 August 1918; Milner to Kemp, 14 August 1918.

52 The following paragraph relies on DND Records, vol. 1848, f. GAQ 12-6, 'Report of the Visit of Investigation of conditions of Canadian Prisoners of War Interned in Holland,

October 1918'; Overseas Military Forces of Canada, *Report of the Ministry* (London: 1918), 465-7; and Charles W. Bishop, *The Canadian Y.M.C.A. in the Great War* (National Council of YMCAs of Canada 1924), 297-9.

53 CAB 24/52, GT4667, memo by Lord Newton, 27 May 1918.

54 Kemp Papers, vol. 154, f. P11, Kemp to N.W. Rowell, 13 June 1918; DEA Records, vol. 3411, f. 1-1918/7, memo from Borden, 29 July 1918; series G1, vol. 1227, f. 1918-964, High Commission to External Affairs, 7 November 1918.

55 Oliver Hezzelwood, ed., *Trinity War Book: A Recital of Service and Sacrifice in the Great War* (Toronto: Ontario Press 1921), 32.

56 Morton, *Silent Battle*, 133; Fred Gies, untitled MS, 3.

57 Percy Hampton, interview by author, Toronto, 25 November 1991; Hezzelwood, ed., *Trinity War Book*, 33.

58 DMD Records, series III B1, vol. 1121, f. P-46-4, War Office to CPRO, 27 October 1917.

59 Ibid., series III A1, vol. 102, f. 10-16-5, Director of Mobilization, War Office to Minister, OMFC, 18 April 1918.

60 DND Records, vol. 1848, f. GAQ 11-16c, memo 'Procedure to be Adopted in Handling Canadian repatriated Prisoners-of-War,' 15 August 1918; Adjutant-General, OMFC, to Gardner, 13 November 1918; Adjutant-General, OMFC, to Gardner and Dod, 19 November 1918.

61 Officers of the Services, 'Religious and Social Activities,' in *Canada and the Great World War*, vol. 6, *Special Services, Heroic Deeds, Etc.*, 149; DMD Records, series III A1, vol. 94, f. 10-12-53, Canadian Red Cross Society to OMFC, 30 November 1918; Mary MacLeod Moore, *The Maple Leaf's Red Cross* (London: Skeffington & Sons n.d.), 124.

62 DEA Records, series G1, vol. 1227, f. 1918-964, memo 'Repatriation of Canadian Civilians, 1918, 1919,' n.d.; series A2, vol. 156, f. C12/14, Colonial Office to High Commission, 27 August 1918.

63 This section relies on Sir James Edmonds, *The Occupation of the Rhineland, 1918-1929* (London: HMSO 1944), 6-32, 48-54.

64 Article 13, Quartermaster-General's Orders, 13 November 1918, in ibid., 349.

65 PRO: WO 144/3, Inter-Allied Armistice Commission Despatch #2 (18 November 1918) and #8 (24 November 1918), by Lt.-Gen. Haking.

66 WO 144/4, Inter-Allied Armistice Commission Despatch #15 (1 December 1918) by Haking; WO 144/5, Inter-Allied Armistice Commission Despatch #25 (11 December 1918), by Haking; Imperial War Museum: Sir Richard Ewart Papers, diary, 14 December 1918, 10 January 1919.

67 Ibid., diary, 17 January 1919.

68 DND Records, reel C-5068, f. HQC 4498, pt. 10, statements by Ptes. R.C. Lever, W. Miller, and A.C. Beesley, n.d.; Edmonds, *The Occupation of the Rhineland*, 57.

69 DND Records, reel C-5068, f. HQC 4498, pt. 10, statement by Pte. R.C. Lever, n.d.; Hezzelwood, ed., *Trinity War Book*, 35.

70 G.D. McLeod Papers, in possession of Libby McNally, Waterdown, ON: Clarence M. Young to C.K. McLeod, 21 August 1972; Lt.-Col. E.W. Mingo, 'Prisoners of War, 1914-1918,' *Journal of the United Services Institute of Nova Scotia* 6 (1933):53; Hampton interview, 25 November 1991.

71 N.L. Wells, 'Repatriation of Prisoners of War,' *The Caduceus* 2/3 (June 1921):12-13.

72 DND Records, vol. 1848, f. GAQ 11-16c, Blake to Adjutant-General, 14 December 1918; memo 'Repatriated Prisoners of War,' 27 November 1918.

73 NAC: Russell M. Smith Papers, diary for 16 December 1918; NAC: H.H. Howland Papers, MG 30 E204, 320.

Chapter 4: The Interwar Years

1 M. Stuart Hunt, *Nova Scotia's Part in the Great War* (Halifax: Nova Scotia Veteran Publishing 1920), 363; Department of National Defence, Director General History: f. BIOG A, transcript of taped interview with Sgt. Colin Alexander, 27.

2 National Archives of Canada (NAC): Department of Militia and Defence (DMD) Records, series III A1, vol. 94, f. 10-12-53, Mewburn to Kemp, 8 January 1919; letter from Christina Knowles, Chairman of the Advisory After-Care Committee for British POWs, *Times* (London), 6 February 1919, 3.

3 House of Commons, Special Committee on Pensions and Returned Soldiers' Problems, Minutes of Proceedings and Evidence #14, 6 May 1936, 364.

4 Gordon Reid, *Poor Bloody Murder* (Oakville: Mosaic Press 1980), 89; NAC: Stephen O'Brien Papers, MG30 E426, 31.

5 C.G. Pether, 'The Returned Prisoner-of-War,' *Lancet*, 5 May 1945, 572.

6 House of Commons, Special Committee on Pensions and Returned Soldiers' Problems, Minutes of Proceedings and Evidence #14, 6 May 1936, 364, 371; P.R. Hampton, interview by author, Toronto, 25 November 1991.

7 NAC: Department of National Defence (DND) Records, vol. 1848, f. GAQ-12-6, Brooke to Perley, 6 September 1917.

8 NAC: Department of External Affairs (DEA) Records, series A2, vol. 303, f. POW 90/15, report by Lt.-Col. Bryan, December 1917, passim.

9 DND Records, vol. 1848, f. GAQ-12-6, 'Report of the Visit of Investigation of Conditions of Canadian Prisoners of War Interned in Holland,' October 1918.

10 Don Corker, interview by author, Campbellville, 29 June 1992; Oral History Archives, Hannah Chair for the History of Medicine, McMaster University: f. HCM-R 21-81, Alfred J. Cleeton, interview by C.G. Roland, 2 December 1981.

11 Desmond Morton, *When Your Number's Up: The Canadian Soldier in the First World War* (Toronto: Random House 1993), 214.

12 DEA Records, series A2, vol. 302, f. POW 90/15, pt. 3, High Commission to Robertson, The Hague, 31 December 1918.

13 'Many Men Stated Dead, Still Alive,' *Vancouver Daily Sun*, 4 January 1919, 1; DND Records, vol. 859, f. HQ 54-21-13-5, pt. 2, undated clipping [*Ottawa Journal*]; Department of Insurance to DMD, 3 February 1919.

14 Ibid., memo from British chargé d'affaires, The Hague, 30 January 1919.

15 'Ottawa Story About Missing Soldiers Was Cruel Hoax,' *Vancouver Daily Sun*, 28 January 1919, 1; DMD Records, series III A1, vol. 101, f. 10-15-3, Adjutant-General, OMFC, to Deputy-Minister, OMFC, 17 February 1919; DMD to Deputy-Minister, OMFC, 18 March 1919.

16 E.W.H. Cruickshank, 'Impressions of Nazi Germany,' *Dalhousie Review* 13 (1933):404; House of Commons, Debates, 27 May 1919, p. 2873; DMD Records, series III A1, vol. 95, f. 10-12-72, OMFC to Kemp, 20 May 1919.

17 DND Records, vol. 859, f. HQ 54-21-13-5, pt. 2, Sir Walter Townley, The Hague, to Curzon, 14 February 1919. It eventually transpired that no Canadians fell into this category.

18 Ibid., f. HQ 54-21-13-5, pt. 3, GWVA, Ottawa Branch to Militia Council, 12 July 1921.

19 Ibid., DMD to DEA, 29 July 1921.

20 Ibid., High Commission to DEA, 4 October 1921.

21 Ibid., vol. 1205, f. HQ 240-1-40, Mrs. Victoria Burma, Toronto, to DMD, 5 December 1922.

22 The correspondence is in NAC: Henri Béland Papers, MG27 II D2. Béland's memoirs were published in English by Briggs and in French by a newspaper in Beauce; at least eleven other Canadian ex-prisoners published books of memoirs in 1918 and 1919. Mary Vipond, 'Best Sellers in English Canada: 1919-1928,' in *Journal of Canadian Fiction* 35/36 (1980):99.

23 'This Is Work of Hun Fiends,' *Vancouver Daily Sun*, 25 January 1919, 1; 'Rescuing Wounded from Prison Camp Within Germany,' *Vancouver Daily Sun*, 20 January 1919, 3.

24 'Tatooed Prussian Eagle on Foreheads of War Prisoners,' *Vancouver Daily Sun*, 6 January 1919, 12.

25 For the background to the 1929 Geneva Conference, see André Durand, *From Sarajevo to Hiroshima: History of the International Committee of the Red Cross* (Geneva: Henry Dunant Institute 1984), 249-52. It is significant that primary responsibility for the protection of POWs shifted from the realm of Hague law, which focuses upon the methods of combat, to Geneva law, which is primarily concerned with the victims of war. See Geoffrey Best, *Humanity in Warfare* (New York: Columbia University Press 1980), 297.

26 George G. Phillimore, 'Some Suggestions for a Draft Code for the Treatment of Prisoners of War,' *Transactions of the Grotius Society* 6 (1920):25-34; NAC: R.B. Bennett Papers, MG26 K, reel M-1045, vol. 304, f. E-301-R, External Affairs memo 'History of the Two Conventions,' undated; Allan Rosas, *The Legal Status of Prisoners of War* (Helsinki: Suomalainen Tiedeakatemia 1976), 76; Public Record Office (PRO): CAB 16/50, 'Proceedings and Memoranda of the Sub-Committee to Consider the Report of the Younger Committee relating to Prisoners of War,' 8 August 1923. Members of the subcommittee included J.M. Spaight, who had written so disparagingly of the status of POWs before the Great War.

27 NAC: Office of the Governor General Records, series G21, reel T-1426, vol. 391, f. 5854, Dominions Office to Byng, 5 December 1924; DEA Records, series G1, vol. 1386, f. 1924-1485, pt. 1, Desbarats to DEA, 7 January 1925.

28 CAB 4/13, CID Paper 648-B, 'Report of the Sub-Committee on the Proposed Preparation of an International Convention for the treatment of Prisoners of War,' 1 December 1925.

29 Office of the Governor General Records, series G21, reel T-1426, vol. 391, f. 5854, Dominions Office to Governor General, 1 August 1925, and reply, 31 May 1926; CAB 4/16, CID Paper 807-B, 'Report on the Amendments suggested by the Governments of the Dominions and of India to the Original Report,' 3 November 1927.

30 CAB 4/18, CID Paper 946-B, 'Report of the Sub-committee on the Amendments suggested by various countries to the Proposed Preparation of an International Convention for the treatment of Prisoners of War,' 22 June 1929.

31 Office of the Governor General Records, series G21, reel T-1426, vol. 391, f. 5854, DEA to Dominions Office, 20 September 1928.

32 DEA Records, series G1, vol. 1386, f. 1924-1485, pt. 1, memo for Prime Minister, 14 March 1929; Desbarats to DEA, 4 April 1929, and reply, 8 April 1929; P.C. 783, 8 May 1929.

33 Robert Speaight, *Vanier. Soldier, Diplomat and Governor General* (Toronto: Collins 1970), 153.

34 Joan Beaumont, 'Rank, Privilege and Prisoners of War,' *War & Society* 1/1 (May 1983):72; NAC: G.P. Vanier Papers, MG32 A2, vol. 7, f. 7-5, W.A. Riddell, 'Report on the Work of the Diplomatic Conference,' 7.

35 Office of the Governor General Records, series G21, reel T-1426, vol. 391, f. 5854, Skelton

to Dominions Office, 7 June 1929.

36 DEA Records, series G1, vol. 1386, f. 1924-1485, pt. 1, Desbarats to DEA, 14 November 1929.

37 The text of the convention can be found in External Affairs, *International Convention Relative to the Treatment of Prisoners of War, Geneva, July 27, 1929* (Ottawa: F.A. Acland 1931).

38 House of Commons, Debates, 19 February 1932, p. 360. The signature was accepted by the House of Commons on 2 March 1932.

39 J.E. Read, 'Modern Warfare and the Laws of War,' *Dalhousie Review* 2/4 (January 1923):488.

40 Mingo, for example, criticized the Hague Conventions for not stipulating a method of inspection, while George Adami recommended that international agreements pay greater attention to the speedy repatriation of wounded soldiers and protected personnel. Both of these concerns were addressed at Geneva. Lt.-Col. E.W. Mingo, 'Prisoners of War 1914-18,' *Journal of the United Services Institute of Nova Scotia* 6 (1933):35; Lt.-Col. J. George Adami, *War Story of the Canadian Army Medical Corps*, vol. 1, *The First Contingent* (Toronto: n.d.), 173.

41 C.P. Stacey, 'Is "Civilized Warfare" Possible?' *Queen's Quarterly* 37/1 (Winter 1930):121.

42 NAC: Robert Manion Papers, MG27 III B7, vol. 67, f. S-300-P, notice from Secretary of State, 18 November 1918.

43 The background to the Reparations Commissions can be found in Royal Commission for the Investigation of Illegal Warfare Claims and for the Return of Sequestered Property in Necessitous Cases, Errol M. McDougall, Commissioner (cited as McDougall Commission), *Interim Report* (Ottawa: King's Printer 1931), 10-14.

44 Royal Commission ... to investigate and report upon all claims which may be submitted to the Commission for the purpose of determining whether they are within the First Annex to Section I of Part VIII of the Treaty of Versailles, James Friel, Commissioner (cited as Friel Commission), *Reparations, volume 1: The Report of the Royal Commission* (Ottawa: King's Printer 1929), 16-17.

45 Friel Commission, *Reparations, volume 2: The Report of the Royal Commission* (Ottawa: King's Printer 1929), 506-7.

46 NAC: Arthur Meighen Papers, MG26 I, reel C-3572, vol. 185, p. 117654, Maltreated Ex-POWs Association, Toronto to Meighen, May 1936.

47 McDougall Commission, *Interim Report*, 5.

48 McDougall Commission, *Report of the Commission on Reparations, 1930-31: Maltreatment of Prisoners of War* (Ottawa: King's Printer 1932), 3-9.

49 Ibid., 12-17.

50 DND Records, vol. 1845, f. GAQ-11-16A, undated report, 4. During the Second World War, POWs would be decorated for such conduct.

51 McDougall Commission, *Maltreatment of Prisoners of War*, 10.

52 NAC: H.H. Howland Papers, MG30 E204, Commissioner's report.

53 Correspondence surrounding the appeal is in DEA Records, series G1, vol. 1639, f. 850.

54 McDougall Commission, *Maltreatment of Prisoners of War*, 18-22; McDougall Commission, *Reparations, 1932: Further Report* (Ottawa: King's Printer 1933), 29-30, 180; McDougall Commission, *Reparations, 1932: Final Report* (Ottawa: King's Printer 1933), 25.

55 McDougall Commission, *Interim Report*, case #1685; McDougall Commission, *Maltreatment of Prisoners of War*, case #1645.

56 The Overseas Military Forces of Canada claimed to have interviewed every returned POW,

paying special attention to ill-treatment and unnecessary punishment, and accumulated a mass of evidence showing 'the many vicissitudes through which the soldier has passed.' Overseas Military Forces of Canada, *Report of the Ministry, Overseas Military Forces of Canada, 1918* (London: 1918), 457. However, only about one in five ex-prisoners were interviewed at the end of the war. Desmond Morton, *Silent Battle: Canadian Prisoners of War in Germany, 1914-1919* (Toronto: Lester Publishing 1992), 138.

57 Mingo, 'Prisoners of War 1914-18,' 53; Bennett Papers, reel M-1310, vol. 620, f. R-950-E, Evans to Bennett, 9 May 1934; McDougall Commission, *Further Report*, case #1990.

58 House of Commons, Debates, 23 June 1931, pp. 2963-4.

59 Bennett Papers, reel M-1309, vol. 620, f. B-950, p. 383591, POWs Association, Toronto to Honourable Members of His Majesty's Government of the Dominion of Canada, undated. The association was quite correct, for the treaty contained no suggestion that any one group of claimants should be given precedence over any other.

60 Bennett Papers, reel M-1399, vol. 708, f. S-300, p. 435039, Pinder to Bennett, 27 February 1932; p. 435043, Kennedy to Bennett, 24 March 1932; McDougall Commission, *Maltreatment of Prisoners of War*, cases #1995 and #1987.

61 NAC: W.L.M. King Papers, MG26 J4, reel C-4288, vol. 230, p. 155743, Davis to King, 14 April 1932; McDougall Commission, *Maltreatment of Prisoners of War*, case #2257. After producing further evidence, Pinder was awarded $1000 in a reassessment of his case.

62 House of Commons, Debates, 26 May 1932, p. 3450.

63 Morton, *Silent Battle*, 153.

64 McDougall Commission, *Maltreatment of Prisoners of War*, cases #2104 and #2055.

65 Special Committee on Pensions and Returned Soldiers' Problems, Minutes of Proceedings and Evidence #14, 6 May 1936.

66 Meighen Papers, reel C-3572, vol. 185, p. 117654, MPOWA, Toronto to Meighen, May 1936.

67 House of Commons, Debates, 30 March 1938, p. 1848.

68 Manion Papers, vol. 67, f. S-300-P, Secretary of State to Ex-POW Association, Toronto, 22 June 1938.

69 Ibid., A. Vidamour, Staffordville, to Manion, 6 February 1939.

70 Morton, *Silent Battle*, 142, 154.

71 National Defence, *Extracts from the Manual of Military Law 1929, Reprinted for Use in the Canadian Army* (Ottawa: King's Printer 1941); National Defence, *King's Regulations and Orders for the Canadian Army* (1939), para. 644, sec. A.

72 J.F. Garswood, interview by author, Windsor, 6 December 1991; R.E. McLaren, interview by author, Hamilton, 18 January 1992; Colonel John Page, interview by author, Waterdown, 11 February 1992.

Chapter 5: The Organizational Framework, 1939-45

1 It is difficult to estimate the number of Canadians captured while serving with other forces. Roughly a hundred Canadians in the RAF were taken prisoner, and perhaps twice as many fell into enemy hands while serving with British Army units. A partial list of neutral internees can be found in Department of National Defence, Director General History: f. 181.005 (D1395). The number of civilian internees was estimated in 1952 by the Advisory Commissioner for War Claims. See *War Claims: Report of the Advisory Commissioner* (Ottawa: Queen's Printer 1954), 40.

2 Argyll and Sutherland Highlanders of Canada Regimental Archives, Hamilton (ASHC):

Donald G. Seldon, interview by W.H. Wiley, Hamilton, 9 June 1986.

3 National Archives of Canada (NAC): Department of External Affairs (DEA) Records, series A6, vol. 429, f. Cas 1/6/1, pt. 4, 'Report on Repatriation to U.K. of Cdn Army Personnel from Germany,' undated, 7. In spite of this, some officials were concerned that the series of British capitulations from 1940 to 1942, including Hong Kong, might lead Allied or neutral nations to think that Commonwealth troops were prone to quick surrender. In this regard, the Chancellor of the Duchy of Lancaster opined that 'it is surely not desirable to proceed on the assumption that the soldier [who is captured] must necessarily be guiltless. Any officer who surrenders is liable to court-martial, but circumstances usually render court-martial impracticable until the war is over, when the universal inclination is to let bygones be bygones, and not spoil the victory by recriminations about the past.' The chancellor's memo concluded on a suggestive note: 'Headlines to-day tell us of fierce fighting in the streets of Veronezh. There was no street fighting reported at Singapore or Tobruk.' Public Record Office (PRO): CAB 66/26, War Cabinet memorandum WP (42) #305 by the Chancellor of the Duchy of Lancaster, 20 July 1942.

4 DEA Records, vol. 2781, f. 621-GE-40, 'Precis of the Report to the War Office on Psychological Aspects of the Rehabilitation of Repatriated POWs by Lieut.-Col. A.T.M. Wilson,' 20 June 1944, sec. A/4e; Directorate of Army Psychiatry Technical Memorandum #13, 'The POW Comes Home,' 10; W.H. Whiles, 'A Study of Neurosis Among Repatriated Prisoners of War,' British Medical Journal, 17 November 1945, 697; A.L. Cochrane, 'Notes on the Psychology of Prisoners of War,' British Medical Journal, 23 February 1946, 284.

5 ASHC: George Soper, interview by Rosanne Giulietti, 12 July 1984; Melvin Junck, interview, Orillia, ON, 16 August 1984.

6 Arthur Crighton, Edmonton, correspondence with author, 21 March 1992.

7 Sir Edwin Leather, interview by author, Hamilton, 14 April 1992. There was apparently nothing for Canadian troops like the cartoon leaflet issued by the American army. See 'Armored Force Cartoons Tell U.S. Soldiers How to Act if Captured,' Life 13/14 (5 October 1942):122-4.

8 M.A. MacAulay, Seattle, correspondence with author, [February 1992]; J. Laurie Cormier, Dieppe, New Brunswick, correspondence with author, 20 June 1992. Towards the end of the war, the Allies also had access to a number of German and Japanese leaflets instructing their soldiers how to interrogate prisoners of war. Examples of these leaflets, which reached External Affairs in December 1944, can be found in DEA Records, vol. 2782, f. 621-HP-40.

9 Dave McIntosh, ed., High Blue Battle (Toronto: Stoddart 1990), 82, 116.

10 Don Wilson, interview by author, Waterdown, 15 June 1992.

11 DEA Records, series A6, vol. 425, f. Cas 1/1, Crerar to High Commission, 23 May 1940; Col. John Page, Waterdown, correspondence with author, 13 February 1992.

12 Maj. S.R. Elliot, Scarlet to Green (Toronto: Canadian Security and Intelligence Association 1989), 399.

13 R.E. McLaren, interview by author, Hamilton, 18 January 1992; F.J.L. Woodcock, interview by author, Grimsby, 24 January 1992. A similar state of affairs existed in the RCN and the RCAF at this stage. Oral History Archives, Hannah Chair for the History of Medicine, McMaster University (HCHM): f. HCM 3-86, Charles M. Fisher, interview by C.G. Roland, Boston, 7 February 1986; J. Earl Taylor, Victoria, correspondence with author, undated.

14 Col. John Page, interview by author, Waterdown, 11 February 1992; Elliot, From Scarlet to Green, 399.

15 Harry Pope, 'Souvenirs de Guerre,' *La Citadelle* 22/1 (February 1986):25; HCHM: f. HCM-R 5-81, Dr. Allen F. Graham, interview by C.G. Roland, Toronto, 5 May 1981.

16 ASHC: Truman Wilcox, interview by Patty Smith, Maynooth, ON, 21 August 1987.

17 Harry Foster Diary, in possession of Tony Foster, Halifax, entry for 23 May 1940. I am grateful to J.L. Granatstein for this reference.

18 See Tony Foster, *Meeting of Generals* (Toronto: Methuen 1986), 323 or Farley Mowat, *And No Birds Sang* (Toronto: McClelland & Stewart 1979), 208.

19 DEA Records, Accession 89-90/029, Box 46, f. 135-A (S), pt. 1, note by Read, 10 July 1944; NAC: Department of National Defence (DND) Records, reel C-5330, f. HQS 9050-4, pt. 5, special meeting at the Directorate of POWs, London, 25 July 1944.

20 The correspondence on this matter is in NAC: H.D.G. Crerar Papers, MG30 E157, vol. 5, f. 6-3.

21 ASHC: W. Smelser, interview by W.H. Wiley, London, 9 July 1986.

22 A.B. Thompson Papers, in possession of Nora Thompson, Penetanguishene: undated news clipping; Air Ministry to Mrs. F. Ritchie, London, November 1939; Les Allison, *Canadians in the Royal Air Force* (Roland, MB: L. Allison 1978), 123.

23 DEA Records, series G1, vol. 1961, f. 842-AC-39, ICRC to Prime Minister, 12 September 1939; ICRC, *Report of the ICRC on its Activities during the Second World War* (Geneva: ICRC 1948), 2:144-5; DEA Records, series A6, vol. 425, f. Cas 1/3/1, pt. 2, DEA to Dominions Office, 16 June 1941.

24 NAC: W.L.M. King Papers, MG26 J1, reel C-4861, vol. 301, p. 255546, Department of the Secretary of State outline, 19 April 1941.

25 DEA Records, series G1, vol. 1961, f. 842-AC-39, pt. 1, Skelton to Sommerville, 11 November 1939.

26 Ibid., meeting minutes, 22 November 1939.

27 Ibid., series A6, vol. 425, f. Cas 1/1, Pearson to British Red Cross, 23 November 1939; Pearson to WCdr. A.P. Campbell, RCAF HQ, 17 May 1940. Pearson took nearly two months to come up with a reply.

28 The correspondence on this matter is in ibid., vol. 2833, f. 1426-C-40c, pt. 1.

29 In 1942, some staffers in External Affairs were having second thoughts about this and advised against basing decisions on POW policy on the fact that there were only a few hundred Canadians in captivity. DEA Records, series G1, vol. 1959, f. 842-U, Scott to Wershof, 5 August 1942.

30 Ibid., vol. 1962, f. 842-AH-39, Coleman to Skelton, 17 October 1940.

31 Ibid., series A6, vol. 426, f. Cas 1/4, pt. 1, draft letter, Dominions Office to High Commission, 1 October 1940; covering letter, Dominions Office to Mayrand, 2 October 1940.

32 Ibid., series G1, vol. 1961, f. 842-AC-39, pt. 1, Coleman to DEA, 13 November 1940; DND Records, reel C-5069, f. HQC 4498-1, pt. 1, High Commission to DEA, 17 December 1940.

33 DEA Records, series A6, vol. 425, f. Cas 1/3/1, pt. 1, CRCS to High Commission, 18 December 1940; C.P. Stacey, *Official History of the Canadian Army in the Second World War*, volume 1, *Six Years of War: The Army in Canada, Britain and the Pacific* (Ottawa: Queen's Printer 1955), 284.

34 Cf. the American and British systems. The US State Department established an Internees Section to handle all POW matters, both for American and enemy prisoners. This section coordinated closely with the American Red Cross, the ICRC, the neutral nations, and the Army and Navy Departments, especially the Office of the Provost Marshal General, which

contained the POW Information Bureau and the Civilian Internees Bureau. The Internees Section also maintained close contact with other US government departments to ensure that privileges requested for American POWs were reciprocally granted to enemy prisoners in the US. Graham H. Stuart, 'Special War Problems Division: Internees Section,' *Department of State Bulletin* 11/264 (16 July 1944):63-74. In Britain, the War Office Directorate of POWs was divided into two sections: PW1 was responsible for enemy POWs, and PW2 took charge of the interpretation of the Geneva Convention, communication with neutral nations and representatives of Allied governments, and correspondence with the Foreign Office's POW Department. DND Records, reel C-5330, f. HQS 9050-3-2, Monthly Directorate Letter #1 (December 1941).

35 NAC: Post Office Department (PO) Records, reel T-1690, vol. 2762, f. 35-27-3, memo by Chief Postal Censor F.E. Jolliffe, 10 December 1940; National War Services, *Annual Report of the Department of National War Services for the Fiscal Year Ending 31 March 1944* (Ottawa 1945), 13; Hamilton Public Library Special Collections (HPL), f. Canadian Red Cross – POWs, clipping dated 15 February 1941.

36 DEA Records, vol. 2883, f. 2125-40, memo by Rive, 12 June 1941.

37 DND Records, reel C-5069, f. HQC 4498-11, Rive to Clarke, 8 April 1942. For further details on External Affairs' responsibilities, see John Hilliker, *Canada's Department of External Affairs*, vol. 1 *The Early Years* (Kingston: McGill-Queen's University Press 1990), 244-5.

38 In 1944, Scott wrote that 'nobody else in the world will look after our civilians except Special Section.' DEA Records, vol. 2833, f. 1426-C-40, pt. 2, Scott to Feaver, 29 February 1944.

39 Ibid., vol. 2883, f. 2125-40, Director of Marine Service, Transport, to Rive, 16 June 1941; series G1, vol. 1961, f. 842-AD-39, pt. 1, National War Services to DEA, 28 August 1941; DND Records, reel C-5069, f. HQC 4498-1, pt. 3, Maag to Rive, 3 October 1941. The change did not solve the problem, however, and even in 1944 relatives sometimes received notification from unofficial sources before they heard from the government. The family of Able Seaman Don Newman, an HMCS *Athabaskan* crewman captured in April 1944, learned of his fate from a ham radio operator in West Palm Beach, Florida, weeks before they heard anything through Canadian channels. *POW Journal*, Spring 1979, 22.

40 NAC: Department of National War Services (DNWS) Records, f. Canadian POWs, pt. 2, brochure 'The Canadian Red Cross,' December 1942, 3; P.C. 17, 5 January 1942.

41 HPL: f. Canadian Red Cross Society – POWs, 'A Message from the Red Cross to the Next of Kin of Canadian and other British POWs,' [January 1942].

42 DNWS Records, accession 85-86/537, box 7, f. Canadian POWs, pt. 1, Ralston to LaFlèche, 4 May 1943.

43 DEA Records, vol. 3018, f. 3745-40, DEA to Naval Services, 18 March 1942; *Gazette* (Montreal), 13 March 1942, 1.

44 It was 1944 before someone pointed out that the SAAG and the POW Next-of-Kin Division defined their respective roles in almost identical terms. DEA Records, vol. 2783, f. 621-JR-40, memo by Scott, 4 January 1944.

45 M.A. MacAulay Papers, Seattle: circular letter to next of kin, undated.

46 DND Records, reel C-5069, f. HQC 4498-11, agenda of 1st CPW meeting, 9 April 1942; f. HQC 4498-10, Clarke to Adjutant-General, 4 January 1943.

47 Don Page, 'Tommy Stone and Psychological Warfare in World War II: Transforming a POW Liability into an Asset,' *Journal of Canadian Studies* 16/3&4 (Fall-Winter 1981):111.

48 DEA Records, series A6, vol. 434, f. Cas 2/1, pt. 4, Scott to Rive, 14 October 1943. On Robertson's reluctance to delegate tasks, see J.L. Granatstein, *A Man of Influence: Norman A. Robertson and Canadian Statecraft, 1929-68* (Toronto: Deneau 1981), 106, and Page, 'Tommy Stone and Psychological Warfare,' 111.

49 DEA Records, series A6, vol. 434, f. Cas 2/1, pt. 4, memo by Read, 21 October 1943.

50 NAC: Department of Veterans Affairs Records, vol. 143, f. Prisoners of War, minutes of meeting, 16 November 1943.

51 In January 1944, Special Section narrowly avoided being drawn into a dispute between the SAAG and the POW Next-of-Kin Division of National War Services over which was the more useful inquiry office, and in July the section escaped a brewing battle between National War Services and the defence departments regarding the dissemination of information on camp conditions. DEA Records, vol. 2783, f. 621-JR-40, memo from Scott, 4 January 1944; memo from Rive, 11 July 1944.

52 Ibid., series A6, vol. 428, f. Cas 1/4, pt. 5, Scott to Feaver, 16 December 1944.

53 In 1942 it was estimated that some 900 different organizations existed to aid prisoners of war. DND Records, reel C-5069, f. HQC 4498-11, minutes of second CPW meeting, 12 May 1942.

54 P.H. Gordon, *Fifty Years in the Canadian Red Cross* (1969), 42.

55 C.P. Shedd, *History of the World's Alliance of YMCAs* (London: SPCK 1955), 557-8; DEA Records, vol. 3018, f. 3745-40, War Office Weekly POW Summary #2 (24 October 1941).

56 Murray G. Ross, *The YMCA in Canada* (Toronto: Ryerson Press 1951), 419-20.

57 DNWS Records, accession 85-86/537, box 7, f. Canadian POWs, pt. 1, Asselin to LaFlèche, 3 March 1943.

58 H.K. Ward Papers, Edmonton: Violet Thistle, B.C. representative, CPOWRA, to Ada Miller, 5 November 1943. The membership rolls of the Manitoba branch are in the W.S. King Papers, in the possession of S. Gordon King, Edmonton.

59 George McGill Papers, in possession of Betty Gillies, Mississauga, ON: undated news clipping; DNWS Records, accession 85-86/537, box 7, f. 1, Asselin to LaFlèche, 3 March 1943. A sample of the newsletter can be found in NAC: Montreal Soldiers' Wives' League Papers, MG28 I311, vol. 2, f. 45.

60 PO Records, reel T-1693, vol. 2766, f. 35-32-1, Maj. E.J. Underwood to Coolican, 18 October 1940.

61 DNWS Records, vol. 17, f. Red Cross POW Parcels, Pifher to Davis, 20 June 1942; accession 85-86/537, box 7, f. Canadian Red Cross Enquiry Bureau, DNWS to Plumptre, 18 January 1943; f. Canadian POWs, The RRC, memo by Pifher, 3 April 1943.

62 PO Records, reel T-1693, vol. 2766, f. 35-32-1, Gordon to Coolican, 8 September 1941.

63 DEA Records, vol. 3018, f. 3745-40, memo 'Prisoner of War Aid of the World's YMCA – Status in Germany' by Rive, 11 February 1942.

64 Ibid., Coleman to DEA, 13 February 1942; W.G. Mills to DEA, 3 March 1942; Acting Deputy-Minister, Army to DEA, 21 February 1942.

65 Ibid., DEA to Canadian Minister, Washington, 14 March 1942; DEA to Davis, 10 March 1942.

66 Ibid., Davis to DEA, 2 April 1942; memo from Rive, 4 April 1942.

67 *Globe* (Toronto), 28 May 1943, 3.

68 NAC: YMCA Papers, MG28 I95, vol. 272, f. 10, S.E. Smith, President, National Council of YMCA to Gordon, 6 June 1942.

69 Ibid., f. 12.

70 DEA Records, series G1, vol. 1962, f..842-AJ-39, Plumptre to DNWS, 5 December 1942.
71 Ibid., f. 842-AN-39c, Routley to Rive, 15 December 1942.
72 McKenzie Porter, *To All Men: The Story of the Canadian Red Cross* (Toronto: McClelland & Stewart 1960), 92.
73 DNWS Records, accession 85-86/537, box 7, f. Canadian POWs, pt. 1, Gordon to LaFlèche, 28 December 1942.
74 Ibid., f. Canadian Red Cross Enquiry Bureau, Mrs. Arthur Ellis to Plumptre, 25 May 1943; Plumptre to LaFlèche, 27 May 1943. The first vice president of the Ontario CPOWRA recalled that CRCS and CPOWRA volunteers were often friends, and that there was some degree of rivalry at the local level. Dorothy McLaren, interview by author, Hamilton, 18 January 1992.
75 DNWS Records, accession 85-86/537, box 7, f. Canadian Red Cross Enquiry Bureau, LaFlèche to Plumptre, 9 June 1943.
76 Ibid., f. Canadian POWs, pt. 1, Asselin to LaFlèche, 3 March 1943.
77 Ibid., 31 May 1943.
78 DEA Records, vol. 2782, f. 621-HR-40, Rive to Clarke, 15 July 1943.
79 The following paragraphs rely on ibid., memo 'Voluntary Organizations Interested in Prisoners of War' by Rive, 27 July 1943.
80 LaFlèche later criticized the Red Cross for having 'incurred considerable unpopularity in influential quarters.' Ibid., memo by Wrong, 8 October 1943.
81 Ibid., series A6, vol. 434, f. Cas 2/1, pt. 4, memo by Scott, 29 September 1943.
82 NAC: Privy Council Office (PCO) Records, series 7C, vol. 14., minutes of Cabinet War Committee meeting #263, 6 October 1943. Two different reorganization schemes were suggested. See DND Records, reel C-5330, f. HQS 9050-1-3, pt. 1, draft letter to Dodds, 15 September 1943; and DEA Records, vol. 2782, f. 621-HR-40, memo 'Re-Organization of Voluntary Relief Societies' by Scott, 15 October 1943.
83 Ibid., vol. 2784, f. 621-LA-40, Asselin to Wartime Prices and Trade Board, 13 April 1944.
84 Ibid., Feaver to Scott, 23 May 1944.
85 DNWS Records, accession 85-86/537, box 7, f. Canadian POWs, pt. 2, memo by Pifher, 12 January 1945.
86 DEA Records, vol. 3397, f. 619-B-40, pt. 1, Rive to Pearson, 2 December 1947.
87 PRO: DO35/997, PW101/151, memo dated 4 September 1941.
88 W. Wynne Mason, *Prisoners of War* (Wellington, New Zealand: Department of Internal Affairs War History Branch 1954), 96-7.
89 DND Records, reel C-5330, f. HQS 9050-4, pt. 1, minutes of first Sub-Committee A meeting, 26 June 1941.
90 Ibid., reel C-5069, f. HQC 4498-1, pt. 1, DEA to High Commission, 30 May 1941; External Affairs, *Annual Report 1941* (Ottawa 1942), 6.
91 PCO Records, series 7C, vol. 10, Cabinet War Committee document #240, memo 'Prisoners of War' by Clarke, 20 July 1942.
92 DND Records, reel C-5330, f. HQS 9050-2, memo by Ralston, 27 May 1943.
93 Ibid., High Commission to DEA, 13 January 1943, and reply, 21 January 1943.
94 Ibid., reel C-5070, f. HQC 4498-14, minutes of third IPOWC meeting, 3 February 1943.
95 Ibid., reel C-5330, f. HQS 9050-3-1, High Commission to DEA, 15 February 1943.
96 Ibid., f. HQS 9050-2, High Commission to DEA, 25 March 1943.
97 Ibid., memo from T.P. Mackenzie, 10 May 1943.
98 Ibid., f. HQS 9050-4, pt. 3, memo for Sub-Committee A 'Machinery for Consultation

between the Allies regarding Prisoners of War,' 10 July 1943; note from US State Department, undated.

99 Ibid., f. HQS 9050-3-5, High Commission to DEA, 15 October 1943; Naesmyth to Mackenzie, 12 November 1943.

100 Ibid., 20 January 1944.

101 As a Canadian civilian internee wrote, 'you can have no idea how comforting it was to all of us in Berlin to feel that competent officials in Canada were striving hard to relieve our state.' DEA Records, vol. 2944, f. 3033-B-40, pt. 2, Doreen Turner, Toronto, to Rive, 15 July 1942.

102 Letter dated 29 September 1948 in Page, 'Tommy Stone and Psychological Warfare,' 111.

Chapter 6: Relief and Release in the European Theatre

1 Charles Clay, 'Parcels for Prisoners: How the International Red Cross is Doing an Important Job,' *Country Guide and Nor-West Farmer* 60 (September 1941):51.

2 Gren Juniper, interview by author, Hamilton, 6 April 1992; C.H. Maxwell, interview by author, Hamilton, 25 October 1991; T. Stewart Ripley Diary, Toronto, 24, 27.

3 Jack Parr, 'Eased into Captivity,' *The Legion*, June 1993, 22; Jim Lang, 'Drop over Utrecht,' in Tony Strachan, ed., *In the Clutch of Circumstance: Experiences of Canadian Prisoners of War* (Victoria: Cappis Press 1985), 87; Kingsley Brown, *Bonds of Wire: A Memoir* (Toronto: Collins 1989), 33.

4 Mills Library Microform Collection, McMaster University (MLMC): Akten der Partei-Kanzlei der NSDAP, teil 1, band 2, fiche 243, letter to Bormann, 3 July 1943; teletype, Propaganda Ministry, Berlin to Münster, 21 July 1943.

5 International Military Tribunal, *Trial of the Major War Criminals* (Nuremberg: IMT 1947), documents 110-R (Order to HSSPFs, 10 August 1943), 3855-PS (Decree by Chief of Sipo and SD, 5 April 1944), 057-PS (Circular letter to political leaders, 30 May 1944), 154-L (Circular order, 25 February 1945).

6 Les Allison and Harry Hayward, *They Shall Grow Not Old* (Brandon, MB: Commonwealth Air Training Plan Museum n.d.), 59. Reports of the suspicious deaths of Canadian airmen can be found in Windsor Municipal Archives: B.J.S. Macdonald Papers, box 4, series I2, f. 10, 'Report of the #1 Canadian War Crimes Investigation Unit on Miscellaneous War Crimes against Members of the Canadian Armed Forces,' pts. 1 and 2.

7 National Archives of Canada (NAC): Department of National Defence (DND) Records, reel C-5339, f. HQS 9050-17-10.

8 The details of the Mallory case can be found in NAC: Department of External Affairs (DEA) Records, vol. 2109, f. 405/4/10; Macdonald Papers, box 4, series I2, f. 10, 'Report of the #1 Canadian War Crimes Investigation Unit on Miscellaneous War Crimes,' pt. 1, 80.

9 Robert V. Waddy, 'My Six Years of War,' in Strachan, ed., *In the Clutch of Circumstance*, 15.

10 DEA Records, series A6, vol. 426, f. Cas 1/4, pt. 1, High Commission to DEA, 16 December 1942; DND Records, reel C-5330, f. HQS 9050-3-4, pt. 1, memo from SAAG, 24 May 1943.

11 Ibid., series C2f, vol. 8021, f. 19-7-1, 'Memo on Protest Policy,' 8 November 1943.

12 Charles Clay, 'Jack is a Prisoner of War,' *National Home Monthly* 42/10 (October 1941):17.

13 Quoted in John Melady, *Escape from Canada! The Untold Story of German POWs in Canada, 1939-1945* (Toronto: Macmillan 1982), 39.

14 Eckehart J. Priebe, *Thank You, Canada: From Messerschmitt Pilot to Canadian Citizen*

(West Vancouver: Condor Publishing 1990), 76; David J. Carter, *Behind Canadian Barbed Wire: Alien, Refugee and Prisoner of War Camps in Canada, 1914-1946* (Calgary: Tumbleweed Press 1980), 177.

15 NAC: Department of National War Services (DNWS) Records, vol. 17, f. Red Cross POW Parcels, Gordon to DNWS, 9 April 1942; DEA Records, vol. 2833, f. 1426-C-40c, pt. 3, H.M. Hueston, Sarnia, to DEA, 2 June 1944. Complaints about the treatment of German POWs also reached Canada from Allied POWs. See ibid., series A6, vol. 427, f. Cas 1/4, pt. 2, War Office to Ignatieff, 4 February 1943.

16 Ibid., vol. 425, f. Cas 1/3/1, pt. 1, Skelton to High Commission, 15 August 1940.

17 Ibid., vol. 427, f. Cas 1/4, pt. 2, External Affairs to High Commission, 17 June 1943; Foreign Office to High Commission, 12 July 1943.

18 Ibid., vol. 2833, f. 1426-C-40c, pt. 2, Read to Consul-General of Switzerland, 20 November 1943; vol. 2783, f. 621-JH-40, Canadian Embassy, Washington, to State Department, 7 February 1944.

19 Ibid., Canadian Embassy, Washington, to DEA, 11 March 1944; Scott to Feaver, 8 July 1944; Canadian Embassy, Washington, to Feaver, 9 September 1944.

20 In another typical incident, Canadians at the naval camp near Bremen were offered parole walks outside the camp, because German POWs in Canada received special privileges. Canada immediately protested the situation, pointing out that the Geneva Convention prohibited the granting of this concession to some prisoners while withholding it from others. The correspondence is in DND Records, series C2f, vol. 8025, f. 23-0.

21 Steve Michell, *They Were Invincible* (Bracebridge, ON: Herald-Gazette Press 1976), 87.

22 DEA Records, vol. 2833, f. 1426-C-40c, pt. 2, Graham to Scott, 4 April 1944.

23 DND Records, reel C-5331, f. HQS 9050-4, pt. 5, minutes of Sub-Committee A 34th meeting, 26 April 1944; DEA Records, vol. 2833, f. 1426-C-40c, pt. 2, Feaver to Scott, 8 May 1944. When Canadian POWs returned home after the war, they verified that Stargard was in fact no better, and perhaps even a little worse, than other camps in which they had been held.

24 C.P. Stacey, *Official History of the Canadian Army in the Second World War*, volume 1, *Six Years of War: The Army in Canada, Britain and the Pacific* (Ottawa: Queen's Printer 1955), 396.

25 NAC: W.L.M. King Papers, MG26 J1, reel C-6809, vol. 329, p. 281184, High Commission to DEA, 3 September 1942; Stacey, *Six Years of War*, 396.

26 Public Record Office (PRO): CAB 65/28, War Cabinet Conclusions #137 (42), 9 October 1942.

27 J.E.R. Wood, *Detour* (London: Falcon Press 1946), 153; John Buxton, 'Below the Tide of War,' *Atlantic Monthly* 177/6 (June 1946):60.

28 John Mellor, *Dieppe – Canada's Forgotten Heroes* (Scarborough, ON: Signet 1979), 137.

29 NAC: J.L. Ralston Papers, MG27 III B11, vol. 65, f. Shackling, High Commission to DEA, 8 October 1942.

30 Ibid., DEA to High Commission, 8 October 1942 (two cables).

31 King Papers, MG26 J1, reel C-6813, vol. 334, Dominions Office to DEA, 8 October 1942; reel C-6809, vol. 329, High Commission to DEA, 9 October 1942. At that time, there were roughly 16,000 German POWs in Canada and fewer than 500 in Britain. CAB 79/24, Joint Intelligence Sub-committee report (42) #434, 10 November 1942.

32 NAC: Privy Council Office (PCO) Records, series 7c, vol. 11, minutes of Cabinet War Committee meeting #197, 9 October 1942.

33 King Papers, MG26 J1, reel C-6813, vol. 334, p. 286350, DEA to Dominions Office, 9 October 1942; p. 286357, DEA to Dominions Office, 10 October 1942.

34 Ibid., p. 286361-2, Dominions Office to DEA, 10 October 1942 (two cables).

35 PCO Records, series 7c, vol. 11, minutes of Cabinet War Committee meeting #198, 10 October 1942; CAB 65/28, War Cabinet Conclusions #139 (42), 12 October 1942.

36 PCO Records, series 7c, vol. 11, Cabinet War Committee document #311, 'Report on Action Taken by NDHQ in Regard to Placing in Chains of German POWs,' 13 October 1942. Nevertheless, Canada did request that Britain inquire through the Protecting Power whether similar incidents had occurred in Germany; this suggests that Internment Operations was willing to use greater force if it was being employed against Canadian POWs. CAB 65/28, War Cabinet Conclusions #140 (42), 13 October 1942.

37 W.L.M. King diary (typescript), fiche 179, 12 October 1942; PCO Records, series 7c, minutes of Cabinet War Committee meeting #199, 14 October 1942.

38 King Papers, MG26 J1, reel C-6805, vol. 322, p. 273904, Prime Minister of Australia to King, 13 October 1942; reel C-6809, vol. 329, High Commission to DEA, 12 December 1942; High Commission to DEA, 12 October 1942; see 'Men in Manacles,' TIME, 19 October 1942, 27, and 'War Trials and Reprisals Against Prisoners,' Christian Century 59/42 (21 October 1942):1277.

39 'Battle of Bowmanville,' TIME, 26 October 1942, 32.

40 King Papers, MG26 J1, reel C-6810, vol. 330, p. 281449, High Commission to DEA, 30 November 1942.

41 PCO Records, series 7c, vol. 11, minutes of Cabinet War Committee meeting #208, 30 November 1942.

42 CAB 65/28, War Cabinet Conclusions #164 (42), 3 December 1942; King Papers, MG26 J1, reel C-6813, vol. 334, p. 286847, Dominions Office to DEA, 3 December 1942; 'Swiss Ask Shackling be Banned,' Globe & Mail (Toronto), 9 December 1942, 1.

43 King diary, fiche 181, 10 December 1942.

44 PCO Records, series 7c, vol. 11, minutes of Cabinet War Committee meeting #211, 16 December 1942.

45 Ibid., vol. 12, minutes of Cabinet War Committee meeting #227, 25 March 1943. Fewer than a third of the 4128 shackled POWs were Canadian; most were from other parts of the Empire. Lester Pearson wrote that nearly all of the shackled POWs were Canadians. Lester B. Pearson, Mike: The Memoirs of the Right Honourable Lester B. Pearson (Toronto: University of Toronto Press 1972), 1:171.

46 The phrase was used by Massey's biographer, Claude Bissell.

47 Michell, They Were Invincible, 21; Art Crighton, 'The Organ Loft,' The Anglican Messenger, December 1991, 9; Ambrose Farnum Diary, Bournemouth: playbill for variety show 'Bandwaggon,' 14 October 1944.

48 Daniel Dancocks, In Enemy Hands: Canadian Prisoners of War, 1939-45 (Edmonton: Hurtig 1983), 103; R.E. McLaren, interview by author, Hamilton, 18 January 1992.

49 Ripley Diary, 65; Farnum Diary, 146.

50 Mark Winston, ed., Spotlight on Sagan (London: n.d.), 27; Roy Turner Diary, Bushey Heath, Hertfordshire, UK, 32, 65.

51 Jim Witte, The One that Didn't Get Away (Bognor Regis: New Horizon 1983), 121; R.A. Bethell Diary, Alton, Programme of Events, 17 June 1944; Dancocks, In Enemy Hands, 102; Bill Cameron, Ottawa, correspondence with author, 18 January 1989.

52 Farnum Diary, 17 December 1944.

53 DEA Records, series A6, vol. 426, f. Cas 1/3/1, pt. 3, British Red Cross to Ignatieff, 25 August 1942; P.R. Reid, *Colditz: The Full Story* (London: Macmillan 1984), 146-7.

54 Ripley Diary, 38.

55 Ian F. MacDonald, interview by author, Windsor, 19 October 1993.

56 Farnum Diary, 90; Gladys E. Smith, *Forty Nights to Freedom* (Winnipeg: Queenston House Publishing 1984), 78.

57 W.A. Sandhals, Terrace, BC, correspondence with author, 23 November 1993; Fred LeReverend, Victoria, correspondence with author, [May 1992]; Farnum Diary, 15 November 1944.

58 NAC: Post Office Department (PO) Records, reel T-1689, vol. 2762, f. 35-27-2, pt. 1, L.G. de Forest, Drumheller, AB, to Tucketts Ltd., Hamilton, 18 July 1941; DEA Records, series G1, vol. 1959, f. 842-S, Robertson to Gordon, 3 December 1941.

59 PO Records, reel T-1689, vol. 2761, f. 35-27-2, pt. 1, High Commission to DEA, 16 September 1942; Second Assistant Postmaster-General, Washington, to Director of Administrative Service, Post Office Department, 22 August 1942.

60 DEA Records, series A6, vol. 426, f. Cas 1/3/1, pt. 3, DEA to Dominions Office, 24 October 1942.

61 Ibid., 22 October 1942. There was still a slight difference in the regulations in that Canadians could send a parcel every ninety days but Americans could send one every sixty days. However, Canadians were allowed to send any amount of games, books, or cigarettes through licensed shops, something that was prohibited in the United States. PO Records, reel T-1689, vol. 2761, f. 35-27-2, pt. 1, DEA to Canadian Minister, Washington, 28 October 1942.

62 DEA Records, series A6, vol. 426, f. Cas 1/3/1, pt. 3, War Office to Ignatieff, [October 1942]. As the War Office wrote to Ignatieff in 1943, 'when the Canadian Red Cross have been dealing with the Germans as long as we have been dealing with them, they will perhaps recognize that once we have started to provide for our prisoners anything in the way of supplies, it is quite useless to hope to persuade the Germans to make good any of their deficiencies.' DND Records, reel C-5069, f. HQC 4498-1, pt. 3, War Office to Ignatieff, 27 February 1943.

63 DEA Records, series A6, vol. 426, f. Cas 1/3/1, pt. 3, minutes of meeting, 29 October 1942.

64 Ibid., minutes of meeting, 29 October 1942.

65 *Gazette* (Montreal), 10 November 1942, 6.

66 DND Records, reel C-5335, f. HQS 9050-12-11, pt. 2, DEA to Asselin, 18 November 1944.

67 PO Records, reel T-1690, vol. 2762, f. 35-27-3, Coolican to Plumptre, 11 June 1943. The original pamphlet can be found in Hamilton Public Library Special Collections (HPL): Post Office Department, *Regulations Concerning Communications with POWs Interned Abroad*, March 1941; DND Records, reel C-5335, f. HQS 9050-12-16, pts. 1 and 2.

68 PO Records, reel T-1688, vol. 2760, f. 35-26-2, Department of National Defence – Army to Coolican, 30 March 1944; f. HQS 9050-12-11, pt. 1.

69 These parcels were for POWs only, not for civilian internees. Internees were supplied by individual relief allowances from the government, in return for providing promises to repay. In this sense, relief for civilian internees was strictly a loan that the government had every intention of collecting after the war. DEA Records, series G1, vol. 1960, f. 842-W, pt. 1, memo 'Relief for Canadian Civilians in Japanese Hands through ICRC' by Rive, 10 February 1944. Having said that, conditions for internees were generally quite accept-

able. In fact, in late 1943 External Affairs decided against pressing for the release of a group of Canadian women because it was realized that conditions in their camp were better than those they would experience if released. Ibid., vol. 2804, f. 841-D-40, memo to Rive, 16 December 1943. For a description of internee conditions, see Jennifer Jerome, 'Life in an Internment Camp for British and American Families,' *Saturday Night* 59/40 (10 June 1944):32.

70 PO Records, reel T-1693, vol. 2766, f. 35-32-1, District Director of Postal Services, Toronto, to Coolican, 16 August 1940.

71 Frederick F. Tisdall, 'Canadian Red Cross Food Parcels for British Prisoners-of-War in Germany,' *Canadian Medical Association Journal* January 1941:77-8.

72 Mackenzie Porter, *To All Men: The Story of the Canadian Red Cross* (Toronto: McClelland & Stewart 1960), 88; P.H. Gordon, *Fifty Years in the Canadian Red Cross* (1967), 70.

73 P.H. Gordon, *Fifty Years in the Canadian Red Cross* (1967), 70; Wartime Information Board, *Facts and Figures Weekly* #69 (1-7 July 1944):5. By contrast, the American Red Cross packed 1.5 million parcels monthly in five centres. MLMC: Records of the War Department General Staff, Operations Division, D&O 320, General Board, U.S. Forces – European Theatre (GBUSF), Study #5, 'American National Red Cross Activities in the European Theatre of Operations,' 24.

74 DEA Records, series G1, vol. 1958, f. 842-D, pt. 2, Canadian Red Cross to Pifher, 29 June 1945.

75 HPL: Red Cross Society scrapbook, vol. 1, clipping dated 4 May 1942; [Toronto Red Cross], *History, Toronto Branch, The Canadian Red Cross Society, 1914-1948* (Toronto: Toronto Red Cross n.d.), 48.

76 André Durand, *From Sarajevo to Hiroshima: History of the ICRC* (Geneva: Henry Dunant Institute 1978), 473-8.

77 Norman Gruenzner, *Postal History of American POWs: World War II, Korea, Vietnam* (State College, PA: American Philatelic Society 1979), 18; J.F. Garswood diary, Windsor, undated clipping in file pocket; PRO: WO 208/3329 #194, report by Flight Lieutenant A.K. Ogilvie.

78 The headquarters staff of the 8th Canadian Infantry Brigade reported finding a stockpile of Red Cross parcels in a wealthy civilian's house in Keppeln during the advance into Germany in 1945. J.A. Roberts, *The Canadian Summer* (Toronto: University of Toronto Bookroom 1981), 119.

79 DND Records, reel C-5069, f. HQC 4498-6, pt. 1, DEA to High Commission, 5 January 1942.

80 DEA Records, series G1, vol. 1962, f. 842-AJ-39, DEA to High Commission, 28 May 1941; series A6, vol. 426, f. Cas 1/3/1, pt. 3, DEA to Dominions Office, 27 January 1942, and reply, 4 February 1942; High Commission to DEA, 17 July 1942.

81 NAC: R.B. Bennett Papers, MG26 K, reel M-3185, vol. 969, p. 614779, Gordon to Bennett, 14 September 1942.

82 DEA Records, vol. 2777, f. 621-DQ-40, pt. 1, minutes of meeting of the Canadian, American, and British Red Cross Societies, 23-24 September 1943. Russian POWs received no outside aid whatsoever, save what enterprising western prisoners were willing to risk throwing to them over the camp fences.

83 PCO Records, series 7c, vol. 15, Cabinet War Committee document #689, 'Increase in Food Parcels for Commonwealth and Allied POWs,' 10 January 1944.

84 Wartime Information Board, *Canada at War* #41 (October 1944):54.

85 *History, Toronto Branch*, 74; Frederick F. Tisdall, 'Final Report on the Canadian Red Cross Food Parcels for Prisoners-of-War,' *Canadian Medical Association Journal* 60 (March 1949):285; Leslie Le Soeuf, *To War Without a Gun* (Western Australia: Artlook 1980), 375; DEA Records, series A6, vol. 429, f. Cas 1/6/1, pt. 4, Ignatieff to Rive, 13 December 1943.

86 Ibid., vol. 2943, f. 3033-40-4, 'Information on Red Cross Matters Derived from the M.S. Gripsholm Repatriation, May-June 1944,' 4; University of Victoria Archives, Canadian Military History Project (CMHP): Clarence F. Henigman interview; Tisdall, 'Final Report,' 280.

87 Staff Sergeant, 'Food Is Main Interest of Prisoners of War,' *Saturday Night* 60/23 (10 February 1945):13; Ripley Diary, 55.

88 Between the beginning of the war and the end of August 1942, over 78,000 POWs (nearly half of them Soviet) had escaped from German captivity; in August 1942 alone, there were over 14,000 escapes. Akten der Partei-Kanzlei der NSDAP, teil 2, band 2, fiche 132, Klemm to Justice Minister Thierack, 12 October 1942.

89 A.B. Thompson Papers, in possession of Nora Thompson, Penetanguishene: Thompson to father, 19 March 1942; Pat Langford Papers, in possession of Dennis Langford, Calgary: WCdr. H.M.A. Day to Mr. and Mrs. Langford, 17 July 1945; Leo Heaps, *The Grey Goose of Arnhem* (Markham: PaperJacks 1977), 81.

90 Information received from Capt. David Ratz, Unit Historical Officer, Lake Superior Scottish Regiment, 12 July 1993; J.M. Veness, Fredericton, correspondence with author, 9 July 1993; Heaps, *The Grey Goose of Arnhem*, 106-7.

91 For a detailed discussion of the problem of escape from one camp, see my article 'The War Behind the Wire: The Battle to Escape from a German Prison Camp,' *Journal of Contemporary History* 28/4 (October 1993):675-93.

92 PRO: WO 208/3441, statement by security officer Thiede.

93 Wood, *Detour*, 65-6, 70.

94 Aidan Crawley, *Escape from Germany* (London: HMSO 1985), 124.

95 C.D. Noble, interview by author, Collingwood, ON, 28 June 1986; Reid, *Colditz: The Full Story*, 71.

96 Dancocks, *In Enemy Hands*, 111.

97 Alfred G. Frei, '"In the End I Just Said O.K.": Political and Moral Dimensions of Escape Aid at the Swiss Border,' *Journal of Modern History* 64/Suppl (December 1992):S68.

98 Crawley, *Escape from Germany*, 138-9, 163.

99 M.R.D. Foot and J.M. Langley, *M.I.9: Escape and Evasion, 1939-1945* (London: Futura Publications 1980), 246; DEA Records, vol. 2944, f. 3033-40, pt. 5, Military Attaché, Stockholm, to War Office, 3 July 1944; *POW Journal*, Winter 1988, 15.

100 IMT, *Trial of the Major War Criminals*, Document 1650-PS (teletype *Aktion Kugel*, Chief of the Sipo and SD to Gestapo offices, 4 March 1944).

101 University of Toronto Archives: Department of Graduate Records, f. A73-0026/269 (50) G.E. McGill.

102 DND Records, reel C-5069, f. HQC 4498-6, pt. 2, report on Calvert shooting, undated; A. Robert Prouse, *Ticket to Hell via Dieppe* (Toronto: Van Nostrand Reinhold 1982), 50; Reid, *Colditz: The Full Story*, 219-20.

103 DND Records, reel C-5339, f. HQS 9050-17-10.

104 DEA Records, vol. 2942, f. 3033-40-1, minutes of first IPOWC meeting, 5 November 1941; memo 'Repatriation of Civilians from Europe,' 10 June 1942.

105 Ibid., vol. 2944, f. 3033-A-40, DEA to High Commission, 30 August 1941.

106 Ibid., memo 'Reciprocal Exchange of Nationals,' undated.

107 Ibid., vol. 2804, f. 841-D-40, Canadian Minister, Washington, to DEA, 23 May 1941.

108 The correspondence on this case is in ibid., vol. 2251, f. 17-AC-40.

109 Ibid., vol. 2944, f. 3033-B-40, pt. 1, note for Rive, 29 May 1942. The sinking of the *Zam Zam* is the subject of a number of accounts. See Charles J.V. Murphy, 'The Sinking of the "ZamZam,"' *Life* 10/25 (23 June 1941):21-6, 70-4, 77-9, and Eugène Nadeau, *La perle au fond du gouffre: Zam-Zam et barbelés* (Montreal: Fides 1963). To some extent, Canada was at the mercy of Germany in these matters. If German authorities decided, for whatever reason, to include a specific individual on an exchange, there was nothing Canada could do.

110 DEA Records, vol. 2943, f. 3033-40-1, memo 'Repatriation of Civilians from Europe,' 10 June 1942.

111 DND Records, vol. 48, f. HQ 240-1-73, Caldecote to DEA, 23 May 1940; *Times*, 8 October 1941, 3; W. Wynne Mason, *Prisoners of War* (Wellington, New Zealand: Department of Internal Affairs War History Branch 1954), 93.

112 DEA Records, vol. 2943, f. 3033-40-1, High Commission to DEA, 18 June 1942.

113 Ibid., memo by Robertson, 17 June 1942.

114 Ibid., minutes of first #1 Repatriation Committee meeting, 24 June 1942; High Commission to DEA, 30 June 1942, 13 July 1942, and 23 July 1942.

115 Ibid., 30 July 1942; Akten der Partei-Kanzlei der NSDAP, teil 1, band 1, fiche 119, memo from German Consulate in Geneva, 20 July 1942.

116 External Affairs Records, vol. 2944, f. 3033-A-40, DEA to High Commission, 23 December 1941.

117 There were six other repatriations, but these were limited agreements between either Britain and Italy or France and Germany and involved only a handful of Canadians. ICRC, *Report of the ICRC on Its Activities During the Second World War* (Geneva: ICRC 1948), 2:378-82.

118 McLaren interview; L.R. Gruggen, interview by author, Hamilton, 3 February 1992.

119 DND Records, reel C-5337, f. HQS 9050-14-10, Canadian Minister, Washington, to DEA, 21 October 1944.

120 DEA Records, vol. 2782, f. 621-HV-40c, minutes of ISCP first provisional meeting, 24 August 1943, and second provisional meeting, 4 October 1943.

121 Ibid., minutes of ISCP fourth provisional meeting, 30 November 1943.

122 Ibid., series A6, vol. 429, f. Cas 1/6/1, pt. 4, memo by Lt.-Col. D.C. Unwin Simson, [November 1943]; ibid., vol. 2782, minutes of ISCP third provisional meeting, 26 October 1943. Clarke would have been mortified had he known the opinions of one Canadian repatriate, who maintained that conditions on the Canadian hospital ship *Lady Nelson* were far inferior to those on the British hospital ship. HCHM: f. HCM 20-83, Howard Bradley, interview by C.G. Roland, London, ON, 29 June 1983.

123 DEA Records, series A6, vol. 430, f. Cas 1/6/2, pt. 1, memo, 'Repatriation of POWs – CMHQ proposals,' 1 December 1943; War Office to Ignatieff, 7 January 1944; f. Cas 1/6/2, pt. 2, DEA to Adjutant-General, 17 March 1944.

124 Ibid., vol. 431, f. Cas 1/6/2, pt. 3, DEA to Dominions Office, 6 May 1944.

125 Ibid., High Commission to DEA, 29 May 1944; War Office to Massey, 30 May 1944; HCHM: f. HCM 33-85, John A. Chapel, interview by C.G. Roland, Leicester, UK, 26 March 1985.

126 McLaren interview; Gruggen interview.

127 NAC: G.L. Magann Papers, MG30 E352, vol. 8, Morris Careless, 'Trip to Gothenburg,' 9.

128 Ibid., diary for 8 September 1944.

129 DEA Records, series A6, vol. 432, f. Cas 1/6/2, pt. 5, Magann to High Commission, 10 September 1944.

130 Ibid., Scott to Rive, 12 September 1944.

131 Ibid., vol. 3585, f. 2364-40c, pt. 15, report by J.K. Cronyn, 7 March 1945. Cronyn's report is immensely entertaining; as the covering letter reads, 'I dump into your hands what unquestionably is the world's worst report. There can be no middle road. This masterpiece either finds its way to the Hoo-Hoo or the P.M.'s hands.' Despite Cronyn's assessment, the report reveals keen insight into the problems involved in repatriation.

132 Ibid., series A6, vol. 435, f. Cas 9/12, report by Group Captain Sampson, 7 February 1945; vol. 3585, f. 2364-40c, pt. 15, report by Cronyn.

133 Ibid., Meagher to Rive, 27 February 1945; report by Cronyn. National Defence had requested twenty-one dock passes for their party.

134 Ibid., Meagher to Rive, 27 February 1945; Wrong to Canadian Consul-General, New York, 9 March 1945.

135 Ibid., vol. 2943, f. 3033-40, pt. 1, High Commission to DEA, 20 December 1943; memo 'Exchange of Civilians with Germany,' 4 January 1944. Interestingly, a visit to one internment camp in July 1942 revealed that only 20 per cent of the internees would accept exchange if it was offered to them. Ibid., vol. 3032, f. 4051-40, summary of *Frontstalag* 122 visit, 28 July 1942.

136 Ibid., Scott to Rive, 7 March 1944. Cf. Scott's earlier complaint that cables received from the ICRC were in French. Ibid., vol. 2833, f. 1426-C-40, pt. 2, Scott to Maag, 26 November 1943. Such comments reflect the definite anglophone bias of External Affairs, which is commented upon in J.L. Granatstein, *The Ottawa Men: The Civil Service Mandarins, 1935-1957* (Toronto: Oxford University Press 1982), 4-5. They also reflect the view that, at least in the eyes of some bureaucrats, it was much more desirable to secure the freedom of an English-Canadian civilian than a French-Canadian civilian.

137 DEA Records, vol. 2943, f. 3033-40, pt. 3, note by Meagher, 8 March 1944.

138 Ibid., f. 3033-40, pt. 3, High Commission to War Office POW Department, 9 June 1944.

139 Ibid., DEA to High Commission, 28 June 1944. The comments of one official in this regard are revealing, in light of the interwar controversy over reparations payments to former civilian internees: 'Prior to the outbreak of war Allied nationals were given ample warning and advice to return to their homes and many did so; these people paid their own way. Many of those remaining in dangerous territory did so for personal or business reasons and it would appear to us that to grant this latter class free passage would seem in the line of rewarding them for ignoring their government's advice or, turned around the other way, penalize [sic] those who did the proper thing and saved the Government a great deal of trouble.' Ibid., vol. 3113, f. 4464-C-40, A.L. Jolliffe, Department of Mines and Resources to DEA. Canada continued to collect repatriation expenses from former civilian internees as late as 1952.

140 Ibid., vol. 2944, f. 3033-40, pt. 5, High Commission to DEA, 12 August 1944. According to Glazebrook, 'whenever a French speaking European wants to claim an extra-European nationality he says he is French Canadian.' Ibid., vol. 2943, f. 3033-40, pt. 4, memo 'Drottningholm Exchange Security Arrangements,' 5 July 1944.

141 Ibid., vol. 2944, f. 3033-40, pt. 5, DEA to High Commission, 21 August 1944.

142 Ibid., f. 3033-40, pt. 6, memo 'Exchange of Civilians at Gothenburg,' 19 September 1944.

143 Ibid., Rive to Scott, 26 September 1944.

144 Ibid., f. 3033-40, pt. 8, DEA to High Commission, 18 January 1945.

145 DND Records, vol. 1845, f. GAQ 11-16c, memo to Deputy Adjutant-General, 4 March 1942; CAB 79/27, minutes of War Cabinet – Chiefs of Staff Committee meeting (43) #149, 11 November 1943.

146 PCO Records, series 7c, vol. 12, Cabinet War Committee Document #383, 'Arrangements for Postwar Repatriation of POWs,' 7 December 1942; minutes of Cabinet War Committee meeting #215, 13 January 1943.

147 For an outline of this plan, see DND Records, reel C-5330, f. HQS 9050-4, pt. 5, memo for Sub-Committee A, 'Plan for the Repatriation of POWs from Germany,' 31 December 1943.

148 DEA Records, series A6, vol. 435, f. Cas 9/12, Deputy Minister of National Defence – Army to DEA, 28 February 1944.

149 Ibid., vol. 2784, f. 621-LU-40, DEA to service HQs, 25 September 1944.

150 Ibid., DEA to High Commission, 13 January 1945.

151 Ibid., vol. 3585, f. 2364-40c, pt. 14, DEA to Canadian Ambassador, Washington, 14 February 1945.

152 Ibid., vol. 2782, f. 621-HV-40c, minutes of tenth provisional ISCP meeting, 26 September 1944.

153 DND Records, reel C-5330, f. HQS 9050-4, pt. 6, memo 'Post-Hostilities Handling of Canadian prisoners in Germany' by Scott, undated.

154 DEA Records, series A6, vol. 435, f. Cas 9/12, '"Eclipse" Memorandum No. 8: The Care and Evacuation of POWs in Greater Germany under "Eclipse" Conditions,' 19 March 1945. Presumably this is the memorandum described by A.J. Evans, one of the ablest PWX contact officers, as 'a terrifying and detailed document containing minute instructions to an immense organisation.' A.J. Evans, *Escape and Liberation 1940-1945* (London: Hodder & Stoughton 1945), 139.

155 CAB 88/23, Combined Chiefs of Staff memorandum #472/4, note by United States Chiefs of Staff, 23 November 1944; PRO: AIR 14/1685, minutes of POW airlift meeting, 28 March 1945.

156 DEA Records, series A6, vol. 428, f. Cas 1/4, pt. 5, High Commission to DEA, 26 August 1944; vol. 2784, f. 621-LY-40, memo 'Negotiations with the USSR regarding Allied POWs coming into Russian Hands' by Rive, 3 February 1945. As a CBC radio talk said, 'the great conference of leaders now taking place is considering high upon the list the protection and repatriation of all prisoners who may fall into the welcoming hands of their brothers in freedom.' Ibid., vol. 2833, f. 1426-C-40, pt. 3, text of talk by L.J. Brockington, 11 February 1945.

157 The following paragraphs rely upon ibid., series A7, vol. 556, f. Cas 9/12/1, reports by Squadron Leader C.G.E. Leafloor and Maj. Nelson Darling, both entitled 'Repatriation from the Russian Zone.'

158 *The Camp*, January 1990, 4; D.A.Y. Merrick, 'From Parachute to Prison,' *Canadian Banker* 53 (1946):212; Tom Thomson, Medicine Hat, correspondence with author, 11 October 1993.

159 ICRC, *Report of the ICRC on Its Activities During the Second World War*, 3:88.

160 DND Records, series C2f, vol. 8021, f. 19-7-2, SAAG monthly report for February 1945, dated 12 March 1945; vol. 8024, f. 21-1, British Minister, Berne, to External Affairs, 17 March 1945; Ted Brocklehurst, 'Excerpts from the Diary of Ted Brocklehurst – POW –

RCAF,' *The POW Journal*, Spring 1985, 15-17.

161 Crawley, *Escape from Germany*, 220-37; Mellor, *Forgotten Heroes*, 184-92.

162 Farnum Diary, 17 December 1944; GCapt. D.E.L. Wilson, 'The March from Luft III,' *The Camp*, June 1988, 9; Akten der Partei-Kanzlei der NSDAP, teil 1, band 1, fiche 036, Führerinformation Nr A I 504, 26 January 1945.

163 Dr. D.W. Clare Diary, Kingsville, ON, 28 January 1945; Brocklehurst, 'Excerpts from the Diary of Ted Brocklehurst,' 17; *POW Journal*, October-December 1980, 22.

164 Roy Loomer Diary, Halifax: entry for 19 April 1945.

165 DEA Records, accession 89-90/029, box 46, f. 135-A(S), pt. 1, Rive to Feaver, 7 October 1944; IMT, *Trial of the Major War Criminals*, document 3786-PS (transcript of Führer conference, 27 January 1945).

166 DEA Records, series A7, vol. 556, f. Cas 9/12/1, report by Lt.-Col. J.H. Mothersill, 5; CAB 88/23, Combined Chiefs of Staff memorandum #472/9 (12 April 1945), SHAEF HQ, Versailles, to War Department, 26 March 1945.

167 Sampson and Mothersill disagreed on this point. Sampson believed that it was a waste of time to attempt to ensure that Canadian POWs were always contacted by Canadian liaison officers, while Mothersill believed that 'at least some consideration should be shown towards Canada in looking solely after her own interests instead of being merely a voice in the wilderness.' He believed that Canadian officers should have been free to travel to meet groups of Canadian POWs, wherever they might accumulate in the SHAEF area. Given a choice of being evacuated immediately or waiting to be greeted by a Canadian contact officer, most repatriated POWs would surely have agreed with Sampson. DEA Records, series A7, vol. 556, f. Cas 9/12/1, report by GCapt. F.A. Sampson, para. 29; report by Mothersill, 5.

168 The only major problem occurred with the evacuation of the camp at Luckenwalde. Liberating Russian troops refused to allow the POWs to leave, and even fired upon American convoys sent to remove the POWs. The reason for the delay was the difficulty in negotiating the administrative arrangements for the return of these prisoners to the western zone, and it was nearly a month before the Russians allowed the camp to be cleared. See ibid., series A6, vol. 435, f. Cas 9/12, report by WCdr. R.C.M. Collard; Nikolai Tolstoy, *Victims of Yalta* (London: Hodder & Stoughton 1977; repr. London: Corgi 1986), 533.

169 Evans, *Escape and Liberation*, 161.

170 H.E. Woolley, *No Time Off for Good Behaviour* (Burnstown, ON: General Store Publishing 1990), 172.

171 ASHC: Clifford Foulds, interview by W.H. Wiley, Hamilton, undated; Roy Clute, interview by W.H. Wiley, Scarborough, undated.

172 CMHP: W.A. Wilson interview; John P. Grogan, *Dieppe and Beyond* (Renfrew: Juniper Books 1982), 113-15.

173 HCHM: HCM 77-85, Roy A. Westaway, interview by C.G. Roland, Burlington, 13 September 1985.

174 DEA Records, series A7, vol. 556, f. Cas 9/12/1, report by Sampson, para. 39-40. Sampson's figures show that three RCAF prisoners were unaccounted for as of 25 June 1945.

175 DEA Records, series A7, vol. 556, f. Cas 9/12/1, report by Mothersill. Figures for Army POWs show that nineteen other ranks were unaccounted for. Reports by the Army liaison officers are appended to Mothersill's report; William H. Cram, Indian Head, Saskatchewan, correspondence with author, 7 July 1992; DEA Records, Lt. D.B. Wilson, 'Report on the Repatriation of RCN Liberated POWs,' undated. Other Allied liaison

officers were also satisfied. See MLMC: GBUSF Study #103, 'The Military Police Activities in Connection with the Evacuation and Detention of POWs, Civilian Internees, and Military Personnel Recovered from the Enemy,' 23.

176 Keith Pettigrew, Edmonton, correspondence with author, [March 1992]; Ripley Diary, 22 April 1945; Maxwell Bates, *A Wilderness of Days* (Victoria: Sono Nis Press 1978), 133.

177 DEA Records, vol. 3401, f. 621-NE-40c, Rive to Robertson, 18 April 1945.

178 HCHM: f. HCM 10-80, Charles T. Robertson, interview by C.G. Roland, Scarborough, 7 July 1980; f. HCM 19-83, Howard Large, interview by C.G. Roland, 29 June 1983.

179 DND Records, vol. 8020, f. 19-0, pt. 3, memo from DEA, 3 July 1945; DEA Records, series G1, vol. 1962, f. 842-AK-39, Brig. W.W. Southam, *Stalag* 7B, to King, 21 January 1944.

Chapter 7: A Tougher Nut: Prisoners of the Japanese

1 Wartime Information Board (WIB), *Facts and Figures Weekly* #133 (23-29 August 1945):4.

2 Argyll and Sutherland Highlanders of Canada Regimental Archives, Hamilton: George Soper, interview by Rosanne Giulietti, Toronto, 12 July 1984.

3 John Luff, quoted in Grant S. Garneau, 'The 1st Battalion of the Royal Rifles of Canada: The Record of a Canadian Infantry Battalion in the Far East, 1941-1945,' in [Lionel Hurd, ed.], *The Royal Rifles of Canada in Hong Kong, 1941-1945* (Sherbrooke: Hong Kong Veterans' Association Quebec-Maritimes Branch 1980), 102.

4 See Charles Burdick and Ursula Moessner, *The German Prisoners-of-War in Japan, 1914-1920* (Lanham, MD: University Press of America 1984).

5 National Archives of Canada (NAC): Department of External Affairs (DEA) Records, series A6, vol. 425, f. Cas 1/1, High Commission to DEA, 12 December 1941.

6 Britain took the Japanese reply to mean that they would observe the spirit but not the letter of the convention. W. Wynne Mason, *Prisoners of War* (Wellington, New Zealand: Department of Internal Affairs War History Branch 1954), 185; Patricia Roy, J.L. Granatstein, Masako Iino, and Hiroko Takamura, *Mutual Hostages: Canadians and Japanese During the Second World War* (Toronto: University of Toronto Press 1990), 68-9. See also C.G. Roland, 'Allied POWs, Japanese Captors and the Geneva Convention,' *War & Society* 9/2 (October 1991):83-101.

7 The government stressed this fact as early as 14 January 1942. See Roy et al., *Mutual Hostages*, 84.

8 NAC: J.L. Ralston Papers, MG27 III B11, vol. 48, f. Hong Kong Cables, pt. 2, High Commission to DEA, 13 January 1942; DEA to Argentine Minister, 9 February 1942.

9 Ibid., Canadian Minister, Argentina, to DEA, 24 February 1942.

10 NAC: Department of National Defence (DND) Records, reel C-5069, f. HQC 4498-6, pt. 2, aide memoire, 13 August 1942.

11 Ibid., reel C-5330, f. HQS 9050-4, pt. 1, minutes of nineteenth Sub-Committee A meeting, 14 April 1943; f. HQS 9050-4, pt. 2, memo for Sub-Committee A, 'Notification of POWs in the Far East,' 2 June 1943. At this time, Britain had received the names of only half of her POWs in the Far East, while Australia had received the names of fewer than a third.

12 Ralston Papers, vol. 48, f. Hong Kong Cables, pt. 1, Robertson to Ralston, 22 January 1942; Public Record Office (PRO): CAB 66/22, War Cabinet memorandum WP(42) #82, 14 February 1942, note by Secretary of War Cabinet.

13 Ralston Papers, vol. 48, f. Hong Kong Cables, pt. 2, High Commission to DEA, 12 February 1942.

14 Ibid., DEA to British Ambassador, Chungking, 16 February 1942.

15 House of Commons, Debates, 10 March 1942, p. 1168.

16 'Our Own Jap Problem' (editorial), *Vancouver Sun*, 10 March 1942, 4. See also 'Remember Hong Kong' (editorial), *Edmonton Bulletin*, 11 March 1942, 6.

17 'These Modern Savages' (editorial), *Spectator* (Hamilton), 11 March 1942, 6; 'The Beasts Seeking Conquest' (editorial), *Globe & Mail* (Toronto), 11 March 1942, 6.

18 Mills Library Microform Collection, McMaster University (MLMC): Magic Documents, reel 1, SRS-617 (summary of 2 June 1942), p. 0386.

19 Oliver Lindsay, *At the Going Down of the Sun: Hong Kong and South-East Asia, 1941-1945* (London: Hamish Hamilton 1981), 90.

20 NAC: W.L.M. King Papers, MG26 J1, reel C-6813, vol. 335, p. 287169, British Ambassador, Chungking, to DEA, 28 December 1942; DND Records, reel C-5069, f. HQC 4498-9-2, High Commission to DEA, 23 January 1943.

21 DEA Records, series G1, vol. 1961, f. 842-AD-39, pt. 2, note by Meagher, 2 July 1943. Reports received about conditions for other Allied POWs confirmed what was said about Canadians. For example, at the Quadrant Conference, Gen. George C. Marshall read a report on the treatment of American POWs in the Philippines made by an airman who had recently escaped. Marshall called the treatment 'inhuman and barbaric in the extreme.' CAB 88/3, minutes of Combined Chiefs of Staff meeting #115, 23 August 1943. Even more compelling were reports from the Allied Translator and Interpreter Section (ATIS), a unit of Gen. Douglas MacArthur's South-West Pacific command that interrogated Japanese POWs and translated captured documents. One such report was a disturbingly graphic account of the beheading of a captured Allied airman, taken from the diary of a Japanese soldier. MLMC: ATIS Papers, SW Pacific Area, fiche 10-SR-153, Spot Report #153, 4 October 1943.

22 ICRC, *Report of the ICRC on Its Activities During the Second World War* (Geneva: ICRC 1948), 1:451. Through the course of the war, ICRC delegates secured permission to visit fewer than half of the prison camps operated by Japan.

23 William Allister, *Where Life and Death Hold Hands* (Toronto: Stoddart 1989), 81-3.

24 DND Records, reel C-5070, f. HQC 4498-15, High Commission to DEA, 16 July 1942.

25 Ibid., reel C-5069, f. HQC 4498-9, pt. 2, High Commission to DEA, 7 and 16 January 1943.

26 Ibid., DEA to High Commission, 17 February 1943.

27 DEA Records, vol. 2830, f. 1426-A-40, Rive to Gordon, 20 June 1942.

28 DND Records, reel C-5330, f. HQS 9050-4, pt. 2, Letson to Ralston, 3 July 1943; SAAG to DEA, 5 July 1943.

29 NAC: Privy Council Office (PCO) Records, series B2, vol. 120, f. W-35-1, Canadian Minister, China, to DEA, 24 July 1943.

30 Ibid., series 7c, vol. 14, minutes of Cabinet War Committee 270th meeting, 24 November 1943.

31 Ibid., vol. 15, Cabinet War Committee document #685, 'Japanese Treatment of POWs: Publicity Campaign,' [January 1944]. Canadian officials were unusually slow in arriving at this decision. When the matter came before Britain's War Cabinet, Canada was the only one of eight Allied governments that requested more time to consider it. CAB 66/46, War Cabinet memorandum WP (44) #51, memo by Secretary of State for Foreign Affairs, 24 January 1944.

32 House of Commons, Debates, 28 January 1944, p. 3-4.

33 WIB, *Facts and Figures Weekly* #79 (10-16 August 1944):5; #80 (17-22 August 1944):2. An equally rosy report on the camp at North Point was published in September.

34 DND Records, reel C-5330, f. HQS 9050-4, pt. 6, DEA to High Commission, 30 September 1944.

35 In April 1945 the Joint Chiefs of Staff announced that all theatre commanders could release atrocity stories without first obtaining the consent of the State Department. MLMC: Records of the Joint Chiefs of Staff, Part 1 1942-5 (JCS1): Pacific Theater, reel 1, p. 0038, JCS memo #504/6 by Chief of Staff, US Army, 25 April 1945. Also in April, British officials drew up a plan code-named Bassington, which involved informing Japan that the Allies were holding a mass of information about Japanese atrocities. This would be used after the war as a sort of black book to discredit the Japanese nation 'or delay the resurgence of Japan as a respectable member of the community of nations.' JCS1: Strategic Issues, reel 12, p. 0236, Combined Chiefs of Staff memo #843 by British Chiefs of Staff, 25 April 1945.

36 DEA Records, vol. 3626, f. 2998-D-40, pt. 7, Maag to DEA, 9 August 1945.

37 Daniel Dancocks, *In Enemy Hands: Canadian POWs, 1939-45* (Edmonton: Hurtig 1983), 255; Colin Standish, 'The Third Draft to Japan,' in Hurd, *The Royal Rifles of Canada*, 330-1.

38 Kenneth Cambon, *Guest of Hirohito* (Vancouver: PW Press 1990), 60-1; Hurd, *The Royal Rifles of Canada*, 141; Dancocks, *In Enemy Hands*, 255.

39 Oral History Archives, Hannah Chair for the History of Medicine, McMaster University (HCHM): f. HCM 8-83, Robert D. Adams, interview by C.G. Roland, Winnipeg, 27 May 1983.

40 Hurd, *The Royal Rifles of Canada*, 350; HCHM: f. HCM 5-90, Donat Bernier, interview by C.G. Roland, Montreal, 9 June 1990; Cambon, *Guest of Hirohito*, 55.

41 Dancocks, *In Enemy Hands*, 252, 259.

42 David Bosanquet, *Escape through China* (Toronto: McClelland & Stewart 1985), 41; Hurd, *The Royal Rifles of Canada*, 94-5.

43 Bob Manchester, on *The Valour and the Horror* (Canadian Broadcasting Corporation/National Film Board 1992).

44 Hurd, *The Royal Rifles of Canada*, 286.

45 Ed Horton, 'A Prisoner of the Japs,' *The Camp*, April 1993, 12.

46 Soper interview.

47 NAC: F.D.F. Martyn Papers, MG30 E324; John Neilson Crawford Papers, MG30 E213.

48 DND Records, reel C-5330, f. HQS 9050-4, pt. 6, memo for Sub-Committee A, 'Morbidity among POWs in the Far East,' 10 January 1945; P. Jones, J. Bradley-Watson, and E.B. Bradbury, 'Health of Prisoners-of-War Evacuated from Hong Kong,' *Lancet*, 17 November 1945, 646.

49 Other Allied nations sustained significantly higher death rates; Australia lost 7412 out of a total of 21,726 prisoners, Britain lost 12,433 out of 50,016, and the United States lost 7107 out of 21,580. R.J. Pritchard and Sonia Zaide, eds., *The Tokyo War Crimes Trials* (New York: Garland Publishing 1981), 6:14902. Cf. casualty figures for prisoners in other theatres in Günter Bischof and Stephen E. Ambrose, eds., *Eisenhower and the German POWs: Facts against Falsehood* (Baton Rouge: Louisiana State University Press 1992), 18-19.

50 External Affairs made a separate request to Japan through the Protecting Power in April 1942. DEA Records, series G1, vol. 1960, f. 842-W, pt. 1, DEA to Canadian Minister, Argentina, 17 April 1942.

51 Ibid., series A6, vol. 433, f. Cas 2/1, pt. 1, Massey to Cranborne, 5 January 1942; High

Commission to DEA, 16 January and 10 February 1942.

52 DND Records, reel C-5069, f. HQC 4498-9, Canadian Minister, Washington, to DEA, 13 March 1942; Ralston Papers, vol. 48, f. Hong Kong Cables, pt. 2, Clarke to Ralston, 22 May 1942.

53 Department of State, *Bulletin* 10/243 (19 February 1944):190.

54 DEA Records, series A6, vol. 433, f. Cas 2/1, pt. 1, DEA to High Commission, 23 March 1942; DND Records, reel C-5069, f. HQC 4498-10, Robertson to Under-Secretary of State, 13 May 1942; NAC: Secretary of State Records, series H4, vol. 811, f. 2469, High Commission to DEA, 11 June 1942.

55 DEA Records, series A6, vol. 433, f. Cas 2/1, pt. 1, Ignatieff to War Office, 15 May 1942; High Commission to DEA, 19 May 1942.

56 Ibid., 1 June 1942; DND Records, reel C-5330, f. 9050-4, pt. 1, memo for Sub-Committee A, 'Relief for POWs and Internees in Far East by Diplomatic Exchange Ships,' 22 September 1943.

57 DEA Records, series G1, vol. 1960, f. 842-W, pt. 1, DEA to Canadian Minister, Washington, 14 September 1942, and reply, 17 September 1942.

58 Ibid., series A6, vol. 433, f. Cas 2/1, pt. 2, DEA to High Commission, 14 October 1942; minutes of meeting between War Office, Foreign Office, British Red Cross, and Canada House, 17 October 1942.

59 Ibid., DEA to Canadian Minister, Washington, 23 October 1942, and reply, 30 October 1942.

60 Ibid., DEA to High Commission, 11 November 1942; Fred L. Israel, ed., *The War Diary of Breckinridge Long* (Lincoln: University of Nebraska Press 1966), entry for 27 August 1942, 280.

61 DEA Records, series A6, vol. 433, f. Cas 2/1, pt. 2, DEA to High Commission, 15 December 1942.

62 DND Records, reel C-5330, f. HQS 9050-1-1, Canadian Minister, Washington, to DEA, 10 December 1942; DEA to High Commission, 15 December 1942.

63 Ibid., reel C-5070, f. HQC 4498-15, minutes of meeting, 7 January 1943.

64 DEA Records, series A6, vol. 433, f. Cas 2/1, pt. 1, DEA to High Commission, 12 March 1942; vol. 426, f. Cas 1/3/4, pt. 1, DEA to High Commission, 2 December 1942.

65 Ibid., War Office to Ignatieff, 15 December 1942; Hurd, *The Royal Rifles of Canada*, 339.

66 PRO: FO 916/769, loose minutes, 16 January 1943.

67 DEA Records, vol. 2777, f. 621-DQ-40, pt. 1, minutes of special Sub-Committee A meeting, 26 January 1943; DND Records, reel C-5070, f. HQC 4498-15, High Commission to DEA, 9 February 1943.

68 DEA Records, series A6, vol. 434, f. Cas 2/1, pt. 3, DEA to High Commission, 17 January 1943.

69 Ibid., 18 February 1943.

70 DND Records, reel C-5070, f. HQC 4498-15, Canadian Minister, Washington, to DEA, 20 February 1943.

71 DEA Records, series A6, vol. 434, f. Cas 2/1, pt. 3, British Minister, Washington, to Foreign Office, [February 1943]; High Commission to DEA, 1 March 1943.

72 PCO Records, series 7c, vol. 12, minutes of Cabinet War Committee meeting #221, 24 February 1943.

73 DND Records, reel C-5330, f. HQS 9050-1-2, memo to the Minister by J. Pembroke, 6 March 1943.

74 PCO Records, series 7c, vol. 12, minutes of Cabinet War Committee meeting #223, 5 March 1943; DND Records, reel C-5330, f. HQS 9050-1-2, Canadian Minister, Washington, to DEA, 12 March 1943, and reply, 17 March 1943.

75 Ibid., minutes sheet, 'Off the Record Discussion between Col. Clarke and Mr. Ryan of the American Red Cross,' 19 April 1943; DEA Records, series A6, vol. 434, f. Cas 2/1. pt. 3, DEA to High Commission, 24 April 1943.

76 Ibid., 22 April 1943; DND Records, reel C-5330, f. HQS 9050-1-2, Canadian Minister, Washington, to DEA, 28 April 1943; f. HQS 9050-1-3, pt. 1, Canadian Minister, Washington, to DEA, 12 May 1943.

77 Ibid., memo by Scott, 13 May 1943.

78 Ibid., Wilgress to DEA, 31 May 1943; DEA to High Commission, 12 June 1943.

79 Ibid., Canadian Minister, Washington, to DEA, 9 July 1943; High Commission to DEA, 29 June 1943.

80 DEA Records, series A6, vol. 434, f. Cas 2/1, pt. 3, Wallinger to Ignatieff, 17 June 1943; DEA to High Commission, 2 July 1943.

81 DND Records, reel C-5330, f. HQS 9050-1-3, Canadian Minister, Washington, to DEA, 22 July 1943.

82 Ibid., High Commission to DEA, 11 August 1943.

83 DEA Records, series A6, vol. 434, f. Cas 2/1, pt. 4, memo by Clarke, 4 August 1943; DND Records, reel C-5330, f. HQS 9050-1-3, pt. 1, Wilgress to DEA, 8 August 1943.

84 Ibid., Clarke to Rive, 7 August 1943; minutes of the meetings, which lasted for more than a week, are in DEA Records, vol. 2777, f. 621-DQ-40.

85 The changes recommended were the substitution of concentrated orange juice for dried fruit, the addition of vitamin pills, and the inclusion of instructions on how to cook rice and soybeans to preserve the mineral content. NAC: Post Office Department Records, reel T-1688, vol. 2760, f. 35-26-1, Tisdall to Routley, 16 June 1943.

86 DND Records, reel C-5330, f. HQS 9050-1-3, pt. 1, Canadian Minister, Washington, to DEA, 14 September 1943; Wilgress to DEA, 17 September 1943.

87 Ibid., Canadian Minister, Washington, to DEA, 2 October 1943.

88 Ibid., 3 and 18 November 1943.

89 DEA Records, series A6, vol. 435, f. Cas 2/1, pt. 5, Scott to Massey, 29 March 1944.

90 DND Records, reel C-5330, f. HQS 9050-1-3, pt. 2, Canadian Embassy, Washington, to DEA, 6 October 1944, and reply, 19 October 1944.

91 Ibid., summary of broadcast from Tokyo, 11 November 1944; memo 'Summary of First Relief Shipment via Soviet Territory for Far East POWs and Civilian Internees,' [December 1944]; Clarke to DEA, 25 November 1944; note from Capt. P.R. Turner, SAAG office, 29 November 1944.

92 Ibid., Rive to DND, 16 April 1945; ICRC, *Report of the ICRC*, 1:459; CAB 66/65, War Cabinet memorandum WP (45) #303, memo by Secretary of State for War, 17 May 1945.

93 ICRC, *Report of the ICRC*, 1:461.

94 Lindsay, *At the Going Down of the Sun*, 82; Russell S. Clark, *An End to Tears* (Sydney: Peter Huston 1946), 153.

95 Horton, 'A Prisoner of the Japs,' 13.

96 NAC: Tom Forsyth Papers, MG30 E181, 'Gleanings from the Diary of a Winnipeg Grenadier,' 42, 46.

97 Dancocks, *In Enemy Hands*, 253-4; Ken Stofer, *Dear Mum: The Story of Victor Edward 'Candy' Syrett* (Victoria: Kenlyn Publishing 1991), 224.

98 Dr. S.M. Banfill, 'Shamshuipo' in Hurd, *The Royal Rifles of Canada*, 312.

99 Garneau, 'The 1st Battalion of the Royal Rifles of Canada,' 107-8.

100 Les Allison and Harry Hayward, *They Shall Grow Not Old* (Brandon, MB: Commonwealth Air Training Plan Museum n.d.), 709-10.

101 Forsyth Papers, 'Gleanings from the Diary of a Winnipeg Grenadier,' entry for 29 January 1942.

102 DND Records, reel C-5337, f. HQS 9050-14-7, pt. 2, Rive to Deputy-Minister of National Defence, Army, 11 April 1944; Canadian Minister, Washington, to DEA, 27 May 1944.

103 Ibid., High Commission to DEA, 3 July 1944.

104 CAB 65/43, War Cabinet Conclusions #98 (44), 28 July 1944.

105 DND Records, reel C-5337, f. HQS 9050-14-7, pt. 2, Canadian Minister, Washington, to DEA, 6 September 1944.

106 Ibid., DEA to High Commission, 28 September 1944; High Commission to DEA, 18 October 1944.

107 Ibid., DEA to High Commission, 24 October 1944 (two cables).

108 CAB 66/57, War Cabinet memorandum WP (44) #650 (15 November 1944), American Embassy, London, to Foreign Office, 9 November 1944; CAB 65/44, War Cabinet conclusions #151 (44), 16 November 1944.

109 Magic Documents, reel 5, SRS-955 (summary of 4 May 1943), p. 0404, Tokyo to Japanese Minister, Berne, undated.

110 King Papers, MG26 J1, reel C-6804, vol. 321, p. 272821, British Minister, Berne to DEA, 30 May 1942; Roy et al., *Mutual Hostages*, 207.

111 WIB, *Facts and Figures Weekly* #35 (8-14 October 1943). There are many accounts of this operation. One that covers the experiences of a number of Canadians is 'Americans' Return,' *Life* (20 December 1943):87-93. According to this article, one of the Canadians was Morris A. Cohen of Edmonton, Sun Yat-Sen's bodyguard and the holder of a slot-machine concession in Canton. See also Kathleen G. Christie, 'M. & V. for Christmas Dinner,' *Canadian Nurse* (December 1967):28-30.

112 DEA Records, vol. 3342, f. 4464-40, pt. 6, Meagher to Rive, 11 April 1944.

113 Ibid., Scott to Rive, 25 April 1944. Scott was referring to the fact that many Canadian missionaries in the Far East did not wish to desert their charges, before, during, or after the war. Roy et al., *Mutual Hostages*, 57-61, 208.

114 DEA Records, vol. 3343, f. 4464-40, pt. 6, note by Robertson, 20 June 1944.

115 DND Records, reel C-5330, f. HQS 9050-4, pt. 3, memo for Sub-Committee A, 'Post War Repatriation of POWs from the Far East,' 6 July 1943.

116 Ibid., reel C-5337, f. HQS 9050-14-15, pt. 1, DEA to Canadian Minister, Washington, 20 September 1944, and reply, 23 September 1944.

117 Ibid., DEA to High Commission, 14 March 1945; CAB 122/692, f. 8/4/4Q, War Cabinet/Chiefs of Staff Committee memo, 11 April 1945.

118 DND Records, reel C-5337, f. HQS 9050-14-15, pt. 1, High Commission to DEA, 16 April 1945.

119 Ibid., DEA to Deputy-Minister of National Defence – Army, 17 April 1945, and reply, 5 May 1945.

120 NAC: Department of National War Services Records, accession 85-86/537, box 7, f. Canadian POWs, pt. 2, Scott to DEA, 31 May 1945.

121 DND Records, reel C-5337, f. HQS 9050-14-15, pt. 1, DEA to High Commission, 16 April 1945.

122 Ibid., reel C-5330, f. HQS 9050-4, pt. 7, DEA to High Commission, 7 June 1945 (two cables).

123 Ibid., reel C-5337, f. HQS 9050-14-15, pt. 1, High Commission to DEA, 20 June 1945, and reply, 25 June 1945.

124 Ibid., f. HQS 9050-14-2, pt. 2, minutes of twelfth ISCP meeting, 28 June 1945.

125 Ibid., reel C-5330, f. HQS 9050-4, pt. 7, minutes of Sub-Committee A 52nd meeting, 3 July 1945.

126 Ibid., reel C-5337, f. HQS 9050-14-15, pt. 1, DEA to Canadian chargé d'affaires, Washington, 4 July 1945.

127 Ibid., reel C-5330, f. HQS 9050-4, pt. 7, minutes of Sub-Committee A 53rd meeting, 17 July 1945, and 55th meeting, 30 July 1945.

128 DEA Records, vol. 2782, f. 621-HV-40c, minutes of thirteenth ISCP meeting, 10 August 1945.

129 DND Records, reel C-5337, f. HQS 9050-15, pt. 7, Canadian Minister, Washington, to DEA, 15 August 1945.

130 CAB 88/39, Combined Chiefs of Staff memorandum #924 (21 September 1945), Commander-in-Chief, U.S. Army Forces, Pacific, to War Department, 5 September 1945.

131 WIB, *Facts and Figures Weekly* #132 (16-22 August 1945):2; External Affairs, *Annual Report 1945* (Ottawa 1946), 6.

132 Allister, *Where Life and Death Hold Hands*, 218; Soper interview; HCHM: f. HCM 5-86, Leonard J. Birchall, interview by C.G. Roland, Kingston, 22 February 1986.

133 Dancocks, *In Enemy Hands*, 272; Forsyth Papers, 'Gleanings from the Diary of a Winnipeg Grenadier,' entry for 25 August 1945.

134 Allister, *Where Life and Death Hold Hands*, 221; HCHM: f. HCM 25-85, Angus McRitchie, interview by C.G. Roland, Winnipeg, 9 March 1985.

135 *Legion*, March 1987, 39.

136 Quoted in Carl Vincent, *No Reason Why: The Canadian Hong Kong Tragedy – An Examination* (Stittsville, ON: Canada's Wings 1981), 214.

137 John E.A. Tayler, Edmonton, correspondence with author, 5 February 1992.

138 NAC: F.W. Ebdon Papers, MG30 E328, f. 8, Canadian Commander's message, undated; Richard S. Malone, *A World in Flames 1944-1945: A Portrait of War, Part Two* (Toronto: Collins 1984), 266-7.

Chapter 8: 'The Debris of Past Wars'

1 Capt. Kim Beattie, 'The Three Sergeants of Stalag 8B,' *Liberty*, 12 August 1944, 45.

2 National Archives of Canada (NAC): Department of National Defence (DND) Records, vol. 6659, f. CPC/4-1-11-6, Periodical Censorship Report #15, 15 March 1945, R.C. Large to friend, 6 November 1944.

3 NAC: Department of External Affairs (DEA) Records, vol. 2777, f. 621-DQ-40, pt. 1, minutes of American Red Cross meeting with British Red Cross, 16 September 1943; vol. 2781, f. 621-GE-40, précis of 'Report to the War Office on Psychological Aspects of the Rehabilitation of Repatriated Prisoners of War,' by Lt.-Col. A.T.M. Wilson, received in Ottawa 20 June 1944; Public Record Office (PRO): CAB 66/54, War Cabinet memorandum WP (44) #456, memo by Secretary of State for War, 22 August 1944.

4 DEA Records, vol. 2781, f. 621-GE-40, Scott to Associate Deputy-Minister of Pensions and National Health, 30 April 1943.

5 A.T.M. Wilson, Martin Doyle, and John Kelnar, 'Group Techniques in a Transitional Community,' *Lancet*, May 1947, 735.

6 NAC: Post Office Department (PO) Records, reel T-1688, vol. 2760, f. 35-26-1, memo 'Rehabilitation of POWs' by WCdr. H.G. Reid, 1 June 1943; DEA Records, vol. 2781, f. 621-GE-40, Scott to SAAG, 8 June 1943.

7 George F. Collie, 'Returned Prisoners: A Suggested Scheme for Rehabilitation,' *The Fortnightly* 153 (June 1943):407-8.

8 Maj. P.H. Newman, 'The Prisoner-of-War Mentality: Its Effects after Repatriation,' *British Medical Journal*, 1 January 1944, 8-10.

9 DEA Records, vol. 2781, f. 621-GE-40, 'Report on Psychological Aspects of the Rehabilitation of Repatriated POWs,' by Wilson.

10 '*Stalag* mentality' was a blanket term given to the various psychological after-effects of captivity that Newman described, the most significant of which (as far as rehabilitation planners were concerned) were skill in passive resistance to authority, fragile self-respect, lack of self-confidence, and various degrees of depression, hostility, and bitterness masked by a façade of cheerfulness.

11 DEA Records, series A6, vol. 435, f. Cas 9/12, Sampson to RCAF HQ, London, 7 January 1945.

12 Ibid., vol. 2782, f. 621-HV-40, minutes of special meeting, 6 March 1945.

13 DND Records, vol. 6659, f. CPC/4-1-11-6, Periodical Censorship Report #15, 15 March 1945, J.H. Bishop to wife, 19 November 1944.

14 NAC: Department of National War Services Records, vol. 2, f. Canadian Legion of the BESL Educational Services, pt. 2, Condensation of Two-Year Report, 1 April 1942 to 31 March 1944, 4.

15 DEA Records, series G1, vol. 1962, f. 842-AN-39, Canadian Red Cross Society Overseas Commissioner to Routley, 15 February 1943; Queen's University Archives: *Principal's Report, 1943-44*, 43; University of Saskatchewan Archives: President's Papers, series 2, vol. 30-31, f. B47, G.W. Simpson, Assistant Dean of Arts and Sciences, to Shirley Plank, Secretary of Correspondence Courses, 12 March 1943.

16 DEA Records, series A7, vol. 556, f. Cas 9/12/1, 'Arrival and Processing in the United Kingdom,' undated; Lt. D.B. Wilson, 'Report on the Repatriation of RCN Liberated POWs,' undated; Bill Mitchell, Guelph, ON, correspondence with author, 22 October 1988.

17 A copy of the pamphlet can be found in DEA Records, vol. 3585, f. 2364-40, pt. 14.

18 WIB, *Facts and Figures Weekly* #19 (18-25 May 1945):5.

19 Charles Badbury, 'How to Treat Returned Prisoners of War,' *Saturday Night* 60/36 (12 May 1945):6. A similar point was made by the British Directorate of Army Psychiatry, which cautioned against public welcomes that might cause ex-POWs to doubt the sincerity of the welcomers. Rather, relatives should greet returning prisoners at home, to fulfil what the Directorate called a POW's 'garden-gate phantasy.' DEA Records, vol. 2781, f. 621-GE-40, Directorate of Army Psychiatry Technical Memorandum #13, 'The Prisoner of War Comes Home' (May 1944), received in Ottawa 4 July 1944.

20 William Allister, *Where Life and Death Hold Hands* (Toronto: Stoddart 1989), 236.

21 Barry Broadfoot, *Six War Years 1939-1945: Memories of Canadians at Home and Abroad* (Toronto: Doubleday 1974), 375.

22 Carl Vincent, *No Reason Why: The Canadian Hong Kong Tragedy – An Examination* (Stittsville, ON: Canada's Wings 1981), 238-9; House of Commons, Minutes of Proceedings and Evidence of the Standing Committee on Veterans Affairs, issue #15, 10 April 1975, 45.

23 George Sweanor, *It's All Pensionable Time: 25 Years in the RCAF* (Port Hope, ON: Gesnor Publications 1981), 221; Dr. Wes Clare, interview by author, Kingsville, 7 December 1991.

24 Allister, *Where Life and Death Hold Hands*, 236.

25 Oral History Archives, Hannah Chair for the History of Medicine, McMaster University (HCHM): f. HCM 37-85, Harold Englehart, interview by C.G. Roland, Rosemount, Quebec, 10 April 1985.

26 Gren Juniper, interview by author, Hamilton, 6 April 1992; R.E. McLaren, interview by author, Hamilton, 18 January 1992; Gord King, Edmonton, correspondence with author, 22 May 1992.

27 H.K. Ward, Edmonton, correspondence with author, 30 November 1991; Daniel Dancocks, *In Enemy Hands: Canadian Prisoners of War, 1939-45* (Edmonton: Hurtig 1983), 279; University of Victoria Archives, Canadian Military History Project, Gerald H. Gibbens interview; Dave Stubbs, correspondence with author, Barrie, [October 1993]; Glenn Gardiner, interview by author, Mississauga, 24 April 1986.

28 HCHM: f. HCM 20-85, Stanley Darch, interview by C.G. Roland, Dundas, 27 February 1985; Argyll and Sutherland Highlanders of Canada Regimental Archives, Hamilton (ASHC): Melvin Junck, interview by W.H. Wiley, 16 August 1984.

29 DND Records, vol. 173, f. 650-92-93, Public Relations Officer, Military District #10, to Maj. P.V. Wade, [November 1945].

30 NAC: H.W. Herridge Papers, MG32 C13, vol. 73, f. 11, Dr. John Crawford, 'The Consequences of Captivity: Their Psychosomatic Aspect'; Manfred Jeffrey and E.J.G. Bradford, 'Neurosis in Escaped Prisoners of War,' *British Journal of Medical Psychology* 20/4 (1946):428; HCHM: f. HCM 4-85, William E. Connolly, interview by C.G. Roland, Burlington, 6 February 1985.

31 House of Commons, Debates, 13 September 1945, 134-5.

32 John Holmes, *The Shaping of Peace: Canada and the Search for World Order*, vol. 1 (Toronto: University of Toronto Press 1979), 133.

33 House of Commons, Debates, 12 April 1946, 809; Philip R. Piccigallo, *The Japanese on Trial: Allied War Crimes Operations in the East, 1945-1951* (Austin: University of Texas Press 1979), 140-1.

34 Patricia Roy, J.L. Granatstein, Masako Iino, and Hiroko Takamura, *Mutual Hostages: Canadians and Japanese during the Second World War* (Toronto: University of Toronto Press 1990), 73.

35 J.M.E. Duchosal, 'The Revision of the Geneva Conventions,' *Political Quarterly* 19/1 (January 1948):33; DEA Records, series G1, vol. 1961, f. 842-AC-39, pt. 2, circular letter, ICRC to National Red Cross Societies, 15 February 1945; vol. 3397, f. 619-B-40, pt. 1, ICRC to Mackenzie King, 25 July 1946; minute sheet, [March 1946].

36 Ibid., Pearson to St. Laurent, 14 February 1948; f. 619-B-40, pt. 3, memo to Cabinet, 4 August 1948.

37 Ibid., series A6, vol. 437, f. CC25/1, pt. 3, 'Report of Canadian Army Representative on the Proposed Amendments to the POWs Convention as discussed at Stockholm,' [September 1948].

38 Ibid., vol. 3397, f. 619-B-40, pt. 1, memo from Barber, 10 February 1947.

39 Ibid., series A6, vol. 437, f. CC25/1, pt. 3, DEA to High Commission, 4 January 1949; External Affairs, *Annual Report 1949* (Ottawa 1950), 103.

40 DEA Records, series A6, vol. 437, f. CC25/1, pt. 5, minutes of meeting, 18 March 1949.

41 NAC: Privy Council Office (PCO) Records, series B2, vol. 120, f. W-43, memo to Cabinet,

26 March 1949.

42 International Committee of the Red Cross, *The Geneva Conventions of August 12, 1949* (Geneva: ICRC 1987).

43 Senate, Debates, 26 May 1964, 555-6; *External Affairs* 17/7 (July 1965):308-9.

44 Maj. W.B. Armstrong, 'International Protection for the Victims of War, Part I,' *Canadian Army Journal* 3/7 (October 1949):12. The articles continued in the November and December 1949 and January and March 1950 issues.

45 Department of National Defence, Director General History (DG Hist): f. 81/279, *Unit Guide to the 1949 Geneva Conventions for the Protection of War Victims*, 1950; P.H. Gordon, *Fifty Years in the Canadian Red Cross* (n.d.), 2.

46 There is virtually nothing written on the experiences of Canadians captured in Korea, a gap that will be filled with the completion in 1994 of Bruce McIntyre's University of Waterloo MA thesis on the subject.

47 Albert D. Biderman, *March to Calumny: The Story of American POWs in the Korean War* (New York: Macmillan 1963), 111. Over 2700 of the 7140 American POWs in Korean died in captivity. Charles A. Stenger, 'American Ex-POWs – Their Numbers,' *Ex-POW Bulletin* (American Ex-Prisoner of War) 38/3 (March 1981):36.

48 Lt.-Col. Herbert F. Wood, *Strange Battleground: The Operations in Korea and their Effects on the Defence Policy of Canada* (Ottawa: Queen's Printer 1966), 250-1. George Griffiths of the Royal Canadian Regiment summed up the feelings of his captors, who apparently did not know whether he was American or Canadian. Griffiths was shown pictures of the American and Canadian flags; when he indicated the Red Ensign, the Chinese soldiers pulled out their bayonets and stabbed the Stars and Stripes. John Melady, *Korea: Canada's Forgotten War* (Toronto: Macmillan 1983), 134.

49 *Brantford Expositor*, 25 August 1953, 2; Melady, *Korea: Canada's Forgotten War*, 136-8.

50 *Vancouver Sun*, 22 August 1953, 2.

51 Jim King, 'Korea,' in Tony Strachan (ed.), *In the Clutch of Circumstance* (Victoria: Cappis Press 1985), 98; Melady, *Korea: Canada's Forgotten War*, 126.

52 *Dundas Star*, 19 August 1953, 1; *Brantford Expositor*, 22 August 1953, 1.

53 *Brantford Expositor*, 22 August 1953, 2.

54 PO Records, vol. 3424, f. 36-26-2, CRCS National Commissioner to Postmaster-General, 24 February 1951.

55 House of Commons, Debates, 27 March 1953, p. 3341. This information was received in December 1951, when North Korea provided a list of 4417 UN POWs, including one Canadian. William H. Vatcher, *Panmunjom: The Story of the Korean Military Armistice Negotiations* (New York: Frederick A. Praeger 1958), 126.

56 The most concise and penetrating examination is Callum A. MacDonald, '"Heroes Behind Barbed Wire": The US, Britain and the POW Issue in the Korean War,' in James Cotton and Ian Neary, eds., *The Korean War in History* (Manchester: Manchester University Press 1989): 135-50.

57 Rosemary Foot, *A Substitute for Victory: The Politics of Peacemaking at the Korean Armistice Talks* (Ithaca: Cornell University Press 1990), 121; Callum A. MacDonald, *Korea: The War Before Vietnam* (London: Macmillan 1986), 146.

58 NAC: Lester B. Pearson Papers, MG26 N8, vol. 1, f. 6, notes on Korean discussions, 4 November 1952.

59 DEA Records, accession 86-87/160, box 18, f. 619-J-40, Chairman of Canadian delegation to DEA, 1 April 1953.

60 DG Hist: f. 112.009 (D98), Canadian Military Mission, Tokyo, to Chief of the General Staff, 6 April 1953.

61 *Telegram* (Toronto), 20 April 1953, 1.

62 PO Records, vol. 3424, f. 36-26-1, Deputy Minister of National Defence – Army to Deputy Postmaster-General, 9 May 1953.

63 DG Hist: f. 112.009 (D98), Canadian Military Mission, Tokyo, to Chief of the General Staff, 21 April 1953; f. 410 B25.011 (D3), taped interview with Private A. Baker.

64 PO Records, vol. 3424, f. 36-26-1, High Commission to DEA, 27 March 1951.

65 *Hamilton Spectator*, 21 April 1953, 1.

66 *Telegram*, 21 April 1953, 6.

67 *Hamilton Spectator*, 22 April 1953, 6.

68 DEA Records, accession 86-87/160, box 18, f. 619-J-40, Canadian Ambassador, Washington, to DEA, 5 May 1953.

69 *Brantford Expositor*, 25 August 1953, 2; Joyce Surman, 'Brighton – Korea War Vet Reminisces,' *POW Journal*, Summer 1988, 20.

70 DG Hist: f. 410 B25.059 (D1), Instructions to #25 Canadian Public Relations Unit, 24 July 1953.

71 *Brantford Expositor*, 25 August 1953, 1; Wood, *Strange Battleground*, 250.

72 DEA Records, accession 86-87/160, box 18, f. 619-J-40, memo from Commonwealth Relations Office, 18 May 1953. The official history of the Royal Canadian Regiment admits that a greater effort was made to convert American POWs but still avers that they withstood pressure poorly compared to other UNC POWs. G.R. Stevens, *The Royal Canadian Regiment*, vol. 2, *1933-1966* (London: London Printing & Lithographing 1967), 279.

73 Hamilton Public Library Special Collections: *Hamilton News* scrapbook, vol. M2, clipping dated 10 August 1953.

74 *Legion*, August 1983, 46; Melady, *Korea: Canada's Forgotten War*, 131.

75 Wood, *Strange Battleground*, 249.

76 PCO Records, series B2, vol. 120, f. W-38, 'Report of the Reparations Claims Sub-committee of the Inter-Departmental Committee on Reparations,' [December 1947]; DND Records, reel C-8425, f. HQS 9050-54-4, Director of Administration to Deputy Adjutant-General, 11 March 1950.

77 Ibid., J.P. Charette to Claxton, 10 February 1950.

78 Ibid., memo from Macklin, 13 March 1950.

79 House of Commons, Debates, 8 April 1952, p. 1300; *War Claims – Report of the Advisory Commission, 25 February 1952* (Ottawa: Queen's Printer 1954), 50-2.

80 P.C. 4267, 9 October 1952; House of Commons, Debates, 16 December 1952, p. 742.

81 Herridge Papers, vol. 73, f. 25-2, HKVA brief, [1958].

82 DEA Records, accession 86-87/160, box 128, f. 10894-40, pt. 2, Deputy Minister of Veterans Affairs to DEA, 7 July 1958. Australia and New Zealand, however, were rather less generous. By 1957, New Zealand had paid each Far East POW £75, plus £5 for working on the Thai railway, while Australia made a lump sum grant of £86 to prisoners of the Japanese, who also had access to a large trust fund for exceptional need. Ibid., New Zealand Department of External Affairs to DEA, 8 August 1958; Australian Department of External Affairs to DEA, 20 October 1958.

83 Herridge Papers, vol. 73, f. 25-2, Secretary of State to HKVA, 3 November 1958, and reply, 12 November 1958.

84 Ibid., Secretary of State to HKVA, 1 December 1958.

85 Veterans Affairs, *Annual Report*, 1971-72, 18; ibid., 1989-90, 24.

86 Herridge Papers, vol. 73, f. 25-2, HKVA brief, 3 December 1963.

87 Ibid., H.J. Richardson, 'Report of the Study of Disabilities and Problems of Hong Kong Veterans, 1964-65.'

88 Ibid., f. 25-1, Submission to the Parliamentary Standing Committee on Veterans Affairs by the HKVA, 17 May 1966.

89 Veterans Affairs, *Report of the Committee to Survey the Work and Organization of the Canadian Pension Commission*, 2:782, 791.

90 Veterans Affairs, *Pensions for Disability and Death Related to Military Service*, August 1969; Vincent, *No Reason Why*, 245-6.

91 DG Hist: f. 72/604, *Report of the Chief War Claims Commissioner*, October 1953.

92 R.S. Dutka, Edmonton, correspondence with author, [January 1992]; J. Keith Pettigrew, Edmonton, correspondence with author, [January 1992].

93 NAC: Douglas M. Smith Papers, MG30 E361, Cliff Chadderton, 'Capital Report,' [1972].

94 J.D. Hermann, *Report to the Minister of Veterans Affairs of a Study on Canadians Who Were Prisoners of War in Europe During World War II* (Ottawa: Queen's Printer 1973), 12.

95 House of Commons, Minutes of Proceedings and Evidence of the Standing Committee on Veterans Affairs, issue #15, 10 April 1975, 5.

96 Ibid., issue #16, 15 April 1975, 14. The NPOWA was quite right. Since 1945, many studies of the residual effects of captivity had been published in medical and psychiatric journals around the world, including over a dozen in Canadian journals.

97 Veterans Affairs, *Annual Report*, 1976-77, 31; ibid., 1977-78, 9.

98 Veterans Affairs, *Annual Report* 1985-86, 13. At least one ex-POW is bitter about the way pensions are assessed. W. Smelser noted that, although Dieppe prisoners were held for longer, their living conditions were not rigorous for much of that period. In contrast, Smelser, who was captured in northwest Europe in 1944, never received a proper issue of clothing, blankets, or rations during his imprisonment. Despite this fact, his pension is considerably lower than that given to an ex-Dieppe POW. ASHC: W. Smelser, interview by W.H. Wiley.

99 J.L. Templeton Papers, in possession of Gladys Templeton, St. John's: Canadian Pension Commission to J. Templeton, 8 June 1987.

100 DEA Records, series A6, vol. 435, f. Cas 9/12, DEA to High Commission, 6 February 1945.

101 DG Hist: f. 80/129, Canadian Armed Forces Manual of Training *Conduct after Capture*, 1960. Three manuals are presently in use: CFP 122 *Manual on the Geneva Conventions of August 12, 1949* (31 August 1973); CFP 318(4) *Unit Guide to the Geneva Conventions* (15 June 1973); and CFP 318(5) *Conduct after Capture* (30 June 1978).

102 Department of National Defence, *Queen's Regulations and Orders* (1968), article 103.09.

103 Brig.-Gen. J.P. Wolfe, 'Changes in the Law of Armed Conflict,' *Canadian Defence Quarterly* 8/3 (Winter 1978-79):16-21, 48.

104 DG Hist: f. 80/616, Maj. Barry A. Read, 'Conduct After Capture: A Canadian Code,' Canadian Forces Command and Staff College, 18 April 1980, 3, 26, 29. Other papers presented at the college have been titled 'A Guiltless Prisoner of War: Does He Exist?' and 'POWs: A Weapon of the Propaganda War.'

105 *Bulletin* (CRCS Ontario Division), April 1991, 3.

106 John M.G. Brown and Thomas G. Ashworth, 'A Secret That Shames Humanity,' *U.S. Veteran News and Report*, 29 May 1989, 2-12.

107 HPL: *Hamilton News* scrapbook, vol. M2, clippings dated 7 March 1952, 13 April 1953, and 26 August 1953; *Spectator*, 20 June 1992.

108 *Spectator*, 28 March 1990, 5.

109 I am grateful to Mr. Chadderton for providing me with copies of the February 1991 submission and three letters to Prime Minister Mulroney outlining the background to the case.

110 *Spectator*, 29 May 1991, 1.

Conclusion

1 See, for example, G. Irene Todd, 'Shop Early for Them,' *Saturday Night* 57/3 (27 September 1941):27; John Mellor, *Dieppe: Canada's Forgotten Heroes* (Scarborough: Signet 1979); Desmond Morton, *Silent Battle: Canadian Prisoners of War in Germany, 1914-1919* (Toronto: Lester Publishing 1992), ix.

2 H.E. Woolley, *No Time Off for Good Behaviour* (Burnstown, ON: General Store Publishing House 1990), 45; Elspeth Huxley, 'War Prisoners Learn to Cook,' *Saturday Night* 57/34 (2 May 1942):23.

3 National Archives of Canada: Department of External Affairs (DEA) Records, series A6, vol. 428, f. Cas 1/4, pt. 5, Scott to Feaver, 6 June 1944.

4 For another comment on this, see John Hilliker, *Canada's Department of External Affairs*, vol. 1, *The Early Years, 1909-1946* (Kingston: McGill-Queen's University Press 1990), 245.

5 DEA Records, vol. 2907, f. 2364-D-40, Ferns to Feaver, 21 June 1944; series A6, vol. 435, f. Cas 9/12, 'Summary of Questionnaire on February 1945 Exchange,' 14 March 1945, 25.

6 Figures provided by Departmental Statistical Unit, Veterans Affairs Canada, 19 February 1993. The *Hamilton Spectator* of 16 March 1993 carried a notice of the death at age 100 of Thomas Gill, a member of the Canadian Mounted Rifles captured at Sanctuary Wood in 1916.

BIBLIOGRAPHY

Primary Sources

Argyll & Sutherland Highlanders of Canada Regimental Archives, Hamilton
Interviews
    Roy B. Clute
    Clifford Foulds
    Melvin Junck
    Donald G. Seldon
    W. Smelser
    George Soper
    Truman Wilcox

Department of National Defence – Director General History
Biographical files
    Department of National Defence
      Records
    Pamphlet collection

Hamilton Public Library Special Collections
    Canadian Red Cross – POWs file
    Canadian Red Cross – scrapbook
    Hamilton News – scrapbook
    Martin Family Papers

House of Lords Record Office, London, UK
    Beaverbrook Papers

Imperial War Museum, London, UK
    Sir Richard Ewart Papers

McMaster University
Mills Library Microform Collection
    Akten der Partei-Kanzlei der NSDAP

Allied Translator and Interpreter
    Section Papers
Joint Chiefs of Staff Records
Magic Documents
Records of the War Department
    General Staff
Oral History Archives, Hannah Chair
for the History of Medicine
(interviews)
    Robert D. Adams
    Donat Bernier
    Leonard J. Birchall
    Howard Bradley
    John A. Chapel
    Alfred J. Cleeton
    William E. Connolly
    Stanley Darch
    Harold W. Englehart
    Charles M. Fisher
    Dr Allen F. Graham
    Howard Large
    Angus McRitchie
    Charles T. Robertson
    Roy A. Westaway
William Ready Division of Archives
and Research Collections
    P.T. Caiger Papers
    World War I Collection

National Archives of Canada
Government Archives Division
    Department of External Affairs Records
    Office of the Governor General Records
    Department of Militia and Defence
      Records
    Department of National Defence
      Records
    Department of National War Services
      Records
    Post Office Department Records
    Privy Council Office Records
    Secretary of State Records
    Department of Veterans Affairs Records
Manuscript Division
    Henri Béland Papers
    R.B. Bennett Papers
    Robert Laird Borden Papers
    William Brooke Family Papers
    Loring Christie Papers
    J.N. Crawford Papers
    H.D.G. Crerar Papers
    F.W. Ebdon Papers
    Tom Forsyth Papers
    John Barton Heron Papers
    H.W. Herridge Papers
    A.E. Hilder Papers
    H.H. Howland Papers
    Sir Edward Kemp Papers
    W.L.M. King Papers
    A.H. Macdonell Papers
    G.L. Magann Papers
    Robert Manion Papers
    F.D.F. Martyn Papers
    Arthur Meighen Papers
    George Albert Mercer Papers
    Montreal Soldiers' Wives' League
      Papers
    Stephen O'Brien Papers
    G.L. Ogilvie Papers
    Lester B. Pearson Papers
    Joseph Pope Papers
    Salamon Pritchard Papers
    William Quinton Papers
    J.L. Ralston Papers
    J. Frederick Ramsay Papers

    Douglas M. Smith Papers
    Russell M. Smith Papers
    G.P. Vanier Papers
    YMCA Papers

Public Record Office, Kew, England
    Air Ministry Records
    Cabinet Office Records
    Dominions Office Records
    Foreign Office Records
    War Office Records

Private Collections
    R.A. Bethell Diary, Alton, ON
    Dr. D.W. Clare Diary, Kingsville, ON
    Arthur Donovan Corker Diary,
      Richmond, BC
    Ambrose Farnum Diary,
      Bournemouth, UK
    Harry Foster Diary, in possession of
      Tony Foster, Halifax
    J.F. Garswood Diary, Windsor
    Fred Gies Manuscript, in possession of
      Bert Konig, Hamilton
    W.S. King Papers, in possession of S.
      Gordon King, Edmonton
    Pat Langford Papers, in possession of
      Dennis Langford, Calgary
    Roy Loomer Diary, Halifax
    M.A. MacAulay Papers, Seattle
    George McGill Papers, in possession of
      Betty Gillies, Mississauga
    G.D. McLeod Papers, in possession of
      Libby McNally, Waterdown, ON
    T. Stewart Ripley Diary, Toronto
    James Templeton Papers, in posses-
      sion of Gladys Templeton, St. John's
    A.B. Thompson Papers, in possession
      of Nora Thompson, Penetanguishene,
      ON
    Roy Turner Diary, Bushey Heath,
      Hertfordshire, UK
    H.K. Ward Papers, Edmonton

Queen's University Archives
    Principal's Reports

University of Saskatchewan Archives
    President's Papers

University of Toronto Archives
  Department of Graduate Records

University of Victoria Archives, Canadian Military History Project (taped interviews)
  Gerald H. Gibbens
  Clarence F. Henigman
  W.A. Wilson

Windsor Municipal Archives
  B.J.S. Macdonald Papers

Correspondence
  Bill Cameron, Ottawa
  J. Laurie Cormier, Dieppe, NB
  Cliff Chadderton, Ottawa
  William H. Cram, Indian Head, SK
  Arthur Crighton, Edmonton
  R.S. Dutka, Edmonton
  S. Gordon King, Edmonton
  Fred LeReverend, Victoria
  M.A. MacAulay, Seattle
  Bill Mitchell, Guelph, ON
  Col. John Page, Waterdown, ON
  J. Keith Pettigrew, Edmonton
  Capt. David Ratz, Thunder Bay
  W.A. Sandhals, Terrace, BC

  Dave Stubbs, Barrie, ON
  John E.A. Tayler, Edmonton
  J. Earl Taylor, Victoria
  Tom Thomson, Medicine Hat, AB
  J.W. Veness, Fredericton
  H.K. Ward, Edmonton

Interviews
  Dr. D.W. Clare, Kingsville, ON
  Don Corker, Campbellville, ON
  Glenn Gardiner, Mississauga
  J.F. Garswood, Windsor
  L.R. Gruggen, Hamilton
  Percy Hampton, Toronto
  Gren Juniper, Hamilton
  Sir Edwin Leather, Hamilton
  C.H. Maxwell, Hamilton
  Ian F. MacDonald, Windsor
  R.E. McLaren, Hamilton
  Dorothy McLaren, Hamilton
  C.D. Noble, Collingwood, ON
  Col. John Page, Waterdown, ON
  George Williams, Milton, ON
  Don Wilson, Waterdown, ON
  F.J.L. Woodcock, Grimsby, ON

Printed and Secondary Sources

Adami, Lt.-Col. J. George. *War Story of the Canadian Army Medical Corps*, vol. 1. Toronto: n.d.

Aitken, Max. *Canada in Flanders: The Official Story of the Canadian Expeditionary Force*, vol. 1. Toronto: Hodder & Stoughton 1916

Alberta Tribune (Calgary)

Allan, Iris. 'A Riel Rebellion Diary,' *Alberta Historical Review* 12/3 (Summer 1964):15-25

Allison, Les. *Canadians in the Royal Air Force*. Roland, MB: L. Allison 1978

—, and Hayward, Harry. *They Shall Grow Not Old: A Book of Remembrance*. Brandon, MB: Commonwealth Air Training Plan Museum n.d.

Allister, William. *Where Life and Death Hold Hands*. Toronto: Stoddart 1989

Armstrong, Maj. W.B. 'International Protection for the Victims of War, Part 1.' *Canadian Army Journal* 3/7 (October 1949):12-16

B.I.M. (British Interned Mürren)

Bates, Maxwell. *A Wilderness of Days: An Artist's Experiences as a Prisoner of War in Germany*. Victoria: Sono Nis Press 1978

Beattie, Capt. Kim. 'The Three Sergeants of Stalag 8B,' *Liberty*, 12 August 1944, 8-9, 45

Beaumont, Joan. 'Rank, Privilege and Prisoners of War.' *War & Society* 1/1 (May 1983):67-94

Best, Geoffrey. *Humanity in Warfare*. New York: Columbia University Press 1980

Biderman, Albert D. *March to Calumny: The Story of American POWs in the Korean War*. New York: Macmillan 1963

Bischof, Günter, and Ambrose, Stephen E., eds. *Eisenhower and the German POWs: Facts Against Falsehood*. Baton Rouge: Louisiana State University Press 1992

Bishop, Charles W. *The Canadian Y.M.C.A. in the Great War: The Official Record of the Activities of the Canadian Y.M.C.A. in Connection with the Great War of 1914-1918*. The National Council of YMCAs of Canada 1924

Bosanquet, David. *Escape Through China*. Toronto: McClelland & Stewart 1985

Bourinot, Arthur S. *Poems*. Toronto: T.H. Best 1921

British Prisoner of War (London)

Broadfoot, Barry. *Six War Years 1939-1945: Memories of Canadians at Home and Abroad*. Toronto: Doubleday 1974

Brown, John M.G., and Ashworth, Thomas. 'A Secret that Shames Humanity,' *U.S. Veteran News and Report*, 29 May 1989, 2-12

Brown, Kingsley. *Bonds of Wire: A Memoir*. Toronto: Collins 1989

Bulletin (Canadian Red Cross, Ontario Division)

Burdick, Charles, and Moessner, Ursula. *The German Prisoners-of-War in Japan, 1914-1920*. Lanham, MD: University Press of America 1984

Busy Man's Magazine (Toronto)

Buxton, John. 'Below the Tide of War,' *Atlantic Monthly* 177/6 (June 1946):41-8

Cambon, Kenneth. *Guest of Hirohito*. Vancouver: PW Press 1990

Camp (Ex-RCAF POW Association)

Canada and the Great World War, 6 vols. Toronto: United Publishers of Canada 1921

Canadian Magazine (Toronto)

[Canadian Red Cross Society]. *Report by the Canadian Red Cross Society of its Operations in the South African War, 1899 to 1902*. Toronto: Canadian Central Council 1903

Carr, Iona K. *A Story of the Canadian Red Cross Information Bureau during the Great War*. 1920

Carter, David J. *Behind Canadian Barbed Wire: Alien, Refugee and Prisoner of War Camps in Canada, 1914-1946*. Calgary: Tumbleweed Press 1980

Casselman, A.C. *Richardson's War of 1812*. Toronto: Historical Publishing 1902

Christian Century (Chicago)

Christie, Kathleen G. 'M. & V. for Christmas Dinner,' *Canadian Nurse*, December 1967, 28-30

Churchill, Winston. *London to Ladysmith via Pretoria*. Toronto: Copp Clark 1900

Clark, Russell S. *An End to Tears*. Sydney: Peter Huston 1946

Clay, Charles. 'Parcels for Prisoners: How the International Red Cross is Doing an Important Job,' *Country Guide and Nor-West Farmer* 60 (September 1941):51

—. 'Jack is a Prisoner of War,' *National Home Monthly* 42/10 (October 1941):17, 49-50

Clink, William L., ed. *Battleford Beleaguered*. Willowdale: William L. Clink 1984

Cochrane, A.L. 'Notes on the Psychology of Prisoners of War,' *British Medical Journal*, 23 February 1946, 282-4

Collie, George F. 'Returned Prisoners: A Suggested Scheme for Rehabilitation,' *The Fortnightly* 153 (June 1943):407-11

Crawley, Aidan. *Escape from Germany*. London: HMSO 1985

Crighton, Art. 'The Organ Loft,' *The Anglican Messenger*, December 1991, 9

Cruickshank, E.W.H. 'Impressions of Nazi Germany,' *Dalhousie Review* 13 (1933):403-16

Dancocks, Daniel. *In Enemy Hands: Canadian Prisoners of War, 1939-45.* Edmonton: Hurtig 1983

Davis, Calvin DeArmond. *The United States and the Second Hague Peace Conference.* Durham, NC: Duke University Press 1975

Douglas, Lt. J. Harvey. *Captured: Sixteen Months as a Prisoner of War.* Toronto: McClelland, Goodchild & Stewart 1918

Duchosal, J.M.E. 'The Revision of the Geneva Convention,' *Political Quarterly* 19/1 (January 1948):32-40

Dundas Star (Dundas, ON)

Durand, André. *From Sarajevo to Hiroshima: History of the International Committee of the Red Cross.* Geneva: Henry Dunant Institute 1978

Duthie, William Smith, ed. *Letters from the Front: Being a Record of the Part Played by Officers of the Bank in the Great War, 1914-1919*, 2 vols. Canadian Imperial Bank of Commerce 1920

Edmonds, Sir James. *The Occupation of the Rhineland, 1918-1929.* London: HMSO 1941

Edmonton Bulletin

Elliot, Maj. S.R. *Scarlet to Green.* Toronto: Canadian Intelligence and Security Association 1989

Ellis, William Hodgson. 'The Adventures of a Prisoner of War,' *Canadian Magazine* 13/3 (July 1899):199-203

Evans, A.J. *Escape and Liberation, 1940-1945.* London: Hodder & Stoughton 1945

Evans, Jack. 'Sixteen Months a War Prisoner,' in *World's War Events*, vol. 2, ed. Francis J. Reynolds, 142-58. New York: P.F. Collier & Son 1921

Expositor (Brantford, ON)

External Affairs (Ottawa)

External Affairs. *Annual Report.* Ottawa 1941, 1945, 1949

—. *International Convention Relative to the Treatment of Prisoners of War, Geneva, July 27, 1929.* Ottawa: King's Printer 1931

Field, A.F. 'Wounded and Captured,' *University Magazine* 18/2 (April 1919):260-9

Foot, M.R.D., and Langley, J.M. *M.I.9: Escape and Evasion, 1939-1945.* London: Futura Publications 1980

Foot, Rosemary. *A Substitute for Victory: The Politics of Peacemaking at the Korean Armistice Talks.* Ithaca, NY: Cornell University Press 1990

Foster, Tony. *Meeting of Generals.* Toronto: Methuen 1986

Free Press (London, ON)

Frei, Alfred G. '"In the End I Just Said O.K.": Political and Moral Dimensions of Escape Aid at the Swiss Border,' *Journal of Modern History* 64/Suppl (December 1992):S68-S84

Garner, James Wilford. *International Law and the World War*, vol. 2. London: Longmans, Green 1920

Gazette (Montreal)

Gerard, James W. *My Four Years in Germany.* New York: George H. Doran 1917

Gibbons, Sgt. Arthur. *A Guest of the Kaiser: The Plain Story of a Lucky Soldier.* Toronto: J.M. Dent & Sons 1919

Globe (Toronto)

Globe & Mail (Toronto)

Gooch, G.P., and Temperley, Harold, eds. *British Documents on the Origins of the War*, vol. 1. London: HMSO 1927

Goodspeed, Maj. D.J. *Battle Royal*. Toronto: Royal Regiment of Canada 1962

Gordon, P.H. *Fifty Years in the Canadian Red Cross*. [1969?]

Granatstein, J.L. *A Man of Influence: Norman A. Robertson and Canadian Statecraft, 1929-1968*. Toronto: Deneau 1981

—. *The Ottawa Men: The Civil Service Mandarins, 1935-57*. Toronto: Oxford University Press 1982

Grant, Capt. Maurice Harold. *History of the War in South Africa*, vol. 4. London: Hurst & Blackett 1910

Grogan, John Patrick. *Dieppe and Beyond for a Dollar and a Half a Day*. Renfrew, ON: Juniper Books 1982

Gruenzner, Norman. *Postal History of American POWs: World War II, Korea, Vietnam*. State College, PA: American Philatelic Society 1979

Halifax Herald

Hart-McHarg, W. *From Quebec to Pretoria with the Royal Canadian Regiment*. Toronto: William Briggs 1902

Heaps, Leo. *The Grey Goose of Arnhem*. Markham: PaperJacks 1977

Hermann, J.D. *Report to the Minister of Veterans Affairs of a Study on Canadians Who Were Prisoners of War in Europe during World War II*. Ottawa: Queen's Printer 1973

Hezzelwood, Oliver, ed. *Trinity War Book: A Recital of Service and Sacrifice in the Great War*. Toronto: Ontario Press 1921

Hilliker, John. *Canada's Department of External Affairs*, vol. 1, *The Early Years, 1909-1946*. Kingston: McGill-Queen's University Press 1990

Hoffman, Conrad. *In the Prison Camps of Germany: A Narrative of 'Y' Service among Prisoners of War*. New York: Association Press 1920

Holmes, John W. *The Shaping of Peace: Canada and the Search for World Order, 1943-1957*, vol. 1. Toronto: University of Toronto Press 1979

Hopkins, J. Castell. *The Canadian Annual Review*. Toronto: Canadian Annual Review Publishing 1917

Hough, Richard. *First Sea Lord: An Authorized Biography of Admiral Lord Fisher*. London: George Allen & Unwin 1969

House of Commons. Debates

—. Special Committee on Pensions and Returned Soldiers' Problems, Minutes and Proceedings

—. Standing Committee on Veterans Affairs, Minutes of Proceedings and Evidence

Hull, William I. *The Two Hague Conferences and Their Contribution to International Law*. Boston: Ginn 1908

Hunt, M. Stuart. *Nova Scotia's Part in the Great War*. Halifax: Nova Scotia Veteran Publishing 1920

[Hurd, Lionel, ed.] *The Royal Rifles of Canada in Hong Kong, 1941-1945*. Sherbrooke: Hong Kong Veterans' Association Quebec-Maritimes Branch 1980

International Committee of the Red Cross. *Report of the International Committee of the Red Cross on Its Activities During the Second World War (September 1, 1939 – June 30, 1947)*, 2 vols. Geneva: International Committee of the Red Cross 1948

—. *The Geneva Conventions of August 12, 1949*. Geneva: International Committee of the Red Cross 1987

International Military Tribunal. *Trial of the Major War Criminals.* International Military Tribunal: Nuremberg 1947

Israel, Fred L., ed. *The War Diary of Breckinridge Long.* Lincoln: University of Nebraska Press 1966

Jackson, Robert. *The Prisoners, 1914-18.* London: Routledge 1989

Jeffrey, Manfred, and Bradford, E.J.G. 'Neurosis in Escaped Prisoners of War,' *British Journal of Medical Psychology* 20/4 (1946):422-35

Jones, P., Bradley-Watson, J., and Bradbury, E.J. 'Health of Prisoners-of-War Evacuated from Hong Kong,' *Lancet,* 17 November 1945, 645-7

Ketchum, J.D. *Ruhleben: A Prison Camp Society.* Toronto: University of Toronto Press 1965

Laird, Donald Harry. *Prisoner Five-One-Eleven.* Toronto: Ontario Press n.d.

Laqueur, Walter, ed. *The Guerrilla Reader.* Scarborough: New American Library 1977

Lee, J. Fitzgerald. 'Prisoners of War,' *Army Quarterly* 3/2 (January 1922):348-56

Legion (Ottawa)

Le Soeuf, Leslie. *To War Without a Gun.* Western Australia: Artlook 1980

Levie, Howard S., ed. *Documents on Prisoners of War.* Newport: Naval War College Press 1979

Life (New York)

Lindsay, Oliver. *At the Going Down of the Sun: Hong Kong and South-East Asia, 1941-1945.* London: Hamish Hamilton 1981

Livingston, F.J. *My Escape from the Boers.* Toronto: William Briggs 1902

MacDonald, Callum A. *Korea: The War Before Vietnam.* London: Macmillan 1986

—. '"Heroes Behind Barbed Wire": The US, Britain and the POW Issue in the Korean War,' in *The Korean War in History,* ed. James Cotton and Ian Neary, 135-50. Manchester: Manchester University Press, 1989

MacDonald, Frank C. *The Kaiser's Guest.* New York: Country Life Press 1918

Macleod, R.C., ed. *'Reminiscences of a Bungle by One of the Bunglers' and Two Other North-West Rebellion Diaries.* Edmonton: University of Alberta Press 1983

Mail and Empire (Toronto)

Malone, Richard S. *A World in Flames 1944-1945: A Portrait of War, Part Two.* Toronto: Collins 1984

Marshall, P.R. 'Two Near VCs of the South African War,' *Organization of Military Museums of Canada Bulletin* 3 (1974):39-50

Marwick, Arthur. *The Deluge: British Society and the First World War.* London: The Bodley Head 1965

Mason, W. Wynne. *Prisoners of War.* Wellington, New Zealand: Department of Internal Affairs War History Branch 1954

Mathieson, William D. *My Grandfather's War: Canadians Remember the First World War, 1914-1918.* Toronto: Macmillan 1981

McCarthy, Daniel J. *The Prisoner of War in Germany: The Care and Treatment of the Prisoner of War with a History of the Development of the Principle of Neutral Inspection and Control.* New York: Moffat, Yard 1918

McClung, Nellie. *Three Times and Out, Told by Private Simmons.* Toronto: Thomas Allen 1918

McIntosh, Dave, ed. *High Blue Battle: The War Diary of No. 1 (401) Fighter Squadron, RCAF.* Toronto: Stoddart 1990

McMullen, Fred, and Evans, Jack. *Out of the Jaws of Hunland.* Toronto: William Briggs 1918

Melady, John. *Escape from Canada!: The Untold Story of German POWs in Canada, 1939-*

1945. Toronto: Macmillan 1981

—. *Korea: Canada's Forgotten War*. Toronto: Macmillan 1983

Mellor, John. *Dieppe: Canada's Forgotten Heroes*. Scarborough: Signet 1979

Melnyk, T.W. *Canadian Flying Operations in South-East Asia, 1941-1945*. Ottawa: Department of National Defence 1976

Merrick, D.A.Y. 'From Parachute to Prison,' *Canadian Banker* 53 (1946):210-12

Merry, D. Bilson. 'My Escape from a German Prison: A Thrilling Experience,' *The Gold Stripe* (Vancouver) 1 (1918):85-7

Michell, Steve. *They Were Invincible: Dieppe and After*. Bracebridge, ON: Herald-Gazette Press 1976

Militia and Defence. *Supplementary Report: Organization, Equipment, Despatch and Service of the Canadian Contingents During the War in South Africa, 1899-1900*. Sessional paper #35a, Ottawa 1901

Miller, Carman. *Painting the Map Red: Canada and the South African War, 1899-1902*. Montreal: Canadian War Museum and McGill-Queen's University Press 1993

Mingo, Lt.-Col. E.W. 'Prisoners of War 1914-1918,' *Journal of the United Services Institute of Nova Scotia* 6 (1933):35-53

Moore, Mary MacLeod. *The Maple Leaf's Red Cross: The War Story of the Canadian Red Cross Overseas*. London: Skeffington & Son [1919?]

Morgan, J.H. *The German War Book: Being 'The Usages of War on Land' Issued by the Great General Staff of the German Army*. London: John Murray 1915

Morrison, E.W.B. *With the Guns in South Africa*. Hamilton: Spectator Printing 1901

Morton, Desmond. *Silent Battle: Canadian Prisoners of War in Germany, 1914-1919*. Toronto: Lester Publishing 1992

Morton, Desmond, and Roy, Reginald H., eds. *Telegrams of the North-West Campaign, 1885*. Toronto: The Champlain Society 1972

—. *When Your Number's Up: The Canadian Soldier in the First World War*. Toronto: Random House 1993

Mosse, George L. *Fallen Soldiers: Reshaping the Memory of the World Wars*. Oxford: Oxford University Press 1990

Mowat, Farley. *And No Birds Sang*. Toronto: McClelland & Stewart 1979

Mowat, R.B. *The Life of Lord Pauncefote*. London: Constable 1929

Mulvaney, Charles Pelham. *The History of the North-West Rebellion of 1885*. Toronto: A.H. Hovey 1885

Nadeau, Eugène. *La perle au fond du gouffre: Zam-Zam et barbelés*. Montréal: Fides 1963

National Defence. *Canadian Prisoners of War and Missing Personnel in the Far East*. Ottawa: King's Printer 1945

—. *Extracts from the Manual of Military Law 1929, Reprinted for Use in the Canadian Army*. Ottawa: King's Printer 1941

—. *King's Regulations and Orders for the Canadian Army, 1939*

—. *Queen's Regulations and Orders, 1968*

National War Services. *Annual Report of the Department of National War Services for the Fiscal Year Ending 31 March 1944*. Ottawa: King's Printer 1945

Newman, Maj. P.H. 'The Prisoner-of-War Mentality: Its Effects after Repatriation,' *British Medical Journal*, 1 January 1944, 8-10

Nicol, Eric, ed. *Dickens of the Mounted: The Astounding Long-lost Letters of Inspector F. Dickens, NWMP, 1874-1886*. Toronto: Douglas Gibson 1989

Nowlan, Alden. *The Mysterious Naked Man*. Toronto: Clarke, Irwin 1969

O'Brien, Jack. *Into the Jaws of Death*. Toronto: McClelland & Stewart 1919

Ontario. Journals of the Legislative Assembly

Overseas Military Forces of Canada. *Report of the Ministry, Overseas Military Forces of Canada, 1918*. London: 1918

P.O.W. Journal (National POW Association)

Page, Don. 'Tommy Stone and Psychological Warfare in World War II: Transforming a POW Liability into an Asset,' *Journal of Canadian Studies* 16/3&4 (Fall-Winter 1981):110-20

Pearson, George. *The Escape of a Princess Pat*. New York: George H. Doran 1918

Pearson, Lester B. *Mike: The Memoirs of the Right Honourable Lester B. Pearson*, vol. 1. Toronto: University of Toronto Press 1971

Pennefather, John P. *Thirteen Years on the Prairies: From Winnipeg to Cold Lake, Fifteen Hundred Miles*. London: Kegan Paul, Trench, Trubner 1892

Pether, C.G. 'The Returned Prisoner-of-War,' *Lancet*, 5 May 1945, 571-2

Phillimore, George G. 'Some Suggestions for a Draft Code for the Treatment of Prisoners of War,' *Transactions of the Grotius Society* 6 (1920):25-34

Piccigallo, Philip R. *The Japanese on Trial: Allied War Crimes Operations in the East, 1945-1951*. Austin: University of Texas Press 1979

Picot, Colonel H.A. *The British Interned in Switzerland*. London: Edward Arnold 1919

Pope, Harry. 'Souvenirs de Guerre,' *La Citadelle* 22/1 (February 1986):24-5

Porter, McKenzie. *To All Men: The Story of the Canadian Red Cross*. Toronto: McClelland & Stewart 1960

Priebe, Eckehart J. *Thank You, Canada: From Messerschmitt Pilot to Canadian Citizen*. West Vancouver: Condor Publishing 1990

Pritchard, R.J., and Zaide, Sonia, eds. *The Tokyo War Crimes Trials*, vol. 6. New York: Garland Publishing 1981

Prouse, A. Robert. *Ticket to Hell via Dieppe: From a Prisoner's Wartime Log, 1942-1945*. Toronto: Van Nostrand Reinhold 1982

Read, J.E. 'Modern Warfare and the Laws of War,' *Dalhousie Review* 2/4 (January 1923):485-9

Reid, Gordon. *Poor Bloody Murder: Personal Memoirs of the First World War*. Oakville: Mosaic Press 1980

Reid, P.R. *Colditz: The Full Story*. London: Macmillan 1984

Repington, Charles à Court. *Vestigia*. London: Constable 1919

Reville, F. Douglas. *History of the County of Brant*, vol. 2. Brantford, ON: Hurley Printing 1920

Roberts, J.A. *A Canadian Summer*. Toronto: University of Toronto Bookroom 1981

Robinson, Ralph. 'Retaliation for the Treatment of Prisoners in the War of 1812,' *American Historical Review* 49/1 (October 1943):65-70

Roland, C.G. 'Allied POWs, Japanese Captors and the Geneva Convention,' *War & Society* 9/2 (October 1991):83-101

Rosas, Allan. *The Legal Status of Prisoners of War: A Study in International Humanitarian Law Applicable in Armed Conflicts*. Helsinki: Suomalainen Tiedeakatemia 1976

Ross, Murray G. *The Y.M.C.A. in Canada: The Chronicle of a Century*. Toronto: Ryerson Press 1951

Roy, Patricia; Granatstein, J.L.; Iino, Masako; and Takamura, Hiroko. *Mutual Hostages:*

Canadians and Japanese during the Second World War. Toronto: University of Toronto Press 1990

Royal Commission ... to investigate and report upon all claims which may be submitted to the commission for the purpose of determining whether they are within the First Annex to Section I of Part VIII of the Treaty of Versailles, James Friel, Commissioner. *Reparations: The Report of the Commissioner*, 2 vols. Ottawa: King's Printer 1929

Royal Commission for the Investigation of Illegal Warfare Claims and for the Return of Sequestered Property in Necessitous Cases, Errol M. McDougall, Commissioner. *Interim Report*. Ottawa: King's Printer 1931

—. *Report of the Commission on Reparations, 1930-31: Maltreatment of Prisoners of War*. Ottawa: King's Printer 1932

—. *Reparations, 1932: Further Report*. Ottawa: King's Printer 1933

—. *Reparations, 1932: Final Report*. Ottawa: King's Printer 1933

Russell, Thomas H. *The World's Greatest War*. Brantford, ON: Bradley-Garretson 1914

Saturday Night (Toronto)

Schull, Joseph. *Rebellion*. Toronto: Macmillan 1971

Scott, James Brown. *The Hague Peace Conferences of 1899 and 1907*, 2 vols. Baltimore: Johns Hopkins Press 1909; repr., New York: Garland Publishing 1972

—. *Diplomatic Correspondence between the United States and Germany*. New York: Oxford University Press 1918

Scudamore, T.V. 'Lighter Episodes in the Life of a Prisoner of War,' *Canadian Defence Quarterly* 7/3 (April 1930):394-406

—. 'Tales of an Interné,' *Canadian Defence Quarterly* 8/1 (October 1930):98-105

—. *Lighter Episodes in the Life of a Prisoner of War*. Aldershot: Gale & Polden 1933

Senate. Debates

Shedd, Clarence Prouty. *History of the World's Alliance of Young Men's Christian Associations*. London: SPCK 1955

Shera, John W. 'Poundmaker's Capture of a Wagon Train,' *Alberta Historical Review* 1/1 (April 1953):7-9

Smith, Gladys E. *Forty Nights to Freedom: The True Prisoner of War Escape Story of Wing Commander Stewart F. Cowan (Ret.)*. Winnipeg: Queenston House Publishing 1984

Spaight, J.M. *War Rights on Land*. London: Macmillan 1911

Speaight, Robert. *Vanier. Soldier, Diplomat and Governor General: A Biography*. Toronto: Collins 1970

Spectator (Hamilton)

Speed, Richard B. *Prisoners, Diplomats, and the Great War: A Study in the Diplomacy of Captivity*. New York: Greenwood Press 1990

Stacey, C.P. 'Is "Civilized Warfare" Possible?' *Queen's Quarterly* 37/1 (Winter 1930):105-21

—. *Official History of the Canadian Army in the Second World War*, vol. 1, *Six Years of War: The Army in Canada, Britain and the Pacific*. Ottawa: Queen's Printer 1955

Statutes of Canada

Steele, Col. S.B. *Forty Years in Canada*. New York: Dodd, Mead 1915

Stevens, G.R. *The Royal Canadian Regiment*, vol. 2, *1933-1966*. London: London Printing and Lithographing 1967

Stofer, Ken. *Dear Mum: The Story of Victor Edward 'Candy' Syrett, a Canadian in the Royal Air Force during World War Two*. Victoria: Kenlyn Publishing 1991

Strachan, Tony, ed. *In the Clutch of Circumstance: Reminiscences of Members of the Canadian*

National Prisoners of War Association. Victoria: Cappis Press 1985

Sweanor, George. *It's All Pensionable Time: 25 Years in the Royal Canadian Air Force*. Port Hope, ON: Gesnor Publications 1981

Taylor, Alonzo Englebert. 'The Diet of Prisoners of War in Germany,' *Journal of the American Medical Association*, 69/19 (10 November 1917):1575-82

Telegram (Toronto)

Thorn, John C. *Three Years a Prisoner in Germany*. Vancouver: Cowan & Brookhouse 1919

TIME (New York)

Times (London)

Tisdall, Dr. Frederick F. 'Canadian Red Cross Food Parcels for British Prisoners-of-war in Germany,' *Canadian Medical Association Journal*, 44 (January 1941):77-8

—, Wilson, Margaret; Mitchell, Joan; Gershaw, Norma; Rouse, Grace; McCreary, J.F.; and Sellers, A.H. 'Final Report on the Canadian Red Cross Society Food Parcels for Prisoners-of-War,' *Canadian Medical Association Journal* 60 (March 1949):279-86

Tolstoy, Nikolai. *Victims of Yalta*. London: Hodder & Stoughton 1977; repr., London: Corgi 1986

Toronto Daily News

Toronto Daily Star

[Toronto Red Cross]. *History, Toronto Branch, The Canadian Red Cross Society, 1914-1948*. Toronto: The Toronto Red Cross [1948]

United Kingdom. House of Commons. *Report of the Committee on Alleged German Outrages*. London: HMSO 1915

—. *An Agreement between the British and German Governments Concerning Combatant and Civilian Prisoners of War* Cmd 8590 (1917)

—. *Report of the Joint Committee to Enquire into the Organisation and Methods of the Central Prisoners of War Committee* Cmd 8615 (1917)

United Kingdom. War Office. *The King's Regulations and Orders for the Army*. London: HMSO 1912; repr., 1914

—. *Manual of Military Law*. London: HMSO 1914; repr., 1916

United States. Department of State. *Bulletin*

The Valour and the Horror, 3 parts. Canadian Broadcasting Corporation/National Film Board 1992

Van Horne, James. *A Narrative of the Captivity and Sufferings of James Van Horne*. Middlebury, VT: 1817; repr., New York: Garland Publishing 1977

Vance, Jonathan. 'The Politics of Camp Life: The Bargaining Process in Two German Prison Camps,' *War & Society* 10/1 (May 1992):109-26

—. 'The War Behind the Wire: The Battle to Escape from a German Prison Camp,' *Journal of Contemporary History* 28/4 (October 1993):675-93

Vancouver Daily Sun

Vatcher, William H. *Panmunjom: The Story of the Korean Military Armistice Negotiations*. New York: Frederick A. Praeger 1958

Veith, Ilza. 'Humane Warfare and Inhuman War: Japan and Its Treatment of War Prisoners,' *Bulletin of the History of Medicine* 19/4 (April 1946):355-74

Veterans Affairs. *Annual Report*. Ottawa 1971-90

—. *Pensions for Disability and Death Related to Military Service*, August 1969

—. *Report of the Committee to Survey the Work and Organization of the Canadian Pension Commission*, 2 vols., 1968

Veterans' Journal (National POW Association)

Vincent, Carl. *No Reason Why: The Canadian Hong Kong Tragedy – An Examination.* Stittsville, ON: Canada's Wings 1981

Vipond, Mary. 'Best Sellers in English Canada: 1919-1928,' *Journal of Canadian Fiction* 35/36 (1980):73-106

Vischer, A.L. *Barbed Wire Disease: A Psychological Study of the Prisoner of War.* London: John Bale, Sons & Danielsson 1919

War Claims – Report of the Advisory Commission, 25 February 1952. Ottawa: Queen's Printer 1954

Wartime Information Board. *Canada at War*

—. *Facts and Figures Weekly*

Webster, Sir Charles, and Frankland, Noble. *The Strategic Air Offensive Against Germany, 1939-1945,* vol. 6. London: HMSO 1961

Wells, N.L. 'Repatriation of Prisoners,' *Caduceus* (Toronto) 2/3 (June 1921):12-13

Whiles, W.H. 'A Study of Neurosis Among Repatriated Prisoners of War,' *British Medical Journal,* 17 November 1945, 697-8

White, Andrew D. *Autobiography of Andrew Dickson White,* vol. 2. New York: Century 1905

Wilson, A.T.M.; Doyle, Martin; and Kelnar, John. 'Group Techniques in a Transitional Community,' *Lancet,* 31 May 1947, 735-8

Winston, Mark, ed. *Spotlight on Sagan.* London: n.d.

Wolfe, Brig.-Gen. J.P. 'Changes in the Law of Armed Conflict,' *Canadian Defence Quarterly* 8/3 (Winter 1978-79):16-21, 48

Witte, J.H. *The One That Didn't Get Away.* Bognor Regis, UK: New Horizon 1983

Wood, Lt.-Col. Herbert Fairlie. *Strange Battleground: The Operations in Korea and Their Effects on the Defence Policy of Canada.* Ottawa: Queen's Printer 1966

Wood, Lt. J.E.R. *Detour: The Story of Oflag IVC.* London: Falcon Press 1946

Wood, William, ed. *Select British Documents of the Canadian War of 1812.* Toronto: The Champlain Society 1928; repr., New York: Greenwood Press 1968

Woolley, H.E. *No Time Off for Good Behaviour.* Burnstown, ON: General Store Publishing 1990